Francis W. Pickens
and the Politics of Destruction

The Fred W. Morrison Series
in Southern Studies

Francis W. Pickens
and the Politics of Destruction

John B. Edmunds, Jr.

The University of North Carolina Press

Chapel Hill and London

© 1986 The University
of North Carolina Press
All rights reserved
Manufactured in the
United States of America

Library of Congress Cataloging-in-Publication Data
Edmunds, John B.
  Francis W. Pickens and the politics of destruction.
  (The Fred W. Morrison series in Southern studies)
  Bibliography: p.
  Includes index.
  1.Pickens, F. W. (Francis Wilkinson), 1805–1869.
2. South Carolina—Governors—Biography.   3. South
Carolina—Politics and government—1775–1865.
I. Title   II. Series.
F273.P57E36   1986   975.7′03′0924 [B]   86-1406
ISBN 0-8078-1699-X

THIS BOOK WAS DIGITALLY PRINTED

To Judge Donald S. Russell

and my wife, Judy.

They made it possible.

Contents

Preface xi

Chapter 1	Young Radical	3
Chapter 2	A Provocative Course	21
Chapter 3	A Vile Association	47
Chapter 4	Harbinger of Doom	71
Chapter 5	A Litany of Destruction	95
Chapter 6	An Insolvable Dilemma	112
Chapter 7	A Mere Office-Seeker	120
Chapter 8	The Rose of Texas	137
Chapter 9	A Fire-Eater Down to the Ground	150
Chapter 10	Governor and Council	167
Chapter 11	"There Can Lay No Peace for Me"	173

Notes 183

Bibliography 223

Index 241

Illustrations

Francis W. Pickens   6

Eliza Simkins Pickens   14

John C. Calhoun   29

William C. Preston   49

Waddy Thompson   65

James H. Hammond   77

Robert Barnwell Rhett   88

Franklin H. Elmore   109

Preston Brooks   129

Andrew Pickens Butler   135

Lucy Pickens   147

Currier and Ives drawing of Pickens   170

Preface

Antebellum South Carolina was unique in the nation. Politics was a passion that was interlaced with calculation and intrigue. In order to escape the boredom and loneliness of the rural southern life, the South Carolina cavalier sought refuge in the game of politics. The sons of Mother Carolina rushed to serve with a zeal unmatched anywhere. The players in the game were few and were connected by social and family bonds. Those struggling to ascend the political ladder had to appeal to the state's oligarchy, not to the contemptible masses. This made for a situation where intrigue held sway, as those in political circles manipulated each other to control the state's political establishment. Seldom were such machinations openly revealed, since to the southern mind appearances counted as much as realities. For years the myth abounded that the office should seek the man, not the reverse. The revelation that a man was a mere office-seeker classed him with the politicians, not the statesmen. In South Carolina a charade was played: beneath the veneer of dignity were office-courting, self-serving men who calculated the path for the fulfillment of their ambitions. There were differences in political philosophy, and those differences did set candidates apart; but the quest for office often caused beliefs to take a back seat.

This is not just a book about Francis Pickens; rather, it uses him as a vehicle to explore the labyrinths of antebellum South Carolina politics. The individuals are themselves fascinating, but coupling them with the most archaic political, social, and economic system in the nation makes for an amazing study. The Carolina temper, driven by mythical romanticism, lost all sense of reality as it found solace in provincialism. In seeking to preserve their parochial society in the face of great change, South Carolina's sons engaged in a politics of destruction that not only wrought havoc with the Union but also destroyed forever their own culture and way of life.

Although numerous works have examined the Palmetto State and those who determined her course, Francis W. Pickens is a figure who has for generations remained in the shadowy recesses of history. He was just as important as his contemporaries James H. Hammond and Robert Barnwell Rhett, yet a full study of his life has never before emerged. His correspondence is scattered in numerous manuscript collections and mainly concentrates on politics. He comes across as an arrogant, disingenuous person who, in his attempts at political intrigue, found himself to be the object of others' manipulations. Constantly in the forefront of controversy, he was embroiled in every movement that made South Carolina unique in the Union. Hoping to inherit John C. Calhoun's mantle of leadership, he had to contend with forces led by the brilliant Hammond and the fire-eater Rhett. Always desirous of a higher political station, he was tripped by his own ambitions and his flawed personality, which garnered for him a host of enemies. The height of his career was reached when he ascended to the South Carolina governorship at the most critical juncture in the nation's history. The state seceded, prepared for and went to war, urged sister states to embrace secession, and embarked on a novel experiment in government. Pickens's term as the Palmetto State's chief executive represented the most extraordinary and difficult governorship in the nation's history.

This study was written as a result of prodding by friends and colleagues. While I was a graduate student at the University of South Carolina, William A. Foran encouraged my interest in South Carolina's antebellum history by bringing to life the individuals and issues that made the Palmetto State so strident. It was Professor Foran who urged me to fill a gap by doing a doctoral study of Pickens. Many years later Walter Edgar, Director of the Institute for Southern Studies at the University of South Carolina, asked me to conduct further research and write a biography of Pickens to complement those of Calhoun, Hammond, and Rhett, since studies of their careers are incomplete without reference to Pickens.

This project would not have been possible without the generosity of Judge Donald S. Russell, the University of South Carolina Venture Fund, and the Carolina Piedmont Foundation at the University of South Carolina–Spartanburg. My friends Ned Anderson and James P. Sloan read the manuscript and gave helpful suggestions. The kind advice and help of Clyde Wilson and his staff, who are currently editing the Calhoun papers, was most appreciated.

The staffs of all the research libraries listed in the bibliography were most helpful. Allen Stokes, Les Inabinett, and Clara Mae Jacobs of the South Caroliniana Library afforded me every courtesy. Mattie Russell and her staff at Duke University uncovered material on Pickens that was never before researched. I was greatly assisted in my efforts by Augustus T. Graydon, Ellen Butler, Jane Greer, and Myrtle Fisher, all of whom kindly gave me access to family papers and pictures in their possession. I am grateful to Lewis Bateman, executive editor of the University of North Carolina Press, who has guided a neophyte skillfully along the path toward publication. To Vernon Burton of the University of Illinois, the author of *In My Father's House Are*

Many Mansions, go my sincere thanks for kindly sharing with me valuable material on Edgefield. Bettis Rainsford and David Parker gave of their time, showing me Edgefield and regaling me with conversation and hospitality.

This project could never have become a reality without the typing skills of Linda Bowen, Shirley Ridgeway, Jan Blackwell, and Renee O'Brian. The computer skills of John Roddy saved countless hours. My wife, Judy, typed, edited, and assisted me in researching the materials; she was a full partner in the undertaking. Were it not for her love, and that of Donald Russell, Pickens would have remained in the shadows.

Francis W. Pickens
and the Politics of Destruction

The Fred W. Morrison Series
in Southern Studies

We are supposed to be weak and divided. Think you that this state of things is to continue? No! We will sooner or later have to contend . . . it is idle to disguise it any longer. We must fight with the Goths and the Vandals over the tombs of our fathers, or allow our country to become a colony of blacks . . . why should we delude ourselves with the false and visionary hopes that we shall be able to avoid the contest.
F. W. Pickens's Notebook, 11 May 1844
F.W.P. (S.C.L.)

A patriot should be accustomed to tolerate every political party, to stand true to his own and to attack his antagonist with eagerness yet without personal animosity. Political antagonists should regard each other like the officers of two opposing armies who do their best to wound and kill each other yet all in honor.
Political Maxim on cover of
Whitfield Brooks's diary

1. Young Radical

South Carolina's secession in December 1860 did not just happen. For over thirty years Palmetto State radicals intent on defending their perceived rights had been ascertaining the best means by which to have their own way or bring down the Union. Their efforts brought on movements that would bring disorder and turmoil to the state and the nation. The individuals who participated were all arrogant, strong-willed figures who, for the sake of appearances, disavowed their love for political office, yet they were always seeking to appease their insatiable ambitions. Although these men varied in their degree of enmity for the Union, their radicalism represented the most extreme states' rights philosophy. South Carolina was small in population and poor in resources; nevertheless, her outlandish behavior and extremism determined that she would emerge as the most provocative state in the Union. Her actions during the nullification controversy and subsequent radical movements prior to secession caused reactions that polarized the sections so dramatically that only the dissolution of the nation and a way of life could result. Since Francis Pickens was involved in all of the state's important political movements, his career can be used as a vehicle to study the individuals, factional intrigues, and political happenings that made South Carolina unique. Not only did the state harbor an unsettled hostility toward the Union, but many of her leaders felt a deep hatred for one another as well. In the final analysis this ongoing animosity prevented cooperation during the Civil War. Constantly battling among themselves, they took pleasure in the failures of old adversaries. Friendships were ephemeral, but enmity long lasting. Adding to this failure of cooperation, and promoting internal instability, South Carolina had also shunned national political parties, fearing that any such allegiances would jeopardize the fierce independence of action which the rural society of the state promoted.

Francis Pickens was a typical Carolina patrician. He embraced the political principles of Thomas Jefferson and, like others of his class, section, and time, was influenced by a romanticism that was reflected by quixotic sentimentality in his public and private life. So desirous was he of rising; yet, like others, he was held in check by John C. Calhoun and by South Carolina's archaic political system. His frustrations were shared by his equally ambitious contemporaries.

Being from rural Edgefield, Pickens was brought up in an area that thrived on politics and fed the obsessions so prevalent at the time. Fiery rhetoric, combined with romantic passion and dogmatic fundamentalism, made for an atmosphere that stifled dissent. South Carolina's tendency toward radicalism was so well known that one of her native sons described her as being "too small to be a nation and too large to be a lunatic asylum!"[1] Thirty years prior to the Civil War, the Palmetto State was the political fiefdom of John C. Calhoun, who so overshadowed other Carolina leaders that important men of lesser charisma and ability have been swept aside as history has devoted full attention to his role as the champion of the South and the author of ultimate secession. Besides Calhoun, South Carolina possessed a galaxy of talented men who served at both the national and state levels. Prior to the Civil War, individuals could be accepted in the state's society through birth, the possession of wealth, marriage, or extraordinary talent. This social structure profoundly affected South Carolina's political makeup, for the General Assembly was composed of the "best men" and controlled the state's oligarchy by electing the governor, United States senators, state judges, presidential electors, and all constitutional officers. "The people" only elected local officials, congressmen, and representatives to the General Assembly; furthermore, even candidates for these posts were always nominated by caucuses composed of the gentry.[2] The antebellum South Carolina gentry was wedded to a stilted code of behavior that placed an emphasis on honor and correct manners. This society existed in the midst of and was propped up by the archaic institution of slavery. Conservative to a fault, the Carolinians had created an atavistic society that was unnatural for the times. The frustration level was acutely high; true feelings could not be openly paraded, since the consequences of revelations could be catastrophic. As long as individuals were perceived as patriots and spokesmen for the public good, they were safe. Overt disagreement could result in serious consequences, since the road left little room for dissent. Violence was sanctioned by the southern code of honor which determined that quarrels be settled by retraction and public apology, or by pistol or whip. The diary and letters to trusted relatives and friends served as a means to unburden oneself of true feelings; ambitions and emotions were recorded, as frustrations were vented.

In this society men of intellect valued education and studied history, the classics, languages, and science while perfecting their rhetoric and style. Politics became the risky game for many in the planter class. Fortunes were wrecked, lives sometimes lost, families divided, and friendships dashed.

Into this setting Francis Wilkinson Pickens was born on 7 April 1807.[3] He began life at his mother's home in St. Paul's Parish, near Charleston, but he spent his youth upstate at Hopewell Plantation, near Pendleton. The Pickens family had been making its mark on South Carolina and the nation since Revolutionary War times. Francis's grandfather was General Andrew Pickens, who was instrumental in the American victory at the Battle of Cowpens and was a leader in numerous skirmishes against the English, Tories, and Indians. Andrew Pickens was elected to the state legislature and to Congress, and he served his nation as commissioner of Indian affairs. Hopewell, his home, became famous as the place where important Indian treaties were signed. Two of the general's sons, Ezekiel and Andrew, Jr. (Francis's father), served in the state legislature. Ezekiel became lieutenant governor, and in 1817 Andrew, Jr., became the first man from upstate to be elected governor of South Carolina.[4]

During his childhood Francis had inculcated in him the value of learning. Although his grandfather never received a formal education, he was well read and made certain that Ezekiel and Andrew had the best education possible. Ezekiel finished first in his class at Princeton, and Andrew was a Phi Beta Kappa scholar at Brown.[5] According to a diary kept by Edward Hooker, a traveler from Connecticut who visited Hopewell, Andrew and his wife, Susan Wilkinson, had an excellent library and a deep appreciation for literature, music, and the arts.[6] From his father the junior Pickens gained an appreciation for learning. Before entering college he had memorized Edmund Burke's great speeches on taxation and reconciliation with the American colonies, and he was so well acquainted with the oratory of Cicero and Demosthenes that he could quote from memory long passages of their speeches. The works of Aristotle and Plato were well known to him, and his knowledge of the works of other classical figures was impressive.[7] In addition to being well versed in the classics, his learning included a stiff introduction to the hard-shell Calvinist theology that was embraced by his father and grandfather. The Pickenses were noted for their piety and strict religious observances.[8] The Old Stone Presbyterian Church (today adjacent to the Clemson University campus) was near their home, and they faithfully attended. For several generations the Pickens, Calhoun, Noble, Anderson, and Bonneau families had lived near each other and had, through numerous marriages, become intertwined. Andrew Pickens, Jr., was John C. Calhoun's first cousin and was also a cousin to Calhoun's wife, Floride Colhoun.[9]

As Andrew became more important in South Carolina political circles, Francis had the opportunity to be in the company of important people, making visits to Charleston and to the state capital, Columbia. As a child he was introduced to John C. Calhoun, who was to have a profound impact upon his

FRANCIS W. PICKENS, portrait by William Scarsborough
(courtesy of the South Caroliniana Library, University of South Carolina)

life. While governor, Andrew Pickens moved his family to Edgefield, where he had built a handsome two-story house that he named Halcyon Grove. Near the village he had extensive property holdings. Like so many other planters of the period, Andrew was constantly looking for new lands on which to plant cotton. After completing his term as governor, he made plans to move his family to a large tract that he had purchased near Selma, Alabama. Calhoun reported that the Pickens family was part of a large migration of Carolinians moving to the rich new lands of the Southwest. The family enjoyed close ties in Alabama; Israel Pickens, a cousin, would be governor of the state, and numerous other friends and kin lived there.[10]

Francis Pickens's long political career was launched at South Carolina College. Returning from Alabama, he entered the institution in January 1825 as a sophomore; he became acquainted with intriguing ideas and with many of the state's future political leaders. He was invited to join the prestigious Clariosophic Society and, shortly after his initiation into its secret mysteries, was elected secretary and kept the minutes, was responsible for all correspondence, and recorded all the debates and orations.[11] Names of significance in South Carolina such as Gist, Huger, Porcher, Miles, Richardson, Lowndes, Simkins, Bonham, Boyce, and Carroll graced the roll of the society during Pickens's term as secretary. His name frequently appeared in the debate book, showing that he often participated in debates or served as the orator for the day, for he found deep satisfaction in impressing his audience with his intellect, cleverness, and knowledge.[12] One of the last debates in which he participated dealt with whether the federal government should refund fines collected from those convicted of disobeying the unconstitutional Sedition Act.[13] Surely this debate must have interested the president of South Carolina College, Thomas Cooper, who had been sentenced under the Alien and Sedition Acts for speaking out against John Adams's administration. At the college Pickens had been studying, in addition to history and the classics, the states' rights doctrines that were being so effectively dispensed by Cooper, whose thoughts had a profound impact on the thinking of Thomas Jefferson. Each week Cooper, lecturing to his students on political economy, brought into play a whole range of subjects that afforded him the opportunity to display his ideas and his extensive learning. Many of his students imbibed Cooper's radical political philosophy, which propounded an ideology of strict construction of the Constitution with the correctness of states' rights.

South Carolina had not always embraced states' rights. Immediately after the War of 1812, the state showed itself to be in the vanguard of national unity, even going so far as to advocate protective tariffs, the Second National Bank of the United States, and federally financed internal improvements. By 1827 the nation was faced with an upcoming presidential election. In the South the undisputed candidate was Andrew Jackson, who had lost the election to John Quincy Adams in 1824 and was determined not to allow the office to elude his grasp again. By this time the South no longer supported tariffs, however, and as cotton became king, the section found itself under attack for keeping humans in bondage. The debates on the tariff and slavery issues made the North appear selfish and heavyhanded. The desire of northern manufacturers to obtain passage of protectionist legislation was seen as a threat, since the South would buy in a protected market and sell in an unprotected one. The blessing of candidate Jackson on the Woolens Bill put Southerners on their guard, and the views of Thomas Cooper gained more adherents. Whereas much of what he had advocated was perceived as mere notions created to tease the minds of impressionable students, for South Carolina his ideas suddenly pointed a way out of a vexing dilemma. Cooper urged that, for South Carolina to be free from the tariff, the state should consider breaking the shackles which bound her to the Union, declaring the Tariff Act void.[14]

Cooper's states' rights philosophy was readily embraced by Pickens. In the summers of 1827 and 1828 Pickens wrote pseudonymous letters to the Charleston *Mercury*, which at the time was edited by a friend, Henry Pinckney. These letters, signed "Sidney," extolled Cooper's philosophy and questioned the government's right to impose a protectionist tariff so "that a miserable, plundering band of grovelling, sordid wretches may fatten at our expense." He argued that when a law of the general government "takes from us our property, without our consent . . . we have the right as a sovereign to declare whether it be law or not."[15] Pickens was echoing Robert Turnbull of Charleston, who, in his "crisis letters" to the *Mercury*, signed "Brutus," was questioning the right of the general government to collect the offensive duties in South Carolina.[16] Pickens's invective proclaimed that he would go to any lengths to protect the interest of the southern minority. He argued that his forefathers had fought England because of oppression, and he proclaimed that the taxing of 7 million by the majority of 12 million was wrong, since it denied the minority protection from an overbearing majority.[17]

In the late winter of 1827 Pickens and a large group of his fellow students decided to put Cooper's philosophy into practice. Each February or March, as a matter of course, disturbances took place over the compulsory commons rule that forced students to eat in Stewards Hall. In March 1827 eighty students refused to eat in commons. Although President Cooper may have sympathized with their rebellion, he could not permit flouting of the regulations; thus some seventy-five students either left the college or were expelled. Pickens left the college before the completion of his senior year, never to return.[18] Preceding his departure, he was honored by being invited to deliver the anniversary address to the Clariosophic Society, where he urged his audience to be wary of "political deception cloaked with the face of patriotism." Exhorting his fellow students to use their great talents in politics, he made a statement to which he would subscribe throughout his life: "The great talents of the nation are drawn into politics. There is nothing that has so strong a charm for ambition as power in government."[19]

Perhaps Pickens decided against returning to college partly because of his pending marriage to Margaret Eliza Simkins, a childhood sweetheart and the daughter of a family friend. Colonel Eldred Simkins was a wealthy landowner from Edgefield who had served South Carolina as lieutenant governor and had succeeded Calhoun in Congress in 1817.[20] He was also Calhoun's "earliest and best friend" and had practiced law with the great Carolinian. Before Christmas 1826 Francis and Eliza had announced their engagement. Calhoun described the future Mrs. Pickens as "quite handsome and a very fine girl," expressing the view that "the union between Francis and Eliza takes place with the hearty consent of old friends."[21] After vows were exchanged on 18 October 1827, Pickens moved back to Edgefield and read law in Simkins's office. His marriage to Eliza proved profitable both financially and politically, for although Pickens had money and property, the marriage to Simkins's eldest child added to his wealth and prestige. Since early childhood he had been inculcated with the pride of his heritage, which dictated that he carry on the honor of his name by involving himself in public affairs. Like others, Pickens was quick to defend the planter society from outside assault, for he loved the land and at every opportunity extolled planting as among the highest callings. William C. Preston, a noted South Carolina statesman, described the traits of a southern leader when he wrote, "The object of a Southern man's life is politics and subsidiary to this end we all practice law."[22] Pickens well fitted Preston's description. He practiced law, and politics became an overriding passion that caused him to neglect family, enterprise, and health. For the South Carolina planter class, the call to service needed to be answered, and if there was no call, it needed to be created.

In the early days of his political career Pickens became associated with three fellow Carolinians who were to have a profound impact on his political life. John C. Calhoun was the unquestioned leader of a trio composed of Pickens, James H. Hammond, and Robert Barnwell Rhett. A study of the careers of these men is a study in the forces that ultimately brought down the Union.

Ambition, jealousy, and arrogance dictated the course of these men's lives, which in turn determined the course of the Palmetto State. Pickens, Hammond, and Rhett composed a triangle that schemed and waited to inherit Calhoun's mantle of leadership. Yet none of them was able to succeed the greatest Carolinian, although each possessed remarkable talent. Calhoun, always desirous of maintaining peace at home, was able for a while to keep his men in harness; eventually, though, their ambitions and jealousies would prove disruptive, and, despite Calhoun's efforts to keep South Carolina at peace, fighting among his lieutenants and their allies would become commonplace.

Like so many other members of the Carolina gentry, Pickens possessed a complex temperament. Living by the chivalric code of honor to which aristocratic Carolinians subscribed and possessing a romantic, moody disposition, he could be extremely "hospitable, generous, kind by nature."[23] On the other hand, he was often overbearing, proud, envious, and stubborn. Intelligence and abundant knowledge he possessed, but he was also a romantic dreamer who often appeared insincere. One contemporary described him as "of a character so contradictory and so inconsistent that it is difficult to estimate."[24]

At the time of his marriage events were taking place that would profoundly affect South Carolina and the nation. The debates on the Woolens Bill and the passage of the Tariff of Abominations would cause many South Carolinians to reevaluate the relationship of the Palmetto State to the nation. In Edgefield more than eight columns of the *Hive* were filled with announcements of pending sheriff's sales; citizens were manifesting their distress at daily public meetings and militia musters.[25] Pickens showed himself to be an early advocate of nullification. Before Calhoun developed his theory of the concurrent majority and secretly penned his "Exposition and Protest," and before the passage of the Tariff of Abominations, Pickens was questioning the right of the federal government to force its will on South Carolina. Determined to educate his fellow Carolinians in the states' rights philosophy, his letters to the Charleston *Mercury* were some of the first published protests. After he had practiced law for a short time, Pickens attempted to participate in the formation of public opinion by writing pseudonymous letters to a new paper created to disseminate the doctrine of nullification. The thrice-weekly Columbia *Southern Times*, edited by a college acquaintance, James H. Hammond, welcomed the "Hampden" letters that so skillfully expressed many Carolinians' growing disenchantment with Andrew Jackson and his administration's tariff policies. Pickens reasoned that the state, acting on behalf of its sovereign people, could prevent the enforcement of repugnant acts within its borders.[26]

With vitriolic rhetoric "Hampden" contended that the tariff was a scheme to enrich the northern manufacturer and merchant at the expense of the southern farmer and planter. Pickens, following in the footsteps of his mentor Cooper, asserted that it was time to calculate the value of the Union. "Disunion," he wrote, "might well be the only means of righting wrongs."[27] The "Hampden" letters were reminiscent of the orations and debates in which Pickens the student had summoned all of his rhetorical skill to make certain that his logic had no flaws. At first the only person who knew the identity of "Hampden" was James Hammond, who by printing the letters was ingratiating himself with Pickens and obtaining badly needed material for his paper. Pickens and Hammond found that they shared similar views on most questions of the period. Hammond, who was trying to break into Carolina society, flattered Pickens by offering to reprint the "Hampden" letters in pamphlet form to "educate the people," who were "below many of our leaders . . . in regard to disunion."[28]

The campaign to enlighten people to the value of nullification began having results. The ideas that had been promulgated by Cooper were rapidly crystallizing the political theories of the South Carolina Nullifiers, and the temper of the state was changing as more Carolinians embraced the radical doctrine. One interesting statistic shows Cooper's impact on the Palmetto State: at the time of secession in 1860, twenty-four of his former students were delegates to the secession convention, and four of his former students, including Pickens, served as governors during the critical period of secession and Civil War.[29] Carolinians were accepting a premise that had been set forth by Thomas Jefferson in 1799 in the Kentucky Resolutions—that a state could declare federal legislation unconstitutional and impede the enforcement of a repugnant act within its borders.[30]

The passage of the Tariff of Abominations and the failure of the Tariff of 1832 significantly to lower rates provoked South Carolina to embrace nullification. Enactment of this legislation was particularly irritating to Southerners; the price of cotton had been tumbling as production of the fiber increased with the opening of new, rich lands in Alabama, Mississippi, and Louisiana. Although overproduction was the main cause of the decline in cotton prices, many Southerners believed that the tariff was to be blamed for their financial ills, since it enhanced the price paid for manufactured goods at a time when the price for cotton was falling.[31]

During the summer of 1828, Calhoun considered the situation and formulated a theory of state sovereignty which was eventually brought forth in his famous "South Carolina Exposition and Protest." This document was Calhoun's attempt to preserve the rights of the state without rupturing the Union.

He traced the development of the Constitution, concluding that the people were sovereign and that, assembled in convention, they could constitutionally nullify acts of the national government.[32] At this time the relationship between Calhoun and Andrew Jackson began to unravel. Calhoun, as vice-president, was to have no role in the new administration. Martin Van Buren, the tariff question, the "Exposition and Protest," the Peggy O'Neill affair, the Seminole Indian letter, the Hayne-Webster debate, and finally the Jefferson Day Dinner of 1830 all acted to distance Calhoun from the president. Division was taking place in the Palmetto State as well, and the friction of this split would profoundly affect the nature of South Carolina politics for the next decade. This schism originated in the nullification crisis as it affected the state's politics.[33] The Unionists were led by James Louis Petigru, Joel R. Poinsett, J. R. Richardson, and two former governors, Henry Middleton and Richard I. Manning. The Nullifiers espoused a variety of opinions on when and how the state should invoke nullification, arguing that the state was sovereign and that delegates elected to a special convention, which could be called by two-thirds of the members of the General Assembly, had the power to decide whether to enforce acts passed by Congress and deemed repugnant to South Carolina. Most Unionists and Nullifiers were unified on one point: the tariff was odious legislation that needed to be repealed, or the Union would be jeopardized. Pickens felt that "the true checking power of all governments is the power to destroy them" and believed that no government "that has the power to collect taxes and declare war can be restrained but by a display of sufficient power to break it up." The more moderate Calhoun took exception to Pickens's radicalism. In order to placate the vice-president, Pickens feigned a modification of his stance by telling Calhoun that he did not desire to see the Union torn apart. "Fortunately," he wrote, "we have the power to restrain it without destroying it."[34] Calhoun continued to urge caution even as anti-Union sentiment was increasing. Pickens continued in the path of Thomas Cooper and calculated the value of the Union. In a letter to Hammond written in May 1830, he confessed that he was "for any extreme, even war to the hilt rather than go down to infamy and slavery with a government of unlimited powers."[35] Pickens's extremist views were being disseminated throughout the state in the *Southern Times*, which had become the official organ for the Nullifiers.[36]

Throughout 1830 the excitement and discontent grew. New frustration levels were reached as South Carolina's impatience with the situation seemed to have no effect. "Hampden" asked, "How long is it for us to suffer this gross injustice and destructive tyranny?"[37] In Washington every attempt at significant tariff reduction was rebuffed. The Palmetto State was seething with anger;

and as the initiative fell to younger men, the power of the Nullifiers grew. They were able to carry the 1830 elections. In late November the first real tests of strength between the Nullifiers and Unionists occurred in the legislature. A contest developed in the race for United States Senate between the incumbent, William Smith, who was known to be a Unionist, and the nullification candidate, Stephen Decatur Miller. Pickens was hopeful that George McDuffie, South Carolina's best-known and most able congressman, would seek the Senate seat. He believed that McDuffie was "the only one that [had] acquired national recognition to come into full and equal contact with Clay and Webster."[38] Despite Pickens's urging, McDuffie, who had succeeded Eldred Simpkins in Congress, preferred to remain in the House. The contest boiled down to one between Miller and Smith, with Miller barely able to oust Smith from his Senate seat. Pickens, Hammond, and other Nullifiers were disappointed with the closeness of the contest; they rationalized that Smith's personal popularity was so great that he was able to gain some Nullifier votes. Their assumption was correct, for in the gubernatorial contest where there was no popular incumbent, the Union candidate, Richard I. Manning, was handily defeated (93-67) by the arch nullifier, James Hamilton, Jr.[39] Nullifiers controlled the legislature, but they still lacked the two-thirds majority needed to call a nullification convention.[40]

As frustration grew, so did the power of the Nullifiers. By the summer of 1831 Calhoun, seeing his presidential prospects declining and his relations with Jackson dead, found it necessary to abandon his moderate position and to adopt the more radical approach. He wrote Hammond that his object was to throw himself entirely upon the South, "to be more Southern if possible." In July 1831, in his Fort Hill letter, South Carolina's most famous son publicly accepted nullification.[41]

In the meantime, the issue of the tariff was joined by the potentially explosive issue of protecting the southern labor system from attack. In January 1831 William Lloyd Garrison launched his notorious *Liberator*; Nat Turner's rebellion took place in Virginia in August. The assaults on slavery heightened the Carolinians' emotions and caused them to associate the tariff and abolition as northern-inspired moves against the South. Calhoun wrote Pickens that he had been "against active operations this summer . . . but events have taken another direction . . . relaxation now would be fatal."[42]

There was talk of compromise on the tariff. Jackson appeared to be following a more states' rights course when he vetoed the Maysville Road Bill and urged some minor tariff adjustments. As Jackson seemed to be making conciliatory gestures, the prevailing sentiment shifted away from radicalism;

ELIZA SIMKINS PICKENS
(courtesy of the Ellen Butler Collection)

Robert Y. Hayne wrote that it was difficult to keep public feeling at a proper pitch.[43] When it became apparent that the administration did not plan to satisfy southern demands by seeking a general reduction of the tariff, the mood rapidly shifted toward radicalism.[44] Calhoun summed up the problem when he wrote Pickens in March 1832: "It is in truth hard to find a middle position where the principle of protection is asserted to be essential on one side and fatal on the other. It involves not the question of concession, but surrender on one side or the other."[45]

By 1832 obstinacy seemed to rule in all parts of the nation. Resistance in South Carolina continued to grow, and there was a real possibility that, without a compromise, the Palmetto State would invoke nullification. Calhoun best expressed the frustration: "I fear we have nothing to hope from the general government and that we must rely on the exercise of our reserved rights for redress."[46] Calhoun's approach was espoused by Pickens, who demonstrated his zeal for nullification by writing a new series of "Sydney" letters to the Charleston *Mercury*. These letters urged the calling of a convention, warned against northern tyranny, and relied upon Pickens's view of history to justify the course South Carolina was pursuing.[47] The calling of a nullification convention had not previously been possible, since there had not been the necessary two-thirds vote in the legislature. Jackson's failure to modify his position and Calhoun's decision to embrace nullification helped place the states' rights supporters in a position to capture overwhelmingly the legislature. In October 1832 Governor James Hamilton, one of the strongest proponents for nullification, created mass rejoicing by calling for an extra session of the General Assembly. There legislators could call a convention before the commencement of the new session of Congress in order to declare the tariff to be "null, void, and no law" in South Carolina.[48]

Elections were held for the legislature on the second Monday and Tuesday in October, and the special session of the legislature convened on 22 October. The elections overwhelmingly favored the Free Trade and State Rights party; by depicting the Unionists as submissionists, they were able to capture the House by a vote of 94-23 and the state Senate by 30-12.[49]

On 25 October the legislature passed an act which called for a convention on the third Monday in November.[50] The preamble of the document ratified by that convention summed up the states' rights philosophy. "We the people of the State of South Carolina in convention assembled, do declare and ordain—that we accede to the Federal compact as an independent and sovereign people."[51] On 24 November the convention declared the tariff "unconstitutional, unequal, and oppressive" and not binding on the state. The nullification ordinance forbade federal officials from collecting customs duties in South Carolina after 1 February 1833.[52] President Jackson issued a stinging proclamation, urging the Carolinians to repudiate their foolish ways and to turn from the brink of treason.[53] Claiming that they had been duped by their "deluded and designing leaders," he argued that the doctrine of nullification was false, since the Union was a consolidation of states, rather than a federation; he left no doubt that he would use force to quell South Carolina.[54] Meanwhile, in order to pass the acts recommended by the nullification convention, the state legislature convened in regular session after the convention adjourned. Jackson's proclamation struck the members of the legislature "with astonishment tho not with alarm."[55]

In keeping with the military fever of the time, on 3 September 1832 Pickens was nominated to run for the South Carolina House of Representatives by a committee composed of representatives of the six militia battalions in Edgefield District. A candidate of the Free Trade and State Rights party, he was elected with no difficulty and was appointed to the committee on federal relations. When the committee chairman, William C. Preston, was elected to the United States Senate in late December 1832, Pickens was catapulted to a position of prominence as chairman of the committee.[56] In this new capacity he made a brief speech against Jackson's proclamation: "The proclamation just read asserted that 'these states were not, and never had been, at any period of their existence Sovereign, or Independent!' This was not historically the truth; for in our Declaration of Independence, it was distinctly proclaimed to the world, that 'these colonies were, and of a right, ought to be free, sovereign and independent states.'"[57] Three decades later, Francis Pickens would again paraphrase the Declaration of Independence when he declared South Carolina to be a "separate, sovereign, free, and independent state."[58] Acting as chairman of the federal relations committee, Pickens authored a retort to Jackson's proclamation in a series of resolutions to the full House, claiming that "The principles, doctrines and purposes, contained in said proclamation are inconsistent with any just idea of limited government, and subversive of the rights of the states and liberties of the people."[59] Hammond said that Pickens's report was "bold and will produce a great shock throughout the union."[60]

All of Pickens's activities served their purpose well. He was becoming well known in his own right, and having famous forebears helped him to advance his political career. The radicalism that was so popular in the state gave him the perfect opportunity to bring forth his own brand of vitriolic radicalism; even though he was young in years, he was ahead of most leaders in the state in this respect. "Sidney" and "Hampden" afforded him opportunities to formulate and disperse his ideas. Pickens's election to the General Assembly and his rise to chairman of the most important committee in the House gave him an immediate opportunity to emerge as a leader in the state. His role became more important in the second phase of nullification. When the legislature reconvened in early December, he was chosen to chair the judiciary committee, and in that capacity he authored legislation to effect the controversial test oath required by the nullification convention. Heated debate arose in the legislature, for this measure required officers in the state militia, judges, and state officeholders (except state legislators) to pledge allegiance to the Palmetto State by agreeing "to obey, execute and enforce" the nullification ordinance.[61] Many Unionist members of the General Assembly opposed the oath, contending that it was unconstitutional since it demanded primary loyalty to South Carolina. Pickens brought forth a committee report which defended the legality of the oath by claiming that the constitution was the "creation of the states.... Therefore, the states were sovereign and allegiance was due to sovereignty."[62]

Reason was giving way to passion, and within the state internecine strife appeared possible as the nullifiers prepared to do battle with the nation. After being notified of his election to the Senate, Calhoun resigned the vice-presidency on 23 December 1832. Robert Y. Hayne, who had resigned his Senate seat and returned to South Carolina, succeeded Governor Hamilton and recommended that the legislature create a state guard of 12,000 men in order to defend the state from the anticipated invasion. Pickens was swept up by the fever of the times and proclaimed, "If we have not the right of secession, we have that of glorious rebellion, and I am prepared to go into it."[63] Since Hayne had served South Carolina as a militia general who had actively commanded troops, he was considered well equipped to lead the state in these perilous times. The new governor appointed Pickens an aide-de-camp with the rank of lieutenant colonel in the militia. Hammond, who was also commissioned a lieutenant colonel by Hayne, wrote his brother, "At all events we continue our military preparations, and shall keep them up until the Force Bill is repealed and probably always."[64]

In spite of all the potential difficulties facing the state, her sons rushed to her aid. Agitation was paramount, and war seemed imminent. The Carolinians' bellicose stance was dramatically revealed in a letter to Pickens from his brother-in-law, Andrew Pickens Butler. "The spirit of the people is prepared to sustain the State," wrote Butler, "I believe that we can march 12,000 in the field at the first tap of the drum.... We may be treated with as much contempt in the papers as our northern friends choose, but the idea that 12,000 men with arms commanded by good and gallant officers has more influence than all our parchment proclamations. The spirit of the people—the military spirit of the people must be kept up. This contest will assume many aspects—it may have to be settled by force—at any rate this is the commencement of a contest that will require military power to battle the affairs of empire."[65]

In order to prepare South Carolina for the apparently inevitable conflict, Pickens was assigned the duty of raising, inspecting, and granting commissions to volunteer companies.[66] From Edgefield District a contingent of over 2,000 men was raised. Further orders directed him to recruit "bodies of mounted minutemen who would prepare . . . in the shortest time possible to proceed to any place which may be designated."[67] Excitement and patriotism attracted men to serve, but gathering arms and munitions proved more difficult. Because South Carolina had shunned manufacturing in favor of the plantation system and cotton culture, the state had no facilities for manufacturing arms and equipment and little money with which to purchase them. The governor lamented that "the demand for arms exceeds five times over the number in possession of the state."[68]

Fortunately, all the military preparations and violent talk were in vain. Henry Clay introduced a compromise tariff measure on 12 February 1833, and Congress passed it on 27 February, thus thwarting the radical nullifiers who were impatient for action. The leading feature of the compromise was to reduce the duties by 10 percent every two years for ten years. This compromise was embraced by the South, since it repudiated protection. At the same time Congress also passed the Force Act, which immensely increased the strength of the federal executive by giving President Jackson the power to enforce the act that had just been repealed. The Nullification Convention accepted the compromise tariff and nullified the Force Act.[69] The military preparations of 1832–33 proved to be the prelude to those of 1860–61. The nullification ordinances were repealed, but South Carolina remained wary. Hayne wrote his officers that although the prospect of war had diminished, "experience has . . . taught us . . . that the best security is to be found in being prepared."[70]

In December 1833 Pickens made a report, as chairman of the committee on federal relations, urging his colleagues to incorporate the test oath as part of the state constitution. His tone showed that, although the tariff was an irritant, slavery was clearly the ultimate and real issue: "We have a peculiar and local institution of our own . . . of great delicacy and momentous concern to the very vitals of our society. . . . The law of state sovereignty is with us the law of state existence. If there be any citizen of South Carolina who . . . should refuse or hesitate to swear allegiance to the mother that has cherished or protected him, he deserves to be an offcast and wanderer upon the earth, without a home and feeling for no country."[71]

The Unionists, led by Alfred Huger, Joel R. Poinsett, and Richard I. Manning, vowed never to raise a fratricidal arm against the Union. Poinsett advised those Unionists who contemplated leaving the state to stay and be buried, if necessary, "in the bloody banner of the stars and stripes" as a protest against the "unconstitutional . . . test oath."[72] The seeds of mistrust were planted and passions inflamed; neither the nation nor South Carolina would ever be the same. Nullification served its purpose in that it forced a change in tariff policy; it also served to move a host of talented and radical South Carolinians into positions of leadership. So long as nullification raged, these men were united in their belief in resistance against the federal government. But after the conflict passed, their own political philosophies and ambitions caused splits in their once united ranks.

One of the most important individuals involved in the nullification controversy was South Carolina's senior representative, George McDuffie, whose political career was ancient. Next to Calhoun, McDuffie was the most revered statesman. Independent of mind and action, he had been the state's leading proponent of nullification in Congress long before Calhoun embraced the cause.[73] Since 1821 McDuffie had enjoyed a brilliant career in Congress; however, pain from an old dueling wound and nervous dyspepsia had caused his health to deteriorate to the point where he decided to retire from Congress and have bestowed on himself the honorific prize of the governorship. The unanimous election of McDuffie was considered to be the first step of reconciliation between Unionists and Nullifiers and the beginning of a new era of harmony in the state.[74] In January 1834 Calhoun informed Pickens of McDuffie's plans to retire and urged his kinsman to consider running for Congress.[75]

Nullification had catapulted Pickens's name before the people of Edgefield District. His appointment as lieutenant colonel and aide-de-camp to the governor helped increase his fame, since he had successfully raised troops and agitated on behalf of nullification. Although he was one of the youngest members of the legislature, he had emerged as a very important leader and had gained national fame by chairing the two most active committees in the House. His speaking out against Jackson and his advocacy of the test oath and South Carolina sovereignty had made him a renowned figure. It was generally suspected that he was the author of the "Hampden" and "Sydney" letters, and it was widely known that he had not been hesitant in humbling the Union. Calhoun appreciated his enthusiasm and talent. Pickens now had all the right credentials, and the situation could not have been better. (Only Whitfield Brooks, a family friend, had shown any inclination to run for Congress on the nullification ticket, but the caucus would put him aside.) Calhoun gave Pickens encouragement when he wrote: "You certainly cannot be censured by anyone for permitting your name to be brought forward . . . and I do hope, that should you appear to be clearly the candidate . . . Mr. Brooks will retire. . . ."[76]

As the foregoing indicates, Pickens and Calhoun were close in many respects. Francis's father had been like a brother to Calhoun. Calhoun's firstborn child was named Andrew Pickens Calhoun, after the general. In letters to Pickens Calhoun frequently requested information about members of his immediate family who were visiting Pickens at Edgewood, his plantation home near Edgefield. Anna, Calhoun's daughter, stayed at Edgewood while attending a female academy in Edgefield.[77] Bonds of loyalty had been forged, and there was no question that Pickens would be Calhoun's man. Arthur Schlesinger wrote, in his *Age of Jackson*, that "in Pickens, the principles of Calhoun . . . stood out with brutal clarity."[78] Calhoun wrote his daughter extolling the virtues of his cousin and telling her that Pickens "will make an excellent member . . . our state now stands so high that we must not let down its reputation."[79] The senator advised Pickens to emulate George McDuffie and not be "too eager, and . . . preserve the peace and harmony of the district at this important crisis."[80] The Pendleton *Messenger* of 1 October 1834 reported McDuffie's retirement and announced Pickens's candidacy.[81] On 18 October a special election was held to fill McDuffie's unexpired term and elect a man to a full term. Pickens overwhelmingly defeated the Union candidate, John S. Pressly, for both.[82] On 8 December Pickens took his seat in the Twenty-third Congress, which has been called the "Star Congress" because of its illustrious membership. In the Senate sat Webster, Clay, and Calhoun, the great triumvirate; among the members of the House were John Quincy Adams, Franklin Pierce, Churchill Cambreling, Millard Fillmore, and James K. Polk. Five members of this Congress would serve as president, five as vice-president, eight as secretary of state, and twenty-five as governors.[83] Pickens won handily because the Union party was unpopular in the Edgefield District, and because he had the support of John C. Calhoun, who "declared him to be the most promising man in the state."[84]

2. A Provocative Course

During the spring of 1834 the battle over nullification was closing, but the seeds of suspicion and disunion were sown. The nullification issue continued to cause disharmony within the state, and for a while Calhoun found himself being led, rather than leading. It was time for factional differences to be put away in order that larger issues facing the state and nation might be addressed.[1] "This is no time for discord," Calhoun wrote to Pickens, "the period is eminently perilous."[2] A South Carolina appellate court's decision to declare unconstitutional the test oath of loyalty that had been required by the nullification convention and upheld by the Palmetto legislature was irritating to the ultra-Nullifiers. This verdict threatened again to open the floodgates of controversy and to disrupt the excitable Carolinians. Calhoun, whose own political plans depended on concert at home, wrote his kinsman, "Take no rash, or violent measure; do nothing that can excite sympathy for our opponents, or endanger the peace of the state . . . let every nerve be exerted to carry the fall election; but in the meantime let all other movements be suspended."[3]

As tenuous peace once again settled over the state, Pickens was given an opportunity to turn from politics to other pursuits. He had recently moved his growing family into his new home at Edgewood plantation. The house, which his father had begun building for him in 1829, was constructed in stages and was of a rambling one-story design on nine-foot stone pylons. It was noted for its large rooms, gleaming mahogany furniture, paintings, and other works of art; the well-stocked library reflected Pickens's love for intellectual pursuits and the good life. The gardens were laid out in a formal English design with statuary and boxwoods, and near the garden was a pond that enhanced the view from the house. The most unique feature of Edgewood was an avenue of intertwined cedars; this route was lighted on festive occasions with bonfires of fat pine to guide guests to the house.[4] Although his cotton crop for 1833 had been "very short" because of wet, cold weather, Pickens continued to add to his acreage by buying more land adjacent to his Edgefield and Selma, Alabama, properties.[5] Like the holding of political office, the acquisition of land and slaves was a visible sign of power and importance. In gaining property Pickens was both fortunate and shrewd. As executor of Eldred Simkins's estate, he managed his wife's property and that of Simkins's other heirs. In

July 1834 he purchased from his mother-in-law 545 acres of land for $4,000. Acting as an agent for his father, who had served as president of the Bank of Alabama (1823–27), Pickens was able to buy several plots of land adjacent to property he controlled. One plot of unimproved land that encompassed almost 1,200 acres was purchased at a sheriff's sale in 1831 for $1,005 "ready cash."[6] In 1836 Andrew Pickens deeded most of his South Carolina property to Francis and gave a large portion of his Alabama holdings to his daughter, Susan, who lived in Alabama and was married to John C. Calhoun's nephew, James M. Calhoun. When Andrew died in 1838, Pickens and his sister inherited more of their father's estate.[7]

By 1839 Pickens owned three plantations in Edgefield District, two in Alabama, and one in Mississippi. His holdings comprised over 9,000 acres of land, abundant livestock, and numerous slaves. In the spring of 1838 he estimated his wealth to be $218,000, proudly calculating that his 189 slaves were worth $101,075, since they "were all of them family Negroes of the very *best kind*."[8] Every year brought an increase in the number of hands he owned. In 1842 the total had reached 267, and by 1847 he recorded that he owned 417 slaves, which made him one of the greatest planters in the South.[9] During this time he acquired 1,025 acres in adjacent Newberry County.[10] As his wealth grew, so did his reputation as a genteel aristocrat.

He was careful that no one abuse his slaves and gave the strictest orders that they be supplied generously with good clothes, blankets, housing, and food. Women and children were to be carefully treated, and all were to receive prompt attention when sick. Although his hands were never to be overworked, they were forbidden to leave the plantation, or to marry off the plantation. Sunday was a day for attending church, but at sundown all slaves were required to be present for roll call.[11]

Pickens kept regular notations of Edgewood happenings in his "Plantation Book." Deaths and births were recorded, tax records kept, and peculiar weather conditions noted. Every spring he entered the dates when the first new potatoes, peas, asparagus, and strawberries were harvested and made special mention of the killing of the first spring lamb. Travel plans and impressions were recorded, as were sadness and jubilation. Each year the bags of cotton, bushels of corn, and number of hams in the smokehouse were painstakingly inventoried in his almost illegible hand.[12]

Land transfer records augment the plantation book in revealing Pickens's business practices. Much of the land he owned was acquired from neighbors and at estate and sheriff's sales. While he served in Congress his acquisition rate diminished, but during the early 1850s there was a resurgence. At this time he borrowed liberally from friends but shunned banks. In January 1860 Pickens did a study of his wealth which revealed that, while being a debtor, he was also a creditor, having extended loans to friends and relations.[13] Good credit, inheritance, and shrewd dealings made him appear wealthier than he was.

As his holdings grew in the 1830s Pickens thrived, becoming more the bon vivant. Edgewood was noted as a place of "genial and lavish entertainment." One friend expressed the view that Pickens combined "courtly hospitality with rural abandon."[14] Behind this appearance of easy living was a keen student of plantation management. Like others of his class, Pickens practiced scientific soil management. He planted pea vines and used marl and manure to keep from depleting his soils. However, he rejected absolute theory in favor of practical management techniques. He understood that different soils required different treatments according to their texture, acidity, and moisture.[15]

Pickens maintained that a successful planter could not rely on hired agents but needed to be his own overseer. In 1849, in an address before the state agricultural society, he stated that the requisites for thrifty farming were "industry, care, and strict economy." In his speech Pickens proclaimed that in South Carolina cotton was not king, since it only accounted for one-fourth of the product of the state's labor. Using the 1840 census as his source, he maintained that the state had a higher level of corn production than either New York or Pennsylvania and that rice production "was equal in value to more than half the foreign exports of flour from every state in the union, until the last seven years."[16]

He defended slavery and connected it with the trait of southern militarism by claiming that the institution made planters constitute themselves into a "permanent 'national guard.' . . . Inured to exposure and to danger, their whole police regulations train them [planters] up to a military organization which is a school for manly and heroic virtues." He dismissed as a myth the assertion that southern planters spent their time in high living and costly indulgences. Planting, he asserted, was a risky gamble that could not succeed except through diligent effort, since the planter was at the mercy of weather, uncertain prices, banks, and a hostile North.[17]

As Pickens's wealth and prestige grew, the strict Calvinism of his grandfather gave way to the more moderate theology of the Episcopal church. In 1833 Pickens became a member of the founding vestry of Trinity Church, Edgefield, helping to raise the money for the church building and for a time paying the rector's salary. In addition to Pickens, Whitfield Brooks (the father of Preston Brooks) and Arthur Wigfall (the brother of Louis T. Wigfall) served on the founding vestry.[18] Pickens showed his disdain for the more evangelical religions when he wrote his sister-in-law, Maria, about the "derangement" of her brother Arthur Simkins, who professed "to be converted." In a facetious letter he described the unsophisticated religious behavior of the country folk who were in the throes of revivalism. He wrote, "There is mad temporal derangement on the subject at present. I suppose every person must have some matter on which they are deranged—I *know* I *have*."[19] Pickens (whose father-in-law had died in 1831) took seriously his role as legal guardian of Eldred Simkins's family. Treating like a brother Arthur Simkins, who was unlucky in love and business, Pickens gave him $12,000 after a series of failures and encouraged him to move to Mississippi. Later he would write to James Edward Colhoun, "My children will not allow me to help him again. I have done for him as if he were my own blood brother, but can do no more."[20]

Before Maria's marriage to James Edward Colhoun, Pickens took a lively interest in her affairs. She was one of his favorite correspondents, and his letters, often written in a light, bantering style, reveal another side of his personality. Usually he would give her advice or write about family affairs. Once he playfully idealized "Southern Belles" as ladies who "indulge in the softer sympathies of nature—who observe what they see and take interest in all around them, who indulge in the feelings and affections of the heart—who utter refined and delicate sentiments . . . who are mild and modest—whose eyes kindle with hope . . . whose bosom heaves with the most elevated and refined affections of the human heart."[21] In another letter Pickens delighted in painting a romantic picture of a dance that he and Eliza gave for the young people, telling Maria of the singing, playing, and moonlight promenading: "Every now and then you could see a young gentleman take a young lady off into a remote corner of the piazza, where he could breathe into her ear the soft but fiery accents of burning love."[22]

Anna Calhoun, the favorite daughter of John C. Calhoun, was another of Pickens's lady friends. It is obvious from the correspondence between Eliza, Maria, Anna, and Pickens that they enjoyed a very close relationship. He warned Maria of the "utter worthlessness and corruption of men," whom he described as "miserable, selfish, contracted little creatures . . . with none of the nobleness and dignity of human nature." He lamented, "When I looked on Anna and yourself this summer and thought of your youth, your sincerity . . . your innocence . . . my heart felt full of tenderness for your fates."[23] In correspondence he begged Anna to remember him in a kind and affectionate manner—not in the "repulsive attitude as . . . an advisor and moral lecturer."[24]

While Pickens was warning Maria and Anna about the debased nature of men, he was becoming aware of the cruelty and intrigue that inevitably accompany politics. His friend Hammond was running for Congress against Franklin Harper Elmore in the neighboring Barnwell District. Hammond wrote of the methods and intrigue being used in an effort to defeat him.[25] Although Pickens had no real opposition in his own congressional race, he was discovering that intrigue was common and that men he considered friendly were not to be relied upon.[26] Pickens's election gave him the unique opportunity to represent the most obstreperous district in the most obstreperous state in the Union. At the time of his election the States' Rights party found itself possessing more power in Congress than ever, and frequently holding the balance of power when the administration and opposition parties came into conflict.[27] A new fragile and temporary alliance had been forged by Clay and Calhoun over the tariff issue. In the midst of this, Andrew Jackson struck another sensitive national nerve when he reckoned on a course to kill the Second National Bank of the United States by vetoing a move to have it rechartered and by removing government deposits. These acts led many to foresee continued cooperation between Clay and Calhoun, which gave rise to speculation that two of Jackson's most bitter foes would be united against him. John Quincy Adams reported that relations between the Nullifiers and National Republicans were cordial and that they worked well together on matters of joint concern.[28] However, a wary Calhoun wrote to Pickens in early 1834, "We . . . are determined to preserve our separate existence. . . . If there is to be union against the administration, it must be union on our ground."[29] Calhoun's views became more palatable to the well to do when they saw Jackson's unyielding designs on the bank, and since Calhoun and his parties held the balance of power, they were more acceptable than previously.[30]

In December 1834 Pickens arrived in Washington as a Nullifier Democrat. The acknowledged leader of the Nullifiers in the House had been McDuffie. Shortly after Pickens arrived, he and Calhoun spent a death watch with Warren R. Davis, who had represented Calhoun's home district of Pendleton and who often spoke on behalf of Calhoun's measures in the House.[31] After Davis's death, Calhoun needed a reliable advocate, and although he was only a freshman legislator, Pickens emerged as Calhoun's chief spokesman in the House. While the bank and all its ramifications were the most absorbing issue of the period and portended the most disastrous consequences for the Union, the new congressman's first act was to request better postal service for his constituents in Edgefield.[32]

Pickens's introduction to national affairs came at a critical period in Franco-

American relations. For years the United States had attempted to procure from the French government money that France acknowledged it owed for maritime spoliations incurred during the Napoleonic Wars. Finally, in 1831, the French agreed to pay 25 million francs in six annual payments, but in the spring of 1834 the French refused to pay the first installment.[33] Andrew Jackson, in his first annual message, warned that the unsettled questions over the claims "continue to furnish a subject of unpleasant discussions and possible collision between the two governments." The Washington *Globe*, Jackson's official organ edited by Francis P. Blair, "speaking by authority," stirred up talk of war.[34] Jackson boasted of reprisals against French property, and in Congress no other matters of importance were transacted. Jackson was urging that $3 million be appropriated to build up American fortifications. In the Senate Calhoun, still filled with the memory of recent threats against the Palmetto State, spoke with passionate intensity against Jackson's request for an appropriation.[35] Although doubting the course that Calhoun pursued and believing that the South's fate was fixed "beyond regeneration except by an appeal to arms and the god of battle," Pickens loyally supported his kinsman in his fight against their mutual enemy Andrew Jackson. On 14 February 1835, on the eve of his maiden speech to the House, Pickens wrote to his cousin Patrick Noble, who was the speaker of the South Carolina House of Representatives: "Mr. Calhoun made his report yesterday, and it elicited much bitterness. . . . I have in the last few days been horrified and excited beyond measure, and I expect tomorrow to get the floor, where I shall speak my sentiment . . . what do you think sir? Are we to have war? . . . Whoever heard of a civilized people going to war for the payment of $5,000,000."[36] The Nullifiers deeply mistrusted Jackson and had no desire to see in his hands more power than he already possessed. John Quincy Adams advanced the proposition that every pressure short of war should be applied against the French. Pickens then took the floor and launched into a speech in which he ridiculed the administration by referring to Jackson as "the high sheriff of the land" who would call out the military "for the ignoble purposes . . . of plunder and murder. . . . Sir, you must first plant the stars and stripes in triumph upon the walls of Paris. With your army of six thousand men, surrounded by four hundred thousand, sir it is folly; it is worse than folly—it is madness."[37]

Until that point William C. Preston, who had gone to the Senate during the height of the nullification controversy, had enjoyed relative harmony of opinion with Calhoun, but the debates over the French question revealed the first fragmentation of their views. The Greenville *Mountaineer*, a Unionist paper long critical of the Nullifiers, brought into question the patriotism of Calhoun and his lieutenants. Congress unanimously voted that the treaty with France be maintained and insisted on its execution.[38] In the course of the debate, the House and the Senate had passed a measure allocating an annual appropriation for the military, but a Senate amendment required that the bill be returned to the House for further action. On the last day of the session the fortification measure again reached the Senate for final approval. The measure had been amended by the addition of $3 million, to be spent at the discretion of the president should the defense of the nation require it. Calhoun and Pickens, always distrustful of Jackson, worried that the president might take the opportunity to involve the nation in a war during the period between congressional sessions. Ultimately the whole measure died for lack of a quorum. The president was furious and blamed Calhoun and his men. The French accepted lack of action on the part of Congress as a conciliatory gesture and eventually agreed to pay.[39] Ironically, a factor in the defeat of the fortification bill involved, in a bizarre way, Pickens, Calhoun, and George Poindexter of Mississippi. Poindexter was president pro tempore of the Senate and a man thoroughly hated by the president.[40] As has been noted, Warren R. Davis, the representative from Calhoun's own Pendleton District, died on 29 January 1835. John Quincy Adams recorded in his diary that "Pickens, the member from South Carolina who comes in the place of McDuffie, announced the decease of his colleague Warren R. Davis. . . . Mr. Pickens pronounced a panegyric upon the deceased. . . . Mr. Pickens moved . . . that the House . . . attend the funeral tomorrow at noon." Adams continued by giving a description of the funeral procession and states, "I heard the snap of a pistol. . . . It was aimed at the President . . . by an insane man named Richard Laurence and it was said he snapped a second pistol; but I heard only one report. They both misfired."[41] President Jackson and those closest to him publicly accused Poindexter of arranging the attempted assassination, and Calhoun and his compatriots were accused of stirring up hatred against the president. Pickens, echoing a popular sentiment in Washington, maintained that the whole matter was nothing more than a plot that had been gotten up for political effect by Jackson himself in order to discredit Calhoun.[42] A Senate committee found no evidence to connect Poindexter with the assassination attempt and determined that his accusers had perjured themselves in order to discredit Poindexter and the Calhoun faction. Sentiment went against Jackson; disgust, mingled with distrust for the administration's tactics, turned many away from supporting Jackson's anti-French measures.[43]

The end to the French problem brought out of limbo the bank question, which would continue to have a profound effect on the course of the nation for a decade. Preceding the 1832 election, some partisans of the Second National Bank had urged a reluctant Nicholas Biddle, the bank's president, to apply for a new charter despite the fact that the 1816 charter would not expire until 1836. Congress passed the necessary legislation to continue the bank, but President Jackson vetoed the bill, much to Biddle's dismay. Biddle then threw all of his influence against Jackson, prompting the president to remove federal deposits from the bank and instead to place the government's revenues in favored state banks, known as "pet banks." This resulted in the national bank's having to restrict loans and contract the money supply, which in turn led to a panic.[44] As George McDuffie, who had been a past spokesman for the bank, observed, "The deposit question will engross the attention of Congress for a considerable time longer," and "public disapprobation is coming in upon the administration in peals."[45]

In South Carolina there were mixed feelings regarding Jackson and the bank. Many were delighted that the bank had been destroyed. Strangely, as the situation became more chaotic, most people placed the blame not on the president but on the "hydra-headed monster," which had the power to destroy them. Prior to 1835 the government faced the problem of increasing surpluses from the sale of western land; the depositing of an ever increasing amount of government funds in favored pet banks was leading to dangerous speculation. The killing of the Second National Bank knocked the props out from under a stabilizing influence, ultimately throwing the Union into a state of depression.[46]

Unlike McDuffie, who had been a longtime supporter of the bank, Pickens had a deep distrust for banks and bankers.[47] Perhaps this was the result of his father's association with the Bank of Alabama, or because many citizens were suspicious of the financial legerdemain that resulted in the banks making profits by manipulating people's money. Pickens believed the national bank to be a northern-based institution that was detrimental to the nation's welfare. He felt that the government should be separated from all banks and should deposit its revenues in its own agencies.[48] Prior to the nullification controversy he saw a natural relationship between those who supported the bank, advocated the abolition of slavery, and pressed for the protectionist tariff. He preached that they were carrying on an undisguised war to plunder the South.[49] The iniquity of banks caused his wrath to be leveled not only against the Bank of the United States, but also against all other banks that were given the benefit of public deposits. Thus, when Jackson's administration entrusted deposits to pet banks,

JOHN C. CALHOUN
(courtesy of the South Caroliniana Library, University of South Carolina)

Pickens condemned the action and became one of the first to advocate the creation of an independent treasury system, separate from banks, that could be utilized for the collection, deposit, and disbursement of government funds.[50]

With the issuance of the specie circular by the president after Congress adjourned in 1836, an economic crash was assured as confidence broke. Martin Van Buren, the chosen successor to Jackson, assumed the leadership of a government that Pickens considered "corrupt and profligate, one in which sin . . . ruled over virtue."[51] Prior to 1837 there had been no popular support for the independent treasury scheme. However, as panic swept the land and banks ceased redeeming their notes in gold and silver, the ideas that Pickens claimed would bring stability out of financial woe enjoyed greater acceptance.[52]

Pickens would use the confusion resulting from the depression in order to change a long-standing political stalemate that resulted from the animosity between Calhoun and Van Buren. For eight years a bitter contest had been waged, culminating in Van Buren's election as president. Yet political realities and a shared philosophy were to make for an unusual rapprochement.[53] In May 1837 the new chief executive called for a special session of Congress to meet in September to deal with the financial crisis. The Van Buren administration wanted to create a system that would provide for the collection, safekeeping, transfer, and disbursement of public money and that would be managed by officers of the government without the aid or intervention of any bank or banks.[54] President Van Buren hoped this course would bring order out of the chaotic fiscal situation and at the same time not ruffle many feathers. In order to do this he had to abandon the banks that had helped elect him. One controversial part of the scheme was that the government would accept and disburse only gold and silver and make use of no bank credit. There was fear that, unless government funds were deposited in banks, the whole banking system would collapse.[55] Since the measure had been advanced by the administration, South Carolinians would presumably be opposed to its passage. In his inaugural address Van Buren held out to the South the promise that he would not sanction any act on the part of Congress that tampered with slavery in the District of Columbia. Ironically, by this gesture Van Buren was appealing not to the Calhoun faction who hated him, but to those in the South who opposed the senator. However, this move pleased all Southerners and made Van Buren more acceptable to the region.[56]

During the Twenty-fourth Congress, which commenced in December 1835, there had been overt harmony among the Carolinians. Calhoun was directing the South Carolina Whig coalition. Pickens, Hammond (who had been elected to the House from the Barnwell District), Waddy Thompson (who took his seat on 16 December, replacing Warren R. Davis from the Pendleton District), Calhoun, and Preston all stayed at Mrs. Lindenberger's boardinghouse on Capitol Hill. Throughout 1836 these men and members of their families often dined together.[57] They shared similar views on abolition, but they began to disagree on foreign relations and the bank question. On 26 February 1836 James Hammond resigned from Congress for health reasons and took his family on a tour of Europe. Pickens and Calhoun continued to dine together regularly, but their relationship with Preston and Thompson began to sour.[58]

At home Calhoun had his share of enemies. Many were angry, believing that the senator had made an alliance with the Whigs and was abandoning this coalition. Old Union men still harbored resentment over the course he had taken on nullification and over his stand on Jackson's fortification measure. Before the 1836 election the Unionist John P. Richardson wrote Pickens that "the state is looking for a new master. It feels that the chains of Calhoun are worn out by long use." Richardson urged Pickens to abandon his loyalty to Calhoun and the Nullifiers and to become the Union candidate for governor.[59] Although Pickens may have been flattered by the prospect of being South Carolina's chief executive at such a young age, he refused to abandon Calhoun, who held the keys to the political aspirations of Carolina's sons.

At this time Pickens found himself disillusioned with the corrupt nature of politics and generally demoralized. The abolition question hit the nation with full force; the southern states were divided; Pickens had to fire his overseer for whipping Negroes; and in the spring of 1836 he almost died from "bilious influenze" which incapacitated him for two months. He did enjoy a good cotton crop; however, he got a poor price for it.[60] Van Buren was also having problems at this time, however, and out of these difficulties Pickens and Calhoun found an opportunity to change their relations with the new administration and to chart a course whereby they could enjoy political ascendancy.[61]

During the spring and summer of 1837 the nation focused on Van Buren's plans to save the economy. The president had called a special session of Congress to meet on the first Monday in September. Early in the spring of 1837 Pickens and Calhoun secretly decided on a provocative course of action. They found that "the counsels of the 'fox' . . . were sounder than the doctrine or practice of the abdicated lion." Earlier invectives were forgotten as plans were made that would tear the fabric of both state and local politics. Those who refused to perform their bidding were to be driven from the councils. This was to be the culmination of the economic clash dividing the Union.[62] Pickens, who was advocating that the government be separated from banks, believed that states' righters needed to abandon their relationship with the Whigs and "play for the old *Original Jackson Party*" in order to regenerate southern power. His South needed to decide whether "cotton should control exchanges and importations, or whether the bank and stock interest should: . . . Break down the swindling bankers . . . and cotton will be the exchange of the commercial world."[63] Through the efforts of Pickens and fellow South Carolinian Joel R. Poinsett, who had become secretary of war, a secret reconciliation of sorts was established between Van Buren and Calhoun, and a plan was devised for a mutual effort to pass the independent treasury measure.[64] It was decided that Pickens in the House and Calhoun in the Senate would lead the fight to divorce the treasury from banks. From Pickens's viewpoint "the states' rights party never had so beautiful a position to occupy as they have at present. As a party it must preserve its independence and separate existence. It is an unnatural alliance for us to sustain."[65] The Whig press would ridicule the unnatural alliance by calling attention to a speech that Pickens had made in the spring, in which he characterized those in the Van Buren administration as "the rooks . . . that have perched themselves in high places of the land, and we sit here beneath, surrounded by their filth."[66]

In June 1837 Pickens wrote Richard K. Crallé, the editor of the Washington *Reformer*, several long, complicated letters in which he outlined his position.[67]

> The more I see the more I am thoroughly satisfied we cannot go for the bank in any shape or form. It is antagonistic to our interest, and besides it cannot be brought within the powers of the Constitution. . . . The government is bankrupt, and it is better for us for it can never be reformed unless it be crippled and poor. The whole banking system is a fraud upon the world, and we must never sustain it. The capitalists of the nonslaveholding states live by it . . . they declare war upon slavery and hold in bondage the labor of the confederacy. . . . It is weakness and vanity in us to attempt to make *such* a government as we have perfect . . . we are interested in making it weak and powerless.[68]

In early September the rumor was being spread that the Nullifiers intended to support the independent treasury. The Baltimore *Merchant*, edited by Duff Green, on 12 September announced that Calhoun supported certain parts of Van Buren's fiscal program.[69] His associate Richard Crallé wrote a long editorial in support of the measure which appeared in the *Reformer* on 14 September.[70] Finally on 22 September the *Merchant* did an adroit somersault by deserting its Whig position, claiming that Calhoun and his men, by supporting the administration, had "captured the Van Buren executive."[71]

While rumors were flying, the House was being organized. Pickens led the first floor fight of the session over the issue of selection of the House printer. He argued that the printing contract should be given to the lowest bidder and not as a reward for partisan political services. He accused the House printers, Blair and Rives, of assailing the independent action of members of the House. Pickens was supported by Henry Wise and the Virginia Whigs. The fight over the printer continued for three days, until on the twelfth ballot Thomas Allen, publisher of the *Madisonian*, was elected.[72] On the heels of this battle the House brought up for debate legislation that gave the treasury the exclusive power to regulate money. The banking interests exploded, as the measure took away from them a very profitable prerogative. In the House of Representatives the administration, led by Speaker of the House James K. Polk and Churchill Cambreling, chairman of the ways and means committee, deferred to Pickens, who introduced several controversial measures.[73] The fight began when Pickens advocated a delay in the payment guaranteed to the states by the distribution act. He argued that the depression had depleted the government's surplus, and that in order to distribute money the government would need to borrow and to levy heavier taxes. His efforts did not go unnoticed. After the House voted to postpone paying the installment, Francis P. Blair, an ancient enemy of the Calhoun faction, praised the Carolinian in his *Globe*, which was understood to be the official organ of the Van Buren administration.[74] On 10 October Pickens made the first speech on behalf of the Divorce Banks bill. This effort, which urged an end to the union of banks and government, was also lauded by the *Globe*, which printed the full text of his address.[75] Pickens was so pleased with his first efforts that he requested that Ogden Niles, the proprietor of *Niles Register*, publish two hundred copies of his speeches.[76] The support of Pickens and Calhoun for the independent treasury measure was to have a profound effect on South Carolina politics. In mid-October the *Globe* began a furious attack on William C. Preston for his stand against the measures, claiming that Preston was acting out of self-interest. His brother John, who had married the very rich daughter of Wade Hampton II, was a close confidant of Nicholas Biddle, president of the hated United States Bank.[77] The strident attacks on Preston and the moves of the Calhoun faction took most of South Carolina's leaders by surprise. In 1834, in order to underscore their contempt for Andrew Jackson and his policies, many Carolinians had joined with the National Republicans to form the Whig party. Pickens and Calhoun had not taken this course. Although they had contempt for Jackson and had made alliances with the Whigs, they held the Whig philosophy to be alien, since it was associated with banks and manufacturing.[78] The thread binding the Whigs and their allies was spun out of hate for Jackson and not out of a common political philosophy; thus the introduction of the independent treasury caused it to snap.

Both Pickens and Calhoun substantiated their moves by proclaiming that the North, through the use of the banking system, exercised unfair control over the South, and that the passage of the independent treasury would "break the last of our commercial shackles."[79] As early as 1834 both Calhoun and Pickens had espoused the divorce philosophy, but they had never been in the position to have their views acted upon. The economic crash forced the desperate Van Buren to seek a solution. The most plausible prospect was for the president to look to the Nullifiers and their strength to help solve his problems. With the help of Pickens, the bitter feud between Van Buren and Calhoun had been overcome, as Calhoun saw an opportunity to assume once again a role as a national leader. When news of the strange new relationship reached the Whigs, they became furious, accusing Pickens and Calhoun of the highest treachery. Dr. Francis Mallory, a Whig representative from Virginia, wrote one of Pickens's closest associates, R. M. T. Hunter, that he remained in a state of disbelief over Calhoun's reversal of position and did not like Calhoun's reconciliation with Van Buren. Mallory believed that Calhoun's desertion of "the Whigs on whom . . . he depended for support . . . will prove ruinous."[80] William C. Preston bitterly accused his colleague of abandoning the Whigs. Calhoun retaliated with the famous remark that he had never been anything "but an honest Nullifier."[81] James L. Petigru, South Carolina's most respected Unionist, wrote, "I shall hear Mr. Calhoun in the Senate, that gentleman has taken a most extraordinary turn . . . and is going to make a speech . . . in favor of the message. All the members from our state will be against him except two: Mr. Pickens and Barnwell Smith, called Mr. Rhett. Nothing can be more monstrous than to support a scheme for doing away with bank paper and of course with credit, and ruining all who are in debt. It is awful—it is so sudden—and . . . so unexpected."[82]

Relations between Calhoun and Preston were growing cold before Calhoun's alliance with Van Buren and his support of the independent treasury scheme. Ironically, ill feelings between the two had intensified during the election of 1836, when Preston, who was up for reelection, was rumored to support Van Buren.[83] In South Carolina a division was growing between the seemingly small faction that supported Calhoun and those powerful state leaders who supported Preston's position, among whom were Langdon Cheves, Petigru, ex-governors Robert Y. Hayne and James Hamilton, and the majority of the House delegation. Of the nine-member South Carolina House delegation, only Pickens and Rhett initially worked for the passage of the bill.[84]

Preston, who controlled the Columbia *Telescope*, began a campaign to organize the state's newspapers against the independent treasury, but he informed his chief lieutenant, Waddy Thompson, that he wanted to preserve "political and personal relations with everybody."[85] As a result of Calhoun's eminence and Preston's caution, the independent treasury men would win the battle for the state. Pickens was denounced as having gone over to the general Democratic party and deserting South Carolina.[86] Throughout September and October 1837, Pickens could be heard debating the issue with the "bitter Whigs." With extravagant rhetoric he pressed the message, "Break down the credit system and the bank and we dictate terms." He deeply believed that the overall object of the North was to plunder the South.[87] After Pickens's most ambitious oratorical effort on the subject on 10 October 1837, John Quincy Adams scorned him in his lively but aciduous memoirs. "The sub-treasury bill was called up by Pickens . . . who made a speech . . . of two hours, with which he has been swelling like a cock turkey . . . Pickens is a fixture in the house of Calhoun, and Van Buren bought him with Calhoun . . . Pickens is a coarse sample of the South Carolina school of orator statesman—pompous, flashy, and shallow."[88] As the leader of the northern Whigs in Congress, the former president naturally held animosity for those who would protect the peculiar institution, which he loathed, and destroy the banks, which he deemed necessary; however, his dislike of Pickens can be better understood from reading the following entry in the diary of Mrs. W. C. Preston, a confirmed enemy: "We learn too that Mr. Pickens goes out of the hall when Henry A. Wise and others of his flock attack South Carolinians, but there is no bolder man than Mr. F. W. Pickens when old Mr. Adams and other avowedly noncombatants attack us."[89]

The measure was brought to a vote on 14 October 1837. Just as Preston had predicted, it narrowly passed in the Senate but failed in the House, 120-107.[90] The ramifications of the split between the Preston forces and those led by Calhoun would profoundly affect South Carolina. At the outset only Blair's *Globe* and Duff Green's *Merchant* were printing editorials supporting Calhoun's position, and Pickens supplied ideas for these.[91] Initially the Calhounites had only two South Carolina newspapers, the Pendleton *Messenger*, which was published in Calhoun's home county, and the influential Charleston *Mer-*

cury, edited by Rhett's brother-in-law, J. A. Stuart. The *Mercury*, taking Calhoun's opposition for granted, castigated Van Buren by harshly criticizing his speech advocating the creation of the independent treasury. However, by the end of September the paper was again in the Calhoun fold.[92] Still, the entire political establishment seemed to be in open revolt against their leader. Intelligent and able men feared that, unless government revenues were deposited in banks, the whole credit and banking system would falter. Throughout the period Calhoun and Pickens remained composed, formulating logical arguments for their position; these were printed in the *Globe* and reprinted in the *Mercury* and other South Carolina newspapers.[93] The Whigs led by Preston and Thompson moved away from a policy of pacifism and bitterly denounced Pickens and Calhoun. Open political warfare was the prospect. George McDuffie warned Preston, Calhoun, Pickens, and Thompson of "the danger of dividing the state into political parties, upon the ground of differences of opinion that prevails among you in relations to the currency and public deposits . . . I think both parties of you are just half right and half wrong."[94] Preston, writing to Waddy Thompson in regard to McDuffie's letter, let his venom flow: "I informed McDuffie that I had no such intentions to divide the state and that I was earnestly inclined to preserve both political and personal relations with everybody *except the scoundrels* . . . I may not have it in my power to avenge the lurking scoundrels, but I shall not readily forget it."[95] The scoundrels were Pickens and Duff Green (whose daughter was married to Calhoun's eldest son, Andrew), Crallé's predecessor as editor of the *United States Telegraph*. Preston believed they had been responsible for defaming him in the newspapers.[96] Pickens's role in the affair became more apparent after an inflammatory letter in which he condemned Preston's friendship with Henry Clay, who was considered unsafe on slavery, was read at a public meeting in Charleston.[97] This further inflamed passions. The correspondence of South Carolina leaders was full of accounts of the rift that was taking such a heavy toll.[98] The desire for vengeance reached mammoth proportions. Preston was accused of being "ungenerous and unpatriotic." Although Preston was unable to wreak immediate vengeance on the "injudicious Mr. Pickens," the affair profoundly affected Pickens's future relationships.[99] The hard feelings and the accusations of underhanded intrigue, coupled with his mercurial personality, would ultimately prove harmful to his career. But Calhoun's magical appeal had not been lost in the battle, and (much to the chagrin of the Whigs) the legislature almost unanimously embraced his course.[100] Pickens, who himself had mastered the art of political intrigue, defamed the Whigs by writing that Preston and Thompson's motive in going against Calhoun was "to make themselves acceptable to Northern men by dividing the South and sacrificing our position. I hope agitation in South Carolina cannot be too strong against them. We will have a great appeal to the people and the excitement will be intense."[101] Pickens was correct—the intense excitement became even more so. Preston, alarmed at what was taking place, attempted to obtain support to start another Charleston newspaper to counteract the *Mercury*.[102] The affair was bringing terrible confusion to South Carolina politics, but it gave Pickens and Rhett the opportunity to feather their own political nests, since they had stayed by Calhoun when others had deserted him. Unfortunately, Calhoun was not considering either man's aspirations; rather, he knew that, in order to promote his own political ambitions, peace needed to be regained and preserved in South Carolina.

The failure of the independent treasury measure in the fall of 1837 depressed Pickens, who told Hammond that he intended to remain "entirely silent this session unless things are forced upon me."[103] Hammond, concerned that the delegation's differences over the independent treasury were proving harmful to the Palmetto State, urged an end to factional hostility so that questions of more momentous import could be faced.[104]

At this time the question of Congress's right to receive petitions urging the abolition of slavery in the District of Columbia was occupying more and more time. The slavery question, coupled with economic difficulties, caused Pickens again to question the value of the Union. "It is my deliberate conviction that we ought to live to ourselves . . . I wish that the nonslaveholding states could take Canada and go to themselves and leave us with Texas to ourselves."[105] Hammond worried, "While we have been employed only in killing one another, our adversaries have quietly pocketed the stakes."[106]

Inactivity was anathema to Pickens. Despite his vow of silence, he was frequently heard in the House as debate resumed on the independent treasury in early 1838. He, Rhett, and Calhoun struggled to close the division in the House, where the delegation was still sharply divided. Waddy Thompson was still standing by his friend Preston and the Whigs. The Calhoun faction feared that representatives Robert Campbell of Georgetown and Hugh Swinton Legaré of Charleston would vote with Thompson against the measure. Franklin H. Elmore had replaced Hammond as the representative from Barnwell District and had allied himself with the Calhoun faction, even though he was a banker.[107] Pickens informed Hammond that "there is much doubt as to the passage of the independent treasury bill. The vote will be close and much depends on our delegation."[108] Rhett and Elmore, working through Rhett's brother Albert, a leader in the General Assembly, were able to influence the

South Carolina legislature to approve resolutions written by Pickens that supported the course of the Calhoun faction.[109] These resolutions, designed to embarrass the opposition, proved counterproductive and had a detrimental effect on Palmetto State politics. Pickens believed that, if differences were put aside and southern members of Congress united to pass the measure, the South would control the balance of power. The real issue, stated Pickens, was not simply a struggle over the subtreasury, but over "whether cotton shall control exchanges and importations, or whether banks and stock interest shall do it."[110]

The efforts to achieve unanimity were futile. Clearly, only a few votes either way would determine whether the bill would pass. Calhoun and Pickens continued to be lauded by one of their oldest and once most detested adversaries, Francis Blair, in his Washington *Globe*.[111] It seemed to John Quincy Adams that the Calhoun men had changed from being "voracious nullifiers to painted administration butterfl[ies]."[112] Mrs. W. C. Preston wrote, "Mr. Calhoun always votes with the administration party; and yet last September, he and friends were in great wrath, because Mr. Preston said Mr. C. was an administration man . . . now . . . his men Pickens, Elmore and Dixon H. Lewis call themselves administration men . . . a year ago they were all against my husband, because he would not abuse Mr. Van Buren or his party."[113]

In order to gather home support and pressure Campbell and Legaré, Pickens asked his cousin, Governor Patrick Noble, to assist him by attending meetings and calling a caucus "to advocate the resolutions that the legislature had passed upholding the independent treasury." Pickens requested Noble to "consult with the Union party too as Richardson is now writing letters on the subject."[114]

The differences between Calhoun and Preston were irreconcilable. Preston's closeness to Clay and his opposition to the anti-bank bill splintered an old relationship that had been built on mutual respect and friendship. Pickens, who had also been close to Preston, now castigated the senator and accused him of lacking "the slightest principles" and desiring to "divide the South and sustain Clay." He urged Noble to help in leading a movement that would force Preston to resign his senate seat, asserting that Preston was "doing more injury to their cause than all of our opponents together."[115]

The bill would soon be brought to a vote again. In the House there were 239 members; a count prior to the last debates on the measure showed that its proponents lacked four of the 120 votes needed.[116] In his last speech on the bill Pickens reiterated his earlier arguments. The most controversial item in the legislation was a section that required the government to make its collections and payments in gold or silver. Opponents argued that, under this arrangement, the debtor class would be placed under an onerous hardship. Hard specie would be scarce, thus credit and currency difficult to obtain. Pickens replied that "it is a poor and contracted declamation to say that collections in gold and silver would break down the prospects of the country." He asserted that the use of hard money would preserve ". . . a stable and fixed standard of value . . . under such a system we could at least have a free and contented people."[117] Shortly after the debate ended, the bill came up for another vote; on 22 June 1838 it was rejected, 125-111.[118]

The Calhoun faction was furious that the South Carolina congressional delegation had split 6-3 on the independent treasury issue and agreed that the price for disobedience to South Carolina's master was to be political death. Hugh Swinton Legaré, the representative from Charleston, realized that he would pay for his opposition by becoming a "Roman sacrifice" and losing his seat. Legaré's prophecy came to pass, both for himself and for Campbell. However, Waddy Thompson, who represented Calhoun's district, was re-elected despite Calhoun's and Pickens's most vigorous efforts.[119]

The independent treasury bill continued to be debated until it finally passed, in the second session of the Twenty-sixth Congress, and was signed into law on 4 July 1840.[120] Ironically, the measure became law because the United States Bank had collapsed in 1839, bringing on a new wave of desperation that caused some of those who had previously opposed the measure to support it.[121]

Calhoun proved that he was still master of South Carolina, and order was preserved, though at heavy cost. The Whig party lost ground and after 1842 failed for several years to elect a congressman or a significant number of state legislators. Preston, the "deadest man" in Congress, resigned his seat on 29 November 1842. As a reward for his service as a faithful administration man, Pickens was offered the ambassadorship to Austria; he did not accept, for much more appealing was the indication that Van Buren's administration would support him for Speaker of the House. However, the personal political price exacted by this choice was to be heavy. He would lose support for future offices that he sought, and years later, when he became governor, many of those who were close to Preston did not readily forget his role in the Calhoun-Preston feud.[122]

Intertwined in all debates on the money question was the provocative question of slavery and its companion issue, the annexation of Texas. Before Pickens entered Congress, a southern furor had been raised in the midst of the nullification controversy by Great Britain's decision to carry out an antislavery crusade, by the launching of William Lloyd Garrison's *Liberator*, and by Nat Turner's slave rebellion.

Before the slavery issue assumed such a momentous role in the life of the nation, Pickens in his "Hampden" letters connected those Northerners who supported the protectionist tariff with those who were pressing the abolition question.[123] Throughout the early 1830s the spirit of emancipation was increasing in the North. In 1834 Calhoun, writing from Washington, informed Pickens that the abolition movement was taking on larger proportions and that the abolitionists were planning to flood Congress with petitions urging that slavery be abolished in the District of Columbia.[124] Calhoun predicted that these moves signaled "the commencement of the work of immediate emancipation over the whole of the South, to which event it will certainly lead, if not promptly met by the entire slaveholding states with the fixed determination to resist at any hazard."[125] The die was cast, and the Union would be shocked time and time again. Slavery became such an intense and passionate issue that both North and South grew determined either to abolish or to protect the peculiar institution.

Just as Calhoun had predicted, petitions praying for the abolition of slavery in the nation's capital were introduced in Congress during the fall and winter of 1835–36. When Pickens entered Congress, the situation was "eminently perilous"; acrimony reigned. Calhoun worried that, if the southern states did not develop a sense of harmony, the "capacity for resisting would daily become weaker." The senator urged that "South Carolina . . . take the lead in all that may be done," for he believed that the slavery issue would bring concert to a Palmetto State ruptured by the nullification controversy. Calhoun hoped that out of national chaos South Carolina would find unity, trusting that James Louis Petigru and "others like him, must be anxious to restore themselves to the state. If so, harmony becomes practical."[126]

On 16 February 1835 some citizens of Rochester, New York, introduced petitions urging Congress to abolish slavery in the District of Columbia. Henry A. Wise, a leader of the Southern Whigs and a proslavery congressman from Virginia, made a speech in the House that left no doubt about the South's inability to compromise or temporize with the new moves against slavery. However, he admonished his colleagues "not to throw a firebrand" into the situation, fearing that "these memorials, so dangerous in their tendency and incendiary in their character," would stir up the nation.[127] These fears proved justified; from both North and South fanatics emerged to inflame public passions. Francis Pickens had been returned unopposed to the Twenty-fourth Congress. His old friend James H. Hammond was the new representative from

Barnwell District. Since Pickens, Hammond, and Calhoun lived at the same boardinghouse, they were in an excellent position to plan a strategy to counter the abolitionists. Throughout 1835 the Carolinians argued that Congress had no constitutional right to concern itself with slavery, since the Constitution expressly sanctioned the institution; thus Congress had no right to receive petitions praying for the abolition of slavery in the District of Columbia.[128] On 18 December 1835, Pickens made his first remarks on the abolition question, assailing William Jackson of Massachusetts for introducing such resolutions. Pickens argued that the House had the perfect right to reject any and all petitions relating to slavery. On 21 January 1836, John Quincy Adams introduced more petitions. Again Pickens rose to his feet and, in a lengthy speech that supported Wise's earlier resolutions, rejected Congress's authority to deal with the slavery question. Pickens attacked numerous individuals and groups whom he considered detrimental to the South's welfare. He began with Van Buren, for his policy of vacillation; then he moved on to the official editor of the Jackson party, the "macabre" Francis P. Blair of the *Globe*, who had become Calhoun's arch enemy. Pickens referred to Blair as "a miserable whipster editor . . . who has fed upon Calumny and fattens upon slander and upon whose countenance envy and malignity hold their cadaverous union. I would loathe to touch this pitiful *thing*, that lives by licking the spittle of men, if it were not that it is understood to represent the Executive Branch of this government."[129] He then turned his thunder upon the British government, which he accused of the highest hypocrisy by holding in bondage "one hundred millions of human beings in her East India possessions." Making a pitch for the support of Irish workingmen in the Northeast, he criticized England for holding in political vassalage Ireland, "the land of genius and eloquence," even as she "violated the rights of property [by] emancipat[ing] a race in the West Indies, only to throw them upon the world, strolling vagrants and vagabonds." Pickens tore into John Quincy Adams, who he claimed gathered strength in fanaticism—"in painting scenes of imaginary evil—in appealing to the passions of the heart and . . . to their religion." He continued by repudiating the doctrine of equality of man, calling upon his Calvinistic heritage to justify his position: "From the days of Moses and the children of Israel—the history of mankind proclaims that there 'is an elect and chosen few,' made the peculiar receptacles of the favors and blessings of an all-wise and all-prevailing providence. This is the world as we find it, and it is not for us to war upon destiny." The speech made several allusions to the "old appeal to the sword," and, in a prophetic summation, predicted that if the abolitionists were not checked it would ultimately be impossible to "avoid the contest."[130]

In the ubiquitous House debates Pickens railed against the "Northern Capitalist," who had declared a war on slavery and intended to hold the South in bondage. Southern congressmen tried to push through a rule that would prohibit abolitionists from introducing petitions for freedom. Pickens, worrying that the "moral power of the world is against us," spoke against the northern press for their "prejudice and denunciation against us," claiming that "their propaganda spreads like the plague and grows blacker and blacker."[131]

The slavery question accomplished what the tariff battle had been unable to, as Nullifiers and Unionists came together to fight the unwinnable battle. Only the bank and subtreasury issues and their kindred problems threatened the southern commonality of purpose. In Congress every issue was affected by the passion of slavery. The simplest matters became complicated as the defense of slavery rode over all. Rhetoric grew bolder. Pickens argued that in every society one class would own another class; he pointed to the northern capitalists who he claimed found slavery repugnant, yet who supported a form of that very institution by permitting wage slavery to exist in their factories.[132] In a debate that John Quincy Adams recorded for posterity, Pickens threatened the abolitionists by claiming that, if they continued to press the abolition question, he would preach insurrection to the northern working class and urge them to revolt against their "capitalistic masters." Adams commented that "all this was delivered with an air of authority and a tone of dogmatism as if he were speaking to his slaves."[133] Caleb Cushing, Adams's well-known colleague from Massachusetts, replied to Pickens by quoting from an earlier speech; using Pickens's own bombastic language, Cushing accused him of leading "a party that is profligate, unprincipled, and detestable."[134]

Southern politicians wanted to prevent the abolition question from being debated, but petitions and memorials were presented with increasing frequency by zealots from the North. Bitterness reigned. Pickens claimed that, since Congress had no power to deal with slavery in the District of Columbia, all papers relating to abolition should lie on the table without being referred or printed.[135]

On 4 February 1836, Congressman Henry L. Pinckney of Charleston, a Nullifier and former editor of the *Mercury*, introduced a series of resolutions from which emerged the famous gag rule. Pinckney first showed the resolutions to Pickens, who begged him not to submit them, as their introduction would confirm the northern belief that Congress *did* have the power to legislate on slavery in the District of Columbia.[136] The resolutions denied Congress any power over slavery in the states, questioned the wisdom of interference with slavery in the District of Columbia, and established the rule that all petitions on the subject should be laid on the table without being printed, referred, or further acted upon. Pinckney's resolutions were made a standing House rule that would be enacted with each opening session. However, the abolitionists were to use the gag rule to their own advantage by linking their cause to the right of petition.[137]

Many Carolinians greeted the resolutions with rage. Pinckney had broken their solid front by conceding that Congress could consider the fate of slavery in the nation's capital. Pinckney was asked to reconsider, but on 8 February he spoke in favor of his resolutions. Pickens helped lead a futile fight against their passage.[138] Administration supporters joined with the abolitionists to carry the resolutions 174-48, establishing that Congress had the power to decide whether it would allow abolition petitions to be submitted in the House.[139] Van Buren's supporters were elated, as this afforded their candidate an escape from the distasteful prospect of having to take a stand on slavery. The foothold that the abolitionists wanted became theirs, not by their own efforts, but by the blunder of a Calhoun lieutenant who had fallen into a Van Buren trap.

Pinckney could hardly have realized the gravity and consequences of his actions. South Carolina exploded. From all sections of the state the Charlestonian was denounced. Pickens accused his colleague of betraying the people's "most sacred rights," referred to him as a "traitor and a dastard," and predicted that the passage of the resolutions would cause the abolition movement "to assume the most serious aspects and force us into a convention."[140] The Edgefield *Advertiser* echoed Pickens, in somewhat softer terms: "He, Pinckney, has no advocate with us . . . we point to a Pickens and a Hammond as true models of Carolina." Former Governor James Hamilton thought Pinckney's course monstrous and utterly inexplicable, "except on the presumption of religious fanaticism."[141]

Pinckney's course was to cost him his seat. He was replaced by Hugh Swinton Legaré, a Unionist who had been urged to run for the seat by James Louis Petigru in order to "play a great role by bringing *back* South Carolina to the Communion of the Holy Church."[142] Legaré was safe on the slave question, but he suffered the same fate as Pinckney for not being in line on the independent treasury issue.[143]

The Pinckney resolutions were not finally passed until 15 May 1836. As a final salvo Pickens, Waddy Thompson, and the Virginia Whigs led by Henry A. Wise "immediately attacked the gag rule with extreme violence and a fiery debate arose." For days Pinckney's resolutions elicited some of the bitterest debates ever held in the House.[144] The *Mercury* lamented their passage: "It yields the Constitutional right to abolish slavery in the District of Columbia

... these abolitionists claimed nothing more, and all the right they ever claimed it has conceded."[145] Duff Green's *U.S. Telegraph* lauded Pickens for his attempts to stop Pinckney and accused the latter of "abominable trickery" by placing southern rights upon a sandy foundation.[146] Ironically, despite the great hate generated by the incident, Pinckney barely lost his congressional seat and showed that he still enjoyed the respect of the independent Charlestonians by being elected their mayor.[147]

At the height of the controversy, the matter of Texas independence was introduced and further exacerbated the slavery problem. In 1835 the Mexican government under Santa Anna decided to tighten its grip on the administration of Texas. During the winter and spring of 1835–36 the Texas revolution was precipitated. The Alamo, Goliad, and finally the Texas victory at San Jacinto in April 1836 set the stage for Texas independence. In a speech delivered on the fortification bill on 23 May 1836, Pickens made one of the earliest pleas for annexation. He claimed not to desire merely to strengthen the slaveholding states—"I scorn to place the annexation of Texas upon any such narrow grounds."[148] Pickens's claims were not believed by his northern colleagues, who saw that in Texas slavery and King Cotton reigned. In 1836 outright annexation proved an impossible goal. Pickens urged the friends of Texas to submit resolutions and petitions urging the recognition of Texas as an independent nation.[149]

In South Carolina Pickens was applauded for his efforts on behalf of slavery. Barbecues and dinners were given in his honor, and Calhoun publicly lauded his kinsman. "Your representative," he proclaimed, "richly merits ... your respect, by the intelligence, abilities and zeal with which he has discharged his public duties. No one could be more faithful to his trust."[150] Despite such praise, the spring and summer of 1836 proved to be a difficult period in Pickens's life. As has been noted, he became seriously ill and for weeks was unable to participate in the affairs of Congress.[151] Part of his difficulty involved a deep state of depression brought on by the "irreversible course in civic virtue."[152] Calhoun urged Pickens to suppress his despondency "and in its place substitute a manly and bold discharge of duty; ... If possible, let us save the liberty of all; but, if not, our own at all events."[153] Pickens decided to remain in Congress and was reelected without opposition.[154]

Although the critical illness of Pickens's mother-in-law prevented him from being present when Congress met in December 1837, events there were to have a profound impact on his future political career.[155] Before gag rules for the session were invoked, John Quincy Adams was able to gain the floor and present memorials about slavery and Texas. This resulted in a "terrible scene" which caused Adams to proclaim "the South and Southern men . . . intolerable." Hugh Swinton Legaré "rose and tried to stop him [Adams]—so did others—all is in vain. We do not know how to manage the inflexible, implacable, furious, and yet crafty old man."[156] William Slade of Vermont followed in Adams's footsteps; ten days later he introduced new memorials advocating the abolition of slavery in the District of Columbia.[157] Many southern delegates retired from the House chamber and held a meeting of their own.[158] At this meeting Robert Barnwell Rhett, who had just entered Congress, and Calhoun urged the calling of a southern convention to devise a permanent and satisfactory solution to the slavery question.[159] Neither Calhoun nor Rhett was successful in arranging a southern convention; however, the whole affair served to project Rhett on to the national scene and placed him in a position to rival Pickens as Calhoun's spokesman in the House. During the sessions that commenced in December 1836 and September 1837, Pickens lived with Calhoun and an unusual assortment of northern representatives at Miss Cochran's boardinghouse. The mess arrangements of the previous term had been most agreeable, but the friction caused by Calhoun's rapprochement with Van Buren had destroyed it.[160] Pickens was given the task of leading the fight against the abolitionist petitions that were presented in the House in early 1837.[161] It was Pickens who led the fight for the independent treasury, and it was Pickens who worked on a reconciliation between Van Buren and Calhoun. Pickens had stood with Calhoun on every issue and had subordinated himself to the senator's will. Calhoun frequently talked of leaving public life, and Pickens hoped to receive the laurels as his reward for faithful service. Yet, with the spectacular arrival of Rhett, Pickens found himself facing an indomitable rival for Calhoun's mantle of leadership, a man who, through the use of family connections and the diligent courting of Calhoun, was to become one of Pickens's political nemeses. Both Rhett and Pickens were able to accommodate the politics of Van Buren and the national Democrats by toning down their zeal for nullification; both men emerged on the right side of such issues as the tariff, abolition, and the independent treasury. Ultimately the two would clash not over issues, but over jealousy and ambition.

During this period numerous problems were besetting Pickens. His wife and mother-in-law were very ill. While the depression and a poor cotton crop caused him to suffer financial difficulties, the difficulties of politics were the ones that demoralized and embittered him. The ongoing fight over the independent treasury spilled over into 1839, and the explosive issue of abolition, along with difficulties with Great Britain and debates on the independent treasury and a new tariff measure, were to dominate Congress. An alliance of sorts had been forged, but so many issues strained it. Moreover, Pickens's support of the Van Buren administration prompted some to claim that he was an opportunist who "not only renounced old friends . . . but leagued with new ones."[162]

3. A Vile Association

The Speaker of the House of Representatives, James K. Polk, had decided to quit Congress in 1839 in order to seek the governorship of Tennessee. The campaign for a new speaker for the upcoming Twenty-sixth Congress, scheduled to convene in December, had begun early in the fall. Although Pickens was not in Washington during the period of early politicking, his chances were considered excellent, since he served as Calhoun's chief spokesman in the House and was also courted by the Van Buren administration. He had led the fight for the independent treasury and had helped bring about the new relationship between the senator and the president.[1] The Van Buren leaders had caucused and decided that Pickens would be their choice. The *Globe* on 30 November announced that "the election of Mr. Pickens would give general satisfaction to the Democratic Party. His honesty and ability are known and appreciated." The New York *Sun* conceded that Pickens would be elected. All of this was done as a move to reaffirm the ever vulnerable alliance of expediency.[2] In spite of reports appearing in some southern newspapers that F. H. Elmore's brother-in-law, Dixon H. Lewis of Alabama, desired the position, the administration's solid backing and Calhoun's presumed support seemed to pave the way for Pickens.[3] Pickens probably worried little about Lewis's candidacy; after all, Calhoun, Rhett, and Hunter lived with him.[4] Unfortunately, a family crisis and business affairs prevented him from being present at the initial caucuses. On 11 August Eliza, who had been ill for some time, gave birth to a son, Eldred; she had failed to recover from the ordeal, and her condition became critical. Afflicted by ulcers and with her patience exhausted, "she frequently wished for death."[5] She was a woman of delicate health who had previously given birth to five daughters and a son. Her son, Andrew, and one daughter, Frances, had died in infancy; Susan, Eliza, Maria, and Rebecca needed her attention, however. In the spring of 1838 Pickens had decided to enlarge Edgewood, and surely all the construction was a taxing irritant for his wife. Servants had to be managed, and during the spring and summer of 1839 parties were given and guests were frequently present. Eliza's role in the life at Edgewood would have been enough to weaken the strongest constitution. Francis was of little help, as he was involved in politics or seeing to his nearly 6,000 acres of land and 189 slaves.

The fall cotton market for 1839 was "quite brisk," with cotton prices bringing 11 to 12 cents a pound in Aiken, South Carolina.[6]

By the beginning of November Eliza's health seemed to be improving, and Pickens, who did not wish to be seen as courting office, took his time returning to Washington to claim the speakership.[7] Although Calhoun had returned late to Washington because of illness in his own family, Pickens believed that the senator wanted one of his men to be speaker, and he knew that he could depend on his colleague and messmate Robert Barnwell Rhett and his friend Franklin H. Elmore—especially since he had endorsed Elmore to fill the position vacated by Hammond.[8] As Pickens explained to Elmore after the balloting was finished, "It seemed to me that those of us who were considered as peculiar friends of each other ought to have acted together in perfect generosity."[9]

When Pickens arrived in Washington, he discovered that Rhett and Elmore had the day before his arrival attempted to manipulate the Democratic caucus in favor of Dixon H. Lewis.[10] At this time the House was in an uproar over whether five Whig representatives who had been certified by the governor of New Jersey should be seated. The New Jersey problem was important; since the Whigs and Democrats were almost evenly divided, the seating of the contested Whig members would affect the organizing of the House for its new session. Pickens became deeply immersed in the debates. Gaining the floor, he maintained that the House had the exclusive right to judge which claimants should be seated. He rejected the argument that the House should honor the election certificates signed by New Jersey officials; they had certified candidates who might not have received the majority vote. The House rejected Pickens's proposals and accepted Rhett's motion, which would provide for hearings and an extensive investigation. The debate sank into an acrimonious party duel. Finally, Pickens proposed that a committee on elections consider the case and make recommendations to the full House. On 13 December he moved that the House instruct the acting clerk to hold elections for speaker and that the New Jersey men be prohibited from taking part in the balloting.[11]

The New Jersey matter revealed the first overt friction between Pickens and Rhett. Not until 13 March 1840 was the New Jersey matter finally resolved. Ironically, in its report to the full House the committee on elections used Pickens's first proposal as the basis for its recommendation. The *Globe* praised the Carolinian and stated that, if the House had followed Pickens's leadership, much bitterness could have been avoided.[12]

However, Pickens's sometimes heavy-handed attacks on his colleagues for putting party before country were to adversely affect his chances of becoming speaker. Shortly before the balloting began, Pickens, Hunter, and Rhett de-

WILLIAM C. PRESTON
(courtesy of the South Caroliniana Library, University of South Carolina)

cided to seek new quarters. They told Calhoun they were dissatisfied with their accommodations and with the "temperance mess."[13] Congressman Aaron Brown, an administration man who lived at the same boardinghouse, was disappointed to see them leave. He regarded the three as "fine fellows and so far have acted with us very well. They are prompt and energetic in their support of the administration—but are very sensitive to any reflections on their sincerity and motives."[14] R. M. T. Hunter commented on what he considered Pickens's feigned sincerity; he confided to his wife that Pickens was the subject of gossip, since he seemed so melancholy over his wife's illness but, on his return to Washington, "was the first man to call upon Ellen BeVine [a noted beauty] who flitted through town last week." Pickens and Hunter moved to a new boardinghouse where a "few discontented men who belong[ed] to neither party" lived, while Rhett sought quarters with members of the uncommitted Georgia delegation.[15] Their motives for leaving had little to do with accommodations; rather, they were a sign of Pickens's animosity for Rhett, and a last-ditch attempt to court the undecided votes.

Together the regular Democrats and the States' Rights men controlled the House. Yet Pickens was destroyed, not by the actions of his former political enemies, or even by the Whigs, but by what he considered to be the treacherous manipulations of "his kind and amiable friends," Rhett, Elmore, and the four-hundred-pound Lewis. While Pickens was in Edgefield they had reckoned on a course to obtain the speakership for Lewis by claiming that Pickens would not be back in Washington in time to assume the position, even though Rhett knew Pickens planned to arrive in Washington the Saturday before Congress convened. When he learned that his "generous friends" had taken the liberty of withdrawing his name, Pickens was furious. An informal count showed that he would have received all of the votes that Lewis garnered, and more. On the eighth ballot Lewis received 113 of the 118 votes necessary for election. Pickens's colleague Sampson H. Butler wrote to Hammond describing the sabotage by Pickens's "very *kind, amiable,* and *disinterested* friends," who withdrew his name out of "*sentimental regard* and *affection.*"[16]

However, the electioneering tactics of Pickens and R. M. T. Hunter proved successful. Hunter's name was submitted, and he was able to gain the support of administration men, States' Rights Democrats, and southern Whigs, thus winning the speakership.[17]

In a confidential letter to James Hammond, who was having his own difficulties with the powerful Rhett machine in South Carolina, Pickens denounced Rhett and Elmore as being the perpetrators "of the vilest intrigue." Hammond, who had long held Rhett and Elmore in disdain and had been warning Pickens of their treachery, "rejoiced that those men have unmasked themselves to you . . . a viler association never attempted to rule over South Carolina. . . . They were never accused of any merit above the lowest cunning . . . God damn them I do and always have . . . I join you heart and hand to put them down." Pickens, in a proper but cold letter to Elmore, lamented that those *"who* I had always acted towards with the greatest liberality and confidence, had not acted towards me in the same manner."[18]

The friction between the Rhett cabal and Pickens was to affect the course of Palmetto State politics. Calhoun proved himself the master of the situation by remaining above the fray; however, he displayed a total lack of loyalty by not supporting Pickens, who had been so faithful to him. For years Pickens had served him well in both public and private matters. He was also his cousin. Political ambition and financial necessity nevertheless dictated that he not be involved. While Pickens was his kinsman, Elmore was his banker, and Rhett was a growing power in South Carolina politics. Ambition dictated that any potentially jeopardizing act must be rejected, even if it meant turning his back on his most loyal lieutenant. Calhoun, who "deeply regretted the whole affair," hoped the speakership would go to John Jones of Virginia so that a contest could be avoided. Strife would dangerously affect his chances for the presidency and jeopardize a favorable outcome in the pending debates on the readjustment of the tariff in 1842.[19]

The underlying causes of the dissension boiled down to envy, jealousy, the desires of both Pickens and Rhett to succeed Calhoun, and a political fight that had its origin in 1834, when Pickens supported Hammond over Elmore in a hotly contested congressional race. Although Pickens supported Elmore to replace Hammond, who had resigned in 1836, he worked to insure that his cousin, Patrick Noble, defeated Elmore's brother, Benjamin, in the 1838 gubernatorial contest. As Pickens and Hammond were to discover, the junto was a political force not to be underestimated. Rhett represented the Beaufort/Colleton District, whereas Elmore represented the Barnwell District, which comprised Barnwell, Orangeburg, Lexington, and Richland counties. The powerful Charleston *Mercury* was published by Rhett's brother-in-law, John A. Stuart, and the Columbia *South Carolinian* was controlled by the Elmores. Rhett's brothers, Albert (who was married to one of Elmore's sisters) and James, were leaders in the state legislature; Elmore's brother, Benjamin, was also in the legislature and was considered powerful in Richland County politics. Franklin Elmore was the president of the Bank of the State of South Carolina and a power in the Nesbitt Iron Manufacturing Company. Elmore's business interests added immeasurably to the power of the junto.[20] Many other powerful politicians in the state embraced the junto; even Calhoun had no desire to give the Rhett-Elmore faction cause to question its loyalty to him, even when it meant going against Pickens, whose loyalty was absolutely without question.

After Pickens's defeat for the speakership, he reckoned on an intriguing course of revenge that was to shake the state to its very foundation. Immediately after his defeat, he wrote confidential letters to those closest to him, expressing his bitter disappointment with Rhett, Lewis, and Elmore.[21] After his initial anger subsided, Pickens worried that he might have gone too far in his condemnation and that he might face dire consequences if Rhett and Elmore were to discover what he had written. Twice he wrote Hammond urging that he not reveal to anyone the contents of his letters.

Word of Pickens's animosity toward those who had engineered his defeat nevertheless filtered back to Rhett and Elmore. Lewis called on Pickens at his Edgefield home and informed him that Elmore and Rhett wanted an explanation of his feelings toward them. There was, after all, a fine line between honorable and dishonorable behavior, and his abusive remarks required proper explanation. In a series of letters to Elmore, Pickens dispassionately set forth his sentiments.[22] Pickens surely wondered how his vituperation had been revealed, for he had written passionate letters only to Hammond and to his close friend and neighbor James P. Carroll. Yet word had reached Rhett in Washington. Although the letter to Carroll was confidential, he had shown it to his brother-in-law Whitfield Brooks and his son Preston. Both men assured Carroll that they had not revealed the contents of Pickens's letter to anyone. In a letter from Louis Wigfall to John L. Manning (whose uncle, John P. Richardson, was being supported for the governor's office by Rhett and Elmore), Wigfall informed Manning of the contents of Pickens's letter to Carroll; it had been revealed by Preston Brooks, who had pumped Carroll for the information and, according to Wigfall, willingly gave it to him. Shortly thereafter Carroll, Whitfield Brooks, Preston Brooks, and Wigfall, the new editor of the Edgefield *Advertiser*, had disagreements over the heated gubernatorial campaign of 1840 and were involved in a series of duels. In one of these both Preston Brooks and Wigfall were wounded; Brooks had to use a cane for the rest of his life. In May 1856 Brooks would use that cane to beat Charles Sumner in the famous Brooks-Sumner affair.[23] Such was the nature of Carolina politics—factionalism, violence, and treachery abounded.

Prior to Pickens's defeat for speaker, he had been approached for assistance in a gubernatorial campaign by James Hammond, who had returned from Europe and was bored with plantation life. Hammond's talents were well known to himself and others. Late in the summer of 1839 he visited with George McDuffie, Judge Andrew Pickens Butler, and Pickens in order to assess his prospects. Hammond hoped that, through Pickens, he could obtain the support of the Calhoun faction, because most of his friends, "Governor [Pierce] Butler, [Wade] Hampton, [James] Adams . . . have unfortunately taken the wrong side on . . . subtreasury."[24] At this time the only announced candidate was Judge David Johnson, an old Unionist, who had a long association with the Whigs. At first Hammond believed that his opponent would be Benjamin Elmore, who had been defeated by Calhoun's and Pickens's cousin, Patrick Noble, in the 1838 governor's race. However, Elmore deferred to John P. Richardson, another Unionist. Calhoun embraced the state's growing sentiment "that the members of the old Union party should be relieved of the disabilities, by which they have so long been excluded from the higher offices of the state; and that confidence should be extended and received by those of both the Old Parties, whose interest and principles are *now* identified in . . . support of the administration and its measures."[25]

What Hammond feared most was the Rhett-Elmore combination, which he felt was capable of duping Calhoun and Pickens. Because he believed that Pickens controlled Calhoun "in all practical matters," it was essential that he have Pickens's support.[26] Before the speaker's race, Pickens had been reticent about committing himself to Hammond's cause. When Hammond described the Rhetts and Elmores as being "third rate—trading politicians going for self alone," Pickens had rejected Hammond's characterization by citing the two as virtuous men who combined wealth and talent.[27] Hammond believed that Pickens was "ignorant of all the intrigues of the day . . . he really does not know what is going on under his nose. Pickens is made a tool of by those very designers whom he fancies he is controlling and directing on everything."[28]

Without consulting Calhoun, Pickens reckoned on a course of vengeance that would involve Hammond as his tool. His previously reserved posture changed to one of active support for Hammond's candidacy.[29] Several of the state's leaders had given Hammond the impression that his chances had diminished since Richardson was introduced by the cabal as its candidate;[30] Pickens's new and enthusiastic support bolstered, for a time, his sagging spirits. Sadly, Hammond was to discover that Pickens was in no position to garner Calhoun's support. He did not fully comprehend that his quest for governor was irritating to Calhoun, who desired harmony in South Carolina. It was Calhoun who had approved the idea for the Nullifiers to bring forth a Union man to signal that past differences should be put away in order to bring unity to strife-torn South Carolina.[31] Hammond, who alternately trusted and damned

Pickens, had no choice but to continue in the hope that Pickens was making things right with the senator. How could he know that Pickens had lost his most favored position with Calhoun, and that Rhett, who had enjoyed such a meteoric rise, still continued to dazzle the senator? Now it was Rhett, not Pickens, who messed with Calhoun; it was Rhett who had Calhoun's ear and served as the conduit through which news from Carolina flowed.[32]

Shortly after the new year began, Hammond learned on good authority that his claim of the governor's office would "not be favorably received at Fort Hill . . . and that the Honorable F. W. Pickens, your particular friend . . . spoke disapprovingly of your pretensions."[33] This intelligence must have mystified Hammond, especially since Pickens continued to urge him forward for the governor's office. Duplicity seemed to be standard in Palmetto State politics. With no signs of action in his behalf, Hammond sank into one of his frequent states of depression, blaming his problems on Pickens.[34] As the year progressed, each man came to view the other as a political liability. Calhoun was irritated with Pickens for his activities on behalf of Hammond and for his refusal to take lightly his defeat for the speakership. Pickens's activities had the potential to disrupt the state at a time when unity was being encouraged. Although the senator refused to express a preference for either Hammond or Richardson, all private reports indicated that he preferred Richardson. From every side Hammond was urged to withdraw, but he continued to emphasize his affinity for the blue cockade of nullification and states' rights.[35] Calhoun was thinking of the future, not the past, and of peace, not strife.

The Nullifiers' *Mercury* of 10 January 1840 endorsed Richardson.[36] Every substantial paper in the state, including Pickens's hometown paper, the Edgefield *Advertiser*, followed the *Mercury*'s lead. Louis T. Wigfall, the *Advertiser*'s twenty-one-year-old editor, reckoned on a course "to see the Hotspur [Hammond] killed"; in his employer's absence, his intriguing mind calculated a way to undo Hammond in the region where he was most popular. Writing to Richardson's nephew, John L. Manning, Wigfall divulged that he intended to go against his employer's wishes and to endorse Richardson in the *Advertiser*.[37] Needless to say, he soon lost his position, but he joined the increasing ranks of men with political influence who were siding with the junto's candidate. Hammond continued to receive conflicting intelligence from Washington. Pickens kept writing letters of support, even telling him that Calhoun secretly preferred him but would not come out for either candidate. Yet other correspondents planted seeds of doubt about the veracity of Pickens's course and led Hammond to believe that "Van Buren, Calhoun, Pickens, Rhett,

Lewis, etc. are acting harmoniously and in perfect concert with one another." Hammond wrote, "If this be true . . . I have been made a dupe by Pickens."[38]

Pickens was anxious about his own political career. He desperately needed the continued good will and support of Calhoun in order to realize his own ambitions. So far he had encountered no opposition since his first race for Congress, but his quest for the Senate was to be full of pitfalls;[39] the path of vengeance was backfiring. For the first time he was receiving news that he might be opposed in his own district. He needed to get right with Calhoun before he was completely debilitated. With Hammond's chances steadily diminishing, it was time for Pickens to desert him. It was becoming clearer to Pickens that he had become the victim of a political plot hatched by Rhett and his cohorts to remove him from contention for the Senate.[40] Envy, revenge, false witness, and ambition—all were combining to bring on a storm that needed to be avoided. By the spring of 1840 Hammond, disgusted with what he considered to be Pickens's treachery, in desperation wrote directly to Calhoun, requesting his endorsement. The senator replied that he would not support either candidate.[41] Finally Pickens, seeing Hammond as a liability, urged him to withdraw so that unity might be preserved. "Withdrawal," he assured Hammond, would place him in "a very high position in the state in the future."[42]

The year 1840 was proving to be another bleak year for Pickens. The realization that Rhett and his associates had dashed his plans and had put together a coalition that was successfully advancing against him was deeply distressing. Pickens lamented: "He [Rhett] has even made him [Calhoun] a little different towards me. . . . I have seen enough to disgust me with the selfish movements of the world. If they do not oppose me this fall I shall resign and follow the paths of honor and virtue for the balance of my life."[43] Hammond, too, lamented that the "treacherous demagogues" were wrecking his plans. In his journal he entered a note of political philosophy appropriately reminiscent of Machiavelli: "Politicians do not form coalitions from principle, but always in hopes of gain—success is indispensable therefore to their purposes, and wise men do not join them unless the chances are . . . at least in their favor."[44] Ironically, these same treacherous demagogues would support Hammond in his successful 1842 bid for the governor's office. For the time being, however, in spite of urging by Pickens and other leaders, Hammond refused to withdraw; he was hopeful that the masses, for whom he expressed unmeasured contempt, would pressure the legislature on his behalf.[45] The voice of the masses was either inaudible or nonexistent. Immediately before the election Judge David Johnson withdrew, and Hammond was defeated by Richardson, 104-47, on 9 December 1840.[46] The results showed that the overwhelming majority of legislators wanted to put away past differences and to cease bickering, at least for the time being.[47]

In Washington Calhoun was determined that his lieutenants should put aside their animosities and unite for the common good. Peace had been made with Van Buren; harmony was being promoted in South Carolina; it was now time to have peace in the family. Rhett, probably at Calhoun's insistence, initiated a meeting with Pickens. On the surface it appeared that peace had been made, even though Rhett's past behavior made a mockery of the friendship he professed to have for Pickens. Ultimately old wounds would fester, and strife would break out again.[48]

The problems and antagonisms that emerged during the 1840 gubernatorial race gave a clue to the political frustrations afflicting the Palmetto State. No other state had taken such a radical course in the nullification period; no other state was so outwardly defensive and sensitive to its perceived honor; no other state was so politically archaic. Within its closed society there was a powerful hierarchy. For years Calhoun had been South Carolina's undisputed leader, and William C. Preston had emerged as his chief antagonist. Both men indicated that they planned to retire from the Senate before the end of 1840. However, the defeat of Van Buren and the election of William Henry Harrison as president caused both senators to postpone their plans. Pickens and Rhett both lusted after Senate seats. As long as both men's desires could be fulfilled, acrimony between them could be kept at a simmering point. Prior to the speaker's race in the fall of 1839, when it appeared likely that Preston would resign, Pickens promised to put aside his own political ambitions and to support Rhett for Preston's seat. Of course, Pickens was banking on Calhoun's retirement to nurture his own great needs. By helping Rhett, Pickens believed he would gain Rhett's support and have no rival for Calhoun's position.[49] Neither senator resigned as expected, but with controversy brewing over the governor's race, it was fortunate that South Carolina did not have to contend with another bitter contest at the very time when Calhoun was promoting harmony. The year 1840 proved to be a political watershed since it marked a real beginning of cooperation between Unionists and Nullifiers. Richardson's election indicated that Carolinians were willing to put away past differences and use their energy to cope with pending problems. The national elections of 1840, the more strident abolition movement, the revival of the tariff question in expectation of readjustment in 1842—all portended disaster. But the most pressing matter facing Carolinians was Calhoun's decision to seek the presidency in 1844. In order for all to go smoothly bruised egos needed to be tended. Albert Rhett invited Hammond to be the junto's 1842 gubernatorial candidate. Since Richardson had been elected in 1840, it had been decided that the position should alternate, and that a Nullifier be chosen in 1842.[50] Consultations among Calhoun, Pickens, and Rhett resulted in the decision that the senator would resign his seat in order to concentrate on the presidency. W. C. Preston had also finally decided to resign. Calhoun thereupon decided that his old friend, George McDuffie, should replace Preston. No one could question McDuffie's eminence, but it was obvious that the sick old man was being run in order to prevent a contest for Preston's seat. Calhoun resigned on 26 November 1842; Preston, who was in Columbia, resigned the next day. Since Calhoun was at his home at Fort Hill, Preston's resignation was received first by the General Assembly.[51] At this time Rhett believed that he had been tapped by Calhoun to be his successor. However, one of those rumored to be contending for the position was Judge Andrew Pickens Butler, whose political star was rising in the state. In order to cast doubts on Butler's loyalty to Calhoun, Rhett, through the use of adroit slander and misrepresentation, intimated that Butler was guilty of "anti-Calhounism" and having "a tendency to Prestonism." This left Butler "flouncing like a harpooned whale" from an attack which William C. Preston described as "indecent and savage."[52] With Butler out of the way, Rhett believed that he would easily win the Senate race. However, the governor's race gave a clue to the mood of the legislature. Many leaders were becoming disgusted with the behavior of Elmore and the Rhetts. At this time there were four men from the Rhett family active in South Carolina politics, and many people perceived them as conniving and overbearing. Hammond was their candidate, and he almost lost his bid for the governorship to Robert F. W. Allston, a respected Union party man. Hammond's own arrogance was a liability; coupled with that of the Rhetts, it nearly made for disaster. McDuffie was elected almost unanimously to succeed Preston, thus avoiding a fight. Four men vied to replace Calhoun; besides Pickens and Rhett, two Union men, William F. Davie and Daniel Huger, aspired to the office.[53] Pickens, who was in Washington, was relying on Hammond to shoulder his cause. Rhett, also in Washington, had his younger brothers taking care of his interests. He was a low state man, had the support of the *Mercury*, and claimed the backing of Calhoun. The deeply respected Daniel Huger had the support of those in the state legislature who felt that there should be both a Nullifier and Union man in the Senate. On the first ballot Huger led the ticket by polling 56 votes; Rhett received 46, Pickens 30, and Davie 29. On the third ballot Pickens, who in the view of many had become too close to the National Democratic party, threw his support to Huger, who was able to defeat Rhett 82–71. Rhett, whom Hammond still called a "pestilent demagogue," had been defeated. Although Pickens received the credit for Rhett's defeat, probably the real mastermind was Calhoun who, as always, was struggling to maintain harmony in order to further his own political plans.[54] However, Pickens had his revenge. Hammond joyfully wrote, "This is the denouement of the plot formed here three years ago by the Rhetts and Richardson to rule the state and has ended now in the prostration of both by each other's means."[55]

While all the excitement in the Palmetto State focused on the gubernatorial race between Hammond and Richardson, Pickens was in Washington, where a controversy continued to alter his relationship with Calhoun. Because Pickens had not been perfectly passive on all questions connected with the speaker's race, had not cheerfully endorsed any candidate presented by the administration, and had not allayed his jealousy arising from the long contest for speaker, Calhoun had become irritated.[56] The senator became even more upset when, in mid-January 1840, Pickens became involved in a crisis that proved embarrassing to Calhoun and to his old political ally, General Duff Green.

For years Green and Calhoun had been close. Green's daughter was married to Calhoun's eldest son, Andrew, and Green had become the official printer for the Calhoun Nullifiers. However, the competition for the position of House printer was for a time to strain relations between the senator and Green. When electioneering for the printer's office began in early 1840, it was obvious that Green was not likely to be elected.[57] Earlier, Calhoun had told him that he planned to stay with the National Democrats and support his old adversary, Francis P. Blair, for the lucrative printing post. At this time the Nullifiers held the balance of power in the House and could determine whether the Whig printers, Gales and Seaton, or the Democratic printers, Blair and Rives, would be selected. On 11 January 1840 the lead story in the Washington *Madisonian*, a paper that spoke for the southern Whigs and their sympathizers, claimed Green had offered to sell his influence to secure the printing office for the printers giving him the most generous bribe. The paper further charged that Green's plans depended on the cooperation of the Nullifiers.[58] Other papers ran the story; charges and countercharges flew. On 13 January Pickens, rising on a point of personal privilege, vehemently protested accusations that the Nullifiers had been involved with Green in a bribery scheme. He disavowed Green and accused those who connected Green with the Nullifiers of being guilty of "artful slander." Upon reading Pickens's remarks, Green wrote both Pickens and Calhoun, assailing them for acting in a "heartless conspiracy against his reputation" and stating that Pickens was acting on behalf of the senator. Calhoun denied that Pickens acted for him and assured Green that he did not intend him "the smallest harm." Pickens claimed that the report of his remarks was not precisely accurate; he had planned not to injure Green, but only to refute the charges as leveled against the Nullifiers. Green published his correspondence with Calhoun and Pickens, along with other documents, in order to deny his guilt in the bribery affair.[59] Although a shaky peace was made with Green, Pickens's overzealous role in the incident, coupled with the divisive speaker's race and his role in the ongoing governor's race between Hammond and Richardson, were weakening the Calhoun-Pickens relationship.

Politics totally dominated the life of South Carolina. The Nullifiers and Unionists had rallied behind Calhoun to support the administration and promote Van Buren for reelection; the deal had been sealed with Calhoun's support of Richardson for governor.[60] The Whigs, led by Preston and Waddy Thompson, remembered well how they had suffered at the hands of Calhoun and Pickens two years previously and were hopeful of upsetting Calhoun's plans of having Van Buren reelected. Preston and Thompson were very active; "party excitement was very bitter and things seemed somewhat uncertain." There was speculation that the Palmetto State Whigs would run a formidable candidate against Pickens, yet none appeared.[61]

During the summer of 1840 Pickens vacationed at the Virginia Springs, but his interest in politics was evidenced by the fact that he busied himself in writing letters to the Edgefield *Advertiser* and to individuals, urging that Harrison be rejected by men of "Southern feeling."[62] Returning to South Carolina, he launched a crusade against the Whigs; in a speech delivered at Greenwood on 23 September he severely lambasted Harrison, Preston, and Thompson.[63] His imprudent oratory almost resulted in a duel with Thompson, who had been one of his earliest friends and confidants until their disagreement over the independent treasury measure. On 2 October 1840 the Pendleton *Messenger* reported on Pickens's Greenwood speech and quoted several passages that Thompson found personally offensive. Thompson wrote Pickens inquiring about these. Pickens, who had not seen the *Messenger*, claimed that his remarks were aimed at Preston and that he could not recall making any remarks that could be construed to be a personal attack, "but merely an intimation of the different consideration in which I hold your *public course*."[64] Thompson wrote that the *Messenger* quotation that he found offensive was the following: "As to Col. Preston's traveling companion and worthy coadjutor in disseminating slander and falsehood under the sanction of an oath, I would not stoop to lift the hide off his back."[65] Pickens then claimed that he had been misquoted. In drafts of the letter Pickens worked and reworked his official reply until he evolved a statement that differed substantially from the one reported by the press. Thompson refused to back off and demanded "an explicit declaration on your part that no personal disrespect or insult was intended by you."[66] The hapless Pickens, not desiring to risk injury or worse, apologized. Thompson had the correspondence and the apology published in the newspapers and disseminated in handbills.[67] The embarrassing affair with Thompson added impetus to Pickens's decision to make his next term in Congress his last.

By 1841 Pickens was totally disgusted "with the utter heartlessness of public life." From every side he was being attacked. Calhoun, disturbed over disharmony in the state, identified Pickens as one of those chiefly responsible. The observant Hammond wrote that "the general impression at Washington and elsewhere seems to be against him [Pickens]." His wife's health was failing again, and his financial plight had forced him to ask Hammond to help arrange a loan. However, had he been able to obtain his ultimate gratification and succeed to the Senate, all thoughts of retirement would have been obliterated.[68]

Shortly before the difficulties with Duff Green, Pickens was elevated to the chairmanship of the House committee on foreign affairs.[69] Numerous important matters were before Congress, but party bickering monopolized the House's energies. The independent treasury was back in committee; the tariff, abolition, and a new measure to distribute revenue to the states aggravated discord. Pickens once more took center stage when the ways and means committee urged the House to appropriate $450,000 for the extension of the Cumberland Road into Indiana, Ohio, and Illinois. In one of his best efforts, Pickens made a strong argument against the expedience and constitutionality of appropriating money for internal improvements in the states. His position cut across party lines but revived sectionalism.[70]

At this time Pickens was recognized as one of the most able orators in Congress, and copies of his speeches were sold by the printers in Washington.[71] In his role as chairman of the committee on foreign affairs he was to emerge as the most controversial figure in the House. For years relations with Great Britain had been deteriorating. In the midst of the continuing national depression, English financiers were calling for payment of huge sums owed them by Americans. The northeastern boundary controversy had resulted in the so-called Aroostook War in 1839. The South was furious over negative British attitude toward slavery and the slave trade. On several occasions American vessels engaged in the domestic coastal slave trade had gone off course, because of a storm or a slave mutiny, and had ended up in the British West Indies, where British authorities had freed their cargoes of slaves.

Western grain farmers deplored the English corn laws, since they effectively cut off a lucrative market for their oversupply of produce. For years Americans living in upper New York had been lending support to a failing Canadian revolt; this the British resented. On 29 December 1837 a British raiding party crossed the Niagara River and burned the *Caroline*, a small steamship that had been engaged in ferrying supplies to the Canadian rebels. Three years later Alexander McLeod, an unpopular Canadian deputy sheriff, was arrested in New York on charges of murder and arson. New York authorities claimed that McLeod had participated in the *Caroline* raid.[72]

Before being appointed to the chairmanship, Pickens had made bellicose remarks about the Maine boundary question.[73] After assuming the chairmanship, Pickens indicated his hostility to the British when the question of U.S. relations with China came before his committee. He again lashed out against British enterprise and spoke in favor of the United States assuming a much more dominant role in the Orient.[74] McLeod's arrest caused Pickens's usually heated rhetoric to turn even more vitriolic. The British Foreign Office, headed by Lord Palmerston, was demanding McLeod's release on the grounds that he could not be held for murder since the expedition in which he allegedly took part was a military action sanctioned by British authorities. In the past all of the heated rhetoric had originated with the Americans; however, the McLeod case, and Pickens's role in it, caused an end to British placidness. The British Foreign Office threatened the most serious consequences if McLeod were not released.[75]

On 21 December 1840 Millard Fillmore, then a Whig representative from New York, introduced a House resolution requesting that Van Buren make available to Congress all diplomatic correspondence concerning the *Caroline* and McLeod Affair. The president refused, and beginning in February 1841 a battle raged in the House. On 13 February Pickens made a report for the House foreign relations committee in which he argued that McLeod should be treated not as a soldier, but as a common criminal. Pickens then lambasted Britain, reciting a litany of complaints. At this juncture the British contemplated putting more vessels on the Great Lakes. Daniel Webster (who would, as secretary of state in the Harrison and Tyler administrations, be the chief negotiator with the British) received a letter from James Alexander Hamilton that accused Pickens of forcing Great Britain "considering the present condition of own differences" to take "the last resort of nations."[76] Pickens was widely denounced. Although he claimed he had not intended to ruffle feathers, but only to awaken the nation to the aims of the British which "know no bounds," he urged the nation to strengthen its defenses. Both the British press and Pickens's perennial enemy John Quincy Adams took up the fight against him. Adams wrote that Pickens's efforts were nothing more than "an inflammatory invective" against the British government.[77] Pickens's remarks were given wide play in England, where they were used "to agitate and influence the public mind, already too much predisposed for violent and rash measures." The *Morning Chronicle*, a government paper, claimed the report threatened war with England. The London *Times* believed that "without the especial interference of the Almighty, any human means of averting war does not seem to be entertained for a moment."[78] One of those most critical of Pickens's report and the strong anti-tariff stand of the South Carolinians was Edward Stanly, a North Carolina Whig who objected to the characterization of those with less bellicose views as men without valor. Remarks made by Pickens and Stanly were reported by the Washington papers. Letters were written, and a confrontation was narrowly avoided thanks to the intercession of mutual friends. Stanly, inferring that Pickens's remarks were calculated to offend, then uttered sentiments felt by others but rarely expressed openly in the House. Although he later apologized, he characterized Pickens as typifying South Carolina's sons in Congress by combining "legislative insolence" with "haughtiness, mixed with contempt."[79]

The debates on the committee reports written by Pickens continued until the end of the special session in September 1841. Pickens claimed that his motive was to prepare people to face the problem of national defense. The Whigs considered the report to be a deliberate attempt on the part of the Democrats to inflame the public against Great Britain. The New York *Observer*, a Democratic party paper, editorialized that Pickens's report was meant for home consumption only, and was designed to allay American fears of the British.[80]

With the inauguration of William Henry Harrison, Daniel Webster replaced John Forsyth as secretary of state and poured oil on troubled waters. McLeod was tried in Utica, New York, and was acquitted on 12 October 1841.[81] The continuing economic crisis, the bank question, and the mistrust of Van Buren had all strengthened the Whig party. While Harrison was inaugurated on 4 March 1841, the real leader of the Whigs continued to be Henry Clay. The debates over the McLeod affair gave the Democrats and Whigs opportunities to exchange accusations; the tariff, states' rights, abolition, and defense all received attention in the heated oratory. The Pickens-Calhoun relationship was further eroded by Pickens's role in the McLeod affair. Calhoun believed his kinsman to be too closely allied with Van Buren and the National Democratic party; in addition, Pickens's violent rhetoric caused many to portray the state as being extreme at a time when Calhoun was promoting the image of moderation and responsibility.[82] The South Carolina House in its late session had passed resolutions applauding the cessation of party feuding and praising Calhoun and his course of leadership.[83] The stage was being set for the senator to make another presidential bid.

The winter and spring of 1841 were proving to be one of the most hectic periods of Pickens's life. In February he made his report of the McLeod affair and the northeast boundary question. Simultaneously, Henry Clay was outlining the Whig program that he intended to push through Congress. William Henry Harrison was inaugurated president; he died on 4 April 1841, after only one month in office.[84] During the campaign Pickens had predicted that the Whigs would gain strength and that Harrison would defeat Clay for the nomination and win the presidency.[85] Pickens greatly feared Clay, for he was advocating an end to the independent treasury system, the creation of a third national bank, and a new high tariff. Most frightening of all, Clay was unsafe on slavery.[86] Pickens, at Edgewood when he received news of Harrison's death, worried that John Tyler would become Clay's tool.[87] President Tyler made it clear that he expected to exercise the full power of his office; however, he kept the cabinet that Harrison had appointed, and in his inaugural address he intimated that he was willing to compromise with Clay. When Congress met for an extra session on 31 May 1841, it was apparent that Clay, after weathering a major conflict in his own party, still controlled the legislative branch by dominating the most important House and Senate committees. Pickens, fearing that ultimately Tyler and Clay would unite, predicted that Calhoun must then "inevitably be the great opposition candidate" for the presidency in 1844. He believed that Van Buren or James Buchanan might also run, making for a three-way contest that would be "bitter and furious to the last degree."[88]

With Clay holding sway over Congress, fears of hostile legislation began to be realized. The Kentuckian came forth with a program that included repeal of the just-passed Subtreasury Act, the incorporation of a new national bank, and the passage of a new protective tariff. In order to help push his program through Congress, Clay made it more palatable to the states by announcing, at the beginning of the Twenty-seventh Congress, a plan to distribute to the states the proceeds from the sale of western lands. If the distribution scheme and its companion measure, the loan bill which authorized the government to borrow $12 million, were passed and if the tariff were allowed to lapse in 1842, then the government would be denied adequate revenues with which to meet its obligations. This, in turn, would encourage the passage of a revenue-producing protective tariff. The Clay plan began its course in Congress when a measure to repeal the Subtreasury Act was introduced on 4 June; on 10 June the distribution bill was brought forth, and on 21 June a bill to incorporate a new United States bank was reported out of committee. The loan bill was introduced by Pickens's arch enemy Millard Fillmore on 24 June. On 14 July Fillmore presented the tariff bill.[89] As the summer progressed, the debate, like the weather, warmed up; Pickens's fiery rhetoric added more heat. On all of Clay's measures the congressman had his say, opposing them all as a "naked and undisguised issue between the speculating and stockholding interests on one side, and the great laboring and land interest of this confederacy on the other."[90] In a speech on the distribution scheme, he attacked those who were pushing Clay's plans as being little better than dogs "licking their chops . . . and wagging their tails . . . and smelling their way into the greasy places of the palace . . . for the bones that might be thrown them—I confess . . . I sicken with disgust and now make an habitual distribution of money from the government and you increase all these disgusting scenes."[91] In the same vein he attacked the loan bill, the repeal of the subtreasury, and the creation of a United States bank.[92] He claimed that the rebirth of a national bank would corrupt the nation's currency. He argued that it would be "engendered in fraud and brought forth in iniquity, the foul offspring of party power and political duplicity," and that the day would come when its "deluded followers shall tear from it the veil that conceals its hideous deformity."[93]

The Calhoun faction forced debate on every section of the bank bill in both houses. The measure passed, but as passions mounted, the nation waited to see if Tyler would veto it. While the president was calculating his course, two other measures passed the House: the tariff and the repeal of the subtreasury. Some believed that Clay's influence would be strong enough to prevent a veto, but they were mistaken. Tyler vetoed the bank bill on 16 August, thus splitting the Whigs and causing unbounded joy among the Nullifiers. After the veto, the pro-bank faction tried to make an accommodation with Tyler. The measure was altered, sent back for debate, and passed again. Again Tyler vetoed the bill, and in so doing he destroyed his cabinet. Clay was crestfallen; however, except for the bank, he had realized most of his aims.[94]

Pickens was elated with Tyler's vetoes, but he confided to Calhoun that the president's course would effectively "imbecile" his administration. He believed that Tyler's actions marked the beginning of the end for the Whig party, thus placing Calhoun and his followers into a more advantageous position in national politics. He informed the senator of the pro-Calhoun sentiment he had found in Virginia and North Carolina and urged him to use the political

WADDY THOMPSON
(courtesy of the South Caroliniana Library, University of South Carolina)

confusion to good advantage by launching his campaign for the presidency immediately, "while the Whigs are reeling and falling under panic and dissolution." Pickens insisted that resolutions of nomination be drawn up for the South Carolina General Assembly to approve, although he hoped that the first nomination would come from the Georgia legislature, "as it would appear natural."[95]

Pickens emerged as one of Calhoun's campaign managers and began an ambitious letter-writing campaign on his behalf. Despite financial worries because of low cotton prices (8 to 9 cents a pound), a drunk overseer, and the loss of most of his corn crop to inclement weather, Pickens's passion for politics overwhelmed him. He corresponded with numerous congressional colleagues, urging them to back Calhoun and asking them for advice and political intelligence. Pickens reported to Calhoun that he received innumerable letters "all breathing the greatest attachment to yourself . . . I know there never was a more important moment for yourself than the present."[96] Bubbling with enthusiasm, Pickens regularly sent Calhoun letters full of information and advice. Daily his optimism seemed to grow as he assessed the senator's prospects. He believed that Calhoun could carry every state except Ohio, Massachusetts, Kentucky, and Maryland; "if Virginia rallies on Tyler, it will make him strong, but in an emergency Clay's friends would defeat him if it became absolutely necessary. They would take you rather than see Tyler succeed."[97]

The letter-writing continued throughout the winter and into the spring of 1842, and from every side came more political intelligence. Pickens was hopeful that Calhoun would resign his senate seat in order to take a more active role in the campaign.[98] Naturally, Pickens still harbored dreams of succeeding his kinsman. However, during the final two months of 1841, his bright optimism paled when a new element was introduced into the situation. Word reached Pickens that Calhoun would not be the only Democrat seeking the nomination: Van Buren's friends wanted him to redeem his loss to the Whigs and make another run for the presidency. Pickens, who was close to many of those in the Van Buren camp, first received the alarming intelligence and alerted Calhoun to the new hazard in his path.[99] Both Calhoun and Pickens realized that in Van Buren they had a formidable opponent who continued to control a great segment of the Democratic party. In a letter inviting Van Buren to stay at his home if he decided to visit South Carolina, Pickens reminded the ex-president of the time when he gave him pills for an upset condition brought on by tension of the extra session of Congress in 1837, subtly imploring him to enjoy life without recourse to either pills or politics.[100]

During the fall and winter of 1841–42, the Van Buren wing of the party was solidifying its ranks by making peace with the manufacturers and courting the abolitionists. In order to improve Calhoun's appeal to northern voters, Pickens was authorized to write to Levi Woodbury, inviting the popular New Hampshire political leader to serve as Calhoun's running mate. In his letter to Woodbury, Pickens optimistically discussed Calhoun's presidential prospects and urged that South Carolina and New Hampshire go into the contest side by side.[101]

As the numerous campaign workers settled down to advising Calhoun, Pickens along with Rhett, Elmore, and R. M. T. Hunter became responsible for the overall direction of the campaign. On 6 January 1842 Pickens left Edgefield for Washington and his last year in Congress. He was disgusted with the disgrace and confusion in the House and yearned to resign and go home.[102] While in Washington he continued his activity on behalf of Calhoun. He wrote to Samuel Ingham, a political power in Pennsylvania, asking for his aid and telling him of the Calhoun faction's difficulties in finding a suitable vice-presidential candidate, since "Silas Wright [senator from New York] and Woodbury are so drilled in the old party traces that '*it*' is very difficult to get any decided stand taken to throw off the old yoke."[103] The first hints that the campaign was not going well appeared in a letter from Pickens to Maria Colhoun, his sister-in-law. He candidly informed her that he hoped Calhoun would be the Democratic nominee but "fear[ed] it would not be so, as the whole country is so sunk and debased in corruption that intrigue and selfishness seem to hold unbounded sway."[104]

The second session of the Twenty-seventh Congress moved at a snail's pace. Attacks on slavery by northern abolitionists, coupled with a ruinous southern depression and the ongoing debates over the tariff, threatened to widen further the sectional split. John Quincy Adams, whom Pickens referred to as "the most extraordinary man on God's footstool," continued to confound the southern members of Congress, who resorted "to every artifice and device to put him down."[105] Pickens's frustrations and fears reached new heights as the attack on slavery became more widespread. Tyler appeared interested in annexing Texas, and England's meddling in the Texas situation, coupled with her strong international antislavery stance, brought on more anxiety and threatened a rupture with Great Britain.[106] Pickens finally confirmed the speculation that he would not run for Congress again, saying that "the sacrifice is too great."[107]

In the spring of 1842 Calhoun had more support from Democratic members of Congress than any other candidate; a canvass of support at the state level also showed him ahead. Nevertheless, problems abounded. There were too many campaign managers, and they were too parochial in their views. The *Mercury* was for a time their only reliable paper, and it lacked a national base. Although Pickens was opposed to starting a paper in Washington because "it would draw the fire of the *Globe* and *Enquirer*," the central committee, composed of Pickens, Hunter, and Lewis, did procure the Washington *Spectator*; its efforts at jousting with the *Globe*, which was supporting Van Buren, proved less than successful, as Pickens predicted. Coordination within the Calhoun ranks was poor, and Calhoun's suggestion that the delegates to the Democratic convention be elected by congressional districts, rather than at large from the states, was not being favorably received by party leaders.[108]

The presidential campaign was not the only matter holding the nation's attention. During the previous session of Congress, all of Clay's measures had been passed except the bank bill. In the meantime, a compromise had been worked out in regard to the Tariff Act and the Land Distribution Act: tariffs would not be raised above the 20 percent level so long as the Land Distribution Act was functional, but if the need for revenue could not be met, then the disbursement of money from public land sales to the states would cease if Congress agreed to raise the tariff.[109] In the spring of 1842 the nation found itself lacking the revenues needed to meet its obligations. In the eyes of the states' rights faction, the Tyler administration had played into the Whigs' hands by asking for increased appropriations and increased loan and treasury notes when a policy of frugality was in order. This situation gave the administration no choice but to ask Congress to impose a higher tariff. Pickens accused the administration of "imbecility" and wrote disparagingly about politicians and their activities. The Whigs, led by Fillmore, tried to force the administration to accept a new tariff measure which contained higher rates and, in violation of the earlier compromise, to permit distribution to continue. Tyler vetoed this scheme. Finally in the late summer the Whigs, with the assistance of some northern Democrats, were able to pass a bill that was acceptable to Tyler but unacceptable to most Southerners.[110]

In South Carolina the agitation, which ordinarily would have been fierce, was softened by the state's leadership. Pickens advised that, if South Carolina followed the same course she had taken a decade earlier, "injudicious agitation" would destroy Calhoun's presidential aspirations.[111]

In addition to working on behalf of Calhoun, Pickens found himself again involved in debate with "that mischievous, bad old man," John Quincy Adams, on congressional reapportionment. Adams introduced a bill designed to reflect recent changes in population. Since South Carolina would lose two seats in the House and the representational shift would favor the North, Pickens railed against Adams's measure. The bill passed anyway, and South Carolina's House delegation was cut from nine members to seven. The same issues of the Edgefield *Advertiser* that reported on Pickens's efforts, toasting him as "our bold indefatigable representative in Congress—always a watchtower of our free institutions—ready and competent to defend them," announced that Francis Pickens would not be a candidate for reelection to Congress. However, he would continue to serve until 17 March 1843.[112]

On 10 August, shortly after the announcement of his retirement, Pickens's young son, Eldred, died of congestive fever. Two days later Eliza succumbed to the same malady, leaving Pickens with four daughters and in a great state of grief. Anna Clemson wrote, "Francis is truly a distressed man and one to be pitied."[113] Pickens recovered slowly from his shock; in his letters he poured out the most passionate and emotional tributes to his deceased wife and pity for himself.

After losing the most important things in his life—his wife, his son, and his opportunities to advance politically—his bitterness was evidenced in letters to James Edward Colhoun. Pickens vowed that he would never again push his name for anything—and he halfheartedly meant it. However, he did confide to Colhoun that George McDuffie intended to serve in the Senate for only two sessions and that he, Pickens, had friends who were determined to nominate him.[114] Pickens returned to Washington in late November to serve out his remaining months in Congress. This time he took his children with him, as "he could not bear to be separated from them so soon after their mother's death."[115]

In March 1843 Pickens returned to Edgewood. He was in a predicament; his girls needed a mother. For a time Maria Colhoun helped him with his family, but this was an unsatisfactory arrangement.[116] Searching for a suitable mate, he decided to court Martha Maria "Cudy" Colhoun, the daughter of John Ewing Colhoun and the niece of James Edward Colhoun and Floride Calhoun. Throughout the summer of 1843 he implored her to marry him, yet every proposal was rebuffed. Finally, in early October, Pickens received a final blow as "Cudy" gave him a "peremptory and final refusal of all advances made by him." Surely her refusal added immensely to his depression. He wrote James Edward, "No language can convey to you the sadness of my heart . . . she has struck the blow, and oh! it has fallen with a heavy hand upon me . . . I had fondly desired to love and cherish her as the idol of all my affections, and I thought I could have ministered in purity and kindness to every wish and desire she might entertain. . . . Oh! God what shall I do?"[117]

At this time Calhoun, acting on behalf of Abel P. Upshur, Tyler's secretary of state, offered Pickens the ambassadorship to France. His desire to remain at home to attend to his domestic situation precluded him from accepting the position.[118] With Pickens's retirement, Robert Barnwell Rhett was the only experienced South Carolinian left in the House. Although Pickens held no national office after March 1843, he remained active in politics as one of Calhoun's campaign managers. In fact, a study of the nature and volume of correspondence from Pickens to Calhoun shows that he had emerged as Calhoun's chief and most reliable advisor. Even though his advice may not always have been appreciated by Calhoun because of its direct and forthright nature, letters reveal that Pickens had an uncanny understanding of the issues, the political leaders, and the emotions of the period. Pickens was Calhoun's man, and his concern for his kinsman transcended political motives. In a letter to James Edward Colhoun, Pickens showed his concern for Calhoun and for his family's financial welfare by suggesting that James Edward help set Calhoun's financial house in order.[119] The movement to commission the world-famous artist Hiram Powers to execute a statue of Calhoun, wearing the toga of a Roman senator, was Pickens's idea; he handled all the arrangements, contributing $400 to the project and helping to raise another $3,000.[120] Ernest M. Lander, in *The Calhoun Family and Thomas Green Clemson*, showed Pickens to be a concerned guardian who liberally gave of his time and resources for Calhoun's benefit. Yet Calhoun did little to assist Pickens in realizing his own political ambitions. With help from Calhoun, Pickens could have been elected speaker of the House of Representatives or to a seat in the Senate; however, Calhoun had a loftier goal—to be president.

4. Harbinger of Doom

In early 1843 the campaign was not going well. Money was in short supply, and coordination was poor. Calhoun worried that Van Buren's successes would destroy his presidential plans.[1] The new tariff measure threatened to become disruptive. Even though Pickens urged Calhoun to "reflect cooly and calmly" upon the steps he might take in the next year, he admitted that he "would appeal to arms and the God of battles sooner than acquiesce permanently" in the principles of the tariff. He urged his kinsman not to make "an open rupture from the great mass of the Republican party" and to "wait and try every reasonable remedy: in hopes of sustaining the highest measures of redress."[2]

In a letter dated 14 July 1843, Pickens outlined all the difficulties that the Calhoun forces were encountering and as if to say, "I told you so" reminded Calhoun of the advice he had given that had not been taken.[3] Pickens felt that Calhoun's chances of receiving the nomination were rapidly diminishing, so he reminded his kinsman of his generosity and work on his behalf.[4] It is obvious that Pickens considered Calhoun to be the problem—he had lost his former ability to capture the public imagination. He still had the same followers, but they, too, had changed. Pickens analyzed the situation: "And where are your men—who are your friends? McDuffie (although honest) is broken down, and will be a splendid failure as soon as he gets into the Senate. Robert Y. Hayne is dead, and James Hamilton might as well be . . . Rhett is energetic, but *entirely* selfish and totally bankrupt—and is looking solely to office. Elmore is in the same condition. Hunter is a pure and intellectual man, but has no action or influence in Virginia. Lewis is energetic and talented, but is carried off by impulse . . . and besides he is too fat to be very active."[5]

The Calhoun forces found that, despite their efforts at containing anti-tariff feelings, the state was on the verge of creating a protest. This would be perceived by the North as another radical move on the part of South Carolina. Pickens suggested to Governor James Hammond, who still clung to the tenets of nullification, that "some sort of resolution ought to be prepared on the subject of the tariff, but let them be temperate and dignified. We ought to pass nothing that would look like a threat."[6] The tariff was becoming the great sore spot that threatened to undo Calhoun's presidential plans. Before the passage of the tariff of 1842, southern leaders had worked diligently but unsuccessfully to control tariff rates. The controversy had splintered the Democratic party, and in 1844 it was to fragment South Carolina. Pickens had warned Van Buren and Democratic leaders that, before peace and harmony could prevail in the party, "all must be joined on the tariff."[7] In light of the tariff and Calhoun's diminishing prospects, the challenge was to keep Calhoun in the race and keep South Carolina from exploding. To exacerbate matters, John Tyler also decided to seek the nomination. Tyler's entrance could only detract from Calhoun's support, since his beliefs were closer to Calhoun's than to Van Buren's. The battle was going to be waged along economic and sectional lines. The Van Buren forces were hurting Calhoun by implying that Calhoun's past support of nullification bordered on treason. A letter from Andrew Jackson urging delegates to the state conventions to support Van Buren over Calhoun was being effectively used.[8] In order to combat the ex-president, Pickens advised that new issues be injected in the campaign, forcing Van Buren on the defensive.[9] However, each day seemed to bring more bad news. The Alabama convention went with Van Buren; even Virginia was leaning toward him, while knowing that the Van Buren policy was to "keep the tariff as it is."[10] The most bothersome problem for the South and the Calhoun forces was the certainty that the now precious gag rule would be rescinded. Rule 21 was an adaptation of the gag rule that had been introduced by Henry Pinckney in 1836. In January 1840, much to the relief of the South, it had become a standing rule and as such forbade any "petition, memorial, resolution or other paper praying for the abolition of slavery" to be received by the House. The Democrats controlled nearly two-thirds of the votes, but the commitment was strong on the part of northern members to have the rule rescinded. The question of Texas annexation had again become a sticky issue and was seen as part of the overall slavery problem.[11]

Many South Carolinians believed that the strength of the Democratic party would protect the peculiar institution and create a tariff policy favoring southern agricultural pursuits. Such proved not to be the case—instead of being protected, southern interests were assailed.[12] When the Twenty-eighth Congress held its first caucuses in early December 1843, it was obvious that Van Buren and his men were in control. Calhoun decided to withdraw from the race and, on 21 December 1843, announced from his home at Fort Hill that he was refusing to let his name go before the convention.[13] However, Joel R. Poinsett, the leader of the Van Buren forces in South Carolina, believed that Calhoun expected his friends to hold him up as a martyr to the abstract principle of the minority and to continue to regard him as a candidate. The *Mercury*, which for months had advertised itself as a Calhoun party paper, furled the flag and on 27

January 1844 dropped Calhoun's name from its masthead.[14] Pickens read Calhoun's message with great interest and care and objected to it, believing it would be counterproductive since it was "too personal agst V. B." He worried that Calhoun's withdrawal could lead to Clay's election, and that, if "we should be compelled to take ultra or extreme measures against the tariff," people would blame Calhoun.[15] In a letter to Hunter, Pickens expressed his quandary: "I know not which will be the greater calamity—the election of Clay or the rotten clique who rule in the Democratic Party. If we have to choose between such rotteness [sic], we will be putrified ourselves. . . . The South can only have strength when maintaining principles."[16]

After Calhoun's abandonment of the fight for the Democratic nomination, some conjectured that he might run as an independent candidate. However, the passage of time and the late publication of his withdrawal letter allowed enthusiasm on his behalf to wane in South Carolina; besides, as Pickens warned, such a move "would badly split the state and produce such division as to destroy us."[17] From Pickens's standpoint the campaign had damaged his relationship with his kinsman. He believed that Calhoun had turned from him, instead putting his faith in and being "cruelly treated by those who have professed exclusive friendship."[18] His candid letters were not altogether designed to curry Calhoun's favor, but to alert him to events that were affecting his presidential aspirations. However, Pickens's arrogant nature was irritating, and as the campaign turned sour, Calhoun little needed his cousin's explanations for defeat.

The Texas situation, which had remained unsettled since 1836, became a campaign issue with Tyler's entrance into the presidential contest. Like most Southerners, Pickens had seen the annexation of the Lone Star Republic as an object "near and dear to [his] heart." Though many people in the North advocated the annexation of Oregon, they viewed the incorporation of Texas in a different light, as a step that would insure the South and slavery more power.[19] When Congress met in March 1843 it was evident that the tariff would not be immediately adjusted, and that the Tyler administration could not gather the support needed to fulfill southern dreams of an annexed Texas. In late 1843 and early 1844 many people were predicting that the "lone star" would become another jewel in Queen Victoria's crown if the United States did not act quickly.[20] In one of Pickens's last speeches in Congress he lambasted those opposed to annexation and proclaimed his desire to see the "lone star . . . add new lustre to that constellation which now blazes . . . over our national boundaries."[21] He wrote Calhoun that "the position of Texas as a British colony would be just cause for war, and if the nonslaveholding states oppose its admission upon the grounds of its strengthening the slaveholding interest then we will be bound in self-respect and self-preservation to join Texas with or without the Union."[22] One of Pickens's greatest worries was that Senators McDuffie and Huger would not adequately represent South Carolina's attitude. Others agreed; the noted literary figure William Gilmore Simms, in a letter to his long-time confidant James Hammond, expressed the sentiment that Calhoun's views on the Texas question would have been better reflected if Pickens and Elmore were in the Senate.[23] Pickens hoped the South Carolina legislature would instruct the independent McDuffie to support the Tyler administration in its quest to make Texas part of the Union by uniting the Texas and Oregon questions, thus obtaining a broader base of support for the annexation of both territories.[24]

While Texas was a matter of intense interest, it was rivaled as a subject of concern by the excitement that was generated by South Carolina's approach to presidential politics. The state convention of the Democratic Republican party met in Columbia on 22 May 1843. Pickens, who had been succeeded in Congress by Armistead Burt of Abbeville, emerged as the leader of the convention; he and Franklin Elmore were elected delegates to the national convention that would occur in Baltimore on 27 May 1844.[25] At the state convention, resolutions were adopted that accepted the Calhoun doctrine of "free trade, low duties, no debt; separation from banks; economy; retrenchment and a strict adherence to the constitution." The convention agreed to support Calhoun but did not promise to support the nominee of the National Democratic party.[26] Calhoun's withdrawal brought on confusion and caused many of the state's leaders to rethink their positions. In early March 1844 Pickens traveled to Charleston to consult with local politicians; while there he called for a caucus and persuaded the group to accept his resolutions instead of those submitted by Elmore. Pickens convinced the caucus that he and Elmore should not attend the Democratic convention, and that Calhoun's name should be held in reserve in case there was a deadlock.[27] The Charleston caucus decided to call for the state central committee to convene in Charleston on 15 March 1844. That committee, knowing that Pickens was acting on behalf of Calhoun, who had taken the position that the state should have nothing to do with the national convention, recognized the need to unify the state. The members decided that Pickens and Elmore would not go to Baltimore, since the Carolinians objected to the methods by which delegates were elected and the national convention organized.[28] It was further agreed that South Carolina had to be vindicated on the fundamental principles of the tariff and abolition before the state party could support the nominees of the national party.[29]

The period immediately after Calhoun's decision not to seek the nomination was exciting yet depressing for Pickens. He attempted to reingratiate himself with his kinsman, inviting the whole Calhoun clan to Edgewood for Christmas to enjoy "a lavish table and old fashioned South Carolina hospitality." Calhoun declined, claiming to have other plans, and spent Christmas at Fort Hill.[30] Since he had been unable to see Calhoun, Pickens wrote him obsequious letters praising his "un-sullied honor" and telling him that he was the victim of a "corrupt and degenerate age" and men who had treated him "cruelly." In letters to Calhoun and to his brother-in-law, James Edward Colhoun, Pickens could not resist pointing an accusing finger at Rhett, whom he characterized as scheming and deceitful.[31] What could be better than assailing Rhett, while promoting himself?

The Peacemaker, the large gun on the new battleship *Princeton*, exploded on 28 February 1844, killing Secretary of the Navy Thomas W. Gilmer, Secretary of State Abel P. Upshur, and Virgil Maxcy, one of Pickens's and Calhoun's dearest friends.[32] The catastrophe left a void in Tyler's cabinet. Pickens believed that he would be offered a position; however, he informed Calhoun that he would refuse, since he held Tyler in contempt. Although no position was offered to Pickens, Calhoun succeeded Upshur.[33]

Other exciting events were taking place in the Pickens and Colhoun families. Maria Simkins Colhoun, the wife of James Edward Colhoun and sister-in-law of Floride Calhoun, was expecting her first child. She had had difficulties in conceiving, and the announcement of her pregnancy was greatly welcomed. While Calhoun was making plans to return to Washington, Maria was planning to leave her plantation, Millwood, near the Savannah River in Abbeville District to spend her confinement at Edgewood. Floride left Fort Hill to be with Maria, and her daughter Anna visited from the Clemson plantation, Cane Brake, whenever she could.[34] On his way to Washington to become secretary of state, Calhoun planned to stop at Edgewood and invited Anna, his son John, and James Edward to meet him there.[35] Shortly after Calhoun's departure, Maria became desperately ill; on 17 April, at the age of twenty-seven, she and her child died in labor. The tragedy so overwhelmed her husband that he sought refuge as a recluse. In a letter to Calhoun, Pickens expressed surprise at James Edward's feelings, admitting that he did not "think it would have overcome him so." Of course, he worried for himself, "as it leaves my little children without a female friend near and dear to counsel and advise them as they rise up into the sorrows and temptations of this life."[36]

In late April 1844 the crops had been planted and seemed to be thriving. The small grain and corn were beautiful, and Pickens had a fine stand of cotton on

700 acres. The plantation was demanding his attention.[37] Although he professed a waning interest in politics, he still had no shortage of advice for Calhoun. The Texas and Oregon questions, the British slave seizures in the West Indies, the tariff, and the presidential race were all discussed.[38] On 20 April 1844 a letter written by Van Buren against the annexation of Texas appeared in the Washington press. James Buchanan, Lewis Cass, and others emerged to contend with Van Buren for the Democratic nomination. To add to the confusion, the Democratic party was split, and plans were being made to have separate Tyler and Van Buren conventions.[39] Throughout the South meetings were called to protest Van Buren's pronouncements against annexation of Texas.[40] In early May Calhoun wrote Pickens urging that meetings be held in the Edgefield district to discuss the future of the Union in light of the Texas situation and to pass resolutions demanding annexation.[41] Pickens, who needed to muster all of his energies on his own behalf, was reticent to act, explaining that he could not call a meeting until sale day (the first Monday in June). Anyway, he reasoned, "I think it well that we do not meet too soon. We ought to see the whole ground and give others in Va., N. C., Geor., and etc. the chance to move if they will, for whenever $S^o\ C^a$ moves first there are thousands who fall back under the everlasting slang of $S^o\ C^a$ ultraism $S^o\ C^a$ Disunion and etc."[42]

Pickens worried about the "blood and ruin that must follow" if the South vacillated on the Texas question. He worried about the drought that threatened his once beautiful crops, and he worried because he had foolishly agreed to offer security for a $5,000 note made by former Tennessee senator Alexander Anderson.[43] In Washington Calhoun, while trying to formulate an acceptable Texas annexation treaty, was astutely observing the political undercurrents and radically changing his approach to presidential politics. It was Calhoun who had decided that the state should not be represented at the Democratic convention in Baltimore; it was Calhoun who, at the eleventh hour, made an about-face by writing Pickens "two extraordinary letters" that caused him to put aside his own concerns and, after consulting with members of the central committee, prepare to go to Washington and Baltimore. Pickens wrote James Edward Colhoun that the whole situation was rather awkward but that he was " 'waiting orders' and will start at a moment's warning . . . Mr. C. says V. B. and Clay can both be beaten and all is confusion at Washington. I have also rec^d letters from members from Miss: and Tenn: to go on and etc."[44]

While Pickens was making his way to Washington, the Democratic convention was being organized in Baltimore. Again Calhoun was being spoken of as a possible candidate, although recent proslavery pronouncements that he had

JAMES H. HAMMOND
(courtesy of the South Caroliniana Library, University of South Carolina)

made as secretary of state had cut off northern support. No moves were being made to place his name in nomination.⁴⁵ The national convention, which officially commenced on 27 May, was organized under the two-thirds rule. This was a victory for the Calhoun faction, since it assured that Van Buren could not be nominated. Andrew Jackson sealed Van Buren's fate when it became known to the convention that he desired to see a pro-Texas candidate become president. The situation became heated and "the most vulgar demagogism" was displayed. Pickens hoped the convention would break up without agreeing.⁴⁶ In order to avoid a deadlock, the Van Buren supporters decided to withdraw their candidate before the ninth ballot, thus avoiding a stalemate.⁴⁷ Pickens and Elmore were working for the nomination of James K. Polk, believing that he was the one man who could unify the party since he was safe on Texas, slavery, and the tariff. After the ninth roll call was completed but before the results were declared official, excitement was building to a peak. The correspondent for the Washington *Spectator* reported that a Maryland delegate "sprang upon his seat" and, after a string of eloquent remarks, said

> there is but one thing wanting to render this reunion of the Republican family complete; the absence of one Democratic and beloved sister "where is South Carolina?" . . . pointing to Mr. Pickens and Mr. Elmore. . . . The cry now from every part of the vast assemblage was absolutely deafening for "South Carolina!" "South Carolina!" "Pickens!" "Elmore!" These gentlemen who were sitting in the rear of the members of the convention rose up together—the shouts redoubled until the building seemed to rock under them. . . . Mr. Pickens . . . returned his grateful acknowledgements in glowing terms stating that he had no right to pledge his state for anyone, but that he was certain that South Carolina would support Polk, making him the unanimous choice of the Democratic party. Pickens then ascended to the podium and sketched ably the great questions in issue. . . . He expressed the most perfect confidence of success and roused and animated the audience for new efforts. . . . Mr. P. closed amid the most enthusiastic applause.⁴⁸

When Pickens wrote James Edward Colhoun giving him an account of events, he was jubilant as he recounted that Calhoun was behind Polk and that Van Buren was overthrown forever. He continued, "Polk is sound with us, rallying on him will give a sound basis to move together."⁴⁹ He wrote H. W. Conner, an owner of the *Mercury*, that "Polk was nominated unanimously and George M. Dallas of Pennsylvania V.P. *We have triumphed.* Polk is nearer to *us* than any public man who was named. He is a *large slaveholder* and *plants cotton—free trade* and *Texas*—states' rights *out* and *out*. We beat the *New Yorkers* and the *dynasty* and they were compelled to come in with a good grace or break the convention of their own making. . . . There was no time at which Mr. Calhoun's name could have been urged without injury to him and his cause . . . see our editors and put them *all right*—take the nomination with zeal and make it our ticket."[50]

Not everyone in South Carolina shared Pickens's enthusiasm. The ex-governor, James Hamilton, would have preferred Tyler (who would be prodded to quit the race by Andrew Jackson after being nominated by a separate Tyler convention) over Polk, whom he considered "scarcely above mediocrity."[51] Governor Hammond believed that the heated feelings which had been generated over the nomination and the Texas question would split the Democratic party into northern and southern divisions and would arrange the sections of the country against each other "permanently. . . what then becomes of the Union. It is gone unless there is providential interposition."[52] However, a sanguine Pickens preached that the defeat of Clay by Polk would mean a victory for Texas, for he doubted that Calhoun would be able to engineer ratification of the annexation treaty.[53] While participating in the events at Baltimore, Pickens became convinced that the South's salvation lay with Polk, and, like a newly converted religious zealot, he intended to spread the gospel. A subtle change was taking place in his loyalties. Like others in South Carolina, he now knew that Calhoun represented an obstacle to the fulfillment of his own ambitions. He was slowly realizing that it was time to connect with a rising star, rather than remain with a setting one.

Unlike the parochial Carolinians, Pickens did not dislike the national party. Since 1837 he had learned to accept the machinations of party politics; he understood that Polk would have to become evasive and compromise his views to be elected. Pickens had long taken a nationalistic position on many issues; indeed, his role in the McLeod affair, the Maine boundary dispute, and his desire to see the Texas and Oregon questions merged caused many in South Carolina to criticize him for being too national.[54] However, Pickens was purely southern on slavery, Texas, and the tariff. When precious southern institutions were attacked, he abandoned nationalism. Although now not as radical as many, believing that problems could be adjudicated within the structure of the Democratic party, he still maintained resistance to northern aggression as a last resort. Pickens hoped (but doubted) that, with Calhoun assuming the secretary of state's office, the Texas problem could be solved and the South kept united in the face of regional dissatisfaction over the failure of a revenue tariff in 1842. When Calhoun failed to realize the annexation of

Texas, Pickens was furious. "The treaty is rejected," he wrote, "great excitement. All is commotion—*we must act* . . . my whole soul is in the cause."[55] The crumbling of Calhoun's Texas dreams served as the catalyst to change the attitude of the Carolinians. Suspicions were aroused and anger rampant.

Rumors indicated that Daniel Huger would give up his Senate seat and return to Charleston. Again Pickens's hopes rose. His name was on everyone's lips because of his prominent role in Calhoun's campaign, in the deliberations of the state party, and in the recent events at Baltimore. He was being invited to address numerous gatherings, and a large portion of the Charleston delegation had pledged to support him to succeed Huger.[56] At this time Major John S. Jeter, the state senator from Edgefield, resigned from the legislature. Pickens was urged to enter the race to succeed Jeter, as it would place him in a better position to run for the U.S. Senate. The *Mercury* praised his candidacy in the most glowing terms, claiming that in "these degenerate times" it was "more honorable to Col. Pickens [to be in the South Carolina Senate] than to occupy the highest station in the country. There are enough men . . . to leave the state for the honors and distinctions of federal office—how few, like him, leave these honors . . . for the more humble and patriotic ones of the state." The Whigs in the Hamburg area planned to "bring out the most violent and bitter opposition" in the form of a longtime enemy, Frank H. Wardlaw. After the electioneering was over in October 1844, a jubilant Pickens recounted the campaign to Calhoun. Despite "the basest means" used against him, he had emerged victorious, 1,816-996.[57]

With the race for the state senate under way and with the work he was doing for Polk, Pickens was back in politics. While the *Mercury* praised his humbleness, he too desired to leave the state for the honors and distinctions of federal office. In his conversations with Calhoun he had been impressed that his kinsman had no desire to return to the Senate; Pickens believed it was time for the state's unchallenged leader to promote his lieutenant. After the circulation of reports that Huger would leave Washington, there were predictions that George McDuffie would also abandon his Senate seat because of his poor health; however, the old man showed no inclination to resign. There were also reports that Calhoun was being pushed to return to the Senate in order to represent the interests of the South.[58]

The summer of 1844 was very hot and dry. Pickens's corn failed to mature, and the cotton was being injured by plant lice and was opening early. On 27 July a storm brought needed rain and cooled the earth.[59] However, in Charleston, Colleton, and Beaufort another storm was brewing that threatened to inflame the political atmosphere and, if not controlled, to bring on revolution.

For months the slavery, Texas, and tariff questions had irritated the state. Although Polk had been nominated and assurances had been given that he favored a revenue tariff, many Palmetto State leaders believed that he was equivocating on the issue. Tempers were aroused when it was reported that he had written the "Kane letter" to Pennsylvania voters, which implied that he was not married to a revenue tariff.[60]

By early June sectionalism had become so great that the leaders of the Methodist Episcopal church had decided to split the denomination along northern and southern lines. The *Mercury* blamed the ruthless intrusion of abolition for the division.[61] At this time the *Mercury*'s senior editor, J. A. Stuart, returned to his press after a self-imposed fourteen-month exile; now the *Mercury* turned more radical, challenging the efforts of Pickens and Elmore on behalf of Polk.[62] The *Mercury*'s masthead continued to proclaim it as a Polk/Dallas paper; however, the paper's radicalism seemed to border on subversion. Several of the state's most important political leaders supplied grist for Stuart's mill by uttering sentiments against the course advocated by Pickens and Elmore. Speeches of Charleston Congressman Isaac Holmes and Senator George McDuffie were published and praised. Stuart's editorials, like McDuffie's speeches, raised the banner of disunion.[63]

On 31 July a dinner was held at Bluffton, in St. Luke's Parish, for the purpose of honoring the state's most obstreperous congressman, Robert Barnwell Rhett. Rhett proceeded to deliver a speech that urged his constituents to look to the glorious days of nullification and calculate once again the value of union. The heat, Rhett's fiery rhetoric, the fiery toast, and fiery spirits combined to create an explosive situation. By repudiating Calhoun's policy and advocating unilateral action, Rhett was threatening to undo all Calhoun had labored to accomplish. The *Mercury* had, in former days, warned those who would challenge Calhoun's authority "that no public man in the state has not fallen from it."[64] However, now even the paper publicly repudiated Calhoun's policy. On 8 August it praised the Blufftonites in an editorial that invited other South Carolinians to follow the lead of St. Luke's Parish and become "RIPE and READY" and like "old St. Luke PASS the Rubicon . . . her watchword is REDRESS or RESISTANCE."[65] The movement was proving infectious, and other Carolina leaders played on the people's anger and suspicion to fan the flames of resistance. In Edgefield District, Congressman Armistead Burt was preaching defiance, and Louis T. Wigfall, "who was for disunion open," in a fire-eating speech to the militia unit he commanded inferred that South Carolina should consider secession if her rights were not redressed.[66] Old leaders such as McDuffie and Rhett joined with Holmes, Wigfall, Burt, and Hammond to wave the banner of disunion and threaten southern unification—at an inopportune time, in the face of the upcoming presidential contest.[67]

A blowup of this magnitude had not been seen since the early 1830s. However, this time one element was missing. In the earlier troubles Calhoun had emerged as a leader of nullification, but now he and his loyal followers were steering a course that repudiated those who advocated resistance. The die was cast; Holmes, writing to Hammond, expressed the view that "the state [had] so frequently reiterated her 'declaration to resist' that she can't back out without dishonor."[68] These words expressed the sentiments of many who believed the time had come to take a final stand. The fire-eaters' inclination to force the issue could not be countenanced; to do so would jeopardize southern unification at a very critical time.[69]

The situation demanded all the skill and prudence the Calhoun party could muster to allay the paradoxical storm that would "vindicate the constitution which Mr. Calhoun had declared is violated."[70] Although Pickens was unhappy with aspects of Polk's campaign, his real fear was that the course of McDuffie, Rhett, and the radicals would bring disorder and defeat upon South Carolina, destroying every prospect of uniting the South.[71] Elmore worried that the upheaval "was producing in the old Union men a disposition to renew old issues . . . in order to force us from our states' rights principles and drive us to a recantation or into a minority."[72] The danger was apparent to all. In a reenactment of Governor Hayne's moves of over a decade before, Governor Hammond, dreaming of a new movement for disunion, requested from the commander of the Citadel guard the plans for the defenses of Fort Moultrie, Fort Johnson, and Castle Pinckney.[73] It was imperative that the situation be defused. The *Mercury*'s influence was being felt in Georgia and Virginia; its implications, that Calhoun was "deserting old friends and if so another must be look[ed] to to save the state," were having a detrimental effect on the other southern states, which were applauding Polk rather than damning him.[74] Pickens advised Calhoun that they needed to act, for otherwise "our cause will in reality be thrown back instead of advanced."[75] Elmore, writing from Charleston, urged Calhoun to publish letters expressing his views on the proper adjustment of the tariff in order to put down the "fretful temper—the fermented feeling" that was brewing.[76] Richard Yeadon, the editor of the Whig-backed Charleston *Courier*, came to the aid of the Calhounites and began an attack on Rhett, McDuffie, Stuart, and the *Mercury*. Rhett was assailed for his "imputations" against Calhoun, and on 15 August the *Courier* charged Stuart with "forwarding despicable projects." This led Stuart to write a full-page editorial in the *Mercury*; he defended his position by claiming that he and the paper were not Rhett's tools, and that being guilty of "Disunionism was not a grave charge when brought against a Southern man."[77]

In the meantime the decision was made to send a well-known Carolinian to the great Democratic meeting in Nashville to ascertain Polk's true position on major questions. The Calhoun party wanted assurances that Polk would dispense with their old adversary, Francis P. Blair and his *Globe*; and, in light of "the Kane letter," they wanted to know whether he would push for a thoroughgoing tariff reform.[78] Originally Pickens had been urged to go to Nashville, but he had refused, on the grounds that he had no one with whom to leave his children. George McDuffie was then approached and agreed to attend, but his radical inclinations and chronic illness forced him to cancel his plans. Calhoun and Elmore urged Pickens to reconsider. An obedient lieutenant, Pickens again obeyed the call and on 10 August began the "dreary trip."[79] When Pickens was contacted, he was making plans to speak on behalf of Polk at a mass meeting in Georgia, and he met with Elmore in Augusta to map out a strategy. He was closer to Polk than any other man in the state, having served with him in Congress; indeed, he would have succeeded Polk as speaker, had it not been for the cruelties of Rhett, Elmore, and Dixon H. Lewis. Pickens's activities were politically risky, for by going against the seemingly popular fringe movements he was gambling with his own political fortunes. However, it was essential that Polk be found safe on the issues of the day; only this could withhold from the fire burning in South Carolina the fuel that would allow it to become an all-consuming conflagration. Pickens also intended to ascertain the role that Calhoun would play as leader of the new administration.[80] He informed Calhoun that he planned to take the "highest ground ag[ain]st the tariff, but at the same time ag[ain]st all separate action of the state at present . . . and . . . we will organize with our Rep[ublican] brethren of the South . . . and consult freely as to the grounds of concerted action."[81]

Concurrent with the Nashville convention, a meeting was held in Charleston at which Rhett was called on to ameliorate his views and yield to those supporting Polk's candidacy. In order to avoid further irritating Calhoun, Rhett did the safe thing and returned to Washington.[82] While in Nashville, Pickens was overwhelmed with cordiality. He met with politicians from every state "in the Valley of the Miss[issippi]." He spent two days at Polk's house, where they compared the 1833 tariff with the 1842 measure, provision by provision, and discussed the importance of Texas, the fate of the *Globe* as the administration paper, and Calhoun's role in the new administration.[83] After the interviews were terminated, an elated Pickens was convinced that "there were no disguises." He wrote Calhoun that Polk was "determined if elected to do all he can to reform the Gov[ernment] and the first thing is to reduce the tariff of 1842 to a revenue measure entirely upon the principles of the compromise [of 1833] act—2nd to introduce strict economy—3rd acquire Texas at all hazards."[84] While in Nashville, Pickens was invited to spend a day with Andrew Jackson at the Hermitage, where he had "*perfectly* satisfactory" conversations with Calhoun's oldest and bitterest adversary. He then "attended other meetings and addressed the people" and discovered that there was still great enthusiasm in Alabama and Tennessee for a presidential bid by Calhoun in 1848.[85]

Pickens, anticipating that portions of his letter to Calhoun might be published, advocated Polk's election and gave a clear warning to the Carolinians: their actions constituted "madness and folly and worse it is *unpatriotic* to separate ourselves and throw off those who are with us in feeling and principles."[86] It was hoped that the tidings Pickens had brought from Nashville could be used to weaken the Bluffton movement, but discontent was not easily put down; the *Mercury* blasted him, while McDuffie, at a barbeque given in his honor, denounced him at Edgefield.[87] McDuffie's speech marked the rhetorical climax of agitation. He asked his audience, "Are you *men*—are you South Carolinians—are you men of '32—are you descendants of those of '76—or, are you *CURS*—which, when kicked, will howl, and then come back and lick the foot that has inflicted the blow. . . . If you are determined upon submission, first take a military force to Columbia, seize upon the records of revolution and of your no less glorious struggle of '32—BURN THEM! That there be nothing left to render your infamy more infamous, by the contrast."[88] Surely Pickens must have been surprised at McDuffie's attack, for on his way back from Nashville he had first gone to Pendleton to see Calhoun; finding Calhoun not home, he decided to visit McDuffie in Abbeville before going on to Edgefield. There he discovered McDuffie's health much improved, and although the old man seemed confused and desiring secession over nullification, Pickens believed that McDuffie had awoken to political realities, and that from him they had little to fear.[89] Despite the efforts of the radicals, Calhoun and his cause prevailed. The subsequent election of Polk and the Democrats' sweep of the state did not end the criticism that was being heaped on Pickens, Elmore, and Calhoun. By this time James Hammond had allied himself with McDuffie; the radicals were urging secession over nullification, and Rhett, who had been reelected to Congress, was in Washington echoing them. Hammond, who saw in Calhoun's moves not concern over the welfare of the state but promotion of his ambitions, welcomed the appearance of a movement against Calhoun's continued domination.[90] About a year before the inauguration of the Bluffton movement, Hammond had become involved in a scandalous relationship with

Wade Hampton's four daughters, his nieces by marriage. Rumors of his "wickedness and folly" were destroying him politically.[91] He believed that Pickens was adding fuel to the ignominious fire in order to "kill [him] out of his way for the Senate."[92] It appeared that the state was calming down on the eve of the new legislative session. Polk was president-elect, the *Mercury* had been "*Wet blanketed* by Calhoun and Co.," and Pickens continued to denounce "the late movement in the state as ultra, unwise, and unpatriotic."[93] Hammond, knowing all the parties involved and the nature of Carolina political intrigue, correctly realized that Pickens saw an opportunity "to break down Rhett as Calhoun is to see."[94] However, Pickens desired to see both Hammond and Rhett broken down, and his letters to Calhoun did not hesitate to condemn them both.

During this period Pickens continued to be Calhoun's primary advisor in South Carolina. Surely he believed that his stand against Rhett, Hammond, Stuart, McDuffie, Holmes, and Burt would place him in high favor. In mid-October, breathing a sigh of relief, Pickens told Calhoun, "I take it for granted all will now be quiet in our state, and if Polk is elected we will wait and give his Adm[inistration] a fair hearing."[95] However, the governor, in spite of his knowledge that the sentiments for ultraism had waned, decided to have a last hurrah before giving up the office. On 26 November Hammond sent the legislature a rebellious message urging disunion on the grounds that the South's security had been trampled by Congress's failure to lower the tariff and to ratify the Texas treaty. His cold, logical mind deduced that the failure of Texas annexation was tantamount to another attack on slavery. Since he envisioned no hope of combined southern resistance, the state would be "defrauded of her rights" if she did not act alone.[96] When a motion was introduced to publish Hammond's message, Pickens (who had just taken his seat in the South Carolina Senate) objected and asserted that the legislature should not endorse a message advocating disunion. He informed the assembly that the new administration could be relied upon to annex Texas and lower tariff rates. Pickens then introduced a series of anti-Hammond, pro-Union resolutions which were believed by the state senators to have been endorsed by Calhoun when in fact they were not.[97] These resolutions passed the Senate unanimously, but they faltered in the House and were relegated to a committee of the whole, where they were intermittently debated throughout the session.[98] Pickens wrote Calhoun that the actions of Hammond and "*others* who are near to you are a deliberate and concerted move against you . . . I conscientiously believe that it is a deliberate desire of some . . . to force us into such a position as to drive you from the cabinet hereafter . . . Mr. Steward [*sic*; John A.

Stuart] said to Robert Seymour a rep. from Charleston yesterday that 'we were to decide whether the state was to lick your toes forever!' "[99] To James Edward Colhoun, Pickens wrote of his triumph, "You see that the aim of the Governor and the clique was to place the state in such a position as to drive Mr. Calhoun out of the cabinet. . . . I think I have turned their words, and my resolutions have passed the Senate unanimously."[100] Hammond dolefully confided to his diary, "Pickens's resolutions passed the Senate today unanimously—a great triumph to him—and another mortifying to me. I must confess, I did not expect unanimity."[101]

In spite of some discontent, the state was still the fiefdom of John C. Calhoun. However, there was now the worrisome problem of how Polk would treat the state and her unquestioned leader. While praising Polk publicly, Pickens in a confidential letter to his cousin expressed the view that, if Polk and the Democratic party in Congress did not treat the state properly, then South Carolina "in her sovereign capacity has the power to protect her citizens in any emergency, and that we do not *waive that* right by waiting *events* at presents."[102] The Charleston *Courier* damned Hammond's message and praised Pickens for his stand on behalf of Polk, "who had received the decided approval of the state for his views on the tariff, Texas, and any other subject of importance to us."[103]

The difference between Pickens and the radicals was one of degree—practical politics versus South Carolina ultra paranoia. Hammond and Rhett, like Pickens, saw Calhoun as an impediment to the realization of their overriding ambitions; and as they perceived the state under attack, they reasoned that they could advance themselves on the wings of friction. Their fears were genuine, and their love for Mother Carolina took precedence over any sentiments held for the Union. Pickens's ambition was just as great; however, he believed that ultimately his goals would be reached by continuing to align himself with Calhoun. Therefore he preached southern unification and was more cautious in his actions and speeches. If southern unification did not materialize, then nullification or secession were options that could be exercised later. At this time everything was going Pickens's way. His conversations and correspondence with Polk led him to believe that Calhoun would occupy an important position in the new administration, probably continuing as secretary of state. One major reason for putting down the Bluffton movement was to stop any agitation that might sully Calhoun's opportunities. Pickens realized that his own political plans depended on Calhoun being out of South Carolina. The recent personal scandal put aside Hammond, he believed. Rhett enjoyed popularity in the low country, but the recent elections showed that ultraism was not favored statewide. The pending retirement of Huger, the precarious health of McDuffie, and the certainty of Calhoun occupying a major role in the administration, coupled with the fact that Rhett and Hammond were politically dead, assured Pickens that the next Senate opening would be his. Hammond explained it best when he wrote "that Pickens and Co." were pursuing their course as a means "to get back into the fold. They want their share of the Federal loaves and Fishes."[104] Hammond believed that, as a result of Pickens's moves, South Carolina would abandon her independent course and be thrown "into the amalgam of the Union."[105] During the waning days of the Bluffton movement, McDuffie, who had refused to cease his ultra activities, urged the speaker of the South Carolina House, William F. Colcock, to denounce Pickens's resolutions and call for a state convention.[106] However, the time had come for the state to fall in line. Radical talk diminished, and the power of the Calhoun forces was revealed again when the Unionist candidate for governor, William Aiken, was elected on 7 December. His opponent, the Blufftonite Whitemarsh Seabrook, protested to Calhoun that he had been denied the coveted office through the efforts of Pickens and his henchmen. He reported that "unfounded charges, logrolling, the untiring labours of interested individuals, inactivity on the part of my friends and above all, money *profusely* expended, were the agents that discomfitted me, and put another into office . . . I will not however particularize. The recital would disgust you . . . Rhett and Elmore are to be trampled under foot, and Pickens the acknowledged leader of the Aiken party, is to go to the U.S. Senate."[107] Like Seabrook, Hammond believed that Pickens's motives were self-serving, designed to secure for himself the Union party influence for the U.S. Senate, "precisely as Rhett elected Richardson for the same purpose." Prophetically, Hammond continued, "Pickens . . . can never be Senator."[108]

In a letter to Calhoun on 18 December, Pickens gently prodded him to answer three previous letters. Calhoun was obtaining intelligence from other sources as well as from Pickens, and what he was hearing and reading upset him. Already Pickens knew from Elmore, who had received a letter from Rhett, that Calhoun was unhappy with the way he was being ignored by Polk and his men. Pickens could also sense that Calhoun was not pleased with affairs in South Carolina. In an attempt to placate his commander Pickens wrote, "Now I do not know what may be the change in views, but I have endeavored to carry out what I supposed to be your views when I parted from you in Charleston . . . I have endeavored to do my duty and thank God I am satisfied as far as my own judgement is concerned."[109] The actions on the part of the radical Carolinians did not seem so distasteful to the secretary of state as

ROBERT BARNWELL RHETT
(courtesy of the South Caroliniana Library, University of South Carolina)

he viewed the whole situation. Forty years of political experience alerted him that all was not right with Polk. However, there was no way that Pickens could know that Calhoun's attitudes were shifting; he was simply a good lieutenant who served himself as he served his master. When Calhoun inquired about the dangerous rift that he understood had developed in the state, Pickens maintained that the *Mercury* and other informants were incorrect and that only a handful of men were "bitter and opposed to the present position of the state." In an obvious attempt to slur Rhett, he maintained that a majority of the votes cast in the late election in the Beaufort and Colleton District "were actually blank." He then confirmed what Calhoun certainly knew: "There are very few (and none from the low country) who can understand or appreciate our relations to any general parties out of the state. They are no more a part of the general Democratic party than if they were out of the Union."[110] Calhoun must have appreciated this statement since, as events were to show, he, too, had little use for the "general Democratic party."

As 1844 was drawing to a close, problems arose that were to compound difficulties in the Palmetto State and briefly give life to radical fires. In Washington the expected was happening: John Quincy Adams, knowing precisely the most effective way to rile the South prior to Polk's becoming president, served notice that he intended to have the gag rule rescinded; on 3 December his motion was brought to the House floor, where it passed, 108-80. The eight-year ban on the acceptance of abolition petitions in the House was thus repealed.[111] Judge Samuel Hoar was sent to Charleston from Massachusetts to test South Carolina's law that ordered Negro seamen be kept in confinement upon disembarking at a South Carolina port.[112] The tariff and Texas had accentuated anger, but the ire of the Carolinians rose to meet hostile actions against their sacred institution. In order to head off extreme resolutions being fabricated by a group of twenty-one radical South Carolina House members under the leadership of Speaker Colcock, Pickens introduced a second set of resolutions in the Senate. The first set of resolutions which he had made against Hammond's message passed the House on the last day of the session. The second set of resolutions passed the Senate unanimously but were lost in the House. Although Pickens called his resolutions "moderate," they were strongly worded, designed to convince the suspicious Carolinians that his language could be as incendiary as Hammond's, McDuffie's, or Rhett's. Although the substance of his resolutions threatened disunion, he did not urge immediate actions. He condemned Adams's movements as a "*flagrant outrage . . . and a step towards dissolution of the Federal Compact.*"[113] Hammond commented that Pickens's resolutions "more openly threatened disunion than any ever proposed by any state. Yet, they passed the Senate unanimously and who proposed them? Why Pickens, he who three weeks before denounced my violence and proposed resolutions of confidence in the Democratic Party and ... the Federal legislature—which this same Senate passed unanimously. What a Change! ... What a complete vindication of my message."[114] Pickens explained that his purpose was not to side with the Bluffton men, but to make slavery a unifying factor and show the nation that the South would fight any attempt to undermine its peculiar institution. In the final hours of the session many legislators were distracted, confused, and weary and were delighted to see Pickens's second resolutions tabled.[115] Already there had been too much strife; adjournment was welcome. Pickens bragged to Calhoun that "my last resolutions on abolition were introduced to prevent ultra moves in the House ... they performed their office fully—all is safe now."[116] William Gilmore Simms viewed Pickens's resolutions differently, reporting that they were tabled because the time was late and the members impatient to adjourn.[117]

During this disruptive session Pickens and Benjamin F. Perry, the nationalist state senator from Greenville, had the first of many disagreements, although they would later become fast friends. At this time Perry and Pickens agreed on the proper state role in regard to the national party; however, Perry's philosophy demanded constant loyalty to the Union, rather than intermittent fealty based on momentary advantage. Pickens as an opportunist joined with the party out of pragmatic, not philosophical, considerations. Perry as a Democrat preached that the power of government should belong to the people. When presidential electors were selected, he urged the legislature to follow the lead of all the other states and cease choosing the state's delegation to the electoral college, claiming that the voters should enjoy this right. Pickens strongly objected, maintaining that such an important function could not be entrusted to the people. He feared that Perry's moves signaled a shift in the thinking of Piedmont upcountry senators, and that Perry might make a popular crusade out of the matter. Therefore he led a fight with lopsided results that showed the time had not yet come to trust South Carolina's government to the people.[118]

The legislature chose Pickens to be a presidential elector, and he cast his ballot for James K. Polk. Polk's victory was not an easy one; he lost his home state and narrowly won in Pennsylvania and New York. He was able to defeat Clay 170-105 in the electoral college, and he received a popular vote of 1,337,242 to Clay's 1,299,012.[119]

The chief difficulty for the president-elect was Calhoun, whose aid in the campaign had been notable.[120] While Polk was planning to dump the Carolinian, Pickens was momentarily diverting himself from his overriding passion for politics to the necessary business of marriage. After Eliza's death in August 1842, he had relied heavily on Maria Colhoun for aid in rearing his daughters. Her death in April 1844 ended this arrangement, and his inability to successfully woo "Cudy" Colhoun dashed his marriage prospects for a time. Finally in December he found a willing mate in Marion Antoinette Dearing of Charleston. Her father was rich; she had been "raised in the best manner by worthy and pious parents, and she has all the diffidence and retiring softness to which I have been so accustomed in life."[121] Private nuptials took place on 9 January 1845 in Charleston; Pickens chose as his groomsmen James Edward Colhoun, Judge Andrew Pickens Butler, and his brother-in-law, Arthur Simkins. There was no honeymoon, as he intended to be back in Aiken the day after his marriage. Pickens considered his marriage to be "*a Duty* I owed myself and my children."[122] He made little mention of Marion except at the time of their wedding and at the time of her death.

The new year brought with it, in addition to a new wife, new and continuing problems. The flames of the radical Bluffton movement had turned to embers, but the sparks of radicalism were still present and violent moves were always possible. The *Mercury* claimed that a great statewide split existed, which William Gilmore Simms described as a contest between Edgefield and Bluffton.[123] South Carolina was shifting her attention from Columbia to Washington. The hope was strong that Polk would fulfill his promises and that slavery agitation would cease, the tariff be adjusted, and Texas annexed. Pickens believed that, with the fulfilling of Polk's pledges and Calhoun's assumption of an important role in the new administration, peace could return to battered South Carolina as she assumed her rightful place in leading the South.[124]

Polk was inaugurated on 4 March 1845. Pickens, who had remained at Edgefield "to wait results," received a letter from Calhoun that surely shocked him. The expectations that the Carolinian would continue as secretary of state, completing the critical negotiations over Texas and Oregon, were not to be fulfilled. Calhoun was to have no role in the new administration.[125] He was offered the ambassadorship to Great Britain, but he never seriously considered taking it. Before Polk left Tennessee for Washington, he had conferred with Andrew Jackson. From Calhoun's perspective, Polk, as a member of the Jackson dynasty, had permitted the ex-president to have a strong say over policy and over those who would sit in the cabinet.[126] Certainly the old flames of hate were still present, despite Pickens's earlier assurances that time had diminished the ill feeling between the two. With good grace, Calhoun retired from Washington to Fort Hill. In his letters he continued to urge Pickens to keep his composure in spite of so many enduring irritations.[127]

Probably at no other time in their relationship was the correspondence between Calhoun and Pickens so prolific. Although there were frequent speculations as to what Polk's moves would be, family affairs dominated their correspondence. Overproduction and England's policy of taxing American grown cotton had forced the price of the fiber down to 4½ cents per pound. The deep decline in cotton prices was playing havoc with the Calhoun clan. In the fall of 1844 Calhoun's son-in-law, Thomas Green Clemson, was confirmed as chargé d'affaires to Brussels. Prior to leaving he and Calhoun's son, Andrew, had a rift over $3,000 that Andrew owed him. Pickens had secured for Clemson the Cane Brake Plantation, which had belonged to Arthur Simkins. An ugly hassle arose, which resulted in Calhoun having to borrow heavily from Elmore's bank. Unfortunately for Pickens, he was caught in the middle of the whole affair and, in trying to please all parties involved, pleased no one.[128] In Clemson's absence, Pickens "despite protestations" found himself having to manage Clemson's plantation. Since Pickens lived over twenty miles away and had to attend to his own affairs, it was a genuine hardship to remain involved with Clemson, whom he found to be an argumentative, difficult person. He helped him because of his great loyalty to Calhoun and his daughter, Anna, but for his efforts received no thanks.[129]

In late March Calhoun returned to South Carolina. For weeks he had been critically ill and unable to carry out the duties of his office. However, he left Washington in an amiable mood, "freed of all responsibility." He hoped that Polk would not be censured for not inviting him to be in the cabinet, since he regarded what had happened as "probably the best for me."[130] He continued to urge peace in South Carolina. Although time was running out, there might be another chance at the presidency.[131]

The Bluffton movement not only had caused a resurgence of radicalism, which had forced Calhoun's men to quell it, but also had precipitated some peculiar political realignments in the state. Pickens and Elmore had stayed with Calhoun and, in supporting Polk, had gone against their onetime allies, Hammond and Rhett. After Calhoun declined the English mission, the post was offered to Elmore, who refused it on the grounds that his banking business required all his attention.[132] The president then approached Pickens: "I deem it proper to appoint a successor to Mr. [Edward] Everett as envoy . . . to Great Britain and now I invite you to accept the station." Unlike Elmore, who wrote a long, polite letter of rejection, Pickens refused the ministership in a short, pointed letter that reminded Polk of his promise to adjust the tariff.[133] This was the third time that Pickens had refused a foreign appointment; he was a strange choice for this particular post, considering his anglophobia and the delicate state of British-American affairs. Calhoun wrote his kinsman that he could not disapprove of his declining the mission, but since southern interests were deeply involved, he desired to see the post filled by a man "true to the South and all its interests."[134] Immediately before Pickens received Calhoun's correspondence, he had read a letter from Duff Green that urged him to recommend that Polk reconsider Calhoun, in order to prevent Van Buren from assuming the ambassadorship.[135] However, it was impossible for Polk and Calhoun to come to terms. Much to Pickens's relief, Van Buren, like Calhoun, adamantly refused the English post. Finally Louis McLane, probably the best choice of all, consented to go.[136] James Hammond, still smarting from his treatment at Pickens's hands, was elated that his foe had refused the appointment, since he was "wholly unfit . . . particularly . . . when it is supposed a war with England on account of the Oregon Territory is not unlikely. Pickens will precipitate matters and bring on a war if it can be done. He is pompous and blustering, which by no means suits the court of St. James."[137] Another enemy remarked, "The refusal of Elmore and Pickens to accept the mission filled me with unqualified satisfaction . . . what can interest me now, that S. C. is partitioned between such a triumvirate as Calhoun—Elmore and Pickens—public and private interests are safe in the ciphers which indicate the values of the numerals—seriously, these three men were foreseen by Shakespeare—some are born to greatness—others attract greatness and others have greatness thrust upon them—and as to Pickens, fortune had done so much for him that his master wouldn't know him."[138]

Many of those who disliked Pickens condemned him, yet some were not hesitant to ask him to appeal to the president on their behalf. He refused to nominate anyone for federal office, however, keeping aloof as a protest against what he considered to be Polk's failure to secure "permanent justice, equality and protection." He believed that, until Polk considered the welfare of the South, there would be no equality in the nation.[139] Although Polk's election was considered a victory for the South and a mandate to carry out Calhoun's plans for the annexation of Texas by the questionable means of a joint resolution, Texas's annexation alone was not enough to secure for Polk's administration the unqualified approval of the Carolinians. Some tended to believe that the president's policy was "to forget his friends and buy up his enemies."[140] Pickens expressed his dissatisfaction in his refusal of the English mission, and South Carolina's sons continued to put their state's interests ahead of those of the nation. Pickens revealed this sentiment when he wrote, "I could not accept any office with the feelings of allegiance I have for my own state."[141] He explained to President Polk that he had supported him not for power and favor but in order to prevent South Carolina from separating from her sister slave states, thus hampering the building of an alliance between the South and West.[142]

In June 1845 George McDuffie suffered a stroke, and this gave rise to speculation that his days in the Senate were numbered.[143] Although Pickens proclaimed to James Edward Colhoun that he "would not turn on his heel to be in the Senate—I care not a fig for the place," in truth his every action was designed to garner a seat. He desperately wanted to succeed his cousin as leader of the state and perhaps the nation. His ambitions were so great and his marriage to the southern code of decorum so strong that self-delusion became a cloak that protected him in face of rejection. With so many ambitious men courting office, and in light of previous rebuffs, strategic planning and political acumen were vital. Rumors always abounded, and by the summer of 1845 they were especially plentiful. Pickens heard that Elmore was being groomed for the Senate; Louis Wigfall, his longtime enemy, was spreading the word that Hammond was much esteemed by Calhoun and was favored to assume McDuffie's place.[144] The Hammond and Calhoun papers show that Wigfall's pronouncements had some veracity. Calhoun, who surely knew of Hammond's personal difficulties, nonetheless urged him forward, remonstrating with him to continue to serve his state.[145] Ostensibly Hammond, like Pickens, was calculating how best to win Calhoun's support for the Senate. For Pickens, the Senate contest was to be a replay of the earlier episode when Calhoun and Preston had resigned and been replaced by Huger and McDuffie. And, just as before, Pickens's ambitions were to go unfulfilled.

5. A Litany of Destruction

By midsummer 1845 the Oregon question, the tariff, agitation over slavery, even the prospects of war with both England and Mexico took a backseat to concerns over the havoc that a prolonged and severe drought was inflicting on South Carolina. Throughout the Southeast the news was bad. Prayers were offered, meetings held, and pending doom acknowledged. The disaster threatened starvation for the poor and deprivation for the more fortunate.

In the state's political circles, however, speculation continued as to who would succeed Huger and McDuffie in the Senate and whether Calhoun would run for the presidency in 1848. Much to the approval of the Calhoun faction, Blair and his *Globe* had not been retained as the official organ of Polk's administration. Its successor, the new Washington *Union*, was already engaged in battle with the Charleston *Mercury* over the Oregon question and Polk's lack of movement on the tariff. Although the *Mercury* was following the Calhoun line and advocating that the nation take a soft posture in regard to Oregon, this was not the view held by most Carolinians.[1]

Calhoun was being urged by his closest advisors, who were making plans for 1848, to "pursue a conciliatory course towards Polk's administration."[2] Although Calhoun continued to differ with Polk, especially over Oregon and the tariff, he was disposed to accept his advisors' recommendations and did nothing to irritate the administration before returning to the Senate.[3] Calhoun was urged to travel "as a private citizen and make no developments by speeches or otherwise."[4] Pickens, knowing that his kinsman was planning to visit his son Andrew in Alabama, urged him to continue his journey and visit New Orleans, Nashville, St. Louis, and Cincinnati.[5] In his reply Calhoun indicated that he did not contemplate going beyond Mobile or New Orleans; as far as he was concerned, "my public life is terminated . . . I shall never return to it, unless the country should demand my services, and then only on the principal of duty." He maintained that, if he took an extensive trip West, he would be "construed as a seeker of public favour."[6]

Calhoun's course gave encouragement to Pickens. Even though Huger had offered to resign his Senate seat so that Calhoun could return to Washington, the Carolinian had made no such moves.[7] As the days of summer passed, Pickens realized that only one vacancy would occur. Contrary to all expectations, McDuffie's health was improving.[8] The *South Carolinian* reported that "Gen. McDuffie with the exception of a slight paralysis . . . is enjoying very good health, that his constituents will not suffer him to resign, and our correspondent adds—'he will probably die a Senator!'"[9] McDuffie's improving health was an impediment to Pickens's ambitions. As a result of attacks from McDuffie at the height of the Bluffton movement, Pickens secretly harbored deep resentment for the senator, whom he considered to have long outlived his usefulness.[10]

Calhoun's revelation that he intended to bow out of public life gave Pickens hope that his senatorial aspirations might finally be realized. He profusely applauded Calhoun's course: "The philosophical and resigned tone of your letter was such to command my deepest respect. I have long seen . . . that the heartless and selfish pursuits of politics were ill calculated to create resignation or contentment, and it is grateful to see one like yourself furnishing such a prominent example to the country."[11]

At this time meetings were being held throughout the state to elect delegates to the great commercial convention. The theme of the Memphis convention was internal improvements; its supporters hoped to forge a South-West alliance whereby the South would support federally financed internal improvements along the Mississippi in exchange for western support for a lower tariff.[12] For months Calhoun had been receiving letters urging that he return to the Senate; however, he seemed firm in his pledge to remain a private citizen. The *Mercury*, in a praise of Blufftonism, castigated those who put faith in Polk, reminding the state and her leaders that "the tariff and the repeal of the 21st rule are still in force upon the Statute Book."[13] On 4 October a large public meeting was held in Charleston to explain the reasons for calling the Memphis railroad convention and to elect delegates. Calhoun and Elmore were appointed by the governor as special delegates to the convention and in mid-October Elmore and James Gadsden, one of the leaders of the convention movement, urged Calhoun to go.[14] At about the same time he received a letter from Pickens adamantly disagreeing with his views on Oregon. Calhoun worried that, if the administration persisted in taking a hard line on this question, a war with Great Britain would result. He believed that the only intelligent course was to leave matters alone. Pickens supported the administration's course; he believed England had no legitimate title to the territory and no desire for war. However, "another appeal to arms," he predicted, "must come sooner or later."[15]

The Oregon question marks the beginning of overt difficulties in the Pickens-Calhoun relationship. In his reply to a letter in which Pickens admitted his support of the administration's handling of the Oregon question, Calhoun assailed Polk for engaging in "consummate and *crowning* folly."[16] Certainly Pickens took Calhoun's criticism of the administration as an affront. In the midst of this correspondence Calhoun admitted that he was having second thoughts and was considering returning to public life. This revelation came to light after Pickens, who had been paid a visit by McDuffie, commented on the dreadful state of McDuffie's health. "It is melancholy," he wrote, "to see him and think of what he was. It is cruel to allow him to exhibit himself in public, and it will sacrifice his noble fame." Pickens continued in the same vein to express resentment toward Daniel Huger, who he claimed was also in his dotage, for requesting that the South Carolina legislature erect a monument to the memory of Andrew Jackson: "We had better first burn the records of nullification which stand out as the most glorious chapter in our history."[17] Calhoun replied that it was to be lamented that McDuffie and Huger were such a great liability to the state and were "being acted on by cowering and designing men." He then devastated Pickens with the news that Huger had offered to resign provided Calhoun would return to Washington; although he was "exceedingly adverse to returning again to public life . . . I do not see . . . how I could decline the duty." He urged Pickens to respect the confidentiality of his letter and encouraged him, as the only one who was privy to his reasonings, to say whether or not he should return to the Senate. In the past many of Pickens's letters had been obsequious, but his reply to Calhoun indicated he was now undergoing a great change. He reiterated that Polk had a duty to perform regarding Oregon. After voicing approval of Calhoun's return to Washington, he observed that everyone knew that Huger was contemplating the move; he should not comment further, since Calhoun had obviously made his decision. However, he did remonstrate with Calhoun to have it "authoritatively announced" that he would forego a run for the presidency if he returned to the Senate, since a rebirth of presidential aspirations would, "instead of producing concert, produce the reverse."

Pickens had told Calhoun what he did not want to hear. Furthermore, he had solicited in his cause their mutual brother-in-law, James Edward Colhoun.[18] Surely the senator realized that Pickens was lumping him together with all the other politicians who used the call to duty as a means of ascending the political ladder. Pickens had committed an unpardonable sin by pointing out that Calhoun had the choice of being a statesman who could triumph in his own genius and "scorn and defy the opposition of heartless and selfish partisans" or a politician trying to grasp for the final time the presidential ring. When Calhoun announced his intention to go to Memphis, everyone realized that he was going West to test the political waters. His triumphal receptions at every stop surely lifted Calhoun's presidential aspirations.[19] Pickens naturally realized that the fulfillment of Calhoun's ambitions would be detrimental to his own. Because rumor had it that McDuffie would be replaced by either Elmore or Hammond, Pickens again saw himself as the victim of selfish intrigue.[20]

While in Memphis Calhoun was unanimously elected permanent president of the convention, and in that capacity he delivered a speech that amazed and angered many Carolinians. While he deprecated the failure of the administration to adjust the obnoxious tariff of 1842, he ignited a fuse in South Carolina by going against his earlier stand and advocating a wide-ranging program of internal improvements sponsored by the government.[21] This speech left no doubt that Calhoun was once again seeking the presidency. In South Carolina there was talk of rebellion. The ultras passed resolutions condemning Calhoun's course and urging that the state "adhere to her principles on the subject of Internal Improvements, and hold that the Federal Government has no right to make any appropriations in aid of railroads, public highways, canals . . . or any other improvements . . . unless plainly and absolutely necessary for the defence of the Union."[22] The ultras wanted no national program of internal improvements and "looked on a separate national existence as being preferable for the South."[23] While Calhoun was making his way back home, the legislature on 26 November 1845, although fully assembled, cast only a small vote for him to succeed Huger, who had resigned earlier in the month. A correspondent for the *Mercury* expressed the sentiments of many when he questioned Calhoun's loyalty to "ancient republican principals." Pickens informed James Edward Colhoun that Rhett had prepared resolutions against Calhoun and that Elmore had written that "all Mr. Calhoun's friends . . . had deserted him and that resolutions would be introduced into that [Virginia] legislature disapproving of his doctrine in his Memphis speech."[24] Pickens had learned long before that much of what Calhoun did was self-serving and that loyalty to him was not reciprocated. Those who had opposed the senator's course in the late Bluffton movement and were criticizing his activities in Memphis had not been called on to explain their moves; they had not suffered for their opposition, and some were even being promoted for higher office. In spite of numerous favors done for Calhoun and his family, Pickens had reaped little gratitude from the senator. He had played a major role in Calhoun's last presidential campaign, and his coffers had been at his kinsman's disposal. He had gone to Baltimore and Nashville at Calhoun's urging; while in the state senate, he had moderated his own views in order to help Calhoun promote harmony. The appointment to the Court of St. James had been tempting, but he had denied himself the honor;

certainly, one consideration leading to his refusal was the fact that Calhoun had also rejected the mission.[25] All of Pickens's political life had centered around the greatest Carolinian, yet Calhoun's life had centered around himself. The denouement had begun unfolding when Pickens realized that he had been shut out of the inner circle and that he would not be considered to succeed McDuffie.

In February 1846 an article appeared in the *Southern Quarterly Review*, which was controlled by some of the most prominent men in South Carolina, criticizing Calhoun's role at the Memphis convention. The article, utilizing passages from a speech Pickens had made five years earlier, which incorporated Calhoun's arguments against federally sponsored programs of internal improvements, made a mockery of Calhoun's new stance. Although Pickens denied that he had a hand in writing the article and asserted that he too "objected to its tune and language" as it affected Calhoun, he did admit that he had seen the article two days prior to its publication and had insisted that some of the most objectionable passages be deleted. He acknowledged that philosophically he did "not differ from the abstract sentiments of the reviewer." Calhoun complained that Pickens had caught Bluffton fever—the seeds of doubt which had been planted long before were sprouting. Ironically, while Pickens continued criticizing those who publicly differed with Calhoun, the one who was falling from grace was not Rhett, McDuffie, Burt, or Hammond, but Pickens, who had defended his master against Blufftonism in 1844 and had constantly informed him of anti-Calhoun acts on the part of others.[26]

Calhoun was nearing sixty-four, and his health had been steadily declining. During the winter and spring of 1845 he had almost died with a respiratory ailment, and public and private concerns were taking their toll.[27] After the Memphis convention he was faced with another revolt, and the tone of Pickens's letters did little to soothe his spirit. Familiarity proved to breed contempt in the relationship. Pickens was too close and too indispensable. The Calhouns turned to him to guarantee their notes, manage their properties, draw up their wills, and perform countless other tasks. Unfortunately, Pickens had become involved in their family fights and had encountered the hostility of Calhoun's sons.[28] Pickens was probably perceived as lording his wealth over them; his advice, both sought and unsought, was irritating. In countless letters he remarked on the perfidious nature of Calhoun's underlings. Certainly, there was truth in Pickens's observations, but his fulsomeness was exasperating. The situation began to worsen as Calhoun realized that Pickens was moving closer to Polk. Letters that Pickens sent to James Edward Colhoun, questioning Calhoun's actions, were seen as treasonous by the senator. Pickens's cordial meetings with Polk in August 1844, the presidential moves in redeeming pledges relating to Texas, Oregon, the administration's printer, internal improvements, and the tariff had helped to inaugurate a shift in allegiance.[29] Calhoun became the chief critic of Polk's foreign policies, and although at the time of his departure from Washington he outwardly expressed no bitterness at not being asked to remain as secretary of state, his letters to those close to him indicated that he was indeed bitter, and that he felt more capable of managing American foreign policy than Polk and Buchanan. It irritated him that much of what Pickens wrote defended Polk's stands.[30] Pickens's thorough distaste for the English influenced him not to place priority on preserving peace with Great Britain.[31] He sided with Polk, who maintained that the only way to treat England was to pursue a bold and firm course.[32] Calhoun believed Polk's course was fraught with lunacy. Pickens did not accept Calhoun's reasonings. He felt that England was too involved in European affairs to fight the United States; besides, she had not gone to war over the Maine boundary dispute, the McLeod affair, or the Texas question.[33]

After Calhoun returned to the Senate, Pickens urged him to cooperate with Polk and warned him that there were those "who have an interest in fomenting trouble between you and the President." He advised Calhoun to trust the president, for he had redeemed his pledges and was in the process of adjusting the tariff.[34] Outward harmony prevailed, but even prior to Calhoun's leaving Tyler's cabinet, his growing enmity for Polk was making genuine cooperation impossible. Although Polk's talk in relation to Oregon had been bellicose, when the question was finally brought to negotiation, Calhoun's ideas predominated in the treaty. It was agreed that the territory should be divided at 49° north latitude, and the Senate, led by Calhoun, ratified the treaty on 12 June 1846.[35]

The tariff debate in the House coincided with the Senate debates on the Oregon boundary treaty. Pickens feared that Calhoun's opposition to Polk's Oregon position would alienate the president and that the division would prevent "harmony or consultation on the tariff."[36] However, after extensive debate, the Walker Tariff passed the Senate on 28 July 1846, and the president signed the measure two days later. On 3 August Polk distressed representatives from the West by vetoing the harbor and river improvements bill. The tariff never would have passed if the internal improvement bill which the West so fervently desired had been struck down first. Passage of the Walker Tariff raised southern hopes, and Calhoun, who had angered many of his constituents over his moderate approach to Oregon and his support for internal improvements, was again the idol of the Palmetto State.[37] The irony was that, in most matters that affected the nation, the president had followed the path that Pickens urged; like Pickens, he held federally supported internal improvements to be unconstitutional.[38] Nevertheless, Calhoun's popularity was soon to sink again, and his already strained relationship with Pickens was to completely break down over policies regarding Mexico.

After Texas annexation finally became a reality, South Carolinians joyfully displayed their approval with demonstrations throughout the state.[39] James Hammond expressed the sentiment of most Southerners: "The annexation of Texas is an event of great magnitude—the greatest of the present day. It strengthens the South and slave interest."[40] However, annexation presented another dilemma, as debate arose with Mexico over the location of the southwestern border. Months before annexation took place, there was speculation that the nation might become involved in a war with Mexico, Great Britain, or both. After Texas agreed to the terms of annexation on 4 July 1845, tension between the United States and Mexican armies stationed along the Rio Grande heightened, and on 25 April 1846 a scouting patrol of eighty American dragoons was ambushed by the Mexicans. The Charleston *Courier*, Edgefield *Advertiser*, and most other South Carolina papers published scathing accounts and editorials regarding the Mexican actions. However, the *Mercury* and several members of the state's congressional delegation, including Congressman Isaac Holmes of Charleston and Senators McDuffie and Calhoun, took a different tack, blaming the Polk administration for confusing the situation by ordering General Zachary Taylor into the Rio Grande region.[41] Calhoun believed that war with Mexico could be avoided and that the United States could still gain the disputed territory. On 11 May 1846 Polk requested a declaration of war; the next day, despite Calhoun's entreaties, war was declared. Calhoun was furious with Polk and became openly defiant.[42]

War caught Pickens by surprise.[43] However, when news of hostilities reached Edgefield, Pickens was at the forefront in urging citizens to support the administration by raising troops for a volunteer company. On 1 June a public meeting was called to give the people of Edgefield District an opportunity to express their opinions in regard to the war. Pickens, unaware of much that was transpiring in Washington, offered six resolutions supporting the administration. Since he and his closest friends, Whitfield and Preston Brooks and M. L. Bonham, whose brother had died at the Alamo, praised Polk so highly and failed to defend Calhoun's course of action, some of those present claimed that by implication Pickens and his friends had slurred Calhoun.[44] Frank Wardlaw (who co-chaired the meeting), Louis T. Wigfall, Joseph Abney (junior editor of the Edgefield *Advertiser*), and Thomas C. Key (editor of the

Hamburg *Journal*) all bore animosity for Pickens and the so-called Edgefield junto for a variety of reasons. Wardlaw was an old political enemy, and Wigfall had many reasons for turning against Pickens: his brother Arthur had not been appointed permanent rector of Trinity Church, they had been on opposing sides in the gubernatorial election of 1840, and Pickens had refused to guarantee his notes. Wigfall's hostility to the Brooks clan was so great that he had engaged in two duels with them.[45] Key and Abney, friends of Wardlaw and Wigfall, were at the time engaged in a lively correspondence with Pickens's successor in Congress, Armistead Burt, who was another Calhoun kinsman and now his closest advisor. Pickens and Burt had had political differences, and during the late Bluffton movement Pickens had been very critical of Burt's role. Even though Wigfall favored war with Mexico, he and his friends saw an opportunity to totally destroy the Pickens-Calhoun relationship, thus preventing Pickens from attempting to run for McDuffie's senate seat.[46] By this time it was common knowledge in the state's political circles that Calhoun was unhappy with Pickens's deep devotion to Polk. The offensive article in the *Southern Quarterly Review* that Calhoun attributed to his cousin and Pickens's "strong infusion of envy, jealousy and vanity" sufficed for his destruction.[47] Pickens and his clique were not the only ones to make speeches and submit resolutions for the approval of the Edgefield masses; Wigfall made an addendum to his resolutions that proclaimed Calhoun's course offered "nothing to condemn and everything to approve." Although Wigfall's resolutions were tabled, since to pass them might cast aspersions on South Carolina's representatives who had voted for war, they did their work well by putting in doubt Pickens's loyalty to Calhoun and confirming Wigfall's allegiance to the Carolinian.[48] Thus, after Calhoun read the state's newspapers and was shown letters by Burt, who had been corresponding with Key, Abney, and Wigfall, he became furious,[49] especially after seeing a letter from Key stating that Pickens had censured him by "insinuations and sarcasm."[50] In order to foment hostile feelings in Washington, Abney wrote Burt that Pickens believed he could make political capital by "entertaining serious opposition to his great partner . . . whom he supposed . . . would be prostrated by his refusing to vote for a declaration of war and that Pickens thought he would be placing himself in line for promotion by the President, and that if he failed of success . . . a door would still be left open by which he could make fair weather with Mr. Calhoun."[51] The conspiracy worked. As Key remarked, Pickens's "political advancement will certainly not be benefitted by this movement and of this Pickens must be aware."[52] Pickens was indeed aware; all he had to do was read the state's newspapers. Calhoun refused to answer Pickens's letters, but to James Edward Colhoun and his daughter, Anna Clemson, he excoriated Pickens in the harshest terms.[53]

What were Pickens's motives? There is no doubt that he was annoyed with Calhoun; but certainly he knew better than to go against him, for, as Benjamin F. Perry explained in his *Reminiscences*, "Calhoun was absolute in South Carolina and all who sought promotion in the state had to follow him and swear by him. He thought for the state and crushed out all independence of thought in those below him."[54] The chief factors that destroyed Pickens were Calhoun's increasing impatience with him and Pickens's own realization that the relationship had not been politically advantageous. However, the ultimate fall came not because Pickens was challenging Calhoun's leadership, but because those who resented Pickens and wanted to prevent him from becoming senator found ways to make his actions appear to be aimed against Calhoun. They were doing to Pickens what Pickens had done to others. Through innuendo, the telling of half-truths, and clever manipulations, they for a time halted Pickens's political advancement. His enemies had capitalized on an opportunity to settle old scores. There is no question that Pickens's arrogance and vanity made him vulnerable, but ultimately a combination of calamities befell him. Acting on the advice of mutual friends, Pickens asked for an interview with the senator to tell his side of the story. He sought out George McDuffie and denied all statements that had been attributed to him. He repeated his disavowal to others, claiming that, when he supposedly made the slurs against Calhoun, he was sick and had only attended the meeting long enough to submit resolutions which were in no way detrimental to Calhoun. He argued that his enemies had succeeded in prejudicing the senator against him by giving "the most extravagant, exaggerated, and false account of everything I said and did at the public meeting in June last."[55] Finally, he was granted an audience with the great Carolinian, but the reception was cold. Calhoun maintained that there was still "an ugly question to be settled between Pickens and others on whose authority the charges were made."[56] Relations were never to be the same. Shortly after the Edgefield meeting, the *Mercury* condemned him and predicted that he would publicly change his position in order to ingratiate himself with Calhoun. Pickens did not change his position in regard to the war, and he did not denounce what he was accused of doing, since he maintained that he had done nothing to incur Calhoun's wrath. However, the damage was done. Perry's Greenville *Mountaineer* asserted that Pickens had "kicked too soon—the lion is not dead yet."[57] Pickens's last words to Calhoun on the subject were that he had done no more than Franklin H. Elmore had done at a meeting in Columbia: "he uttered precisely the same sentiments that I did, and advocated exactly the same resolutions in substance, and yet not a word of complaint has been suggested against him for his course . . . I have *been by you* when you *needed friends*, and when to *stand by you* was *no gain* to any man . . . However, separated our spheres may hereafter be, yet you *shall*, as you have *ever* done, commend my highest regard and admiration."[58]

For the next two years Pickens kept trying to restore his relationship with the senator. In early 1847 Floride Calhoun invited him to visit Fort Hill. By this time Marion had given birth to Jennie, Pickens's fifth daughter. Since he had received such a cordial invitation, and since Calhoun had written in late December that relations stood "where they have so long stood," he decided to make the visit. Instead of graciously receiving Pickens and his wife and infant daughter, Calhoun refused to meet them; when he did come in for dinner, he acted "outrageously for a gentleman in his own house."[59]

By August 1846 there was no doubt that McDuffie's health had finally broken for good. The end of the congressional session in November would mark the end of his career. Although Pickens was widely mentioned as a successor, along with Hammond, Elmore, Rhett, and Judge Andrew Pickens Butler, the loss of Calhoun's favor had drastically diminished his chances. The best indicator of Pickens's political demise occurred when Ker Boyce, a noted figure in state politics who headed the Charleston Bank, announced in the *Mercury* that he was supporting his rival banker, Franklin H. Elmore, for the Senate. Boyce's endorsement of Elmore showed that loyalty was not a trait of Carolina politics. Boyce was deeply indebted to Pickens and his family for helping his bank prosper; however, in order to court Calhoun and to get Elmore out of Charleston, so "that the Bank of $S^o\ C^a$ may go down and his banks be omnipotent," Boyce supported Elmore.[60] Pickens worried that, if Elmore were elected, his absence would cause the Bank of South Carolina to fail and "all its debtors be published." Expecting that his concerns would be relayed to Calhoun, he shared his fears with James Edward Colhoun. Pickens knew that Calhoun was in debt to Elmore's bank and that its demise would adversely affect the senator's precarious financial situation.[61] Pickens probably hoped that, if the top contenders faltered, he might still have a chance for the seat. Hammond, next to Elmore the most popular candidate, was being pushed by McDuffie. However, Hammond's personal indiscretions could be counted on to put him out of the race. A few days before the balloting began, Elmore did withdraw, citing pressing business commitments. Hammond led on the first two votes but slipped on the third ballot, and on 23 November 1846 the legislature selected Andrew Pickens Butler, who had stayed above the late controversies.⁶² The taint on Pickens was too great; according to Joseph Abney, one of the "anonymous scribblers" who had done so much to destroy him, "Pickens was perfectly flat, more than dead—I believe he is dead in his own district."⁶³ At this time Pickens's sorrow was joy to many. He had a long list of enemies who were delighted with his plight and who reveled "that the blustering puppy [was] killed off."⁶⁴

Some peculiar changes were taking place in state politics. Although relations between the president and Calhoun continued to decline, most South Carolinians were kindly disposed toward Polk. The new tariff was a southern measure, and Polk's stands on Oregon and the Mexican War were popular. However, most Palmetto politicians were very careful not to offend Calhoun. Although Rhett was still out of favor for his activities during the Bluffton movement, he was taking steps to return himself to the senator's good graces by supporting Calhoun's arguments in favor of limited federally financed internal improvements. Unlike Pickens, who had been accused of using the *Southern Quarterly Review* to defame Calhoun, Rhett used the same journal to defend Calhoun's course.⁶⁵

James Hammond also learned his lesson. Although he differed with Calhoun on the war and internal improvements, he refused to speak out. He understood that Calhoun "overshadows us. . . . He is the King in our game whom we cannot abandon and cannot protect. If we shield him from 'check,' he immediately throws himself into a 'stale-mate' and blocks every movement."⁶⁶ As Pickens's plight proved, there was nothing to gain and everything to lose by opposing Calhoun. Hammond, like Rhett, made moves to stay in Calhoun's favor, and unlike Pickens, who opposed Calhoun's Oregon stand, Hammond used enthusiastic support of the senator's position as a vehicle of reconciliation.⁶⁷ Pickens desperately desired to reestablish harmonious relations with his cousin, but, except for a few inconsequential letters, their correspondence dried up. In early April 1848 Pickens informed his kinsman that he had purchased a mule and a mare for the Clemson plantation; he continued, "I will do anything that a gentleman ought to do for Anna . . . I would have done so all along, but for the very *extraordinary treatment* I met with at your house last fall, which I have too much self-respect to forget."⁶⁸ Pickens used the Clemson homecoming from Brussels as an opportunity to make one last attempt at family reconciliation. In an impassioned meeting with Anna, in which "he was deeply agitated and affected and . . . shed tears and if not sincere in what he says is the greatest actor and hypocrite that ever existed," he tried to explain away the whole affair by claiming that "artful persons had disunited your father and myself." Anna concluded: "I do not doubt that his independence of you, bad counsels, and the excitement of the moment to say even perhaps what is stated but *I do not believe that he does not know it himself*. This may appear a paradox to you but our powers of self-deception are wonderful. . . . His account of the matter is this. He denies ever making the statement or using the words attributed to him. He says they were given in a letter not signed but written by Wigfall to injure him because he had refused going his security."[69] Anna's petition on behalf of Pickens was rejected by her father, who wrote that he had never been influenced by persons hostile to Pickens and that he was "above being influenced by such attempts; for no one has ever done so much to '*endeavor to*' influence me that way as himself."[70] How wrong Calhoun was—and Anna knew it—but the truth was not to help Pickens. There is an interesting footnote to the affair. Precisely when the Hamburg *Journal* and the Edgefield *Advertiser* were publishing so-called accounts of the Edgefield meeting at which Pickens was accused of defaming Calhoun, a sheriff's sale was taking place at Wigfall's. One of those who bought at the sale was Pickens.[71] Joseph Abney, the junior editor of the *Advertiser*, was "deposed" for his part in the affair and left for the war.[72] Even as Wigfall, "a disgraced man," was leaving South Carolina for Marshall, Texas, he could not resist stabbing Pickens again; in a letter to Burt he wrote, "The *Advertiser* is to be made the organ of the party and Polk and Patriotism is the tune that is to be played on it. Pickens is in the village everyday talking—talking and etc."[73] Although the split with Calhoun was final, Pickens was to have further relations with Wigfall, even when he resided hundreds of miles from Edgefield.

While Pickens was enduring his agony, harmony seemed to be returning to South Carolina. The state rallied against a formidable new attack on slavery and, with Calhoun at the helm, a single-minded purpose developed. As in the past when events were not to her liking, she inevitably threatened disunion. Ironically, manifest destiny, which was to absorb sectional energy and prevent a national rupture, was the cause of the difficulties. Congress had been in session for over eight months, and most members yearned for adjournment when Polk attempted to force through an additional measure. His expansionistic eye landed on California, and he reckoned on a course to obtain the territory from Mexico. Because money was needed to carry out his plans, on 8 August 1846 he requested that Congress appropriate $2 million to be used in negotiating a treaty with Mexico. Although Congress was not told that the funds were to be used for this purpose, the president's plans were obvious to all. When a proposal to deny the money unless slavery was prohibited in any new territory gained from Mexico was introduced in the House by David Wilmot of Pennsylvania, debate on the measure became heated. Although Wilmot was no abolitionist and Polk could not fathom "the connection slavery had with making peace with Mexico," the nation trembled. The abolitionists saw an opportunity to disrupt southern desires for hegemony.[74] For years the abolitionists had been attacking slavery, but, with the advent of the Wilmot Proviso, it would be impossible to keep South Carolina in check. As late as the summer of 1845 James Hammond doubted the propriety of organizing for the purpose of defending slavery. "South Carolina," he wrote, "belongs to Calhoun. He will not agitate, Elmore will not agitate—Pickens will not agitate and these three men . . . carry the state in their breeches pocket."[75] However, the new situation sent an indescribable shock throughout the South as the realization struck that slavery would be harder than ever to defend.[76] The South was now a minority region in every respect. With the incorporation of Wisconsin and Iowa into the Union, not only were the House and the electoral college controlled by the North, but the Senate as well. There was a growing disposition on the part of the majority to declare the complete exclusion of slavery in all remaining territory.[77] In the South consolidation took place, and men who had differed in the past put those views aside in order to insure that slavery would not be abolished from any new territory gained from Mexico. Pickens, in a letter to James Buchanan, summed up the southern position: the South could not accept the Wilmot Proviso, for to do so would mean changing the terms of national equality. That the South could never do "without feeling our degradation."[78]

The war and the debate surrounding extension of the peculiar institution into the territories overshadowed the upcoming contest for the presidency. In light of Polk's promise to be a one-term president, Calhoun's supporters were again pushing him forward. Although Polk and Calhoun agreed that the proviso was disruptive, they remained far apart on the Mexican War. However, Calhoun continued as the spokesman for the South, and in that capacity he looked to the creation of a southern party to help unify the region, undermine the abolitionists, and give new life to his presidential aspirations. The decision was made to establish in Washington a pro-Calhoun, proslavery newspaper. Elmore was given the task of chairing a committee to raise funds for the new organ. One of those on whom they intended to rely for financial backing was Pickens; but he remained aloof, informing his onetime brother-in-law, Senator Andrew Pickens Butler, that he was "out and out opposed to the movement—denouncing it as a scheme for [Calhoun's] personal objects."[79] By this time Pickens had gone entirely over to Polk. He praised the president's course and predicted "that after the bitterness and prejudice have died away, posterity will remember with gratitude and admiration the patriotism, wisdom and firmness of your administration. Your measures will form a bright page in history."[80] Then Pickens, who had earned early notoriety as one of the most vociferous fire-eaters, praised the "firmness and decision" that enabled Polk to put down "fanatics on one side and agitators on the other."[81]

The split was final: Pickens's honor prevented him from being used. Whereas Calhoun had spurned political parties, Pickens now embraced the Democratic party and decided to participate in the presidential contest that was on the horizon.[82] The war and abolition, the bitter debates in Congress, and the inevitable passage of time insured that Calhoun's chances for the presidency were forever lost. Since the contest would be a prime factor in setting the course for the country and could well determine the fate of the Union, interest grew unusually high as the campaign approached. Calhoun had urged upon the South the destruction of all national party distinctions and the formation of a southern party that had as its sole object the defense of slavery, but the time for this had not come.[83] Many people in South Carolina, like Pickens, were wary of Calhoun's approach, fearing that the North would retaliate with an antislavery party that would cause a political breakdown. Additionally, there was the worry that, if South Carolina took the lead, it would divide the South and insure disastrous defeat.[84] In the fall of 1847 meetings were held throughout the state; Unionist and Nullifiers, Whigs and Democrats, radicals and moderates all joined in condemning the Wilmot Proviso and the moves against slavery.[85]

The war with Mexico ended in May 1848; however, bitter political battles continued to be waged. Slavery was the issue, and disunion the ultimate result. Pickens believed that South Carolina needed to participate in the Democratic convention in order for the state to be in a position to select leaders "at this peculiar time who have the iron will and intrepid spirit to defend our institution." Calhoun urged caution, however, believing that "South Carolina ought not to move until we see the game and those that play it."[86] As a protest, the Palmetto State took the same course it had taken in 1840 and 1844 and refused to send a delegation to the convention. Armistead Burt, echoing Calhoun, preached that the first duty of the South was self-preservation and not loyalty to the Democratic party. However, Pickens, Perry, and many others believed that unilateral abandonment of the Democratic party would hinder the state from acting in concert with other states.[87] The nomination of Lewis Cass of Michigan displeased many Southerners, who believed that he was unsafe on the slavery question. Although admitting that he was not kindly disposed to the institution, he allayed the fears of many by claiming that he opposed the

A Litany of Destruction

FRANKLIN H. ELMORE
(courtesy of the South Caroliniana Library, University of South Carolina)

Wilmot Proviso and that he believed Congress should not decide whether slavery should be permitted in the territories.[88] The Whigs nominated the hero of the Mexican War, General Zachary Taylor. Calhoun, speaking through the Pendleton *Messenger*, expressed dissatisfaction with both candidates, claiming that both "held opinions at war with the cherished principles of the state." However, most of the state's politicians and newspapers took sides. The Edgefield *Advertiser* and Perry's Greenville *Mountaineer* strongly endorsed Cass and in every issue denounced Taylor and praised the Democrats.[89]

Many Democrats believed that since Taylor was a Southerner and a Louisiana slaveholder, he would be safer on the slavery question. The *Mercury* reported that great numbers of Charlestonians preferred Taylor and were holding large meetings on his behalf. Unfortunately, his refusal to come out against the Wilmot Proviso made him unacceptable to most Carolinians.[90] On 9 August 1848 the Free Soil party, whose goal was to stop the expansion of slavery, held its convention and nominated Martin Van Buren. For the first time there was a political party dedicated to stopping the spread of slavery. South Carolina felt threatened. The situation was fittingly summed up in a toast offered at a Fourth of July celebration in St. Paul's Parish: "General Cass and General Taylor: the horns of a dilemma to Southern patriots."[91]

Calhoun continued to urge the state to take no part in the election and to work for nonpartisan unity of the South, but, as the Edgefield *Advertiser* noted, "the people of the state are breaking away from the position of neutrality sought to be imposed upon them by some of their politicians."[92] Robert Barnwell Rhett, in a well-attended meeting at Charleston's Hibernian Hall, claimed that support of Taylor was "utterly inconsistent with the principles of South Carolina."[93] Shortly before Rhett made these pronouncements, Pickens, who had decided two years previously not to stand for reelection to the South Carolina Senate as a sign that he had given up political activity, emerged as a leader in the Cass campaign. He was invited to address the Democratic Association in Athens, Georgia, but had to decline because his wife was ill. In a letter published in the Athens *Southern Banner* and republished in the *Advertiser*, he urged his readers to support the Democratic ticket, praising Polk's stand on internal improvements, the Mexican War, and expansionism.[94] Although both Pickens and Rhett disapproved of Cass's support of the "doctrine of territorial sovereignty," they took charge of his campaign in South Carolina.[95] In the Charleston area the Whigs made inroads, and Isaac Holmes, running as a Taylor man, was returned to Congress. However, when the legislature met in special session to choose presidential electors, Cass defeated Taylor, 127-27.[96]

Shortly before the legislature convened for the presidential election, the Columbia *South Carolinian* published a letter from George McDuffie nominating Pickens for governor. McDuffie, who was now a frequent visitor to Edgewood, traced Pickens's career in the most flattering terms and praised his "intelligence and urbanity" and his refusal to accept the ambassadorship to the "two most splendid courts of Europe—both of which were refused distinctly on the ground that he could not conscientiously take benefit of the Federal Government so long as his state was denied equal rights with all her confederates."[97] The nomination was designed to give a lift to Pickens's sagging political fortunes. William Gilmore Simms claimed that, by supporting Cass, Pickens hoped "to throw Mr. Calhoun aside or give him a mortal stab." Even though the Democrats prevailed in South Carolina without aid or comfort from Calhoun, the senator remained supreme in the state. When the gubernatorial race commenced, Pickens's name was not even considered by the legislature, in spite of a statewide endorsement by McDuffie and others. The contest was overwhelmingly won by Whitemarsh Seabrook, whom Pickens had helped to defeat in the 1844 gubernatorial race.[98] Simms claimed that Taylor's victory over Cass nationally meant that "neither Rhett nor Pickens [could] possibly realize their thirty pieces of silver." Instead of Pickens giving Calhoun "a mortal stab," the reverse proved to be the case.[99] Again Calhoun demonstrated that he was master over the Carolinians, and that no one could ascend the state's hierarchy except through him.

6. An Insolvable Dilemma

The North, so far as we can judge from all components of public opinion—the Press—resolutions of state legislatures—and the actual vote of representatives in Congress—have determined that slavery should not be introduced into any country that the fortune of war or the terms of a treaty, may obtain for us from Mexico."[1] This was the picture painted by Armistead Burt on the eve of the presidential contest. As abolitionist sentiment grew, it was matched by equally strong southern indignation. The unsettling question of slavery absorbed all other issues. In South Carolina songs of defiance were sung:

> Yes, Yes, the direful storm is brewing
> Soon in its rage to burst amain
> And blight each lovely Southern Plain
> With desolation and ruin
> Arise—Arise ye Brave
> Our banners be unfurl'd
> We will swear our rights to save
> Proclaim it to the World.[2]

Committees of safety and vigilance were formed, and in every hamlet Southern Rights Associations elected delegates to a statewide convention to be held in Columbia. Each time the Wilmot Proviso was brought up in Congress, it passed in the House but failed in the Senate; on each occasion the number of congressmen voting for the proviso increased. Taylor's election ushered in more Whig representatives, who now controlled the House, 115-110.[3]

Talk of disunion was omnipresent. Armistead Burt, in a speech given at Abbeville, urged the South to work in concert and hold a convention of slaveholding states to prevent the destruction of their sacred institution. Pickens continually worried that, if South Carolina took a lead in promoting a southern convention, thousands would "fall back under the everlasting charge of South Carolina ultraism and South Carolina disunion."[4] However, there was also the fear that, if moves were not made to unite the South, northern assaults would become even more prevalent.

Seabrook's election as governor was a triumph for the growing number of people who believed that South Carolina should act alone if southern unification could not be quickly attained.[5] Most Southerners still believed that southern cooperation was essential in order to counter the persistent North. The Palmetto State legislature mandated that a states' rights convention be called to consider an appropriate course of action should Congress pass the Wilmot Proviso. The Virginia legislature had taken the lead by declaring that, upon passage of the Wilmot Proviso or any act that abolished slavery or the slave trade in the District of Columbia, the governor should immediately convene the legislature to consider measures of redress.[6] In South Carolina all flirting with the Union ceased. Pickens, who had been noted as a South Carolina nationalist, reversed his course and recalled the glories of 1832, when he was at the forefront of the nullification movement. The situation was imminently more perilous, since slavery, and not the tariff, was now the issue; for a while at least, it appeared that southern cooperation was possible. The South Carolina press was strident, and the legislature directed that the number of rifles in the state's possession be increased to 12,000.[7]

The statewide meeting of committees of safety and vigilance was called by the Richland District committee to be held in Columbia on 14 May 1849. The central committee consisted of five members: Pickens, Elmore, Wade Hampton, James Gadsden, and D. J. McCord. Pickens introduced resolutions urging the Palmetto State to follow Virginia's lead and adopt resolutions to call the legislature into session for the consideration of the mode and measure of redress should Congress continue to interfere with slavery.[8] Although there was a great deal of talk about separate state action, Pickens contended that it was necessary to cooperate with "sister states, identified with us in interest and feeling—our institutions are the same and our destiny must be the same."[9] The Palmetto State was again calculating the value of the Union, but Pickens considered the situation so perilous that he recommended South Carolina "avoid doing anything calculated to isolate [the state] from her sister southern states." Nothing, he believed, could do more harm than if South Carolina was perceived to be leading the South out of the Union.[10]

During the hot summer of 1849 paranoia was rampant and rumors abounded; the central committee of safety reported that strange, unknown individuals had been seen in the state, and quantities of abolitionist literature had arrived in the mails. There was a general belief that northern agents had been sent to foment slave insurrections. The central committee, after several of "those black hearted villians" had been discovered, issued an open letter warning the public of grave dangers: "There is no disguise which an enemy are not ready to assume in order to work mischief, and we urge caution against everyone, who under the pretense of religion or humanity, could use that sacred good to cover his mischievous designs."[11]

At this juncture, after covert prompting from South Carolina, Mississippi called for a southern convention to meet in Nashville in June 1850 for the purpose of adopting resistance to northern attacks. Mississippi had done what South Carolina could not do, for South Carolina was in no position to be the initiator of a southern movement if that movement was to prove successful.[12] In November 1849 Calhoun publicly praised the Mississippi legislature: "Without union and concert of union, there can be no effectual resistance and without a convention there can be no union and concert. Such is and has been my opinion in every stage of the abolition agitation."[13]

During its regular session in December 1849 the General Assembly took steps to elect four delegates at large to attend the Nashville convention, and the voters of each congressional district were invited to send two representatives.[14] In the same session the legislature resolved that passage of the Wilmot Proviso or abolition of slavery in the District of Columbia would be tantamount to a dissolution of the Union. Langdon Cheves, Franklin H. Elmore, Robert W. Barnwell, and James Hammond were selected to represent the state at large. Calhoun's influence was clearly seen in the balloting; Rhett and Pickens came in seventh and eighth, respectively, a sign that Calhoun did not favor their election.[15] Calhoun praised the convention as "the first great step toward meeting the aggressions of the North."[16] The *Mercury* warned the North that the South must be respected, "and that the present generation of Southern temper is not the bravado of a bullying coward . . . but the calm and firm resolution of a brave and determined people."[17]

The situation went from bad to worse. In 1850 the House contained an even larger number of abolitionists, and their cries against slavery were shriller than ever. In the Senate there was a similar situation, but the grand old men, Calhoun, Clay, and Webster, seemed to act as a restraining factor. When Clay presented his famous compromise proposals on 29 January 1850, many Southerners assailed them and accused him of being a northern partisan. From the southern viewpoint the chief problem lay in Clay's proposal to exclude slavery from the California territory. The addition of another free state would further diminish southern power.[18] Calhoun was too ill to hear Clay present his resolutions, but four weeks later the old nullifier replied. In his address, read by James Mason of Virginia, the dying senator expressed the conviction that the Union could not be saved by Clay's plan. Calhoun offered no compromise; however, he warned the nation that a settlement would have to be made on the principles of justice and that only the North could initiate such a settlement. Calhoun died on 31 March 1850 and was finally laid to rest in Charleston four weeks later. His death left the South leaderless; confusion reigned, and compromise was doubtful. In light of this situation the forthcoming Nashville convention took on greater importance.[19]

Since the days of nullification, Pickens, Rhett, Hammond, and Elmore had all desired to inherit Calhoun's coveted mantle of leadership. However, none of them was of sufficient status to take his place. Governor Seabrook had to appoint an interim successor to the senator. In order not to involve himself in a controversy, he first offered the position to ex-governor James Hamilton, who was declared ineligible since he did not meet the state's residency requirements. He then turned to the eminent Langdon Cheves, who had for years absented himself from the controversies in South Carolina politics. Cheves cited age as the reason for his refusal.[20] Seabrook then invited Elmore to assume the interim position, and, after much deliberation, he resigned the presidency of the bank in order to accept.[21] Elmore soon died and was replaced for the interim by Robert Barnwell, who announced that he did not plan to run for the next term. Thus there developed in the legislature a contest between Rhett and Hammond.[22]

Calhoun's death demonstrated how totally out of favor Pickens was. When the Charleston city council selected two men to eulogize the deceased senator at ceremonies to be held in November, it bestowed the honor on Hammond and Elmore; the legislature, at the urging of Governor Seabrook, invited Rhett to eulogize Calhoun before a joint session. Pickens was totally ignored; he seemed as dead as his old mentor. Only in Edgefield District did he command any attention, and there only because his friend W. F. Durisoe published the Edgefield *Advertiser*, which continued to promote him politically.[23] It must have irritated Pickens to see Hammond's and Rhett's stars rise, especially since he felt that he had done so much for Calhoun. At the time when the state's newspapers were full of lament and praise for the dead senator, a letter from Hiram Powers appeared announcing completion of the statue of Calhoun that Pickens had commissioned. Powers wrote that the statue portrayed Calhoun as "the disinterested and stern statesman of the South."[24] Surely Pickens would have agreed with Powers's interpretation, since he, more than anyone, had felt the master's wrath and had paid more than anyone for his transgressions. Ironically, his efforts on behalf of Calhoun during the Bluffton movement had alienated Seabrook, who was now in a position to affect his political prospects. Hammond had paid for his indiscretions, Rhett for his radicalism. However, as the senatorial election in December 1850 showed, both men were now in contention for the highest honors that the state could bestow. A contest developed between Hammond's newfound course of moderation versus Rhett's old doctrine of anti-submission. But Hammond was no Calhoun, and the state as a result of the events of 1850 would not truckle to submission. As a result of his radical stand, Rhett would go to the Senate.[25]

Out of the ashes of banishment Pickens began to forge a new beginning. Unfortunately, he had many handicaps to overcome. In the past he had failed to realize that his fierce attacks upon his political rivals could be fatal to his own prospects. Memories were long and enemies many. His inattention to the future consequences of his past acts had lost him the good will of the state's power brokers; and, unlike Rhett and Hammond, he had relied upon Calhoun's organization, failing to develop a network of his own. Although he was well known nationally, his national connections were now liabilities in light of the North's attacks on the South.

Many Southerners believed that the Southern Rights Convention would show the rest of the nation that the South was formidable and united. Throughout the South, meetings were being held to decide upon candidates to be sent to Nashville. In Edgefield the citizens were formulating their plans. Pickens urged that the two delegates elected from his congressional district remain uninstructed so that they might be flexible.[26] California was the problem on everyone's mind. Clay, in his compromise, had urged that the territory be admitted as a free state. Pickens objected on principle. He doubted that slavery would ever take hold in California, since the soil and production would not suit their "peculiar labor," but he argued that Southerners, if they so desired, should have the right to own slaves in the territory. On 6 May Pickens was chosen unanimously to represent his congressional district in Nashville.[27] At this time he was continuing to follow the moderate line. He preached that the Union was worth saving, provided southern rights and honor did not perish in the attempt. On 3 June the Nashville convention was called to order, but the enthusiasm that had prevailed six months earlier had already waned. Only nine states were represented, and many of those with less than full delegations.[28] The plan for concerted action failed because Clay's measures were attractive to the border states, which had turned against the convention. Although many Southerners urged that the convention be postponed, delay would have been seen as abandonment.[29]

The delegates began their deliberations in an atmosphere of gloom. Just a year earlier, Virginia had boldly announced that adoption of the Wilmot Proviso was just cause for disunion; now the state had only six representatives present. Most of the South Carolina delegates were content to sit and not be heard. The moderates wanted to see what type of compromise, if any, would emerge from Congress, which was sitting while the convention was in session.[30] Although Hammond and other members of the South Carolina delegation decided on a course of silence, Pickens and Rhett, who represented their districts rather than the state at large, decided to make themselves heard. In what Hammond described as two "grandiloquent speeches much admired by the mob," Pickens proposed a set of resolutions designed to limit the power of Congress over slavery and the slave trade.[31] He proclaimed that Congress had no authority to stop the emigration of slaves into territory won by the arms of all the states, and that the slaveholding states should take "the earliest and most decided measures of concert and united action in order to preserve their peace." As a last resort, the states could fall back on "their separate sovereignty and independence" in order to thwart northern designs. Pickens remonstrated with his fellow delegates to reject any moves designed to interfere with slavery by claiming that such moves could only end in "convulsions and ruin." When the convention reconvened for its second session in November 1850, Pickens's resolutions were adopted as part of the preamble of the convention.[32]

Unlike Rhett, who put little faith in southern cooperation and advocated separate state action, Pickens continued for a time to cling to the belief that southern unity would force the North to stop her agitation. Hammond, speaking for the majority of the delegation and trying to don the mantle of Calhoun, advocated a policy of moderation. "Our policy," he wrote, "was to show that we were reasonable and ready to go as far back to unite with any party of resistance as honor and safety would permit."[33] The moderates were enjoying apparent success until Rhett charismatically rekindled the embers of radicalism. Late in the fall of 1850 Pickens, fearing that the moves in Congress signaled a new and disastrous attack on slavery, did a reversal and began flirting with the rhetoric of revolution, proclaiming: "Equality now! Equality forever! or Independence!" Secession was the talk of the times.[34]

The Nashville convention proved to be a disappointment for the ultras. The delegates agreed to reconvene on the sixth Monday after the adjournment of Congress; but the death of Calhoun had removed a check from the Carolinians, and the fire-eaters, led by Rhett, were gaining ascendancy. The convention came out for equality in California and proposed that the old Missouri Compromise line continue to the Pacific, with Southerners assured the right of colonization south of it.[35] Pickens's Nashville resolutions stated that "the Federal Government [had] no constitutional right to prohibit the emigration of the citizens of these Southern States with any of their property into any of the territories of the Union."³⁶ The Palmetto State was impatient for results—the moderates were suppressed, and the radical line became popular. When it became obvious that Congress was going to pass the so-called compromise measures, even the more conservative Carolinians began to change their views; believing that the North was taking all the kernels and leaving only the shells for the South, they cried that acceptance of Clay's compromise was surrender to the abolitionists. Sentiment was growing that the time had come for South Carolina to leave the Union unilaterally, rather than to submit.³⁷ In a speech full of allegory made in Columbia, Pickens revealed the dilemma that the state was facing, since most Southerners feared disunion and welcomed a compromise. "South Carolina makes no move," he observed, "there she stands in a defensive attitude, with her lance couched, and not a feather quivering in her plume." South Carolina was in the awkward position of making no move because she had none to make. The people waited.³⁸

By November 1850 many of the state's newspapers, led by the *Mercury* and the *Advertiser*, were actively advocating separate state action. Realistically, such a move was impossible. At the second session of the Nashville convention Langdon Cheves acted as spokesman for the South Carolina delegation. He had remained silent during the first session, but now he urged the convention to adopt a recommendation for southern secession. Even though the convention refused to champion such a move, it did accept a portion of the preamble of the convention in which Pickens advocated the right of secession provided southern rights were not protected.³⁹

The South Carolina legislature, after seeing the results of the convention and knowing the sentiments of other southern states, realized that the state stood alone in advocating secession. Most legislators agreed that inaction was the best policy to pursue. The Edgefield *Advertiser* expressed the sentiments of many when it bitterly editorialized: "The proceedings of the legislature, thus far indicate no immediate action, to redress her wrongs, will be taken by the state. Her position, however, towards the Federal Government, is no longer a matter of doubt. Her people have imbibed a deep and settled hostility towards the Union."⁴⁰

Although the events of 1850 had given rise to feelings of hopelessness and frustration, they were beneficial to Pickens's career. His election as a member of the Central Committee of Vigilance and Safety and as a delegate to the Southern Rights Convention gave him the opportunity to emerge from political limbo. Again his name was in the press and before the people. At the Nashville convention he had reestablished political bonds with leaders within and outside South Carolina. He was again being mentioned as a possible gubernatorial candidate. However, the time was not yet right, and honor to Calhoun's name demanded rejection of Pickens. The other most prominently mentioned candidates were Robert Barnwell and John H. Means. Because Barnwell, who had succeeded Calhoun as interim senator, renounced any desire for the office, the race was between Means, who was known as a staunch defender of South Carolina rights, and Pickens. Although Means defeated Pickens on the second ballot, 88-67, this gubernatorial contest marked the inauguration of a new political status for Pickens. At this same time Rhett defeated Hammond for the Senate, showing that South Carolinians still clung to their radical heritage at a time when a moderating influence was sweeping the rest of the South.[41] Nevertheless, most of the state's important leaders, including Barnwell and Cheves, determined that the state should not be isolated.[42]

South Carolina was in a quandary. Most legislators desired a state secession convention, but in order to achieve this end two-thirds of them had to vote for it, and this could not be accomplished.[43] After ten months without Calhoun, South Carolina found herself leaderless. Hammond revealed a newfound appreciation for the deceased leader and confided to his diary, "Mr. Calhoun by his vast superiority of mind and influence at home—kept them down and crushed dissension."[44] But now dissension reigned, and South Carolinians were frustrated and angry. Many felt that the time for secession had come.

7. A Mere Office-Seeker

The acceptance of the Compromise of 1850 by President Millard Fillmore signaled that it was time for South Carolina to unite with her sister southern states and prepare for separation.¹ Governor Whitemarsh Seabrook urged caution; in order to be prepared, he requested that the state continue to strengthen the militia. General agitation was a phenomenon in South Carolina but not throughout the South. The legislature was late in electing a governor to succeed Seabrook, and other business was delayed while debates ranged over what posture South Carolina should assume to combat the impossible situation.² The General Assembly argued that a state convention should be called, as suggested by the rump of the Southern Rights Convention which had reconvened in Nashville in November 1850. South Carolina hoped that all this would lead to the development of a southern congress which could speak with a single voice. Each congressional district was urged to elect two delegates to this congress (which would never meet).³ Voters were urged to elect men who would be true to South Carolina's ideals. There was the widespread feeling that congressional oppression would force the South to unite, but that the Palmetto State would and could resort to independent state action if that did not come to pass. The election for delegates to the state convention was to be held on the second Monday in February 1851, even though the legislature had determined that the convention would not meet for a year. Pickens, M. L. Bonham, F. H. Wardlaw, and three others were delegates from Edgefield. Of the one hundred sixty-nine men elected to this convention, about one-third were against separate state secession.⁴

The newspapers reflected the mood by publishing numerous letters and editorials on both sides of the issue. By this time most South Carolinians desired secession, but many feared a solitary journey. Although Pickens had just been defeated in the gubernatorial race, he was again being spoken of as a candidate for the Senate. A. P. Butler, his fellow vestryman at Trinity Church, Edgefield, was rumored to be contemplating retirement, and a likely successor was rumored to be Pickens.⁵ Although the rumors proved groundless and Pickens's hopes met with frustration, he was to play an important role in the events that were unfolding.

The passage of time was a critical factor in determining South Carolina's course. Judging from the election of men to the state convention, in early 1851 the voters were overwhelmingly in favor of separate state secession. However, the passage of time was giving more moderate elements an opportunity to rally. The ultras were led by the Charleston *Mercury* and the Edgefield *Advertiser*, which was now being edited by Pickens's brother-in-law, Arthur Simkins. Countering the calls for immediate unilateral separation were the Columbia *South Carolinian*, the Charleston *Courier*, and the upstate papers, the Yorkville *Miscellany* and the new Greenville *Southern Patriot*. Published by the state's most prominent Unionist, Benjamin F. Perry, the *Southern Patriot* editorialized that separate state secession would prove ruinous and "that by going off alone we shall injure no one but ourselves."[6] In another editorial he reasoned that, if South Carolina had the right to secede, then "we assume the position that districts have equally a perfectly and guaranteed right to withdraw from a state . . . we claim the privilege of secession . . . but will be content to be admitted as a county in . . . North Carolina."[7]

At this time Pickens was in a philosophical state of flux. At the first Nashville convention he vehemently opposed Clay's pending compromise and spoke on behalf of southern unity to force Congress to extend the Missouri Compromise line to the Pacific. In a speech delivered at Spartanburg, South Carolina, in August 1850 and in a letter written to Perry in late October, he still embraced the cooperationist standard.[8] However, the dismal failure of the second session of the Nashville convention and its inability to bring on southern unity, combined with the inclination of many Southerners to accept the Compromise of 1850 as final, demonstrated to him that southern cooperation and secession would not come to pass. Pickens became more radical in his views, advocating a qualified doctrine of cooperation, if possible, while upholding the necessity of immediate independent secession.

On 7 July 1851 a large public meeting in Edgefield allowed the opponents and proponents of separate state secession an opportunity to air their views. Preston Brooks, whose family had been close to Pickens for years, emerged as the spokesman for those who opposed secession. He used the arguments against separate state secession that Pickens had made in Spartanburg a year earlier.[9] Pickens answered Brooks by claiming that the state had been patient and had yielded "every emotion of pride and everything, but a sacrifice of principle to procure cooperation." He contended that, in order not to be a "degraded people," it might "become our sacred duty to act alone." Then he sketched for his audience the history of their rights and argued that the reserve clause in the Constitution did not make for an amalgamated people. "The state acceded to the compact, so it can secede in like manner. Without the right and power the reserved sovereignty and independence of the states is all rabid declamation and swelling assumption."[10]

Pickens, echoing the state's other hotspurs, seemed never to have weighed the consequences of separate state secession for South Carolina. In order to feed their own insatiable egos, the spoiled children of Mother Carolina were willing to risk their very existence in their quest to preserve the peculiar institution and what they perceived to be their sacred honor. Their pomposity was suicidal, much like that of duelists. The *Southern Patriot* and the collaborating Yorkville *Miscellany* continued to excoriate the radicals and the *Mercury*. On 20 September 1851 the *Miscellany* ridiculed Rhett's publication, in a sarcastic parody of Alexander Pope's "Rape of the Lock":

> With anger foaming and vengeance full,
> Why bellowith the Merc'ry like a bull?
> Say goddess, could a few humorous stripes
> Make it so furious, kick about its types:
> Spin round his pandemonium like a
> Top, and, Thundering, to its centre
> Shake the shop?
> Could wit's keen twig produce so dire a din?
> And dwells such softness in a printer's skin?
> Let dogs delight to bark and bite,
> For God hath made them so:
> Let bears and lions growl and fight
> For tis their nature too.
> But, Mercury, you should never let
> Such angry passions rise:
> Your little hands were never made,
>   *to crack necks*.[11]

Other papers warned that separate state action would be disastrous. The Columbia *South Carolinian* and the Charleston *Courier*, although softer in tone than the *Southern Patriot*, followed a similar course. By the fall of 1851 the ardor for secession was cooling. Pickens hoped that the state convention scheduled to meet on 26 April 1852 would move South Carolina to break with the Union. He preached that South Carolina's strength lay in her unity, and that if the Palmetto State took the lead, the other southern states would follow.[12] Pickens's logic was flawed: South Carolina was *not* unified, and the South was not about to risk all to placate her radical cavaliers.

In October, as a move to sample public opinion, delegates were to be elected to a southern congress that had been proposed by the South Carolina General Assembly. The electioneering was heated, as Unionists and Cooperationists attempted to prove that South Carolinians were not ready to take a step leading to unilateral separation.[13] The *Unionville Journal* noted, in a pro-secession editorial which urged South Carolina to take the fateful step, "Georgia has long since taken her stand for the Union by submitting to the past. Alabama has declared in favor of the detestable Compromise and Mississippi has endorsed the abolition policy of the Fillmore Dynasty." The choice lay with South Carolina whether to prevail or submit.[14] The Edgefield *Advertiser* published the names of the Honorable F. W. Pickens and Drayton Nance, Esq., on its masthead, promoting them as the paper's candidates, and called on the ghost of Calhoun by quoting from his last declaration. The paper implored the people of Carolina to heed his words and to let them "sink deep into your hearts. 'If California is admitted, and no other states will act, South Carolina, MUST ACT ALONE.'"[15] In spite of the efforts of the secessionists, the *Advertiser* admitted that "immediate action was beaten rather badly throughout the state."[16] Pickens and Nance won handily in the town of Edgefield but lost the election to Dr. J. J. Wardlaw and Henry Summer by a district-wide vote of 939 to 938.[17] Preston Brooks was the original nominee of the Cooperationists in Edgefield District, but at the last moment had his name dropped from the ticket.[18] The election showed that, despite irritation, anxiety, and perceived oppression, the alternative of independent separation was not the sane course in 1851. Pickens revealed his distress with the state's lack of action. "See how we have been disgraced," he wrote to James Edward Colhoun, "our leaders have dragged us down into the mire of submission . . . the state has been cruelly betrayed."[19] To Judge Hugh Miller of Pontotoc, Mississippi, he expressed the belief that with the submission of South Carolina the South would "sink into degradation and ruin. A slaveholding race, unless they are brave and independent, are the weakest of all races. . . . If the South had struck at the right time and altogether, they might have saved their rights and Union. . . . There must be no spleen and no despair. We must be conciliatory to our people at home who have differed from us. . . . Those who think the storm has finally passed, see but little. We are the commencement of great events and but a few years may develop them fully."[20]

The changing of Pickens's position from moderate to radical was, in a political sense, an error. Just as he seemed to be recovering from the hex that the break with Calhoun had placed on him, he moved counter to the state's prevailing mood. Another low point in his life had been reached. Adding to his gloom was the fact that the spring of 1851 had been very cold and wet. The summer was very dry, except for some severe thunderstorms. The unfriendly weather assured that his cotton crop "never made."[21] His wife's health was still feeble, and now his political career again appeared in jeopardy.[22]

At this time poignant symbols of defeat faced South Carolina from every side. The Union appeared stronger than ever, and southern cooperation seemed futile.[23] The southern congress that South Carolina had hoped to create was dead, since other southern states refused to participate. The state convention for which delegates had been elected a year earlier was meeting in Columbia, "admidst a severe storm of wind and rain, which the Union men said was an indication that the elements were enraged and weeping at the object of assembling the sovereign power of the state."[24] The convention accomplished nothing, and a committee of twenty-one, of which Pickens was a member, was formed to report on its "essential business." There was no business to report, however, and the convention adjourned having accomplished but one thing: Robert Barnwell Rhett resigned his Senate seat, protesting that he was no longer a proper representative of the position and policy of South Carolina, which had shown itself, by the convention's inaction, to be "in favor of Absolute submission."[25] Perry praised Rhett's move as "the brightest feather in his cap. . . . who will be his successor no one knows. Messrs. Pickens, Richardson, Seabrook, Barnwell, Young, DeSaussure, and others have been spoken of as most likely to receive the temporary appointment."[26]

Governor Means offered the seat to W. F. DeSaussure, who became interim senator until the general elections in November. At this time Pickens was being nominated for two positions. Armistead Burt did not plan to seek reelection to the House, and on 15 June 1852 the Edgefield *Advertiser* published letters nominating Pickens and Preston Brooks for Burt's seat. On 30 June the *Advertiser* republished a letter that appeared in the Marion *Star*, signed "free trade and State Rights," which urged that Pickens be considered for the United States Senate.[27]

The Cooperationist-Unionist coalition had won for the time being. Men who had not been in Calhoun's clique began to emerge as leaders in the state, foremost among them James L. Orr, Benjamin F. Perry, and Preston Brooks. Factional strife was subsiding, as was talk of secession. On 1 June 1852 the National Democratic party held its convention in Baltimore and nominated Franklin Pierce of New Hampshire for the presidency. Again South Carolina refused to be represented, but (as had been customary since 1840) the state supported the Democratic candidate. Pickens, who had served with Pierce in Congress, was gratified that his former colleague had been nominated; however, he received some questioning criticism for his stand. It was difficult for some of the more radical elements to understand how a man who had been counted as a separate-state secessionist just a few weeks earlier could now support a New Hampshire Democrat.[28] Pickens's views on Pierce were influenced by his friend and neighbor, Milledge L. Bonham, who had served under Pierce in the Mexican War. Pickens believed that the nomination of the "Young Hickory of the Granite Hills" offered a reprieve for the South. During the electioneering Pickens and his family left Edgefield for a long vacation at the Virginia springs.[29]

While the national campaign was being waged between Pierce and Winfield Scott, South Carolina was faced with a political drama of its own. Pickens was being prominently mentioned as a possible successor to DeSaussure in the Senate. When the balloting began, he made a strong showing but quickly slipped; a little-known Cooperationist named Josiah J. Evans, who was being supported by Perry and James L. Orr, emerged the victor.[30] There were obvious reasons why Pickens lost. Edgefield had already laid claim to A. P. Butler, and two senators from the same town would have been unprecedented. The reins of power had been jerked from the radicals. The state appeared ready to accept reality and return to the Union.[31]

Once again the Senate had eluded Pickens. Since spring he had been frequently mentioned as a possible successor to Burt. Prior to the Senate race many of his friends were urging him to consider returning to Congress, but he seemed reluctant to enter the contest, especially since Preston Brooks, who was close to Perry and Orr, would be his chief opponent. The situation was impossible. Pickens was being encouraged to run, and he wanted the office. In a casual conversation with Brooks he had indicated that he would *not* run; to show his good faith, he wrote a letter to the *Advertiser* withdrawing his name.[32] However, public meetings were held, and letters sent to the newspaper urging Pickens to reconsider.[33] On New Year's Day 1853 Pickens wrote an old friend Beaufort T. Watts, the perpetual secretary to South Carolina governors, that he could not run for Congress "as they saw my name for governor and then recently for U. S. Senate—I did not feel that it was right to allow my name to be run again, when there were so many younger men furnishing themselves in opposition." He concluded, "No circumstances shall ever induce me to introduce my name for any office whatsoever."[34] Nevertheless, after more prompting by friends and being told "that the papers all over the state are looking upon your refusal to run as a public misfortune," he began to waver.[35] He finally agreed to allow his name to be put forth for consideration, provided he would not have to enter the canvass personally.[36] Preston Brooks was furious with Pickens; in a circular printed to describe his side of the affair, he invited "Cassius," an anonymous letter-writer to the *Advertiser* who was supporting Pickens, to the field of honor immediately after the election.[37] Brooks claimed Pickens was taking an unfair course and asserted that "it was a notorious fact" that Pickens had "for the last eight years been a standing candidate for either governor or senator."[38] Pickens admitted that he had not planned to run but explained about "the earnest entreaty of many citizens from various quarters and from the best friends I have in the world. I was prevailed upon to allow them to run me."[39] The affair left deep scars. Whitfield Brooks, Preston's father, and J. P. Carroll, his uncle, were Pickens's closest friends; along with M. L. Bonham, N. L. Griffin, and Arthur Simkins, they comprised Pickens's Edgefield junto. On 9 March the *Advertiser* announced the results of the election, which had been held on 21 February 1853. Brooks had defeated Pickens by some six hundred votes. Arthur Simkins editorialized that Pickens had no cause for "Mortification . . . from the beginning to the end of the matter he has had no desire to go to Congress."[40]

Surely Pickens's disastrous defeat was a deep embarrassment. For the third time in two years he had run unsuccessfully for a major office. The first two defeats were at the hands of the legislature and could be blamed on the prevailing political situation, so in many ways his last defeat must have been the most painful, as it was at the hands of his neighbors and former constituents. His defeat caused him to reassess. The radical stand he had taken earlier had netted him nothing but mortification. The fact that the state was being led by the moderates showed him that major ideological changes were in order. Pickens was a man who could adjust himself to the cause of the moment. His passion was mighty, but ephemeral.

The excitement of 1847–52 had left the state exhausted. Pickens's defeats by Josiah Evans and Brooks demonstrated that ultraism was dead for the moment, and that the people wanted peace. The races for the legislature generated little excitement, and the unanimous election of John L. Manning as governor in 1852 showed that South Carolina was tired of her habitually radical role.[41] Political calm was to be short lived, as James L. Orr, the state's new leader, reckoned on a course that would abandon South Carolina's self-imposed isolationism and inaugurate a new beginning that would entail a close relationship with the National Democratic party. Closely associated with Orr in his strategies were Benjamin F. Perry and the congressman from the Fourth District, Preston Brooks.[42]

Pickens showed a renewed interest in planting and other entrepreneurial pursuits. Between 1853 and 1857, using money borrowed from friends and neighbors, he bought over 2,000 acres of land from men like Preston Brooks, Waddy Thompson, and M. L. Bonham. Some of this land was acquired in an area known as Potterville, near the town of Edgefield. Here, like several others, Pickens established a pottery works which employed several slaves in the creation of a crude porcelain ware that today is highly prized.[43]

By 1854 Pickens was accommodating himself to the politics of the state's new leaders. Perry's *Southern Patriot* was urging that he run for governor.[44] He wrote the paper asking it to inform its readers that he had not sanctioned anyone to nominate him.[45] An accompanying letter to Perry revealed that Pickens was in a state of apathy, feeling that his name was "distasteful to those who control the state." He claimed he had no intention of being a candidate for "anything . . . at present I desire to repose in private obscurity."[46] The late elections showed that the Cooperationists were gaining control of the state, with Brooks, James L. Orr, and Senator A. P. Butler numbered among them. Although Perry was a Unionist, he had ties to the Cooperationists and was considered influential. Pickens's lack of success as a radical caused him to embrace the now moderate mood that prevailed in the state. By the end of 1854 he was squarely in the nationalist camp and was again embracing the National Democratic party. Southerners were pleased with the Pierce administration's support for the Fugitive Slave Act, and with the fact that (for the time being) the problems over the tariff had been resolved and the fight for internal improvements given up. The passage of the Kansas-Nebraska Act caused many people to believe that the abolition movement had been checked. At this time South Carolina was calmer than she had been for years, and many citizens believed that the state could safely remain in the Union.[47] In the fall of 1855 Orr and Perry proposed that the state throw off the Calhoun doctrine of party nonalignment and elect delegates to the upcoming Democratic national convention.[48] Since 1832 and the Nullification movement, South Carolina had been independent in regard to its relations with national parties. Although the Palmetto State had overwhelmingly voted for Democratic presidential candidates, she had no formal ties to the party.[49] The proposal by the Nationalists was unique and, to many, objectionable. Traditions were being broken by the moves of Orr, Perry, Brooks, and Pickens. Although many of the state's newspapers referred to these men as Unionists, they were not Unionists in the northern sense. Their first allegiance was to the Palmetto State; however, they desired to work with Northerners as long as the state's interests were protected.[50] Traditions were being set aside, and for South Carolinians, who intermingled romantic fiction with reality and who worshipped customs, legends, and the past, the new moves were proving difficult to accept. Whether the motives of Pickens, Perry, and Orr were deemed altruistic or selfish depended upon one's philosophy.

After Pickens's unsuccessful campaign for Congress, he was faced with personal problems that affected his political course. His wife had never enjoyed robust health, and during her marriage it steadily declined. In addition to their daughter, Jennie, she had to care for Rebecca, his youngest daughter from his previous marriage. Susan and Eliza were married by the time of Marion's death, at the age of twenty-nine, on 17 August 1853. Life had been too hard for his wife; the few letters in which Pickens mentioned her always refer to her failing health. The trips to Alabama, Glenn Springs, or the North taxed her slight energy. Her death brought no emotional outburst from Pickens. Already he had found death to be no stranger. His first wife, Eliza, and his nearly three-year-old son, Eldred, had died simultaneously of congestive fever. Another son, Andrew, had died at the age of two, and a daughter, Frances, died at seven months. Pickens's two sisters-in-law also died young. Maria, the wife of James Edward Colhoun, died when she was twenty-eight, and Susan, the first wife of Senator A. P. Butler, had died in May 1830 at the age of nineteen.[51]

Pickens's decision to join with Perry and Orr came after his wife's death, which gave him the freedom to involve himself more fully in political happenings. From the summer of 1853 to 1858 was a period of frequent travel for Pickens and members of his family, who visited New York, New Hampshire, Newport, St. Augustine, and the ever popular Virginia Springs. During this period the last vestiges of his relationship with the Calhouns disappeared. After his break with Calhoun, he continued to oversee Anna Clemson's plantation. He provided for overseers, erected buildings, and sold the crops; as with a faithful steward, no money was accepted or expected. Regardless of people's opinions of Pickens, he was totally honest and faithful to obligations. His correspondence with Thomas Clemson, who was a mining engineer and in that capacity frequently traveling, continued well after Calhoun's death. In 1856 Clemson wrote to Pickens, angrily berating him for not saving certain articles from his plantation—which Pickens had sold at a handsome profit and from which Pickens refused the real estate commission to which he was entitled. Pickens accounted for his actions, and at that point their relationship ceased.[52] Clemson had been the worst sort of friend. During the period of difficulties between Calhoun and Pickens, Clemson made cruel statements about Pickens to his father-in-law; yet he continued to call on Pickens for help in managing his lands.[53] Gratitude was not a strong trait among the Calhouns. The severing

PRESTON BROOKS
(courtesy of the South Caroliniana Library, University of South Carolina)

of relations between Pickens and Clemson helped Pickens put to rest the ghost of Calhoun which had been haunting him for so long.

A month prior to his wife's death, Pickens received a letter from his old friend, James Buchanan, who was serving President Pierce as ambassador to Great Britain. He invited Pickens and his family to visit him in London and reminded the Carolinian of "the days of Auld Lang Syne" and the "happy hours" they had spent together. He urged Pickens, with his "fine talents," to emerge from retirement and reenter politics.[54] Ironically, Pickens's return to public life would have a profound effect on the course of the nation in 1860–61 and would cause Buchanan difficulties that he would be unprepared to face.

The Nationalists were building their party. Most of South Carolina's newspapers were opposed to their plans to associate with the National Democratic party and accused them of being willing to sell out South Carolina in order to obtain party success; nevertheless, the Nationalists planned to hold a state convention to select delegates to the national Democratic convention.[55] The state convention, which had been called by forty members of the legislature, met in Columbia on 5 May in order to select delegates to attend the national gathering in Cincinnati. The *Mercury* scorned the Unionists by printing a speech of Calhoun's; it warned the Carolinians that political conventions were "the mere tool of cliques of demagogues . . . the bare mention of the thing is enough to sicken a man who looks upon politics, not as a trade, but as the practical science of just government."[56] The Yorkville *Enquirer*, however, sustained the Nationalists and maintained that "the Democratic Party in the United States, is the only national organization, which had recognized the right of the South in the Federal Compact."[57] Orr argued that South Carolina had been represented at Baltimore in 1844 by Pickens and Elmore at Calhoun's insistence; the arguments against participation were null, since the state had suffered no dire results.[58] Again agitation was threatening rare harmony in the state.

The convention was organized, reported the *Mercury*, "by the election of the Honorable F. W. Pickens, to act as president. He took his seat amid loud cheers, and forthwith proceeded to deliver a speech as remarkable in its positions, as in the source from which it emanated. The last time . . . Mr. Pickens spoke was in a caucus of the secession party during the session of the state convention of 1852. It was a spirited and able effort in the vindication of the . . . States Rights Party."[59] The *Mercury* characterized those who backed the convention as being nothing more than political brokers, mere office-seekers and sacrificers of the state's interest.[60]

The historic split between upcountry and low country was demonstrated. The coastal regions sent few delegates to the convention, while all but two upcountry districts were represented.[61] Pickens, John L. Manning, Andrew G. Magrath, and J. M. Gadberry were selected to serve as delegates to the national convention. Pickens defended the convention's course, stating that, since South Carolina had decided to stay in the Union, it would be foolish to bind herself to a policy of isolation. He advocated cooperation with a unified South and with conservative northern Democrats, believing that the national government could be controlled, and he did an about face by urging the legislature to permit the voters to choose presidential electors. He asserted that it had to be this policy or secession.[62]

Soon after the adjournment of the state convention, Pickens prepared to depart for Cincinnati. He urged Manning to attend and informed him that Magrath from Charleston had decided against going because in "certain Quarters of the state . . . there is much bitterness against us. I was in Charleston and found there many who were very hostile."[63]

The Cincinnati convention convened on 2 June 1856, eleven days after the famous Brooks-Sumner affair which rose out of debates over the Kansas problem. The passage of the Kansas-Nebraska Act caused a furor in the North, and the wrath of the abolitionists was revealed in their actions and speeches.[64] By the spring of 1856 "Bleeding Kansas" emerged as the major problem facing the nation. As passions rose, talk became reckless. Charles Sumner, a senator from Massachusetts, made his famous "crime against Kansas" speech characterizing Stephen A. Douglas, the author of the Kansas-Nebraska Act, and Senator A. P. Butler as the Sancho Panza and Don Quixote of slavery. Butler was Don Quixote and slavery was Dulcinea, "his hideous mistress—the harlot slavery." Sumner declared it the duty of "the Republican Party of the Union . . . to dislodge from the high places that tyrannical sectionalism of which the senator from South Carolina is one of the maddest zealots."[65] Several days after the tirade ended, Preston Brooks came to his fellow Edgefielder's aid, punishing Sumner for his remarks against Butler and South Carolina by severely beating him with his cane.[66] While the incident further exacerbated hostilities between the sections and influenced the outcome of the Democratic convention by increasing partisan bitterness, it served to increase dramatically Brooks's popularity at home. In February Brooks had written, "If the entire South failed to endorse, sustain and demand the reelection of General Pierce, it will be guilty of suicidal ingratitude."[67] At Cincinnati the South Carolina delegation stood solidly behind Pierce for fourteen ballots;

when it became obvious that Pierce could not be renominated, the delegates, according to plans, switched to Stephen A. Douglas on the fifteenth and sixteenth ballots. Douglas withdrew, and the Palmetto delegates threw their support to Pickens's old friend James Buchanan, who was then nominated.[68] Although Buchanan's nomination was not greeted with great enthusiasm in South Carolina, Pickens considered the election and control of the Pennsylvanian to be of paramount importance. He knew from long and friendly association that the Democratic nominee was safe on the slavery issue. Pickens's chief worry was that Buchanan could be manipulated by "selfish and designing men" who would "lead the country into inextricable difficulties."[69] As in the days when he had helped Calhoun, Polk, and Cass, Pickens began a letter-writing campaign on behalf of Buchanan. His interest in Democratic party politics is revealed in his letters to those political leaders whom he knew well. At this time he was frustrated and angry with those in the Palmetto State who failed to see the value of the Union and who continued to preach the doctrine of isolationism and "loudly professed provincial patriotism." He believed that, if South Carolina assumed her place in the Union, she would enjoy "proper concert" within the nation and could emerge as the responsible leader of the South.[70] As a result of Pickens's new responsible role in state politics, he and Manning were elected by the legislature to serve as presidential electors at large from South Carolina.[71] Pickens's unqualified support of Buchanan made him unpopular with many elements in the Palmetto State.[72] He had gained the unsavory reputation as an office-seeker, and his moves on behalf of Buchanan and the National Democratic party reinforced that view. Buchanan's election was assured, since the new Republican party was in no position to have its candidate, the California hero John C. Frémont, elected. James L. Orr, who had drawn close to Pickens and was now a powerful figure in the Democratic party, requested that President Buchanan appoint Pickens secretary of the treasury. Buchanan replied that he had not ascertained "whether in the arrangement of the cabinet I shall be able to give S. C. a place."[73] Pickens feared that those who opposed him would stop at nothing to deny him in his quest for office by claiming that he had no support in South Carolina and that he was being "put forward by a handful of 'broken down politicians.'"[74] His belief that Buchanan would not appoint him to the cabinet was confirmed when he received further correspondence from Orr.[75] Pickens rationalized that it was best that he not be in the cabinet, since his appointment would cause more factional strife in ever turbulent South Carolina. In a letter to Manning, Pickens perceptively observed that, although there were numerous southern leaders who desired that he play a role in the new administration, the radicals and old Calhounites with whom he had broken continued to undercut him. He then launched into a passage that explained his views:

> A man in the cabinet will have to yield small points in order to gain more important ones. I would be denounced by the factions and ultras in our state . . . for there is no man whom they more bitterly dislike on account of my differing with Mr. Calhoun . . . then I was opposed to the call of our last convention . . . to form the state prematurely into ultra position . . . I told them firmly the questions were too delicate and too violent to be agitated for demagogical purposes . . . for these things they have never forgiven me and never will. Time has shown that I was right and they were wrong, and that makes it more galling . . . as for myself if I am not to be selected for principle I scorn to go at all. I ask no personal favor by an appointment—I want no friends of mine to squeeze me into any cabinet and have so written.[76]

No cabinet position was forthcoming, but there were indications that Pickens would be offered a foreign appointment. In the meantime some deaths occurred which were to affect Pickens's plans. On 27 January 1857 Preston Brooks died unexpectedly at the age of thirty-eight; on 25 May, Edgefield lost another son with the death of A. P. Butler.[77] Before Butler's death Pickens had understood from reliable sources that he would receive an important foreign appointment. The *Mercury* reported that Pickens would be offered the ministership to either Mexico or Spain, but the paper said he would be unsuited to fill either post since "in our delicate situation the representative to those countries should have knowledge of the Spanish language." Newspaper clippings in Pickens's notebook reveal that he was again being spoken of for an appointment to the Court of St. James.[78] On 6 June 1857, sandwiched between news and commentary dealing with the *Dred Scott* decision, the continuing Kansas problem, James L. Orr's mission to Kansas, and Congressman Laurence Keitt's speech on Kansas, the *Mercury* announced that Pickens had been offered the ambassadorship to Russia. Pickens had maintained that whether or not he received an appointment from the Buchanan administration was "all a matter of perfect indifference to me—I shall not lift a finger in the matter—I have no favors to ask of any man or set of men living."[79]

Pickens admitted that he disdained any office without real power or prestige, and from his perspective a foreign appointment provided no opportunity to participate in the exciting domestic events that were taking place.[80] When the Russian mission was offered to him, he hesitated, since the rumor mills proclaimed that there was a strong possibility that he might again be offered the prestigious English post.[81] While Pickens was in the throes of deliberation, Senator Butler died, throwing the state into a tailspin. Butler had been very ill since the time of Brooks's death, and the realization that his health was failing caused the state's politicians to calculate their moves. James Hammond, who was being mentioned as a possible successor to Brooks in the Fourth District, announced that he would not oppose M. L. Bonham for a seat in the House, thus indicating he was a candidate for the Senate. Rumors abounded that James L. Orr also had senatorial aspirations, but he was making plans to become Speaker of the House.[82] While the election to replace Butler would not be held until November, if Pickens was going to make the race, he had to ascertain his chances and gain needed support. He realized that his late political activities on behalf of the National Democrats and his earlier desertion of the radical secessionists would hurt his standing in the low country.[83]

When the expected letter from the president arrived, formally tendering him the mission to Russia, Pickens officially declined the post. In a separate and personal letter, he explained to Buchanan that "the death of Judge Butler has thrown the state into great confusion and I have for years promised my friends, to allow them to run me for the Senate the first vacancy that occurred. . . . I suppose there is every reasonable prospect of their electing me." In the same letter Pickens implied that, if by some quirk of fate he were not elected to the Senate, he would go to Russia "providing it is entirely compatible with the public service and agreeable to you to hold it open."[84] Preceding Butler's death, Pickens was writing letters to acquaintances expressing the need for the Unionists to elect a man to the Senate "to give us control of the state and bring sound wholesome politics into operation again—with firmness enough to resist extravagant ultraism at home and . . . boldness enough to resist aggression."[85]

His prospects of success were good, since Orr, Manning, and Perry were helping him in his campaign. The election was one of the most important ever held in South Carolina, as it would decide the relative strengths of the National Democrats and the Secessionists. Strong opposition greeted Pickens—both Rhett and Hammond entered the competition, making it a race between men who had been friends and rivals and who all had grudges to bear. Rhett was supported by the ultras, whose philosophies were daily enjoying less credibility. Hammond, who had been out of state politics for almost a decade, was entering the contest with unknown political views. He could claim both upcountry and low as home; he had made no enemies during the late controversies; and he was being pushed by factions that contained both moderates and radicals, making him a formidable candidate.

ANDREW PICKENS BUTLER,
portrait in the Edgefield County Courthouse

Pickens, who had not *openly* run for office since his break with Calhoun, entered the race preaching wise moderation and an end to provincial prejudice.[86] He enjoyed the support of newspapers that were friendly to Orr and Perry. The *Advertiser*, the *Southern Patriot*, and the Yorkville *Miscellany* supported his candidacy. However, there was strong opposition from the low-country planters and old Calhoun men. Even some upcountry elements mistrusted him. In a letter to Perry he revealed that a new newspaper, the *True Carolinian*, published in James L. Orr's hometown of Anderson, had accused him of being an office-seeker who was not to be trusted on the vital issue of slavery. Pickens refuted the paper's charge: "I, born with the institution over me for three generations on both sides, not to be trusted! At one time I owned over 500 Negroes." To the charge that he was a notorious office-seeker, he replied that he had "refused more high Federal Offices than any man ever did in America."[87] The Lancaster *Ledger*, a Unionist paper in the Perry camp, came to Pickens's defense by holding him up as "firm, practical, and sagacious, but above all . . . one whose sympathies, pursuits, and interests are fully and completely identified with the largest and most important class of our citizens, the planters and farmers of the soil."[88]

In letters, conversations, and speeches Pickens continued to expound the concepts of "southern unity; free consultation with sympathetic northerners and adherence to the constitution and the union of our common country." Unlike other Carolinians, Pickens now looked to the Constitution as the salvation of southern interest, not as the destroyer.

8. The Rose of Texas

She was preeminent for her beauty, intelligence and accomplishments. She was, most deservedly, the belle of the South."[1] These words written by Benjamin F. Perry reveal that Lucy Petaway Holcombe, the lady whom Pickens met at White Sulphur Springs, Virginia, while vacationing there in the summer of 1857, was in no sense ordinary. Her fame as the celebrated beauty of the period was widespread, and when Pickens met her, every other pursuit gave way to his desire for her.

Pickens was going through a middle-age crisis, and his notebook reveals that he was lonely and melancholy. While on a trip to Florida in the spring of 1855, he wrote of how sweet the journey up the St. John's River would have been if he had had "some lovely being with whom to repose." His loneliness was manifested in his poetry and other writings. While in New York City in September 1855, he spent the day visiting the tombs at Greenwood Cemetery and "wandering through the enchanting spot—I apparently love gayety and laughter, but in truth, I love the very depths of melancholy too."[2]

The vulnerable Mr. Pickens was completely infatuated with Miss Holcombe, who was visiting the Springs from Marshall, Texas. Throughout the fall of 1857 his energies were diverted from political pursuits to amorous ones, as he persistently courted the "Rose of Texas." He sent her numerous letters but received few in reply. For a lock of her titian hair, Pickens sent "white and spotless pearls as an emblem of . . . pure and delicate love."[3] Pickens was now fifty and seeking a wife, but never had he imagined that he would have the opportunity to court such a magnificent, spirited, and intelligent beauty as the "lovely lady Lucy." They became secretly engaged shortly after meeting in August; the engagement was tenuous, however, especially after Lucy returned to Texas and informed her father. The courting continued through the winter and spring of 1857–58.

Actually, Lucy was intent on capturing a man like Pickens, and she had even gone to the Springs with her mother for that express purpose. Earlier in her life she had known love, but her beau, Lieutenant Crittenden, was executed after being captured in August 1851, while participating with General Narciso Lopez in an expedition to Cuba.[4] In memory of Crittenden and Lopez, Lucy wrote a romantic account of the starstruck expedition. Choosing the pen name H. M. Hardiman, she entitled her tale *The Free Flag of Cuba: or the Martyr-*

dom of Lopez. A Tale of the Liberating Expedition of 1851.[5] Shortly before coming to White Sulphur Springs, Miss Holcombe had severed a relationship with one George Lee, who had fallen on hard times. Lee wrote to Lucy's father: "I believe she loves me well and will be glad to know that I always love her and yet perhaps it is best that we parted—she is fitter to grace a court than to keep a poor stock raiser's cabin."[6]

Ambition and wealth, rather than love, dictated Lucy's thoughts of marriage to Pickens, a man twice her age. Pickens wrote her that he was certain to be elected to the Senate, but "I believe I would turn now from any political office in the world, and be by your side in your mother's garden . . . if it were not for the obligation of honor that I incurred *before* I *knew* you."[7] Pickens was soon to have his wish; the days in the garden (with all its thorns) were to be his, but the coveted office was to be Hammond's. Pickens's defeat was not a sign that South Carolina had turned to radicalism; actually the opposite was the case. Rhett, the best-known radical in the state, received only six votes. Hammond defeated Pickens 85-59 on the third ballot. Pickens had "but a small share of . . . personal popularity," and many people doubted his sincerity, especially in light of his abrupt switch from secessionist to nationalist. Orr had failed to involve himself as Pickens had hoped; and Hammond, a man with unknown views, appealed to many as an excellent compromise candidate.[8]

Frustration dogged Pickens at every turn, and, as after every defeat, he vowed never again to seek public office. With a deep lament Pickens expressed his reverence for Mother Carolina: "She is my mother, and although repelled and repudiated by her; yet I will proudly lay my head upon her bosom, even though her heart may never beat for me."[9] Pickens's melancholia was so great that after his defeat he considered leaving South Carolina and moving to some land he owned near New Orleans.[10]

Many Carolinians were disappointed with Hammond. The ultras who supported him expected him to redeem South Carolina's past prestige "and stay the tide of degradation."[11] Hammond realized that the state was in no mood to turn back to radicalism. Even the *Mercury* was now taking a more moderate stance by advocating southern unity within the Democratic party.[12] Pickens, seeing that Hammond's course was following his own philosophy, wrote, "I feel complimented that Governor Hammond comes out and covers the same ground I always approved."[13]

In the midst of Pickens's political reflections there was Lucy. She was becoming another frustrating element in his life, one that threatened to undo him completely. His political frustrations were nothing compared to the disappointment he faced in his relations with Miss Holcombe and her family. Her parents were bitterly opposed to the marriage, and her letters, when she wrote, had taken on a cold aura. His letters to her demonstrated his acute melancholia over the impossible situation. Beverley Holcombe probably opposed his daughter's pending marriage for several reasons: Pickens was too old, Edgefield too far, and just possibly the Holcombes' neighbor, Louis Wigfall, was undermining Pickens with the Holcombe family.

Pickens's letters were introduced by salutations that revealed his mood. They ranged from "My dear friend" to "My dear Miss Lucy" to "My dearest lady bird." Many of his letters were full of lovesick phrasing and exclamations more appropriate for a romantic sixteen-year-old than for a sophisticated man of fifty. His passion and incurable romanticism were manifest in every sentence: "I love you with painful solitude—I love wildly, blindly, madly it is for you to bless—or turn me, cold—cheerless, without hope and without mercy upon a dark and dreary world"—"Oh! bury what I have told you in your heart," etc.[14]

Lucy was also in a disagreeable situation. She was naturally reluctant to marry an average-looking bewigged man twice her age, with daughters older than she was. But Pickens had made tantalizing promises that were in line with her ambitious nature. Before his Senate defeat, he had held out to her a place in Washington society, and there was still the possibility that she might dazzle a European court. She was twenty-six and, despite her beauty and independence, was fast entering the frightening age bracket of the spinster. There was Pickens's wealth to be considered. He had hundreds of acres of land in Alabama and Mississippi, in addition to his Carolina holdings. Edgewood, with its 2,250 acres of land in cultivation, hundreds of slaves, and large plantation house of unusual rambling Victorian style set in a formal English garden, was considered a showplace by many.[15]

Lucy's equivocation caused Pickens major problems. He had not told his daughters about his situation. Much to his sorrow, his daughter Maria was engaged to marry Matthew C. Butler, a future U.S. senator but at the time a man whom Pickens regarded as having few prospects. Butler was the nephew of the late Senator A. P. Butler and Commodore Matthew C. Perry, who had won fame by opening up Japan for trade with the United States. Pickens refused to allow Maria to set a date for her wedding, since it might interfere with his own plans.[16] Having received an anonymous letter that accused Lucy of simply having her amusement with him and informing him that Lucy never intended to marry him unless he was "a U.S. Senator or went to England," he became convinced that his engagement was terminated and thereupon permitted Maria to set her wedding date.[17]

Buchanan had held the Russian post open for Pickens and, after his defeat for the Senate, reissued the offer. This time Pickens accepted, feeling that his defeats in both politics and love had made a sojourn abroad necessary. He informed Lucy of his decision, telling her that he intended to sail around the middle of April. He closed his letter to her, "I suppose as you seem to desire it, this terminates our correspondence."[18] An earlier letter revealed Pickens's frustration with the situation: "You were too proud and ambitious to throw yourself away on a disappointed politician. . . . It is now 56 days since you wrote me . . . yet, I have written you twice a week and sometimes oftener. Your last two letters were ominous . . . you wrote all your family were bitterly opposed to me."[19] A great and unexpected surprise now awaited Pickens—Lucy suddenly accepted his proposal, and they were married at the Holcombe home on 26 April 1858.[20] The couple made a quick visit to Edgewood so that Pickens could oversee spring cotton planting, and then they sailed from New York on 28 May.[21]

Word of Pickens's appointment delighted Hammond and his associates, since Hammond's term was for only two years. The idea of another race with Pickens was not a happy prospect. Marcellus, Hammond's brother, feared that Pickens would never sail and that there would be "a hard struggle next time . . . watch him or rather let [Laurence] Keitt do it."[22] However, James Gadsden urged Hammond not to worry, as Pickens "will be frozen up in the Gulf of Finland."[23] Surely the Hammonds breathed sighs of relief when Pickens finally set sail.

Pickens discovered that the administration was uninformative and uncooperative about arrangements concerning his pay, duties, accommodations, etc. He therefore relied upon his friend Milledge Bonham, who had succeeded Preston Brooks in Congress, to assist him with his problems. He informed Bonham that he planned "to discharge his duties . . . in a faithful and unostentatious way."[24] Little did he know that, with Lucy in tow, being unostentatious would be impossible. The entourage consisted of Pickens, Lucy, two daughters, two slaves, and a friend, John E. Bacon, a childless widower who was to act as secretary of legation. Lucy adored jewels, furs, and ornate clothes. In London, Paris, Berlin, and St. Petersburg, the Pickenses made their mark.[25] There were audiences with Queen Victoria and Napoleon III; they arrived in St. Petersburg on 6 July and met the Czar on 18 July.

The attention of the Russian court and the thirty-eight-year-old Alexander II focused on Lucy. Alexander was particularly susceptible to feminine charm, having fallen out of love with his wife, and Lucy's uncommon beauty fascinated him.[26] When it became known that Lucy was pregnant, the czar invited her to spend her confinement in special quarters in the Winter Palace. Alexander's unusual behavior gave rise to speculation that he, and not Pickens, was the father of the girl born on 14 March 1859. This is highly improbable, since the czar did not even meet the Pickenses until mid-July, and all indications were that Eugenia Dorothea Holcombe Pickens ("Douschka") was a full-term baby; however, there is no question that the czar was infatuated with her.[27]

Life for the Pickenses seemed gay, although from the beginning Lucy was acutely homesick. They were invited to participate in the gorgeous and magnificent baptismal ceremonies of the son of the Grand Duke Constantine, and during the winter of 1859 the Pickens family spent much of their time at the Winter Palace, which Pickens described as "the enchanted palace of Aladdin, right out of a fairy tale." He enjoyed the splendor and magnificence that surrounded him and the skating and sleigh rides on the frozen Neva River. He found life in Russia to be expensive. He had busts of himself and Lucy sculpted. Fine clothes, furs, clocks, jewelry, and furniture were purchased. Lucy's tastes were expensive, and when Pickens calculated his worth, he discovered that he had been deluding himself. When he subtracted his obligations from his liquid assets, he was over $17,000 in debt.[28]

While abroad he continued to be interested in happenings at home. A letter published in the Columbia *South Carolinian* was reprinted by most papers in the state; in it Pickens refuted and denounced statements about Calhoun and Polk made by Calhoun's arch enemy, Thomas Hart Benton, in his memoirs, *Thirty Years' View*.[29] Edward Noble, a kinsman from Abbeville, wrote that the defense of Calhoun might have been more effective if it had been written while Benton, who had just recently died, were still living.[30] Pickens's motives were designed not solely to correct the historical record, but also to mollify the feelings of Calhoun's friends, who he believed continued to keep him from rising in the state. When he learned that the South Carolina legislature contemplated placing busts of the Revolutionary War generals Marion and Sumter in niches in the new statehouse, he worried that the political and personal animosity that many of the legislators felt for him would prevent his grandfather from receiving the honors Pickens thought due him.[31]

During his stay in Russia, Pickens continued to correspond with friends and acquaintances in hopes that their replies would keep him abreast of political happenings at home. His letters and a long discourse on his impressions of Russia showed that he was a keen observer and had become interested in Russian history, politics, and institutions. He was acutely concerned with Alexander's moves to free the serfs, especially in light of the worldwide attacks on slavery. Russian religious practices held a fascination for him, and he compared the mysticism and theology of the Eastern Orthodox Church with the practices of the Protestant and Catholic churches with which he was familiar. As a Carolina aristocrat, he naturally had great interest in the way the Russian nobility lived and functioned. He contrasted the Russian aristocrat to his southern counterpart and found both similar in temperament and disposition.[32]

His luxury to observe was cut short by the outbreak of war between France and Austria in the spring of 1859. For a time it appeared that the war would envelop all of Europe. Pickens had written Secretary of State Lewis Cass that he was certain Russia would enter the war on the side of France. He confessed that he was delighted to see war clouds form and hostilities commence, since he believed that war would so involve all European nations that every move made by the United States to settle "all American interests connected with Cuba, Mexico, and Central America to our entire satisfaction" could not be challenged. However, Pickens's grandiose hopes perished with the advent of peace in the middle of July.[33]

During the inhospitable fall and winter, the luster of the first year in Russia started wearing thin. Pickens and Lucy wanted to leave the land of the Romanovs, but the volatile European situation prevented them from returning home.[34] The Russians were hospitable, but other factors mitigated against staying. John Brown's raid on Harpers Ferry took place in October 1859, and agitation over the slave question had resumed. Bleeding Kansas had captured everyone's attention, and the "Black" Republican party was gaining strength. During the fall of 1859 Pickens had been near death with an unknown illness, and he worried about the potential health effects of the coming Russian winter. But most of all he wanted to participate in upcoming political happenings that would determine the fate of the nation.[35]

Lucy's acute homesickness, compounded by her depression at not giving birth to a son, intensified her desire to leave. She had hated Russia from the beginning, and her constant nagging was becoming intolerable. She reminded Pickens of the sacrifice she had made by marrying him and told him that if he loved her he would permit her to go. The birth of "Douschka" and news that her mother was ill caused her to yearn even more fervently for home;[36] she admitted to her mother that she "begged him on [her] knees to let [her] go." She acknowledged that Pickens "swore on the Bible, he would buy a place in Texas . . . and he would give it over to me and he would also help my father to pay his debts . . . but if I should not go, he would do these things to repay me and show that he loved me."[37]

The whole Russian experience showed Lucy to have been an emancipated woman at heart. She knew herself to be more talented than her husband, and she had no doubts about her wit and abilities to charm. She nursed her own child, was fluent in French, an excellent musician, and an accomplished writer. Pickens's refusal to let her leave Russia angered her; she had no fear and resented his paternalistic attitude. Although she admitted that Pickens was "really an excellent man," she confided to her sister that she resented him and his attitudes. "But my dear sister the *best* of men are selfish and incapable of sacrifice even for the person they love best on earth. . . . He (like all other men) loves his own comfort and happiness better than mine." Later she expressed her sentiments by writing to Pickens "that [he] would make any human being miserable."[38]

The ambassador found himself in a difficult situation. In addition to an expensive, ill-tempered, cajoling wife, he discovered that his business affairs at home were in a state of disrepair. His plantations were not doing well in his absence, as poor management and poor weather resulted in poor crops.[39] Besides these hardships, there were personal problems that caused him much anxiety. His daughter Rebecca had married John Bacon, the secretary of legation, under questionable circumstances that brought "pain and mortification to her father."[40] Another personal matter proved to be expensive as well as potentially embarrassing. In 1842, while on a trip to New Orleans, Pickens "got into a scrape" with a girl who he claimed "acted more imprudently than I did." For years he had been giving "the old woman" money to raise "that boy." Since Pickens was out of the country, he asked Bonham to be his agent and to send money to the mother of his illegitimate son. It was an awkward situation. He wrote Bonham, "I have given him money since 1843—every year. Of course all this is between us. I am sorry to trouble you . . . when I succeeded McDuffie I did the same and more for him and perhaps your successor may have to do it for you, if he is a gentleman in the true sense of the term."[41] Although Pickens tried to keep his private mortifications secret, he learned from Bonham, who was in Congress with Hammond, that Hammond was aware of Pickens's illegitimate son and was using the matter to discredit him. Pickens regretted that "Hammond should for a moment have received unfavorable impressions 'of me.' . . . If a man's character depends upon maids or low women, he would indeed be damned to this world as well as the next."[42]

The time away from home seemed to have modified his bitterness over his past political failures. Hammond's conservative course in the Senate elicited approving statements from Pickens, who hoped that radicalism could be stifled, southern rights protected, and "all divisions healed."[43] He believed it essential for the nation to remain united if it was to be a power in the world.[44]

He felt that he had served the nationalistic cause through his political stands, but that he had netted for himself deep opposition from South Carolina leaders, who had caused the "state to even turn the back of her hand to him." He believed himself to have been the human sacrifice that had set South Carolina on "a more common sense and dignified course . . . than she has pursued for years past."[45] Pickens was accurate in his self-appraisal; yet, outside South Carolina, he enjoyed a following that appreciated his abilities and views.

As the fateful year 1860 approached, Pickens's mind turned to presidential politics. One of those frequently mentioned for the presidency was James L. Orr, and the Carolinians held high hopes for his success in the Democratic convention scheduled to meet in Charleston in late April. Pickens maintained that, regardless of who was nominated, peace and "cordial harmony" were essential if the Democratic party was to survive the difficult times ahead.[46]

Although the chances of nominating a Southerner were slight, Pickens harbored hopes of ascending to the presidency himself. He enjoyed a favorable reputation outside South Carolina, being known as a moderate who had bucked the radical leadership in his own state to support men like Polk, Cass, and Buchanan. Certainly his hopes seemed less inconceivable when he began to receive letters from important leaders telling him that neither Douglas nor Buchanan would receive the nomination.[47] Throughout the winter of 1859–60 letters came from W. M. Churchwell, a confidant of Buchanan, and George N. Sanders, who enjoyed a reputation in political circles as the president-maker, stating that he was considered an acceptable aspirant.[48]

Perhaps Pickens looked to historical precedent to bolster his dreams. Both Buchanan and Lewis Cass had won the Democratic nomination after serving abroad; Polk, like Pickens, had been relatively unsuccessful in state politics. The holding of the convention in Charleston and the possibility of obtaining Buchanan's support for the office were factors in his favor. On 6 February 1860, Pickens wrote the president a subtle letter which left no doubt that he wanted Buchanan's backing for the White House; he asserted that the nomination of a Northerner would divide the party and that the way to avoid "great danger" was to select a Southerner who "has the nerve to do what is *right* for the country."[49]

The ambassador to Russia was not totally aware that there had been a rebirth of radicalism in South Carolina and that events had taken a turn which would insure fragmentation of the Democratic party. The chaos was becoming so great that Buchanan believed it essential for Pickens, who had told Cass that he planned to leave Russia in time to be home in August, to alter his plans and "come at once and enter into the most important struggle that has ever been in this country, he [Buchanan] thinks you ought to be here now, that your influence is needed in South Carolina . . . your presence here could inspire your friends with confidence and your known conservative position would give you much power in modeling the political future of the Democratic Party, which is divided, demoralized and distracted."[50] Pickens nevertheless stayed at his post, maintaining the need for continued vigilance,[51] even though he was still being mentioned for the presidency.[52] On the eve of the Charleston convention, the correspondent for the New York *Journal of Commerce* reported that some of the delegates wanted to place Pickens's name in nomination. The paper described Pickens as "conservative as such was kept down in his own state. He is a high-minded, honorable, patriotic and able man."[53]

The Charleston convention commenced its proceedings under very trying circumstances on 23 April 1860. The Republican party was daily gaining strength, and the Democrats were badly split. Stephen A. Douglas commanded a majority, but his refusal to support a territorial slave code cost him southern support. The Democrats' failures to agree on a platform acceptable to the South resulted in Alabama leading South Carolina and other southern states out of the convention. The convention adjourned, and the rump agreed to reconvene in Baltimore.[54] The Republicans were jubilant; the Democrats were disgusted. Churchwell relayed the news to Pickens, telling him of the "treachery of pretended friends" and of the demise "of the only national party in the country."[55]

On 17 April 1860 Pickens resigned his post, but leaving Russia proved more difficult than expected. Although he hoped to be home by the end of summer, the president failed to appoint a successor. The months were waning for the Buchanan administration, and the unexpected turn of events forced the president to consider domestic problems his first priority. Pickens worried that, if he did not leave Russia before the end of summer, the intense cold would prevent him from returning home at all.[56]

Not until August did Pickens receive word that he was relieved and could leave St. Petersburg. He had to round up Lucy and Douschka, who had taken Jennie to a boarding school in Frankfurt. John Bacon and his wife had already returned to the United States.[57] Aside from a colorful episode involving an American confidence artist who had been befriended by William Seward, "the distinguished Senator from New York," Pickens's last days in Russia were spent in making preparations to return home.[58] His mind was focused on the upcoming presidential election and its ramifications. He was ready "at the first tap of the drum . . . for my home and country." Although he wrote Bonham that he had no plans to seek public office, he left no doubt that he wanted to "take [his] responsibility in the great events and in whatever may occur."[59] Pickens and his entourage set sail from Southampton on 23 October.[60]

While he was making his way home, the national political situation deteriorated further. The want of Democratic unanimity was giving great encouragement to the Republican leaders, who felt confident of carrying the day. The nation was being brought "towards the point of 'fever heat.' "[61] The future of the Union was seemingly the only topic for discussion in the Palmetto State. Rhett and the fire-eaters were once again active as the prospect of Abraham Lincoln's election came closer. The situation was changing; other southern states were hardening their positions, and no matter what stance Carolinians had previously taken, they were all coming together to protect their way of life.[62] The failure of the Democratic convention to nominate a universally acceptable candidate showed, as Buchanan stated in an interview with a reporter of the New York *Journal of Commerce*, that it would be easier to mix oil and water than to expect the sections to unite.[63] Radicalism was magnetic. As Mary Boykin Chesnut observed, "Nobody could live in [South Carolina] unless he were a fire-eater."[64]

Pickens kept in touch with the situation through newspapers and letters and formulated his own thoughts about the events unfolding in America. From Warsaw he wrote Arthur Simkins, "We have nothing *to fear but ourselves*. There was a time, only some forty years ago, when very many even in southern states believed slavery to be a grievous national evil . . . the steady and stupendous strides we have made in . . . our mighty productions, have dispelled all those sentimental ideas . . . with our resources, with our population, with our territory, we can stand above and defy the world . . . slavery . . . cannot be extinguished, nor can we be subjugated but through our own discord, and selfish division."[65] Pickens's letter was published in the *Advertiser* on 31 October 1860 and served to remind Carolinians that one of their most experienced leaders would soon be available to serve Mother Carolina.

Secession talk was rampant. The certainty of Lincoln's election added fuel to the radical fires, and movements of the most extreme nature were launched in the Palmetto State. One such association, known as the Minute Men, was led by kinsmen of Pickens and former Governor James Adams; it was holding secret meetings throughout the state in which "champagne flowed freely" and "very inflammatory speeches were made." In Edgefield nearly four hundred members wore the blue cockade as an emblem of defiance and membership. Vows were made to march on Washington to prevent the inauguration of Lincoln in the event of his election.[66] The *Mercury*, now under the editorship of Robert Barnwell Rhett, Jr., reported on the activities of rifle and militia

LUCY PICKENS
(courtesy of Jane Greer)

units in the Charleston area and fanned the flames of rebellion in every issue, proclaiming Lincoln's election as tantamount to the extinction of slavery.[67] The state legislature was being urged to convene to take South Carolina out of the Union. At meetings throughout the state eloquent oratory confirmed that the prevailing passion was for disunion.[68] The *Mercury* of 8 November announced the election of Lincoln, the activities of resistance meetings, the unfurling of a red flag with the Palmetto and a lone star, and the meeting of the legislature in special session to make plans for a secession convention. The same issue of the paper announced the arrival of the "Honorable F. W. Pickens, lady and family" in New York on 5 November.[69]

South Carolina had come full circle since the heated days of nullification. The tariff issue had failed to unite the South for rebellion, but the mere threat of attacks on slavery by the "Black Republicans" brought on a wave of discontent that showed South Carolina to be capable of the most extreme and precipitous actions.

Pickens had gained the reputation of being conservative in his views concerning the relations between South Carolina and the Union. However, at this time his love for Mother Carolina was greater than his sentiments for the Union. He realized that the nation had never faced a problem so "fraught with graver or more momentous considerations"; however, he urged his fellow Carolinians to put aside "spasmodic timidity" and defend slavery at all peril.[70] To older citizens his fiery comments may have called to mind the rhetoric of an earlier period, when he enjoyed the place at Calhoun's right hand.

While returning home on board the *Adriatic* Pickens posed as a moderate who was distressed that so many Europeans were laughing at South Carolina's pretensions. He told several of his fellow passengers that the Carolinians were being foolishly precipitous and that he planned to use his influence on behalf of moderation.[71] Although Pickens was probably embarrassed for his state, his statements about southern defiance were not inconsistent with conservative views. A South Carolina moderate was not moderate in the national sense. Pickens deeply believed in the right of secession; however, he had long felt that separate state secession would be foolhardy. His views on slavery were no different from those he had held since he first entered public life, and he continued to believe that southern cooperation was essential. Most of the so-called South Carolina moderates were willing to support and participate in the federal government so long as the institution of slavery was not molested. The victory of a Republican party that espoused the belief that slavery was an evil that should be eventually eradicated caused South Carolina moderates to alter their views. The Edgefield *Advertiser* had been counted as a moderate paper, but by the fall of 1860 it was strongly behind ultra movements.[72] Radicalism had completely enveloped South Carolina. With the election of Lincoln, anger gave way to rage. The threats that had been uttered in years past were soon to reach fruition—the Palmetto State was in the process of becoming the Palmetto Republic.

9. A Fire-Eater Down to the Ground

"No Black Republican President . . . should ever execute any law within our borders unless at the point of a bayonet and over the dead bodies of our slain sons."[1] These words spoken by James L. Orr, who had a reputation as one of the most conservative South Carolina nationalists, indicated that the Palmetto State was on the verge of acts that were to change the nation's destiny. William Porcher Miles, who had served his state in Congress, wrote that he was "sick and disgusted with all the bluster and threats and manifestos and resolutions . . . let us act if we mean to act without talking."[2] R. S. Holt wrote his brother, Buchanan's postmaster general, that southern leaders were in no position to stop secession. "It is a movement," he explained, "not of leaders, but of the masses . . . the conviction is strong and universal, and I share it fully, that submission by the South is now death . . . she must resist or perish miserable, ignobly and speedily."[3]

The scene was set, and secessionist talk filled the air. Radical South Carolina looked to Mississippi and Alabama to inaugurate disunion, but these states were more cautious. By the middle of November several members of the South Carolina congressional delegation had resigned, and federal district judge Andrew G. Magrath had dramatically showed his hostility to the Union by ripping off his judicial robes in his courtroom.[4] The General Assembly decided not to wait for the other southern states to move, but determined to call for an election to be held on 6 December to choose delegates to a state convention scheduled for 17 December 1860.[5]

In the midst of this furor Pickens returned home. On his way to Edgefield he stopped in Washington, where he had a lengthy meeting with President Buchanan. In early September, before departing from Russia, Pickens had written to the president, praising him and deploring the vile persecution being heaped on him by those who "were bound to you by ties of obligation and friendship." He informed the president that he was deeply in his debt and that he desired to meet with him when he arrived in Washington.[6] Buchanan asked Pickens to use his influence on behalf of moderation. Initially Pickens proposed that South Carolina work in concert with other southern states and that secession be delayed until Buchanan left office.[7] However, as Pickens comprehended the massive scope of the secession movement he more readily accommodated himself to the majority sentiment.

Soon after arriving in Edgefield, Pickens was invited to address a large prosecession meeting. He was accompanied to the rostrum by his son-in-law, Matthew C. Butler, and his friends J. P. Carroll and Martin Gary. Butler and Gary were in the legislature and would play an important role in the gubernatorial race. Pickens began his speech in a cool, dispassionate manner by enumerating the wrongs that had been perpetrated on the South. He explained that secession was the "clear and indisputable right of a sovereign people"; he preached that in Italy the great Garibaldi was fighting against a tyranny much like that of the incoming Republican administration, which to South Carolina represented a "government of plunder and power." He then urged that the secession ordinance be passed immediately, but that it not take effect until the inauguration of that "hostile incoming government." Pickens then let his emotion flow, spellbinding his audience with the passion of his rhetoric as he called upon his countrymen to put away their differences. "If I know the pulse of South Carolina—if I know the pulse of Southern men. The great heart of the South is beating steadily to the march of Southern Independence—Independence, now and *forever*, rather than bear in peace the ignominious bondage whose shadow is already insultingly thrown over our path."[8] The crowd cheered his words, and the thrill of being politically alive drove Pickens to new heights. Prior to coming home, Pickens confessed that he had "prayed . . . to God to avert the pending ruin and save the country from degradation and sorrow." However, after surveying the situation, he concluded that he had "but little faith, save in Providence" that the nation could be saved.[9] Now Pickens prayed that South Carolina would leave the Union, along with other southern states. He defended his previous political stance by explaining that he had not favored secession, believing South Carolina had the obligation to discharge her duties under the compact so long as it could be done "consistently with our rights and honor."[10]

Letters to the state's newspapers were nominating men to succeed William Gist, whose gubernatorial term was expiring. The *Courier* put in nomination Senator James Chesnut; the *Mercury* was naturally supporting Robert Barnwell Rhett. Several letters to the *Advertiser* promoted Pickens.[11] At the same time, he was being nominated as a candidate for election to the secession convention. Maintaining that placing his name on the ballot would be unfair to those who had been nominated prior to his arriving home, he refused.[12] Every move he was making was clever—by avoiding involvement in Edgefield politics, he was staying out of a potentially divisive local fray; nor could he be accused of being an office-seeker. After his speech in Edgefield, Pickens was afforded the high honor of addressing the South Carolina General Assembly.

The timing was perfect. He was touted as an elder statesman who had served his state well for three decades. The ghost of Calhoun seemed to have disappeared, and the speech he delivered on the cold evening of 30 November warmed the imaginations of his listeners. Much of his address was a rehash of his Edgefield speech; however, his symbolic allusions to "Mother Carolina" aroused the passions of the romantic Carolinians. "I come as a son to lay my head upon the bosom of my mother—to hear her heart beat—beat with glorious and noble accents worthy of her past and glorious future." No longer did he advocate waiting for Lincoln to take office before seceding. He appealed to the hot-blooded Carolinians when he stated, "I would be willing to appeal to the god of battles—if need be, cover the state with ruin, conflagration and blood rather than submit."[13] He was not only telling the attentive lawmakers what they wanted to hear, but was also helping to pave his own way to the governor's office, where he would assist in leading South Carolina down the road to "ruin, conflagration and blood."

To his diary George Templeton Strong acknowledged his fear that Pickens had contracted "this foul disunion disease which is frightfully contagious; however, (like other cachectic, asthenic distempers and fevers, and the like) . . . its making steady and rapid progress in . . . every slaveholding state."[14] The keenly observant Mary Boykin Chesnut, whose husband had recently resigned his seat in the U.S. Senate as a sign of protest against the election of Lincoln, commented on Pickens's reversal. "Wigfall," she wrote, "says before he left Washington Pickens . . . and Trescot were openly against secession. Trescot does not pretend to like it now . . . but . . . Pickens is a fire-eater down to the ground."[15]

As the time approached for the legislature to elect a new governor, the newspapers were fully defending secession. The *Mercury* was telling of the woeful state of harbor defenses and reminding its readers that Fort Moultrie was occupied by soldiers of the United States. A smallpox epidemic was revealed to be in Columbia, and news of legislative happenings was reported.[16] It was widely predicted that Robert Barnwell Rhett, the so-called Father of Secession, would be elected governor; but there were many leaders who opposed his election, feeling that his views were too radical. David L. Wardlaw, an eminent jurist, summed up the feelings of many when he wrote, "For God's sake and the sake of our beloved state don't let Rhett be elected governor."[17]

On 12 December the General Assembly, whose complexion had changed dramatically since 1850, began the gubernatorial selection process. For four days and seven ballots the contest waxed and waned. At first it appeared that a deadlock was in the making, with Pickens and Benjamin J. Johnson each receiving 52 votes on the first and second ballots. For a while it appeared that Pickens would suffer the same fate that had befallen him in other contests, but his managers, led by M. C. Butler, kept him in the race. On the fifth ballot Rhett withdrew; on the seventh, Pickens emerged victorious.[18] The Columbia reporter for the Charleston *Courier* commented, "All rejoice that F. W. Pickens is elected governor at last. All parties are reconciled to the result."[19] At 2 p.m. on Monday, 17 December, Pickens was inaugurated. He delivered a short speech to the assembled legislators in which he castigated the North for electing Lincoln; he then announced that he was ready to take the oath of office and "swear undivided allegiance to South Carolina."[20] Three days later Pickens was in Charleston, where he and D. F. Jamison, president of the secession convention, went to St. Andrews Hall to announce that the ordinance of secession had been unanimously passed.[21] The applause was thunderous. Never had he seen anything to rival the intense excitement of the moment; and for a time he may have actually believed that he enjoyed personal popularity. Actually, Pickens had been put forth as a compromise candidate in order to stop factional bickering. He was a logical choice, since he was an able orator and a proponent of southern nationalism who enjoyed the confidence of other southern leaders, and since he had had the fortune of being out of state politics during the critical months before secession. Thoughtful people realized that South Carolina could not stand alone. Pickens had the reputation of being moderate and responsible, and these qualities were needed in order for the radical experiment to succeed.

    Francis Pickens was at the pinnacle of his career. However, all his ability, sagacity, and ephemeral popularity were sacrificed because of his flawed personality. His father had the reputation of being "sternly virtuous, and upright . . . a man of abilities—but his mien is rather authoritative—and he is so independent of opinion as to appear somewhat dogmatic."[22] Unfortunately, Pickens inherited these traits. His aloofness and overbearing personality were real handicaps. Egoism and arrogance were not uncommon in Carolina cavaliers, but Pickens demonstrated these traits to the fullest. He gained notoriety as a pedant. Past political intrigues and battles had caused many of the state's most prominent families to dislike him; furthermore, many women in the Palmetto State were jealous and envious of his beautiful and clever wife. Mrs. Chesnut, whose family and friends had never liked Pickens, alluded to his faulty personality in her diary. Pickens himself frequently admitted that he was his own greatest handicap: "I believe it my destiny," he wrote, "to be disliked by all who know me well."[23] His election ended a sixteen-year-old unwritten agreement that provided for alternation of the governorship between upcountry and low country. He succeeded W. H. Gist of Union, and he would be succeeded by his closest friend, M. L. Bonham of Edgefield. Bonham expressed the view of many Carolinians: "We see that Pickens is elected but do not know what it indicates."[24]

"All are for action now," according to one contemporary. Passions were high as the "South Carolinians . . . exasperated and heated themselves into a fever that only bloodletting could ever cure."[25] Pickens was to experience problems that no other governor in any state had ever encountered. Some were caused by natural misunderstandings; others by outside influences. Unfortunately, the new governor lacked the charisma so essential for success in public life. He was a man of ideas, an acute observer, but not a man of firm action.[26]

Talk was plentiful and rhetoric eloquent, but South Carolina was ill prepared to face the future. The secession convention had proclaimed the state independent. The *Mercury* labeled dispatches coming from the North as foreign news, and the Palmetto State was referred to by some as the "Palmetto Republic." Three days before the proclamation of secession, the state's brand-new governor attempted to solve a problem that was irritating the Carolinians. The federal forts in Charleston Harbor were regarded as both a threat and an insult. The *Mercury* had already alerted its readers to the potential problems that these fortifications could cause; Rhett warned Buchanan that, if he sent additional troops to Charleston, "it will be bloody."[27] Unfortunately, Pickens's first efforts at negotiation were almost fatal. In early December several members of the state's congressional delegation had negotiated a temporary arrangement with Buchanan, in which the president agreed that the military status of the forts in Charleston Harbor would not be changed without giving the Carolinians advance notice.[28] Pickens almost upset this arrangement. In an ill-timed letter he claimed that the federal arsenal had been turned over to South Carolina, and that the forts in the harbor were making ready to turn their guns on Charleston. He proposed that, to quiet the Carolinians' apprehensions, Buchanan allow him to send a small force to take possession of the uninhabited Fort Sumter. The president became alarmed, especially when he learned that armed vessels were patrolling the approaches to Sumter. Buchanan called in William H. Trescot, who was acting unofficially as South Carolina's representative in Washington, and questioned him on the meaning of Pickens's letter. Trescot was furious. Wishing to have the crucial situation lie in limbo until the state could send commissioners to bargain for the forts, he dispatched a telegram to Pickens urging him to withdraw his letter. This was done, but Pickens proved that his zeal was stronger than his discretion.[29] He later explained to the legislature that his motive in sending the controversial letter had been "to ascertain . . . the real intention of the President in relation to the occupation of the forts in the harbor, and to shape his course accordingly."[30]

South Carolina and her new governor appeared to be deserting the path of caution. In order to get a better fix on the situation, Buchanan sent his friend Caleb Cushing to South Carolina. He hoped Cushing might be able to talk some sense to the Carolinians.[31] The frustration and anger in Washington matched that in Charleston. From one of South Carolina's leading citizens, A. P. Hayne, Buchanan received a letter thanking him for his forbearance and telling him, "Every Southern heart feels that the South owes you a debt of gratitude!" A note written by Buchanan's secretary at the bottom of the letter asked, *"How have they paid it?"*[32]

James Buchanan knew that only outright surrender would calm the enraged Carolinians. For years he had dealt with Pickens and other Carolina leaders, and already he had lost a great deal of personal prestige by appearing to pander to them. He had relieved Colonel John Gardner from command of Fort Moultrie, and he had not reinforced the fort, as many people had demanded. He had accepted the resignations of his oldest and most trusted advisors rather than consent to use force to quell the Carolinians.[33] As the nation's dilemma was unfolding, the enthusiasm of the delegates to the secession convention was infectious; the Carolinians manifested their enthusiasm at being free from the Union by firing cannons, ringing bells, and cheering. Pickens informed Cushing that there was to be no turning back—there was no hope for the Union.[34] On Monday, 24 December 1860, Pickens issued this statement: as "Governor and Commander in Chief in and over the state of South Carolina—By virtue of the authority in me vested, Do hereby proclaim to the world that this state is, as she has a right to be, a Separate Sovereign, Free and Independent State; and; as such has a right to levy war, conclude peace, negotiate treaties, leagues or covenants, and do all acts whatsoever that rightfully appertain to a free and independent state."[35] Several days earlier he had vowed, in extemporaneous remarks to the Palmetto Minute Men of Charleston (who had come to serenade him), that he was prepared to meet every issue, and he affirmed that any attempt by the federal government to reinforce the forts would result in war.[36] The convention, which was still meeting, ordered Pickens to "prevent any garrisoning of the fortresses or the mounting of guns thereon." It further resolved that any attempt by the United States to build up the fortifications would be regarded "as an overt act of hostility."[37]

The first such act occurred during the evening of 26 December. Pickens had followed the advice to "exercise the utmost vigilance."[38] Charleston Harbor was constantly patrolled in order to prevent any movement from Moultrie to Sumter by the small federal force under its new commander, Major Robert Anderson.

The impatient Charlestonians had already begun to heap abuse on the new governor, since he had failed to order the seizure of the forts, but Trescot had assured Pickens that Fort Sumter would not be occupied by the Union.[39] However, Trescot's reassuring letter and Pickens's constant vigil did not prevent Major Anderson from moving his entire force from the untenable Fort Moultrie to the bastion of Sumter,[40] making Pickens the object of bitter ridicule. Mary Boykin Chesnut, who was close to the Preston clan, castigated the governor in her diary: "Major Anderson has moved into Fort Sumter while Governor Pickens slept serenely. One of the things which depressed me was the kind of men put in office at the crisis, invariably some sleeping dead head long forgotten or passed over. Young and active spirits ignored. Places for worn out politicians seemed the rule when our only hope is to use all the talents God has given."[41] It seemed to poor Pickens that all his enemies had united against him. He had been assured that Anderson would make no move to take Sumter. However, there was one positive result—Sumter had now become a southern problem, not just a South Carolina problem.[42]

Pickens began to take immediate steps to salvage the situation and his reputation. Instead of waiting for the commissioners whom South Carolina had sent to Washington to negotiate for the forts, he took matters into his own hands. He met with Charles Macbeth, the mayor of Charleston, and requested that the navigation lights in the harbor be extinguished.[43] He dispatched his aide, Colonel J. Johnston Pettigrew, to request Anderson to return his forces to Fort Moultrie.[44] Colonel Walter Gwynn was ordered to reconnoiter the approaches to Charleston Harbor and recommend where gun emplacements should be built. Pickens expressed his frustration at not having enough large guns of sufficient range to protect the Carolina coast. He planned to place his few cannons on an "interior line at points where the rivers grow narrow," and he decided that it was impossible to defend the Port Royal area with his limited means.[45] On the bottom of the letter containing Colonel Gwynn's recommendations, Pickens penned a fatalistic sentence: "The enemy is too powerful and skillful on water."[46] Even as Pickens was ordering the defenses around Charleston improved, he moved with remarkable speed to occupy Castle Pinckney, one of the forts over which South Carolina was negotiating.[47] It was federal property, and Pickens, by ordering it seized, was committing an act of aggression against the United States. This action has since been cited as a monstrous blunder, but the clamor of public opinion left the governor no alternative at the time. Fort Moultrie was occupied shortly after the seizure of Castle Pinckney. Pickens also ordered Morris Island in Charleston Harbor fortified and at the same time ordered the occupation of the United States arsenal and other federal properties.[48]

In Washington, Trescot and Pickens's old friend R. M. T. Hunter, now a senator from Virginia, were urging the president to order Anderson back to Fort Moultrie and to force Joseph Holt, now secretary of war, out of the administration. They were unsuccessful, and the situation took a turn for the worse.[49]

In spite of the criticism Pickens was receiving, the convention gave him extraordinary powers and created an executive council to act as his cabinet. This council, consisting of the lieutenant governor and four other members, represented the convention within the administration and was to serve as an aid and restraint upon Pickens. Council members were to be nominated by the chief executive and confirmed by the convention. Initially this council acted simply as an advisory board, with the governor retaining the right of final decision. On 30 December 1860, Pickens chose A. G. Magrath as secretary of state, D. F. Jamison as secretary of war, C. G. Memminger as secretary of the treasury, A. G. Garlington as secretary of the interior, and the lieutenant governor, W. W. Harllee, as postmaster.[50]

The convention authorized the governor to levy war, negotiate treaties, and send and receive ambassadors; his appointive powers were also greatly increased. Pickens was responsible for negotiating with Buchanan and for sending commissioners to other southern states to urge secession. He had been transformed from a relatively powerless governor to the executive head of the sovereign Palmetto Republic.

In the early days of his administration Pickens was confronted by problems he could hardly have foreseen. He had to review all intelligence and engineering reports. South Carolina needed to erect coastal defenses and provide troops to man them. Everyone in the new republic seemed to want a commission or a position in the new government. The state militia was inadequate and had to be armed, trained, and provided with leadership. Before South Carolina joined the Confederacy, all logistical problems were the direct responsibility of the state's chief executive. In order for the independent state to be recognized by foreign powers, representatives needed to be contacted and courted. Pickens tried his hand at personal diplomacy by attempting to form a relationship with Russia, the foreign power he knew best.[51]

South Carolina had embarked on a new and dangerous experiment, and with no plans to provide the state with a government adequate to her needs. The problems confronting the governor would have been incalculable, even if secession had occurred under the most favorable circumstances. With war clouds on the horizon and a local populace in a frenzy, the pressures were immeasurable.

"The Charlestonians are surrounding us with batteries on every point of land in the vicinity," reported Captain Abner Doubleday of the Fort Sumter garrison, "this is done with the hope of preventing any vessel from coming to our assistance with a view to force us ultimately to surrender the Fort."[52] Great energy was being expended on both sides to prepare the forts for certain conflict. In a confidential letter written in mid-January to Baron Stoeckle, the Russian minister to the United States, Pickens stated, "We are prepared to maintain our position—I have seven hundred troops in possession of Morris Island with a strong battery commanding the harbor in advance of Fort Sumter and I have 900 troops on Sullivan's Island and in Fort Moultrie, and 800 at Fort Johnson and 200 in Castle Pinckney, and we can put 20,000 men into this city in two days . . . and I have 65,000 men . . . in this state ready for action and the state will be able to put 125,000 into the field."[53]

Finally, after numerous meetings and requests for opinions, Buchanan decided that Fort Sumter should be reinforced. In his characteristic way, he took a long time to implement his decision. At first he planned to send a warship to rescue the Fort, but he was dissuaded from taking such bold action. Instead he arranged to have a merchant vessel, the *Star of the West*, carry reinforcements to Charleston Harbor. The ship set sail on 5 January 1861, bound officially for New Orleans.[54] Ironically, Pickens learned of the sailing from his old enemy, Louis Wigfall, who was then a U.S. senator from Texas. He telegraphed Pickens that the vessel should be expected in South Carolina waters, and on 9 January an action took place that ordinarily would have precipitated war.[55] On that morning the *Star of the West* entered Charleston Harbor; the guns on Morris Island and Fort Moultrie fired on the ship, scoring several ineffectual hits, but Major Anderson did not permit Fort Sumter's guns to retaliate. However, Anderson warned Pickens that, if the act were not disclaimed, he would "regard it as an act of war, and that [he would not] . . . permit any vessel to pass within the range of the guns of [his] fort." The governor explained that he had an understanding with Anderson's "government": if Union troops were sent to reinforce Fort Sumter, it would be regarded as an act of hostility. He continued, "In regard to your threat in regard to vessels. It is only necessary for me to say that you must judge your responsibility."[56] Robert Toombs, a senator from Georgia, wrote from Washington that he approved of

Pickens's course and that "the administration is dead broken down . . . The old gentleman is alternately wreaking, wracking, cursing and railing. At one moment he exacts pity and anon contempt."[57] The legislature unanimously approved Pickens's course in regard to the *Star of the West* and Fort Sumter. It pledged "earnest, vigorous, and unhesitating support" for every measure adopted for the defense of the state.[58]

Other southern leaders were urging Pickens to proceed with caution. Jefferson Davis, whose home state of Mississippi had recently seceded, reminded Pickens that "the little garrison . . . presses on nothing but a point of pride."[59] It was easy for Davis to give advice, since he did not have to contend with the angry Carolinians. From all sides Pickens was being pressed to take Sumter; yet, despite his bravado, Pickens realized that the harbor's defenses were in a miserable state. He decided to play for time by conducting negotiations with Anderson and the outgoing Buchanan administration. On 11 January he demanded that Fort Sumter be turned over to South Carolina. Anderson could not comply with Pickens's request, but he suggested that the whole matter be referred to Washington.[60] Anderson's suggestion was a reprieve for Pickens, since it carried with it the promise that the major would not use his cannon until he received instructions from Washington.[61] The time needed for Anderson's courier and Pickens's representative, Attorney General Isaac W. Hayne, to reach Washington and return was put to good use. Hayne was instructed to warn Buchanan that future attempts to reinforce the fort and continued occupation of Sumter would inevitably lead to a "bloody issue."[62] On the same day that the *Star of the West* was shelled, the governor called together three engineering officers and an officer of ordnance "to consider and report the most favorable plan for operating upon Fort Sumter, so as to reduce the fortress, by batteries or other means."[63]

Hayne was delayed from meeting with the president. Ten southern senators intervened, feeling that Pickens's letter to Buchanan was too rash and might lead to conflict, and that prudence would postpone hostilities until the Confederate government could be formed.[64] In Charleston the harbor fortifications were strengthened at a feverish pace. Pickens planned to take the fort if necessary, but unlike Rhett and the *Mercury*, who were daily advocating the storming of the fortress, the governor desired to prevent bloodshed if possible. Many politicians from other southern states that had seceded or were on the verge of secession knew that the explosive Sumter problem would probably lead to civil war, but they urged South Carolina to continue to follow a policy of forbearance. The great hope was that hostility could be avoided until after the convention that was scheduled to assemble in mid-February in Montgomery, Alabama, to consider the formation of a confederation of southern states.[65]

A desperate Buchanan agreed that hostilities would best be avoided, at least during the waning days of his presidency. He made it clear in his interview with Hayne that he had no power to make agreements and that he was bound by law to protect public property. However, he implied that he was satisfied with the status quo, provided no hostile action was commenced against the fort.[66]

Buchanan may have been content to leave matters unresolved, but Pickens could not afford to do likewise. Pressures were mounting in direct proportion to the rising anger of the Carolinians. Pickens's complicated maneuvering even included an offer to purchase Fort Sumter. The president made it clear that he had no more right to sell the fort to South Carolina than to sell the capitol to Maryland.[67]

The Charlestonians were being reminded of the insulting situation by the vociferous *Mercury*, which daily advocated that South Carolina avoid entering a new confederation until Anderson was removed from the fort.[68] By mid-January the *Mercury*'s editorials had become acutely strident: "Will South Carolina sit quietly with folded arms, and see a fort garrisoned by our enemies, and in their possession, armed with power to forbid ingress and egress to vessels into and out of the harbor? NEVER!"[69]

Pickens was receiving conflicting advice from all quarters. William L. Yancey, the best-known Alabama fire-eater, was one of the many radicals who desired to see South Carolina commence immediate operations against the fort; cooler heads were urging Pickens to refrain from moves that would increase tensions until after the confederacy was formed. Jefferson Davis wrote from Washington that "the occurrence of the *Star of the West* seems to me to put you in the best condition for delay, so long as the Government permits that matter to rest where it is . . . your friends here think you can well afford to stand still so far as the presence of the garrison is concerned, and if things continue as they are for a month, we shall be in a condition to speak with a voice which all must hear and heed."[70] Governor J. E. Brown of Georgia also advised Pickens against precipitous action. If war commenced while Buchanan was in office, he said, it would unite northern Democrats and Republicans against the South.[71]

In a confidential letter to Davis, Pickens explained that he had no plans to take Sumter. "It is a very strong fortress," he wrote, "and in the most commanding position. I found everything in utter confusion, when I came into office, and really no military supplies."[72]

Pickens remained subject to conflicting pressures. Leaders of other seceding states were urging caution, but in South Carolina the overwhelming sentiment was for an immediate storming of the fortress. The Columbia *Southern Guardian* asked: "Why not is Fort Sumter attacked?"[73] Pickens was accused of being negligent and using poor judgment. One observer believed that there would be no fight over Sumter as the "determined policy of Pickens [is] to avoid a fight even if by so doing the honor of the state is sacrificed. Fort Sumter should have been taken weeks ago. He has had men and arms sufficient for besieging it . . . but now it could be disaster, and the lifeblood of the flower now stops the gain . . . but do you not see that this dilemma is the . . . result of his own negligence and bad management. . . . The state . . . is being disgraced every day. There are many men . . . who would rather die than suffer their state disgraced."[74] Henry William Ravenel, a prominent South Carolina botanist and planter, wrote, "There is great disatisfaction prevailing in the city [Charleston] at the course of Governor Pickens . . . in all his official acts. He is overbearing, haughty and rude, and has given offense in numerous cases. He has caused many resignations and has made himself so unpopular since his election, that were it not for the critical state of affairs now existing, he would be called to account and perhaps impeached."[75]

Pickens was in a dilemma not of his own making. On 16 January Hayne had told A. G. Magrath, South Carolina's secretary of state, that most southern leaders favored procrastination.[76] Not until 6 February did conferences between Hayne and Buchanan break down; Hayne returned to South Carolina to urge the governor to order an immediate attack.[77] Although Pickens desperately wanted to take the fort in order to glorify his beloved Mother Carolina and to stop the increasing criticism, he knew that to do so would be folly. Thus he continued to stall and suffer the wrath of the fire-eaters. The journals of the executive council show that the problem of Sumter and defense of Charleston were all absorbing.[78] The correspondence was prolific, full of reports, advice, intelligence, support, criticism, and new problems. On 6 February the order was given to General R. G. M. Dunovant to ready all batteries and posts for a forty-eight-hour bombardment.[79] News of Pickens's latest moves were made known throughout the South, and again southern leaders urged him not to attack. Former President John Tyler of Virginia cautioned Pickens to move slowly. Pickens replied that he would wait as long as possible, but he could not sacrifice the rights of South Carolina.[80] At this time the Confederacy was being organized in Montgomery, Alabama. Pickens was stalling, hoping that, with the advent of the new government, South Carolina's problem would become a Confederate one. However, procrastination was becoming increasingly difficult. While Hayne was in Washington the governor had an excuse for remaining inactive, but now Hayne was home, claiming that he had been insulted in Washington and preaching instant war.[81] Pickens wrote to J. Thompson Mason, a secessionist and the collector of the port of Baltimore, indicating that he longed for the problem of Sumter to be lifted from his shoulders. He suggested that Maryland and Virginia secede and seize Washington.

Pickens demonstrated that he was ready for action, but not in Charleston.[82] The South Carolina delegates in Montgomery presented the provisional Confederate government with its first problem: a clear ultimatum either to unite and accept Fort Sumter as a common obligation, or to let South Carolina take the fort.[83] Robert Toombs, secretary of state of the newly formed Confederacy, urged that Sumter not be attacked without the consent of the Confederate government.[84] Pickens saw a way out of his difficulties. He wrote Toombs, "If your Congress will by any public or specific declaration, indicate jurisdiction . . . then I could not hesitate to abide most cheerfully by your control."[85]

On 12 February the provisional Confederate congress telegraphed Pickens that the new Confederate government had "taken charge of the questions and difficulties existing between the states of the Confederacy and the government of the United States relating to the occupation of the forts, navy yards and other public establishments." In reply to this intelligence Pickens wired the Montgomery congress urging that Fort Sumter be taken before Lincoln assumed the presidency. At the same time he wrote Howell Cobb, the president of the Confederate congress, a long letter informing him that South Carolina had completed measures necessary for the taking of Fort Sumter. He reasoned that war might be averted "by making the capture of Fort Sumter a fact accomplished during the continuance of the present Administration." He explained, "Mr. Buchanan cannot resist, because he has not the power. Mr. Lincoln may not attack, because the cause of the quarrel will have been, or may be considered by him as past."[86]

On 1 March, L. P. Walker, the secretary of war in the new Confederacy, confirmed the decision to shoulder the burden of Sumter.[87] Pickens was delighted. It was now his turn to play the role of fire-eater. Throwing caution to the wind, he urged that the fort be taken immediately and informed Toombs that he was eager to assist in the action.[88] Many South Carolinians believed that Jefferson Davis would continue to delay, but with the arrival of P. G. T. Beauregard in Charleston on 6 March, action seemed imminent.

By the end of March all was in readiness. Pickens wrote Lucy, who was in Texas visiting her family, that he had five hundred men ready to storm the fort.[89] To the Citadel cadets he made a fiery speech "while about half drunk" in which he reiterated the promise so frequently made regarding the irritating bastion in the harbor.[90] Meanwhile, Lincoln had been sworn in on 4 March, and in his inaugural address he vowed to "hold, occupy and possess the property and places belonging to the government."[91] Negotiations with the new president were to no avail. Anderson's mail and provisions were cut off, and Pickens had done an admirable job of obtaining the powder and shot necessary for the reduction of Sumter.[92] When Lincoln ultimately determined to provision the fort, the inevitable occurred.[93]

Beauregard, believing that it was "manifestly an imperative necessity" to reduce the fort before the fort and fleet could combine against him, ordered firing to commence on 12 April 1861.[94] Pickens appeared jubilant as he, along with Beauregard, witnessed the surrender and evacuation of Sumter.[95] The governor's vindicated passion overflowed as he addressed the assembled masses. Before the cannonade, Pickens's name had been anathema to many people; after the bombardment, those who had cursed him applauded. Never known for his humility, Pickens puffed with pride as he waxed eloquent from the balcony of the Charleston Hotel on Sunday, 14 April. In a speech full of "I"s, he stated that the "triumphant and victorious results" were not attributable to his skill. Nevertheless, he did not fail to remind the populace that "I was determined to maintain our separate independence and freedom at any and every hazard . . . when I knew we were prepared, I was ready to strike . . . we have rallied; we have met them . . . let it lead to what it might, even if it leads to blood and ruin . . . we have defeated their twenty millions, we have met them and conquered them. We have humbled the flag of the United States before the Palmetto and Confederate. . . . But today it has been humbled before the glorious little state of South Carolina."[96] The *New York Times* editorialized: "The curtain has fallen upon the first act of the great tragedy of the age. Fort Sumter has been surrendered, and the stars and stripes of the American Republic give place to the felon flag of the Southern Confederates."[97] The gay days of the Carolinians who had forced the Yankees out of Sumter were numbered; nevertheless, in the closing days of April excitement and joy ruled in the Palmetto State.[98]

The governor's brief moments of popularity faded quickly. The need for the state's executive council lessened as the Confederate government at Montgomery became responsible for diplomatic, economic, and military affairs. On 3 April, at the request of Pickens, the South Carolina convention formally ratified the Constitution of the Confederate States and ended the Palmetto State's sovereignty.[99]

As the convention approached *sine die* adjournment, questions arose as to its future role. Some held that, since the Confederate Constitution had been ratified, the convention had completed its work and should be dissolved; others believed it should adjourn but be subject to recall by the convention president, D. F. Jamison, prior to 1 January 1862. The latter group won the day. In case of an emergency the convention could be called back into session.[100]

The resolution of the Sumter question did not end Pickens's problems. Most Confederate soldiers at the war's outset were volunteers from state militia regiments. Since South Carolina had been preparing for conflict longer than the other southern states, her regiments were better organized and equipped. Although many of the state troops were needed for coastal defense, the Confederate government decided to send 8,000 South Carolina troops to Virginia, where they were expected to meet the Union army.[101] Men volunteered by the thousands. Pickens encouraged the troops to serve the Confederacy, but he was emphatic that South Carolina's troops could not serve more than twelve months or be sent outside the state without his approval. When Pickens, as commander in chief, consented to allow the troops to go to Virginia, where secession had not yet occurred, he was bitterly criticized.[102]

Military affairs occupied the governor throughout the spring and summer of 1861. The problem of coastal defenses became absorbing. Although the Confederate government ostensibly was in charge of defending the coast, Pickens assumed the primary role of supplying troops, labor, and arms for the effort.[103] A study of Pickens's papers in the Library of Congress, the South Carolina Archives, and the Caroliniana Library reveals that Pickens was besieged with problems that demanded decisions and that often forced him to deal with vain Carolina cavaliers who were quick to advise and criticize. His failure to consult with Carolina leaders became a sore point and caused his unpopularity within the aristocracy to grow. D. F. Jamison, the president of the convention, became one of the governor's chief critics, and secretary of state Andrew G. Magrath disassociated himself from the chief executive. Beaufort T. Watts resigned as gubernatorial secretary because of a supposed slight; William H. Trescot called attention to Pickens's blunders.[104] William Gilmore Simms complained to Hammond, "Pickens is such an ass that he will drive away from him every decent counselor. . . . His vanity throws him open to the most contemptible advisors, all who flatter, can rule him. He has caused the most infinite degree of blundering and has offended many."[105]

The new advisors to whom Simms referred were Franklin J. Moses, the future scalawag governor of South Carolina, the poet Paul H. Hayne, and

Lucy, whose beauty, cleverness, and charm proved to be her husband's best asset. In her diary Mary Boykin Chesnut frequently mentions Lucy. One of those to whom William Gilmore Simms wrote complaining about Pickens was William Porcher Miles, who may have disliked Pickens but was infatuated with Lucy. Upon first meeting Lucy at the Isaac Haynes's, Mrs. Chesnut described a scene in which Miles was "begging in dumb show for three violets she had in her breastpin. She is a consummate actress and he well up in the part of male flirt. So it was well done." Mrs. Chesnut, after giving a sample of the dialogue, brought all into perspective: "And so we fool on, into the black cloud ahead of us."[106] As the situation grew darker, Pickens's popularity continued to wane. Certainly his egoism and vanity compounded his problems, but anyone who held his awesome responsibility would have met the same fate, given the people, politics, and circumstances. In late May 1861 he declared martial law in the coastal regions, in a futile effort to secure the area against infiltration and attack.[107] South Carolina's troops had to be provisioned, not only with war materials, but with foodstuffs, medicine, and other essentials. Pickens had little use for "a people who would hesitate to defend their rights, because of expense."[108] Flying in the face of human nature, Pickens ordered the unpopular procurement officers to requisition needed goods.[109] Another source of difficulty was the matter of appointments. It was impossible to honor all requests, and the giving of satisfaction to some caused dissatisfaction in others. Some of the criticism of Pickens was no doubt valid. He was frequently overcautious; yet sometimes he tended to be dramatic and impetuous.[110]

Throughout the summer and fall of 1861 public hostility continued. In his annual message to the legislature on 5 November 1861, the governor made no attempt to rally the people. Instead, he recalled the glories of secession and the fall of Fort Sumter.[111] Two days later the United States fleet under the command of Samuel F. DuPont easily took Port Royal. Twelve thousand Union troops landed, quickly gaining control of one of the richest areas of the state. Plantations were abandoned, and large quantities of cotton were lost.[112] The invasion revealed that South Carolina was woefully unprepared. For a time it appeared that Union soldiers might even take Charleston.[113] Pickens was rebuked; Mrs. Chesnut revealed that news of the invasion "could only be traced to that 'reliable man' whose blunders are proverbial."[114] Henry Ravenel expressed the view that Pickens had made himself "so unpopular since his election, that he would not probably get a vote if the election were held now. Conceit, arrogance, inconstancy, petulence, ignorance . . . and dictatorial abuse of his position are ascribed to him. I meet with no one who has a word to say in his favor."[115] Langdon Cheves, Jr., one of the defenders of the Port

Royal area, criticized the governor for his unbending, all-knowing manner. The Charleston *Courier*, which at times had been friendly to Pickens, recounted the events leading up to the invasion and accused Pickens of "doing nothing for the benefit of the state, but much to produce confusion, conflicting and incomprehensible orders were emanating from the military department, and indiscreet and injurious proclamations from the Executive. Everything was in confusion and everybody complaining."[116]

By this time Pickens had left Charleston and set up office in the unfriendly capital, Columbia. There lived the Hamptons, Prestons, and Haynes; frequently the Chesnuts, Mannings, and Wigfalls were also in town. Pickens's personality and past animosities prevented him from being accepted. After the fall of Port Royal he became the butt of their jokes, as they seemed to revel in the state's misery. Pickens was faced with a seemingly impossible task. All confidence in his administration had waned with the reversals in fortunes, and when he made a call for volunteers on 15 November, there was little response. Compounding this difficulty was the scarcity of arms and ammunition.[117] The governor asked the legislature to amend the militia laws, making all male citizens between the ages of eighteen and forty-five liable for twelve months service in or out of the state.[118] If men did not volunteer for service, the law permitted the governor to draft them. Two days after the passage of the measure Pickens called for 12,000 volunteers and threatened to resort to the draft if they were not forthcoming. Prior to the invasion he had been asking the Confederate government for help; after the invasion his pleas became frantic. South Carolina had given much to the Confederacy, but little was being returned.[119]

10. Governor and Council

On 14 December 1861, at the height of the crisis, D. F. Jamison decided to exercise his option before it expired. On 27 December the third session of the secession convention commenced, under the most demoralizing circumstances. A raging fire had consumed the best parts of Charleston; troops were not volunteering; arms were not to be had; the governor was regarded by many as incompetent. The convention, which still enjoyed public confidence, believed that drastic action was needed to strengthen the executive. On 7 January 1862 it issued an ordinance creating the Second Executive Council, composed of the governor, the lieutenant governor, and three members elected by the convention.[1] Although Pickens was the focal point for discontent, he was not entirely at fault. Many of the most able state leaders were at the front, and even had there been the most competent leadership, the results probably would have been little different, given the paucity of resources and the strains on the state government.

The new executive council was an experiment unique in American political history.[2] Pickens and a minority of the convention opposed its creation, since this new council (unlike its predecessor) gave the convention and the council decisive control over the governor. The council in effect usurped all powers that had previously been given to the governor. It would have control of military affairs, power to declare martial law, to arrest and detain disloyal and disaffected persons, to impress private property, and to spend public monies.[3]

The council was comprised of Pickens, Lieutenant Governor W. W. Harllee, ex-United States Senator James Chesnut (the husband of Mary Boykin Chesnut), Isaac Hayne, who had served as state attorney general since 1848, and former Governor William H. Gist.[4]

Pickens was furious. He had expected some regulation, but not complete emasculation. In a letter to A. G. Magrath he cast doubt on the legitimacy of the council[5] and in no uncertain terms expressed his discontent to the convention: "The ordinance you have just passed, will . . . weaken the Executive as created by the constitution. I understand from the ordinance that no appointment, even the humblest kind, is to be made, except by a deliberate vote of the new council to be created . . . I do not know if all orders to be issued, relating to the military, are first to be submitted to a vote of the council. If so, there will be great imbecility in acting as commander-in-chief."[6]

Jamison tried to placate the now powerless governor by informing him that patriotism required that he submit gracefully and that in reality the governor's office had gained, not lost, power: "You seem to consider this as detracting the powers of the *Governor*, by dispensing what belonged to one among five. I have considered it as adding to the power of the Governor by making him ex-officio head of a body to which *new powers* have been delegated embracing most of the powers of the convention. . . . In my judgment [it is] an elevation and give[s] you higher power and greater responsibility than a mere governor, under the constitution, ever could have."[7]

On 9 January, at the first meeting, it was obvious that Chesnut, Hayne, and Gist intended to cooperate to run the council. Pickens protested, but to no avail. On a motion from Chesnut the council organized administrative units. Chesnut was made chief of the department of military; Hayne became chief of the department of justice and police; Harllee and Gist were joint heads of the department of treasury and finance.[8] From the outset antagonism grew between Pickens and the other members of the council. Although Pickens tried to lead, Hayne and Chesnut had usurped the executive.[9]

The hostility between Chesnut and Pickens is revealed in Mary Chesnut's diary. On the very day when the council was organized, Mrs. Chesnut called on Mrs. Pickens. "We flattered each other as far as that sort of thing can be done. She is young, lovely, clever—and old Pick's third wife. She cannot fail to hate us. Mr. C. Put as A sort of watch and ward over her husband."[10] The hostility grew as Pickens saw that the council intended to strip him of his constitutional power. On 28 January Mrs. Chesnut saw Lucy at a party at the home of Dr. Robert Gibbes. The meeting of the two women demonstrated the all-absorbing nature of the "Council War." "The governor's lady was there—she received in state. She did not rise from her chair as we spoke to her—we are only of the governor's council. Young Moses—Franklin Jr.—is secretary to Governor Pickens. He hung over the lovely Lucy, standing or bending over her from the back of her chair. It suggested the devil whispering in Eve's ear in the primeval days."[11]

Foster Marshall, a friend of Pickens's from near Charleston, advised the governor to call the legislature back into session and to resign as a protest.[12] Although the Yankees were in Beaufort, for many Carolinians the war was being fought in Columbia, as the battle raged between Pickens and the council. When Pickens presented a plan for the mobilization and conscription of more troops, the council rejected his ideas in favor of ones submitted by Chesnut.[13]

By June, Hayne and Pickens became so antagonistic that they exchanged castigating letters which were published in the newspapers.[14] Pickens could only complain: "I am deprived of all power to act at all, I cannot even issue a proclamation without authority . . . I have not a particle of power to do anything."[15]

The difficulties with the council caused Pickens to sink into a melancholy state. In late January, while Lucy was being the "Fleur de Luce" and conquering hearts in Columbia, Pickens was at Edgewood suffering from acute depression. On a cold and rainy January night, after a few drinks, he began to rummage through desks looking for his old letters. Upon discovering some letters Lucy had received from "other gentlemen writers," he decided to write his wife a letter demonstrating his childlike passion and his current uncertainties. Although he posed as a sophisticate who was "insensitive to fear," he revealed that he was a frightened, unsure man who had great difficulty manifesting passion for "the whole country" that he loved so much. While he wanted history to remember him favorably, he believed himself to be an "abused man" who was hated by "all bad and selfish men." He poured out his feelings for his country to his wife, resorting to oft-repeated reminiscences. Pickens's romantic phraseology demonstrated what a truly pitiful man he was; like his state, he was filled with despair. He admitted that he had "wept and prayed on my knees to God to avert the pending ruin and to save my country from degradation and sorrow."[16] Surely he prayed that he, too, would be saved from impending doom. Possibly providence heard his prayers; as the war progressed, the council became despised for its increasingly repressive actions. Although Pickens sponsored and voted for many of the measures that were passed by the "five headed governor," he received none of the odium aimed at the council.

During this difficult period Pickens's greatest asset was Lucy, whose reputation had grown as his had diminished. She became known as the "Queen of the Confederacy." Christopher G. Memminger, who had served in the first executive council and had been appointed by Jefferson Davis as the Confederate secretary of the treasury, adorned Confederate currency with her picture. A brigade was named in her honor, and her captivating charm appealed to the demoralized Carolinians.[17]

Many actions of the executive council were absolutely necessary. Troops were drafted, slave labor impressed, liquor prohibited, salt rationed, and supplies requisitioned.[18] Pickens may have been unpopular, but the council's actions were more so.[19] On 1 May the Charleston *Daily Courier* took up the cause, accusing the convention and the council of usurping power. "It is no

Currier and Ives drawing of Pickens
(courtesy of the South Caroliniana Library, University of South Carolina)

council," the paper editorialized, "but a conclave of four additional governors, forced on the Executive by an appointment in which he had no choice or voice—rather an oligarchy, assuming all power, executive, legislative and judicial, the very definition and essence of despotism." Throughout May and June the actions of the extraordinary body were lambasted by the *Courier*.[20] Other papers also took up the hue and cry; the Columbia *South Carolinian* and the Edgefield *Advertiser* came to Pickens's aid, with editorial comment and published letters from his supporters.[21] During the summer the *Courier* continued its assault on the convention and council by claiming that many former opponents of the governor were now admitting to his ability and skill.[22] In her diary Mrs. Chesnut, claiming that the difficulties lay in "Pickens's miserable jealousy," defended the council by recounting all the actions her husband had taken to salvage the situation.[23] Nevertheless, the council's efforts were the cause of its undoing. Meetings were held throughout the state to protest "the five headed dictatorship" and pledge support to the governor. The newspapers became more strident; hundreds of denunciations were published.[24] Voices of the defenders of the experiment were lost in the clamor of criticism. Growing numbers of Carolinians demanded that the convention be reconvened and the council abolished. The general feeling was that the council's every action did violence to the individualism that had long been the conscious pride and boast of Carolinians.[25] Pickens, realizing that the tide had turned, publicly joined the contest by asserting that the convention had illegally usurped his authority. On 1 August a letter to Isaac Hayne appeared in the Charleston *Daily Courier*; therein Pickens, with a rebirth of courage, showed his defiance of the convention and council: "I take this occasion to inform you that I am not responsible to the Chief of Justice and Police, nor to the Executive Council, and shall sternly defy the arrogance of one and the power of both in any event that may arise."[26] On 27 August, President Jamison issued a call for the convention to be reconvened on 9 September; twenty members of the convention had signed a petition requesting that the convention meet.[27] A committee of twenty-one of its members was assigned the task of reviewing the council's record. Although the committee was impressed with the council's labors, the public was not. Thus the convention decided that the future of the council should be left to the legislature, and the body adjourned on 17 September, a few weeks before elections for the legislature were to be held.[28]

In his opening message to the new General Assembly, Pickens laboriously explained the existing state of affairs. He then attacked the convention, claiming that the ordinances creating the executive council were "an unnecessary and arbitrary establishment of an unusual and irregular government which lacked constitutionality" as it "utterly annihilated his role as Commander-in-Chief."[29] The legislature, like the governor, had no love for the council, feeling that it had usurped legislative powers as well. The day after Pickens left office, the legislature abolished the executive council and declared all of its acts, resolutions, and proceedings invalid. Pickens emerged from the controversy with popularity greater than ever.[30] Ironically, one measure that caused the council to lose popularity was a plan to confiscate all gold and silver in private hands and to issue paper money against it. Pickens had advocated the measure, but the council, not the governor, received the criticism for it.[31]

As Pickens's term was coming to an end, there was talk of prolonging his governorship, but this idea was denounced as unconstitutional.[32] The *Mercury* reminded its readers that the controversial council had been created because of the governor's difficulties.[33] There followed an attempt to secure him a seat in the Confederate Senate, but Senator James L. Orr refused to resign his seat in order to take the governorship.[34]

Pickens was succeeded by his closest friend, Milledge Bonham, who had served in Congress and as leader of the South Carolina militia. General Bonham became the third successive upcountry governor. His election was a vote of confidence for Pickens, since the two men were so closely associated and shared similar views. Fate had played strange tricks: Pickens emerged with newfound popularity as another Edgefield man was elected governor.

Pickens returned home on 18 December 1862. Critics charged that his governorship was marked by confusion and instability, and there is no question that he was at times impetuous, verbose, and bombastic. However, it is difficult to conclude that anyone else could have done better under the circumstances. Unfortunately for Pickens, his personality and numerous old enemies detracted from his reputation. After he retired, he would discover that fame is ephemeral and gratitude fleeting.

11. "There Can Lay No Peace for Me"

Francis Pickens may have rejoiced that he was free from the rancor of politics as he waited for the train to take him back to Edgefield on that cold December day, but Lucy was surely disappointed to leave Columbia with its concerts, dinner parties, political intrigues, and other amusements.[1] She had enjoyed being first lady of the sovereign state of South Carolina. Now there would be no more affairs of state with throngs of liveried servants, no more welcoming of wounded heroes, no more flirting with the men in Columbia. Now it was back to Edgefield, "the dim unknown of the interior."[2] Lucy had been demoted from being the first lady to being the mistress of a large upcountry plantation. When Pickens was younger, the plantation had been a place of joy and easy living. The slaves at Edgewood continued to labor with little supervision; however, the war, a substantial diminution in the acreage planted, and uncertain markets combined to change the mode of life. The slaves continued to be well treated but were fewer than previously. There were financial difficulties as banks continued to discount the Confederate currency. During the summer of 1864 Pickens found life increasingly difficult, with "bread getting as important as powder." In order to show his patriotism, the former governor continued to send more of his slaves to the coast to help build badly needed fortifications.[3]

The period between the end of Pickens's governorship and the end of the war became one of great demoralization. The gleam of life faded, and dreams of a southern nation were ending in defeat. In May 1863 Arthur Simkins, whose newspaper had been of immeasurable help in promoting Pickens, died of congestive fever, the same malady that had killed his sisters.[4] The *Advertiser*'s columns were full of death as the human costs of the war mounted. In the midst of the pages of sadness was a bit of pride for Pickens when the paper announced that his son-in-law, Matthew C. Butler, had been promoted to general by the Confederacy.[5] However, as the news became grimmer, Pickens became more fatalistic. A movement to reelect him as governor seemed to do little to bolster his spirits. (The movement failed, since the state constitution mandated a four-year interval between terms.[6]) Toward the war's end the former governor discovered the fleeting nature of fame: on a trip to Richmond in June 1864 a detective had to attest for his passport. He commented to his wife, "My name was the passport for thousands two years ago, and now so humble that a city detective has to vouch for my character."[7]

Naturally Pickens continued to evince an interest in the war. One of his greatest fears was that the Union forces would be successful in the West and become able to attack the state from the mountains as well as from the sea. He saw little evidence that the Davis government was stopping the northern threat, and in a letter to Wigfall, reminiscent of those castigating letters which had earlier been written about him, the ex-governor lambasted the Confederate president.[8]

As 1864 drew to a close, the legislature was meeting to select Bonham's successor, Andrew G. Magrath.[9] Pickens was in Edgefield "patiently awaiting the catastrophe." There was talk of South Carolina joining with North Carolina and Georgia and seceding from the Confederacy. However, Pickens advised Magrath that all was finished and that for South Carolina to continue fighting would be senseless.[10]

Sherman's march through South Carolina forced Magrath to flee Columbia, and on 17 February 1865 the city was occupied by federal troops.[11] James L. Orr reported to Pickens that the cause was lost: "Our armies are broken up— our soldiers are heartily sick and tired of war—our supplies are entirely cut off . . . our seaports are all closed—our lines of railroad are broken up and we could not feed an army if we had it."[12] Mrs. Chesnut commented: "It was a lively, rushing young set South Carolina put to the fore. They knew it was a time of danger . . . they expected to win by activity, energy, enthusiasm. Then came the wet blankets; Pickens, old Orr, halfhearted in the cause . . . now the old men are posing. Wrapping Caesar's mantle about their heads, ready to fall with dignity. While those gallant youths who dashed so gayly to the front lie mostly in bloody graves."[13]

For Edgefield the termination of war inaugurated a period of unpredictability. Many feared land confiscation. The new economic relations between blacks, ruined planters, and yeoman farmers began a process that would destroy the old way of life and forever change the values of the community. Although Edgefield suffered no physical damage from the Union invasion of the state, the work of war was everywhere visible. Homeless refugees, penniless widows, and maimed veterans gave testimony to war's horror.[14] At the age of twenty-nine Pickens's son-in-law, Major General Matthew C. Butler, returned to Edgefield, having lost a leg; he found his seventy slaves freed and a debt of $15,000, with Maria and three children to support.[15]

Although seeing the effects of war all around him, Pickens disavowed any role in the defeat. In a letter congratulating Perry on his selection by President Andrew Johnson as provisional governor, Pickens blamed all on "the utter incompetency and imbecility of those at the head of our affairs."[16] Pickens believed that the death of slavery would result in the death of thousands of Negroes who were unaccustomed to caring for themselves.

The summer of 1865 was so dry that the wells, like the crops, were failing. "Everybody pressing for money, like hungry wolves—there can lay no peace for me"[17]—these words described Pickens's financial situation, but the matter that seemed to worry him most was his uncertain personal status. As he read the newspapers in the spring, he noted the arrests of Jefferson Davis, Governor Magrath, and R. M. T. Hunter.[18] He surely worried for himself. Destitution was everywhere, and in Edgefield all business was suspended as "the pomp and circumstance of war faded away like unremembered fantasies of an idle dream." The dream became a nightmare as the district was occupied on 21 June by the 33rd Regiment, United States Colored Troops. For Pickens and his neighbors the occupation was an unsettling experience.[19] A few days before the Union troops marched into Edgefield, Pickens was elected chairman of the district Democratic central executive committee. The future political role of the freedmen deeply concerned the committee. Although some believed that the blacks could be controlled by the former Confederates, they were in for a rude awakening.[20]

In an effort to protect his freedom and be readmitted as a U.S. citizen, the former governor tried to court Andrew Johnson and Benjamin Perry. On 8 July he wrote both men similar letters, urging immediate reconstruction of South Carolina so that the state might enjoy "the protection of the constitution and laws of the United States." He worried about the "*sudden* emancipation of four millions of helpless human beings amongst us . . . I trust," he wrote President Johnson, "that harmony and kindness may be preserved between the two races."[21] Certainly he was hopeful that the administration would treat him with the same kindness he advocated for his own former slaves. Perry assured him that he would be pardoned if he would consent to become a candidate for the South Carolina constitutional convention, which had been called to rewrite the state's constitution to reflect the realities of defeat.[22] Pickens, relying on Perry's word, decided to humble himself by seeking an office that many Carolinians shunned as demeaning. In the past the former governor had avoided asking politicians for help; now, however, desperation caused him to rely upon Perry not only for his own pardon, but for a position for John Bacon, his son-in-law, as well.[23] For Pickens this was a time of sadness, confusion, and disbelief. He made labor contracts with many of his former slaves, for which they received housing, clothing, food, a small sum, and usually a portion of the crop.[24] Although during the summer matters were "put pretty right by the soldiers," he feared matters would "go poorly when the contract begins to work for me. Then they object and never heard of it before."[25] Other concerns were omnipresent. Since he had not been pardoned, he discovered that Union authorities opened his mail; although he complained, he found himself powerless. A calculation of his wealth showed that all he possessed were his household possessions, Lucy's jewelry, his land, and great obligations.[26]

In August, while Lucy was in Texas, the former governor visited his daughters and traveled to Greenville to meet Perry and take the oath of allegiance to the United States. When he arrived back in Edgefield, he discovered there was confusion over the legitimacy of his election to the constitutional convention, since he had failed to gain a pardon. He attempted to use this awkward situation to press Perry to renew efforts on his behalf.[27] On the basis of Perry's promise, Pickens was seated as a delegate at the convention, which met at the First Baptist Church in Columbia on 13 September. Sidney Andrews, a special correspondent for the Boston *Daily Advertiser*, described in detail the happenings at the convention. He reported on the unprepossessing makeup of the convention and revealed that James L. Orr and Pickens were the only two delegates who enjoyed national reputations.[28] One of Pickens's oldest colleagues, Judge David L. Wardlaw, was elected president of the convention, and Pickens emerged as one of the most vocal delegates. Ironically, it was Francis Pickens, who had bragged to the masses on the day of Fort Sumter's surrender that South Carolina had "humbled the flag that no nation on earth ever before humbled," who moved that the "ordinance passed in convention, 20th December, 1860, withdrawing this state from the Union, be . . . repealed."[29] Pickens did obeisance as he pronounced in a very feeling manner the death of Mother Carolina: "It doesn't become South Carolina to vapor, or swell or strut or brag or threat or swagger; she points to her burned cities, her desolate plantations, her mourning hearts, her unnumbered graves, her widows and orphans, her own torn and bleeding body—this she says the work of war; and she bids us bind up her wounds and pour in the oil of peace . . . and we must do it, even if it means that in so doing we go backwards!"[30]

Sidney Andrews described the former governor as being "a battered old wreck—short and squarely built, with a large and squarish head, a broad and flat face, a small and insignificant nose, round and piggish eyes, and broad high forehead. He has bristly iron-gray moustache and chin whiskers, and wears a brown wig—whereby there is a peculiar and noticeable contrast. His voice is feeble, his manner colloquial, his air jaunty. . . . He eats his humble pie with some ostentation, and is specially solicitous that nothing shall be done to offend His Excellency the Provisional Governor, or His Excellency the President of the United States."[31] The Columbia *Phoenix* reported that it was Pickens who endorsed Andrew Johnson's administration by introducing resolutions to repeal the ordinance of secession, abolish slavery, and attach to the state constitution a bill of rights.[32]

On 27 September the convention adjourned after formulating a new constitution which gave to the people many of the functions formerly reserved by the legislature.[33] While the convention was meeting, the South Carolina College board of trustees, of which Pickens was a member, was called into emergency session to consider ways to reopen the institution.[34] After the meetings in Columbia, Pickens returned home, still hoping for a pardon. Throughout the fall he continued to press Perry. He had upheld his part of the bargain, and others of high rank were earning reprieves. He continued to worry that his land would be confiscated and his contracts questioned. He was frightened to speak out, even though, maintaining his age-old love for political activity, he desired to participate. On 30 October 1865 the General Assembly met to elect candidates to the U.S. Senate. Perry was the overwhelming choice for the long term, and J. L. Manning was elected to the short term. Pickens was not absent from the balloting,[35] despite the failure of repeated requests from Perry and the governor elect, James L. Orr, for his amnesty. Pickens questioned the president's fairness, especially since both Bonham and Wade Hampton had been pardoned.[36]

Perhaps, in refusing Pickens's pardon, Andrew Johnson recalled his own statements during the 1864 presidential campaign, when he proclaimed the leaders of the South to be traitors and called for their destruction. Pickens was to him the arch traitor, since he represented the state that had planted the seeds of secession and destruction. On numerous occasions Johnson had argued that "the traitor has ceased to be a citizen [and] treason must be made odious and traitors must be punished and impoverished."[37]

At this time Pickens noted changes taking place in Washington that would impose new conditions on South Carolina. He realized that his situation was connected to these events, and that Andrew Johnson could not afford an issue with the "Rabid Republicans." Thus, for Pickens, "things look[ed] very gloomy."[38]

Also disturbing to Pickens were rumors that the new military governor of

South Carolina, General D. E. (Dan) Sickles, planned to move many of the freedmen out of the Edgefield District because they were receiving harsh treatment and excessively low wages. Pickens protested that removal of the freedmen would ruin him and his neighbors. He requested Governor Orr to urge the Freedman's Bureau to validate contracts that permitted paying fieldhands $12.50 a month, a rate substantially below that paid in Texas and Louisiana. Pickens maintained that the refusal of the Freedman's Bureau to approve contracts would "utterly ruin and disorganize all agricultural labor and destroy our prospects of any crops." He worried that, since he had not been pardoned and was paying the prevailing wage, the provost marshal would disallow his 143 contracts with his former slaves. He predicted that, if steps were not taken to settle the labor question, a "reign of terror" would be forthcoming.[39]

In June 1866 a reporter for a New Orleans newspaper asked the former governor to comment on the status of affairs in South Carolina. Pickens revealed that he was planting only half of his usual 850 acres, and that he believed the new labor system would ultimately destroy the planter class, since it would give the yeoman farmers a new opportunity to hire labor. He pointed out that already a great portion of the cotton harvest was coming from "the branches and creeks and hills of the great interior."

As Pickens discussed the demise of the plantation system, he seemed to be alluding to his own death. He disclosed that his health was worse and that he found getting about increasingly difficult.[40] For his health's sake he traveled to Baltimore and White Sulphur Springs during the summer of 1866, but the strains of life continued to have their effect.[41] He became uncharacteristically thoughtless. Paul Hamilton Hayne, whose family had relied upon Pickens's charity for over a year, revealed that Pickens had become "cruel, hard and unfeeling."[42] Actually, the former governor was obsessed with the tragedy of life. In notes for an inspirational talk he planned to give, entitled "Hope Not Without Cause," he maintained that for the South there was hope, but that for him "the watch of life" had "run down." He wrote of the nation's current period of tribulation as being like a bad marriage; like "a man and his scolding wife—they meet together again, only to quarrel and scratch."[43]

As Radical Reconstruction took hold, the Edgefield *Advertiser*, edited now by James Bacon, railed against the policies of the radicals and condemned the government for not granting amnesty to the South's most distinguished citizens.[44] During this time the former slaves began to participate in government. Edgefield's white citizens met to discuss their options and discovered that they had none, except to refrain from participating. "Radical Black Republicans" forced their rule on the South. Seemingly all energy and passion were focused on the blacks, as their economic and political roles changed.

Pickens's last years continued to be troubled ones. In the fall of 1867 he found himself embroiled in a controversy. Several parties laid claim to cotton that had been raised by two men who had leased land from him; each had promised a portion of the crop to sharecropping freedmen in return for their labor. He worried that he and the former slaves were being bilked out of their share of the crops, and that the freedmen would become violent as they discovered they had been duped "by designing low men."[45]

Pickens's continued failure to receive amnesty prevented him from publicly voicing his sentiments. A year before his death, he could only watch mutely as South Carolina was tortured with "the horrors of negro supremacy."[46] In his last letter to Perry he poured out his frustrations and worried that, if the radicals were not repudiated by the 1868 elections, the nation would be ruined. Rhetorically asking Perry, "What are we to do?," he answered his own question by suggesting that white Southerners band together "to endeavor to save what little we have, and to protect, if *possible*, our *women* and *children* . . . the danger in the South will be no government at all." Pickens, who had claimed at the outset of the war that he was insensible to fear, revealed in the last months of his life intense apprehension for the future "of my ruined state." "I now begin to look down the slopes of life," he wrote, "and all I now desire is to find some green spot whereon to rest my wearied limbs, as I travel down the hill of life, and gaze into that *long vista in which there* is no *change*. This is my personal feeling as to myself, but of course I feel for my state. True our extreme poverty may be our protection in the dark events before us, but I pray that we may be saved from the horror of anarchy and reckless negro rule. . . . I think we are in a more critical condition than we have yet encountered. The people are sick with despondency, and poverty and ruin . . . fills all with gloom."[47]

For Carolinians, the election of Ulysses S. Grant in November 1868 signaled that Pickens's predictions were coming to pass. He had prophesied at the end of the bloody conflict that the state would be "greatly drained and pass through even deeper degradation."[48] To his wife he wrote, "Our country is dead; my heart is so sad."[49] In a speech delivered before the Euphradian and Clariosophic Societies in 1855, "On the Influence of Government upon the Nature and Destiny of Man," Pickens had alluded to the writings of two ancient historians, Thucydides and Herodotus, and had given examples of how a conquered people should be treated. He had intended to illustrate the difference between ancient and modern civilization by showing that "absolute power and physical force were the basis of the former; while [in] all modern society there is a secret and undefinable responsibility to moral and intellectual power which soothes . . . each sense and sensibility of man."[50]

As Pickens lay dying, he may have recalled this antebellum comparison and thought of his country being controlled by "absolute power and physical force." As a result of the state's suffering, a new era would shake South Carolina's political establishment. However, for Pickens his blessing was death, on 25 January 1869.

Pickens died a man without a country. He had longed for pardon, and his lament was accentuated as he saw his state suffer great humiliation. His death marked the end of a political career that spanned the most interesting era of southern history. In many respects Pickens typified South Carolina planters of his day. He had attended South Carolina College, planted cotton, practiced law, and chosen politics as an all-consuming avocation. Like other Carolinians, he believed himself to be a stirring orator in the classical tradition. Above all else, he desired to inherit Calhoun's mantle of political leadership. Although he was talented, he possessed neither the personality nor the rationality required of such a successor. Unlike Calhoun, who had the strength to modify the state's political course, Pickens showed himself to be a mirror that reflected the state's prevailing mood. His lack of a consistent political course proved damaging, for he gained a reputation as a mere office-seeker. South Carolina's secession and the Civil War gave him ample opportunities to prove his leadership. Although he was frequently assailed by myriad enemies, it is doubtful that anyone else could have handled the position better, considering the war, South Carolina's poverty, the heightened and unclear political situation, the paucity of the population and resources, and the egocentric nature of the Carolina cavaliers. Unfortunately, his inability to demonstrate personal warmth, coupled with unpleasant past political dealings, made Pickens unpopular. Before he entered Congress he showed himself to be a fire-eater who wanted South Carolina to remain in the Union only as long as the Union would bow to the state's will. For thirty years compromises were made, and the Palmetto State enjoyed its peculiar mode of life within the Union. But the end of compromise and the inculcation of a rebellious spirit brought forth Pickens's true nature.

In his speech "On the Influence of Government upon the Nature and Destiny of Man," he claimed that history is predestined and that any man is but a cog in the society and time in which he is born. He failed to mention that individuals do indeed affect history. Francis W. Pickens and his fellow Carolinians, through their actions and rhetoric, planted the seeds and nurtured a revolution that brought forth the fruit of national destruction. Their legacy has been captured in the saddest, yet most exciting, chapter of the nation's history.

Notes

Abbreviations

C.U.	Clemson University
D.U.L.	Duke University Library
L.C.	Library of Congress
S.C.L.	South Caroliniana Library
S.H.C.	Southern Historical Collection (at U.N.C.)
U.N.C.	University of North Carolina
U.Va.	University of Virginia
W. & L.	Washington and Lee University
M.B.C.	Mary Boykin Chesnut
J.C.C.	John Caldwell Calhoun
J.E.C.	James Edward Colhoun
F.H.E.	Franklin Harper Elmore
J.H.H.	James Henry Hammond
L.P.H.	Lucy P. Holcombe
F.W.P.	Francis Wilkinson Pickens
J.K.P.	James K. Polk
W.C.P.	William C. Preston
W.M.C.	Williams–Manning–Chesnut Papers

Chapter 1. Young Radical

1. This statement has been attributed to James Louis Petigru, a noted South Carolina Unionist.
2. Greenburg, "Representation and Isolation," pp. 723–43.
3. *Dictionary of American Biography*, s.v. "Pickens, Francis," lists his birthdate as 7 Apr. 1805; however, his obituary and his tombstone cite 1807. Youmans, *Sketch of the Life of Pickens*, pp. 1–2.
4. Waring, *Pickens: The Fighting Elder*, pp. 50–51, 108, 121, 136, 140–91.
5. Ibid., pp. 3, 189, 190, 203.
6. Hooker, "Excerpts from the Diary," pp. 901–2.
7. Youmans, *Sketch of the Life of Pickens*, pp. 5–7.
8. Waring, *Pickens: The Fighting Elder*, p. 202. Hooker, "Excerpts from the Diary," pp. 900–902. F.W.P. to William Gilmore Simms, 28 June 1844, F.W.P. (N.Y. Public Library).
9. Calhoun, *Papers*, I, 4, 431–34.
10. J.C.C. to J.E.C., 7 May 1820, in Calhoun, *Papers*, V, 95–97. Andrew Pickens

to J.C.C., 20 June 1823, ibid., pp. 126–27. F.W.P. to Benjamin F. Perry, 24 Apr. 1859, Perry Papers (Alabama Archives). U.S. Department of Interior, "National Register of Historic Places," "Description of Halcyon Grove" in National Register file, S.C. Department of Archives and History.

11. Clariosophic Society Record of Members for 1827.
12. Clariosophic Society Record of Debates for 1827.
13. Ibid., 24 Feb. 1827.
14. Malone, *Public Life of Thomas Cooper*, pp. 281–337. Speech of Thomas Cooper in *Mercury*, 27 July 1827.
15. *Mercury*, 12, 17 July 1828. Hayne, "Politics in South Carolina." For an excellent study of the southern view of states' rights, see Carpenter, *The South as a Conscious Minority*.
16. The "Crisis Letters" written by Robert Turnbull appeared in the *Mercury* on a regular basis from July to Dec. 1827.
17. *Mercury*, 12 July 1828.
18. Hollis, *South Carolina College*, pp. 90–92. *Catalog of S.C. College*, 1806–1835. *D.A.B.*, s.v. "Pickens, Francis."
19. "Anniversary Address Delivered to the Clariosophic Society, South Carolina College, 2 Feb. 1827."
20. F.W.P. to Maria Colhoun, 25 Sept. 1842, F.W.P. (S.C.L.). Lander, *Calhoun Family and Clemson*, pp. 13–14.
21. J.C.C. to J.E.C., 27 Dec. 1826, 26 Aug. 1827; in Calhoun, *Correspondence*, pp. 238–39, 247–51.
22. W. C. Preston to George Ticknor, 21 Mar. 1824, W.C.P. (S.C.L.).
23. Crawford, *History of the Fall of Fort Sumter*, p. 4.
24. Ibid.
25. *Mercury*, 17 July 1828; July–Dec. 1828 passim.
26. Edgefield *Carolinian*, 8, 20 Mar., 13 Apr. 1830; reprinted from Columbia *Southern Times*. F.W.P. to J.H.H., 8 Mar. 1830, J.H.H. (L.C.).
27. F.W.P. to J.H.H., 8 Mar. 1830, J.H.H. (L.C.).
28. F.W.P. to J.H.H., 13 Mar., 26 June, 14 July 1830, ibid. Merritt, *Hammond*, p. 16. Tucker, "Hammond," pp. 47–131. Faust, *Hammond and the Old South*, pp. 51–54. "At the same time I believe that the great body of our intelligent citizens are far ahead of our would be leaders . . . who don't want to be branded with the taint of disunion" (F.W.P. to J.H.H., 13 Mar. 1830, J.H.H. [L.C.]).
29. Hollis, *South Carolina College*, pp. 94–96.
30. Freehling, *Prelude to Civil War*, pp. 207–10.
31. Houston, *Critical Study of Nullification*, preface.
32. Wiltse, *Calhoun, Nullifier*, p. 52.
33. Ochenkowski, "Origin of Nullification," pp. 121–53.
34. F.W.P. to J.C.C., 22 Apr., 24 May 1829, in Calhoun, *Papers*, XI, 46–47.
35. F.W.P. to J.H.H., 13 May 1830, J.H.H. (L.C.). *D.A.B.*, s.v. "Pickens, Francis."
36. Merritt, *Hammond*, pp. 15–16.
37. Edgefield *Carolinian*, 20 Mar. 1830.
38. F.W.P. to J.H.H., 26 June 1830, J.H.H. (L.C.).

39. F.W.P. to J.H.H., 26 June, 14 July 1830, ibid. Columbia *Southern Times*, 1 Dec. 1830. Tucker, "Hammond," pp. 56–58.

40. Freehling, *Prelude to Civil War*, pp. 210–18. Boucher, *Nullification Controversy*, pp. 88–110, 164–207. Columbia *Southern Times*, 14 Oct., 11 Nov. 1830.

41. J.C.C. to J.H.H., 16 May 1831, in Calhoun, *Papers*, XI, 382–83. J.C.C. to F. W. Symmes, 26 July 1831, ibid., pp. 413–39. J.C.C. to F.W.P., 1 Aug. 1831, ibid., pp. 445–46. Wiltse, *Calhoun, Nullifier*, pp. 113–16.

42. J.C.C. to F.W.P., 1 Aug. 1831, in Calhoun, *Papers*, XI, 445–46.

43. Faust, *Hammond and the Old South*, pp. 49–50.

44. Wiltse, *Calhoun, Nullifier*, p. 125.

45. J.C.C. to F.W.P., 2 Mar. 1832, in Calhoun, *Papers*, XI, 358–59.

46. Ibid.

47. *Mercury*, 17, 18, 19, 20 Oct. 1832.

48. Boucher, *Nullification Controversy*, pp. 208–27.

49. *Mercury*, 16, 17, 18, 26 Oct. 1832. Election returns: Nullifiers, 24,165; Union Party, 16,664.

50. *Mercury*, 22 Nov. 1832.

51. Draft of Nullification Ordinance in F.W.P. (D.U.L.) and *Mercury*, 24, 27, 29, 30 Nov. 1832.

52. *Mercury*, 29, 30 Nov. 1832.

53. *Niles National Register*, 15 Dec. 1832, p. 261.

54. P. M. Butler to J.H.H., 18 Dec. 1832, J.H.H. (L.C.). Tucker, "Hammond," p. 131.

55. J.C.C. to F.W.P., 5 June 1834, in Calhoun, *Papers*, XI, 331–32. Boucher, *Nullification Controversy*, pp. 316–66.

56. Edgefield *Carolinian*, 6 Sept. 1832. *Mercury*, 13 Sept. 1832. Pickens's Autobiographical Sketch in Pickens-Dugas Papers (S.H.C, U.N.C). Hayne, "Politics in South Carolina: Pickens," p. 10.

57. Hayne, "Politics in South Carolina: Pickens," p. 10.

58. Proclamation of Governor Francis W. Pickens, Charleston *Daily Courier*, 23 Dec. 1860.

59. *South Carolina Senate and House Journals*, 1832, p. 29.

60. J.H.H. to Marcellus Hammond, 1832, J.H.H. (S.C.L.).

61. *Mercury*, 7 Dec. 1832. "A Bill to carry into effect in part an ordinance to nullify certain acts of Congress of the United States," in Miscellaneous South Carolina Papers (W. & L.).

62. Hayne, "Politics in South Carolina: Pickens," pp. 11–12. Youmans, *Pickens*, p. 8.

63. Freehling, *Prelude to Civil War*, pp. 267–68.

64. Pickens was commissioned on 21 Dec. 1832. "Commission of F. W. Pickens to Rank of Lt. Colonel in South Carolina Militia," document in F.W.P. (W. & L.). On back of document Pickens wrote and signed the Test Oath on 27 Dec. 1832. J.H.H. to Marcellus Hammond, 27 Mar. 1833, J.H.H. (L.C.).

65. A. P. Butler to F.W.P., 30 Dec. 1832, F.W.P. (D.U.L.).

66. Robert Y. Hayne to F.W.P., 21 Dec. 1832, "Letters on the Nullification Movement in South Carolina," pp. 752–55.

67. S. W. Bowie to F.W.P., 16 Jan. 1833, F.W.P. (D.U.L.). R. Y. Hayne to F.W.P., 21 Dec. 1832, "Letters on the Nullification Movement in S.C.," pp. 752–55.

68. R. Y. Hayne to F.W.P., 12 Feb. 1833, "Letters on the Nullification Movement in S.C.," part 2, p. 92.

69. Boucher, *Nullification Controversy*. J.H.H. to Marcellus Hammond, 27 Mar. 1833, J.H.H. (L.C.).

70. R. Y. Hayne to J.H.H., 27 Mar. 1833, J.H.H. (L.C.). Hayne to F.W.P., 12 Feb. 1833, "Letters on Nullification," part 2, pp. 97–99.

71. *Mercury*, 14 Dec. 1833. The report was given on 10 Dec. 1833. Wallace, *South Carolina: Short History*, p. 405.

72. Wallace, *South Carolina: Short History*, pp. 404–5.

73. J.C.C. to F.W.P., 20 Jan. 1834, in Calhoun, *Papers*, XI, 227–28. "McDuffie rejected as pure solecism Calhoun's contention that a state could nullify an Act of Congress by virtue of any power derived from the Constitution. He placed the right on higher ground, that a state was sovereign" (Houston, *Critical Study of Nullification*, p. 9). Pickens believed "We have a moral power under the Constitution that can give us entire redress. I believe in the sovereignty of the states in their reserved powers . . . I will go to any extreme to break down the system of unconstitutional deception" (F.W.P. to J.H.H., 13 Mar. 1830, J.H.H. [L.C.]).

74. George McDuffie to Armistead Burt, 3 May 1834, Burt Papers (D.U.L.). J.C.C. to F.W.P., 4 Jan. 1834, in Calhoun, *Papers*, XII, 196–98 *U.S. Telegraph*, 16 Dec. 1834, 17 Jan. 1835. Although everyone expected McDuffie to die, he remained very active in state politics for almost two decades.

75. J.C.C. to F.W.P., 20 Jan. 1834, in Calhoun, *Papers*, XII, 227–28. McDuffie to A. Burt, 3 May 1834, Burt Papers (D.U.L.).

76. J.C.C. to F.W.P., 4 Jan. 1834, in Calhoun, *Papers*, XII, 196–98. Whitfield Brooks was the father of Preston Brooks, of Brooks-Sumner affair fame.

77. Lander, *Calhoun Family and Clemson*, p. 4. The relationship of Pickens with Calhoun and his family is well illustrated in this work.

78. Schlesinger, *The Age of Jackson*, p. 403.

79. J.C.C. to Anna Maria Calhoun, 18 Feb. 1834, in Calhoun, *Papers*, IX, 238.

80. J.C.C. to F.W.P., 20 Jan. 1834, ibid., XII, 227–28.

81. Pendleton *Messenger*, 1 Oct. 1834.

82. Ibid., 22 Oct. 1834.

83. Wise, *Life of Wise*, p. 42.

84. *D.A.B.*, S.V. "Pickens, Francis."

Chapter 2. A Provocative Course

1. J.C.C. to F.W.P., 15 Apr. 1834, in Calhoun, *Papers*, XII, 299–300.
2. Ibid.
3. J.C.C. to F.W.P., 5 June 1834, ibid., pp. 331–32.
4. Lander, *Calhoun Family and Clemson*, p. 14. Bull, "Lucy Pickens," p. 13. U.S. Department of the Interior, National Register of Historic Places, Nomination Form, "Edgewood—The Pickens House," OMB No. 1024–0018.

5. F.W.P. to Maria Simkins, 15 Sept. 1833; F.W.P. to Eliza Pickens, 12 Feb. 1834; F.W.P. (S.C.L.).

6. Edgefield County, Records of the Clerk of Court, deed transfers in book 46, pp. 32–34, 55, 213, 507. For a study of Andrew Pickens as president of the Bank of the State of Alabama, see Brantly, *Banking in Alabama*.

7. Edgefield County, Probate Records Box, South Carolina Archives, Box 44, package 1830. Will made 9 Sept. 1836, Dallas County, Ala. Land and slaves transferred by deed to F.W.P. and Susan P. Calhoun, 28 Aug. 1836.

8. U.S. Census, 1840, Edgefield Court House, Edgefield County (South Carolina Archives). Pickens's Plantation Book, entry for 29 Apr. 1839, F.W.P. (D.U.L.).

9. Pickens's Plantation Book, 1 Jan. 1842, 23 Apr. 1847.

10. Ibid., May 1845.

11. "Account of Meat for the Year 1839" and "General Directions as to the Treatment of Negroes, 1839," ibid.

12. Ibid., passim.

13. "Resources for January 1860," F.W.P. (D.U.L.). This document shows he owed $57,768 and had resources, including notes due him, of $40,727. Pickens does not calculate the value of his land or slaves in the figure, but he does include the value of his crops. For land transfers, see deed books H.H.H., I.I.I., J.J.J., and O.O.O. Twelve transfers are noted in Edgefield County, Records of the Clerk of Court. The census for 1860 showed that Pickens owned $45,000 worth of real estate and $244,201 worth of personal estate.

14. Lander, *Calhoun Family and Clemson*, p. 14.

15. "An Address by Francis W. Pickens Before the South Carolina Agricultural Society, November 29, 1849" (S.C.L.). Pickens, "The Growth and Consumption of Cotton," *Southern Quarterly Review*, 1848, pp. 103–36.

16. Ibid.

17. Ibid.

18. Thomas, *Historical Account of the Protestant Episcopal Church*, pp. 559–61. Brooks became famous for beating Charles Sumner; L. T. Wigfall became a U.S. senator from Texas. In the Trinity Church Vestry Register, 1834–1905, there is this note written after the death of Pickens: "The death of Gov. Pickens was almost the death of the Parish."

19. F.W.P. to Maria Simkins, 21 Aug. 1834, F.W.P. (S.C.L.).

20. Lander, *Calhoun Family and Clemson*, pp. 55–56. F.W.P. to J.E.C., 5 May 1842, F.W.P. (S.C.L.).

21. F.W.P. to Maria Simkins, 15 Sept. 1833, F.W.P. (S.C.L.). Describing the "Belle," he urged her to read the following: "Well written books particularly on the taste, such as Burke on the sublime and beautiful—the nos. of Addison in the Spectator—Cicero's letters—the best novels of Scott . . . study Milton, Pope and Shakespeare. (Byron is corrupt although splendid)—read Virgil and Homer—read in History, the Bible, Rolin . . . Plutarch, Gibbon . . . Robertson's Charles 5th. Robertson's Scotland, Homer . . . Ramsay's U.S. Ramsay's South Carolina."

22. Lander, *Calhoun Family and Clemson*, pp. 14–15. F.W.P. to Maria Simkins, 28 Apr. 1839, F.W.P. (S.C.L.).

23. F.W.P. to Maria Simkins, 15 Sept. 1833, F.W.P. (S.C.L.).

24. F.W.P. to Anna Calhoun, 21 Aug. 1837, F.W.P. (L.C.).
25. F.W.P. to J.H.H., 2 Dec. 1834, J.H.H. (L.C.).
26. F.W.P. to Waddy Thompson, Mon. ——, 1834, Thompson Papers (D.U.L.).
27. J.C.C. to F.W.P., 12 Dec. 1833, in Calhoun, *Papers*, XII, 191–93.
28. Wiltse, *Calhoun, Nullifier*, pp. 209–12.
29. J.C.C. to F.W.P., 4 Jan. 1834, in Calhoun, *Papers*, XII, 196–98.
30. Wiltse, *Calhoun, Nullifier*, pp. 223–36.
31. Adams, *Diary*, IX, 202–8. *U.S. Telegraph*, 30, 31 Jan. 1835.
32. J.E.C. to F.W.P., 29 Mar. 1834, F.W.P. (S.C.L.). F.W.P. to W. T. Barry, Postmaster General of U.S., F.W.P. (D.U.L.).
33. *U.S. Telegraph*, Oct. 1834–Apr. 1835, passim. Bailey, *A Diplomatic History of the American People*, pp. 195–98. McCormick, "Louis McLane," in *American Secretaries of State and Their Diplomacy*, IV, 281–89.
34. *Mercury*, 30 Dec. 1835. *Globe*, Dec. 1834–Feb. 1835, passim.
35. Greenville *Mountaineer*, 21 Feb. 1835.
36. F.W.P. to Patrick Noble, 14 Feb. 1835, Noble Papers (S.C.L.).
37. *Debates of Congress*, XI, part 2, 24th Cong., 28 Feb. 1835, pp. 34–35.
38. Greenville *Mountaineer*, 21 Feb. 1835.
39. Wiltse, *Calhoun, Nullifier*, p. 293. *Register of Debates*, 23rd Cong., 2nd sess., pp. 730–46, 1661–63. McCormick, "Louis McLane."
40. *U.S. Telegraph*, 31 Jan., 9, 12, 28 Feb., 5 Mar. 1835. F.W.P. to P. Noble, 10 Feb. 1835, Noble Papers (S.C.L.).
41. Adams, *Diary*, pp. 231–32. *U.S. Telegraph*, 31 Jan. 1835.
42. F.W.P. to P. Noble, 10 Feb. 1835, Noble Papers (S.C.L.). *U.S. Telegraph*, 9 Feb. 1835.
43. Wiltse, *Calhoun, Nullifier*, pp. 224–46. *U.S. Telegraph*, 12, 28 Feb. 1835.
44. Taylor, *Jackson versus Biddle*, pp. 1–6.
45. George McDuffie to F.W.P., 31 Dec. 1833, F.W.P. (S.C.L.).
46. Taylor, *Jackson versus Biddle*, pp. 1–6.
47. Green, *George McDuffie*, pp. 125–38.
48. McDuffie to J.C.C., 29 Oct. 1837, in Calhoun, *Papers*, XIII, 631–35.
49. Ibid.
50. Speech of F.W.P. on "Separation of Government from All Banks," 10 Oct. 1837 (S.C.L.).
51. F.W.P. to P. Noble, 14 Feb. 1835, Noble Papers (S.C.L.).
52. Lesesne, *Bank of South Carolina*, pp. 39–41.
53. Grayson, "Autobiography," ed. Bass, Robert D., p. 193.
54. Hammond, *Banks and Politics in America*, pp. 487–99.
55. Ibid.
56. Wiltse, *Calhoun, Nullifier*, pp. 344–45.
57. F.W.P. to J.H.H., 9 Oct., 19 Nov. 1835, J.H.H. (L.C.).
58. J.C.C. to Anna Calhoun, 8 Sept. 1837, in Calhoun, *Papers*, XIII, 536–38. Merritt, *Hammond*, pp. 40–42.
59. John P. Richardson to F.W.P., 8 Sept. 1835, F.W.P. (S.C.L.).
60. F.W.P. to J.H.H., 1 Aug. 1835; J.H.H. to Marcellus Hammond, 2 Apr. 1836; J.C.C. to J.H.H., 20 June 1836; all in J.H.H. (L.C.). J.C.C. to F.W.P., 17 Aug.

Notes to Pages 31–35

1836, 17 July 1835, 19 May 1835, in Calhoun, *Papers*, XIII, 278–80, 243–45; XII, 534–36, 542–44. J.C.C. to J.H.H., 19 June 1836, J.H.H. (L.C.). Grayson, "Autobiography," p. 193.

61. F.W.P. to J.H.H., 6 Aug. 1836, J.H.H. (L.C.). F.W.P. to R. Crallé, 18 June 1837, F.W.P. (D.U.L.).

62. F.W.P. to R. Crallé, 18 June 1837, F.W.P. (D.U.L.).

63. F.W.P. to R. Crallé, 18, 28 June 1837, F.W.P. (D.U.L.). Schlesinger, *Age of Jackson*, p. 244.

64. Lynch, *An Epoch and Man*, pp. 442–45.

65. F.W.P. to R. Crallé, 28 June 1837, F.W.P. (D.U.L.).

66. *Congressional Globe*, 25th Cong., 1, V, 29 Sept. 1837, p. 173. Speech of Hon. F. W. Pickens to "Divorce Government from All Banks," 10 Oct. 1837. Adams, *Diary*, IX, 397. F.W.P. to Maria Simkins, 16 Dec. 1837, F.W.P. (S.C.L.). James L. Petigru to Waddy Thompson, 12 Oct. 1838, Thompson Papers (S.C.L.).

67. F.W.P. to Crallé, 18, 28, 30 June 1837, F.W.P. (D.U.L.).

68. F.W.P. to Crallé, 28 June 1837, ibid.

69. *Merchant*, 12 Sept. 1837.

70. *Reformer*, 14 Sept. 1837.

71. *Merchant*, 22 Sept. 1837.

72. Ibid., 7, 8, 9 Sept. 1837. *Globe*, 7 Sept. 1837.

73. Adams, *Diary*, IX, 398. Youmans, *Sketch of the Life of Pickens*, p. 9. Wiltse, *Calhoun, Nullifier*, p. 356. F.W.P. to B. F. Perry, 24 Apr. 1859, Perry Papers (Alabama Archives). Pickens's Autobiographical Sketch, MS fragment, Pickens-Dugas Papers (S.H.C., U.N.C.).

74. *Globe*, 30 Sept. 1837.

75. Ibid., 10, 12, 18 Oct. 1837.

76. Ibid., 28, 29, 30 Sept., 1, 10, 12 Oct. 1837. F.W.P. to Ogden Niles, 7 Oct. 1837, F.W.P. (D.U.L.).

77. *Globe*, 6, 17 Oct. 1837.

78. Wiltse, *Calhoun, Nullifier*, pp. 352–57. F.W.P. to Anna Calhoun, 15 Feb. 1838, F.W.P. (S.C.L.).

79. J.C.C. to J.E.C., 7 Sept. 1837, F.W.P. (S.C.L.).

80. Dr. Francis Mallory to R. M. T. Hunter, 12 Jan. 1840, in Hunter, *Correspondence*, II, 31–33.

81. J.C.C. to Anna Maria Calhoun, 8 Sept. 1837, in Calhoun, *Papers*, XIII, 537–38.

82. J. L. Petigru to Mrs. Jane Petigru North, 17 Sept. 1837, in Petigru, *Life, Letters and Speeches of Petigru*, pp. 190–91. Coit, *Calhoun*, pp. 336–37. Robert Barnwell Smith changed his name to Rhett.

83. Lander, "Calhoun-Preston Feud," pp. 24–25.

84. Ibid., pp. 26–28.

85. W.C.P. to Thompson, Sat. 4 ———, 1837, Thompson Papers (S.C.L.). *Globe*, 6, 17 Oct. 1837.

86. F.W.P. to B. F. Perry, 24 Apr. 1859, Perry Papers (Alabama Archives.).

87. Adams, *Diary*, IX, 398. F.W.P. to Crallé, 18, 28 June 1837. *Congressional Globe*, 25th Cong., part 1, V, 2 Oct. 1837, pp. 92–95.

88. Adams, *Diary*, IX, 398–99. Merritt, *Hammond*, p. 45. Wiltse, *Calhoun, Nullifier*, p. 356.
89. Diary of Louise Penelope Davis Preston, W.C.P. (S.C.L.).
90. Lander, "Calhoun-Preston Feud." Wiltse, *Calhoun, Nullifier*, pp. 359–61. W.C.P. to Waddy Thompson, Sat. 4 _____, 1837, Thompson Papers (S.C.L.).
91. F.W.P. to R. Crallé, 5, 18, 28 June 1837, Pickens Papers (D.U.L.).
92. *Mercury*, 11, 12 Sept. 1837. On 20 Sept. the *Mercury* admitted that Calhoun had sided with the president and changed its course accordingly.
93. Lander, "Calhoun-Preston Feud," p. 27n. Charleston *Mercury*, Sept., Oct., Nov. 1837, passim.
94. George McDuffie to Waddy Thompson, 2 Oct. 1837, Thompson Papers (S.C.L.).
95. W.C.P. to Waddy Thompson, Sat. 4 _____, 1837, ibid.
96. Ibid. The *Reformer* was the successor to the *U.S. Telegraph*.
97. F.H.E. to F.W.P., Mar. 1839, F.W.P. (D.U.L.).
98. Lander, "Calhoun-Preston Feud," pp. 24–37.
99. Ibid., p. 29. W.C.P. to Thompson, n.d. [1837], Thompson Papers (S.C.L.).
100. *Globe*, 16, 18, 20 Dec. 1837.
101. F.W.P. to Patrick Noble, 30 June 1838, Noble Papers (S.C.L.).
102. W.C.P. to Thompson, Sat. 4 _____, 1837, Thompson Papers (S.C.L.).
103. F.W.P. to J.H.H., 15 Jan. 1838, J.H.H. (L.C.).
104. Hammond Diary, "Heidelburg," 1837, ibid.
105. F.W.P. to J.H.H., 15 Jan. 1838, ibid.
106. Hammond Diary, "Heidelburg," 1837, ibid.
107. F.W.P. to J.H.H., 9 Feb. 1838, ibid. White, *Rhett*, pp. 41–42.
108. F.W.P. to J.H.H., 9 Feb. 1838, J.H.H. (L.C.).
109. F.W.P. to Patrick Noble, 23 May 1838, Noble Papers (S.C.L.).
110. F.W.P. to J.H.H., 9 Feb. 1838, J.H.H. (L.C.). F.W.P. to P. Noble, 22 May, 30 June 1838, Noble Papers (S.C.L.). White, *Rhett*, p. 35.
111. Diary of Mrs. W. C. P., Fri. _____, 1838, W.C.P. (S.C.L.). For the next three years the *Globe* would be very attentive to Pickens.
112. Adams, *Diary*, IX, 396.
113. Diary of Mrs. W. C. P., Fri. _____, 1838, W.C.P. (S.C.L.).
114. F.W.P. to P. Noble, 22, 23 May 1838, Noble Papers (S.C.L.).
115. Ibid. F.W.P. to J.H.H., 9 Feb. 1838, J.H.H. (L.C.).
116. F.W.P. to Noble, 22 May 1838, Noble Papers (S.C.L.).
117. *Congressional Globe*, 25th Cong., 2nd sess., VII, 19 June 1838, p. 428.
118. F.W.P. to Noble, 30 June 1838, Noble Papers (S.C.L.). H. S. Legaré to Alfred Huger, 23 Sept. 1838, Legaré Papers (S.C.L.). *Congressional Globe*, 25th Cong., 2nd sess., VII, 19 June 1838, p. 428.
119. H. S. Legaré to Waddy Thompson, 13 Aug. 1838, Legaré Papers (S.C.L.). F.W.P. to Noble, 30 June 1838, Noble Papers (S.C.L.). Wiltse, *Calhoun, Nullifier*, p. 478.
120. *Congressional Globe*, 26th Cong., 2nd sess., VIII, 30 June 1840, p. 495.
121. Hammond, *Banks and Politics*, pp. 517–18.

122. F.W.P. to J.C.C., 13 Dec. 1841, in Calhoun, *Correspondence*, pp. 1100–1101. Lander, "Calhoun-Preston Feud," pp. 35–37.
123. "Hampden," Edgefield *Carolinian*, 6 Mar. 1830.
124. McDuffie to F.W.P., 31 Dec. 1833, F.W.P. (S.C.L.). J.C.C. to F.W.P., 4 Jan., 15 Apr. 1834, in Calhoun, *Papers*, XII, 196–98, 299–300.
125. J.C.C. to F.W.P., 15 Apr. 1834, in Calhoun, *Papers*, XII, 195–98.
126. J.C.C. to F.W.P., 19 May 1835, ibid., pp. 534–36.
127. Wise, *Life of Wise*, pp. 46–48.
128. Merritt, *Hammond*, pp. 34–36. Youmans, *Sketch of the Life of Pickens*, p. 9.
129. "Speech of Mr. Pickens of South Carolina in House of Representatives, 21 Jan. 1836, on the Abolition Question" and *Register of Debates in Congress*, 24th Cong., 1st sess., XII, pp. 1985–86, 2239–53.
130. Ibid. Youmans, *Sketch of the Life of Pickens*, p. 10. James H. Hammond showed very early in his career "envy and jealousy" of his supposed best friend when he wrote his brother, "I am glad you are gratified with my speech which is said by our friends . . . to be the best on the subject. I don't think that is extravagant praise, for neither [illegible] Mr. Pickens are to my mind any thing great" (J.H.H. to Marcellus Hammond, 20 Feb. 1836, J.H.H. [L.C.]).
131. *Congressional Globe*, 24th Cong., 1st sess., 1836, pp. 285–89.
132. Adams, *Diary*, IX, 387–89.
133. Ibid., p. 399.
134. Ibid., p. 406.
135. *Niles Weekly Register*, 31 Dec. 1835.
136. *Globe*, 18 Sept. 1837. *Register of Debates*, 24th Cong., 1st sess., pp. 2482–83. Wiltse, *Calhoun, Nullifier*, pp. 283–84.
137. Craven, *Coming of the Civil War*, p. 176.
138. Wiltse, *Calhoun, Nullifier*, p. 284. J.H.H. to Marcellus Hammond, 20 Feb. 1836, J.H.H. (S.C.L.).
139. Wiltse, *Calhoun, Nullifier*, pp. 283–89.
140. F.W.P. to P. Noble, 7 Mar. 1836, Noble Papers (S.C.L.).
141. Edgefield *Advertiser*, 24 Feb. 1836. James Hamilton to J.H.H., 10 Feb. 1836, J.H.H. (L.C.).
142. J. L. Petigru to H. S. Legaré, 31 May 1835, Legaré Papers (S.C.L.).
143. H. S. Legaré to Waddy Thompson, 13 Aug. 1838, ibid. F.W.P. to P. Noble, 30 June 1838, Noble Papers (S.C.L.). Wiltse, *Calhoun, Nullifier*, p. 478.
144. Adams, *Diary*, p. 283.
145. Wiltse, *Calhoun, Nullifier*, p. 286.
146. *U.S. Telegraph*, 2, 20, 28 July 1836.
147. *Globe*, 9, 18 Sept. 1837.
148. "Speech of Mr. Pickens of South Carolina on the Fortification Bill," 23 May 1836.
149. *Congressional Globe*, 24th Cong., 1st sess., 21 Feb. 1836, p. 240.
150. J.C.C. to B. M. Blocker, D. Holland, W. Ballman, J. C. Allen, and J. Goumillion, Edgefield *Advertiser*, 29 Sept. 1836. Refusing an invitation to attend a din-

ner honoring Pickens, Louis T. Wigfall commented on a similiar affair: "You recall that I mentioned we were to have a 'great barbeque' the 15th of this month in honour of the Hon. F. W. Pickens. The above mentioned affair transpires next Thursday. In addition to seeing fifteen hundred of the sovereign people devour meat enough to kill five thousand hungry dragoons—In addition to the pleasure Col. P's speech will offer you (if you survive it) which will not be less than two hours long . . . you will have the pleasure of seeing . . . the Belle of Augusta" (L. T. Wigfall to Langdon Cheves, Jr., 12 Sept. 1836, Cheves Papers [S.C.L.]).

151. J.C.C. to J.H.H., 19 June 1836, J.H.H. (L.C.). J.C.C. to F.W.P., 17 July 1836, in Calhoun, *Papers*, XIII, 259–60, 54n.

152. Calhoun, *Papers*, XIII, xxii. F.W.P. to J.H.H., 17 June 1836, J.H.H. (L.C.). J.C.C. to F.W.P., 17 Aug. 1836, in Calhoun, *Papers*, XIII, 278–79.

153. J.C.C. to F.W.P., 17 Aug. 1836, in Calhoun, *Papers*, XIII, 259–60.

154. J.H.H. to Marcellus Hammond, 20 Oct. 1836, J.H.H. (L.C.).

155. Lander, *Calhoun Family and Clemson*, p. 14. White, *Rhett*, p. 37.

156. H. S. Legaré to Mary S. Legaré, 14 Dec. 1837, Legaré Papers (S.C.L.).

157. White, *Rhett*, p. 37.

158. Ibid. *Niles Weekly Register*, 26 Dec. 1837.

159. White, *Rhett*, p. 37.

160. J.C.C. to Anna Maria Calhoun, 8 Sept. 1837, in Calhoun, *Papers*, XIII, 536–37.

161. J.C.C. to Nathan Loughborough, 16 Jan. 1837, in Calhoun, *Papers*, XIII, 363–64.

162. F.W.P. to Maria Colhoun, 18 Oct. 1839, F.W.P. (S.C.L.). P. M. Butler to J.H.H., 16 June 1838; Hammond Diary, 27 June 1839; both in J.H.H. (L.C.).

Chapter 3. A Vile Association

1. David Hubbard to J.K.P., 23 Oct. 1839; Cave Johnson to J.K.P., 10 Nov. 1839; Harvey M. Watterson to J.K.P., 29 Nov. 1839; all in Polk, *Correspondence*, V. W. B. Campbell to Gov. David Campbell of Virginia, 2 Dec. 1839, Campbell Papers (D.U.L.). George Fitzhugh to R. M. T. Hunter, 15 Dec. 1839, in Hunter Papers (U.Va.). F.W.P. to J.H.H., 15 Dec. 1839, J.H.H. (L.C.).

2. *Globe*, 30 Nov. 1839. New York *Sun*, reprinted in *Globe*, 4 Dec. 1839. Aaron V. Brown to J.K.P., 7 Dec. 1839; Harvey M. Watterson to J.K.P., 29 Nov. 1839; both in Polk, *Correspondence*, V. George Fitzhugh to R. M. T. Hunter, 15 Dec. 1839, in Hunter, *Correspondence*, p. 30. J.C.C. to Anna M. Clemson, 18 Dec. 1839, J.C.C. (C.U.).

3. David Hubbard to J.K.P., 23 Oct. 1839; Harvey M. Watterson to J.K.P., 29 Nov. 1839; both in Polk, *Correspondence*, V. J.C.C. to Anna M. Clemson, 18 Dec. 1839, J.C.C. (C.U.).

4. R. M. T. Hunter to Mrs. R. M. T. Hunter, 8 Dec. 1839, Hunter Papers (U.Va.).

5. R. M. T. Hunter to Mrs. R. M. T. Hunter, 23 May 1839, ibid. F.W.P. to J.E.C., 7 Sept., 2, 23 Oct. 1839, F.W.P. (S.C.L.). Maria Colhoun to J.E.C., 4 Oct. 1839, J.E.C. Papers (S.C.L.). Lander, *Calhoun Family and Clemson*, p. 21.

6. Pickens's Plantation Journal, 22 Apr. 1839. F.W.P. to Lewis Sims, 22 Oct. 1839, F.W.P. (D.U.L.). J.E.C. to J.C.C., 3 May 1838, in Calhoun, *Papers*, XIV, 287. Lander, *Calhoun Family and Clemson*, pp. 14–15.

7. F.W.P. to J.E.C., 23 Oct. 1839, F.W.P. (S.C.L.).

8. F.W.P. to F.H.E., 18 Jan. 1840, F.W.P. (W. & L.). M. L. Bonham to F.W.P., 8 March 1840, F.W.P. (D.U.L.). Lander, *Calhoun Family and Clemson*, pp. 20–21.

9. F.W.P. to F.H.E., 18 Jan. 1840, F.W.P. (W. & L.).

10. Ibid.

11. *Globe*, 2, 3, 4, 5, 6, 7, 10, 11, 13, 20 Dec. 1839. Speech of Mr. Bayard, 8 Jan., 24 Feb 1840. Speech of F.W.P. in *Globe*, 11 Mar. 1840. *Congressional Globe*, Appendix, 26th Cong., 1st sess., pp. 217–19. J.C.C. to Orestes A. Bronson, 30 Dec. 1839, in Calhoun, *Papers*, XV, 24–25.

12. *Globe*, 11, 13 May 1840. Speech of Mr. Bell in *Globe*, 3 Mar. 1840.

13. J.C.C. to Anna M. Clemson, 18 Dec. 1839, J.C.C. (C.U.). Lander, *Calhoun Family and Clemson*, p. 21.

14. Aaron Brown to J.K.P., 7 Dec. 1839, in Polk, *Correspondence*, V.

15. R. M. T. Hunter to Mrs. R. M. T. Hunter, 3 Dec. 1939, Hunter Papers (U.Va.). Cave Johnson to J.K.P., 16 Dec. 1839, in Polk, *Correspondence*, V.

16. F.W.P. to F.H.E., 18 Jan. 1840, F.W.P. (W. & L.). Sampson Hale Butler to J.H.H., 30 Dec. 1839, J.H.H. (L.C.). *Congressional Globe*, 26th Cong., 1st sess., VIII, 53–56. W. B. Campbell to Gov. David Campbell of Virginia, 17 Dec. 1839, Campbell Papers (D.U.L.). J.C.C. to Anna M. Clemson, 18 Dec. 1839, J.C.C. (C.U.). Hammond Diary, 22 Dec. 1839, J.H.H. (S.C.L.).

17. *Congressional Globe*, 26th Cong., 1st sess., VIII, 43–47. Wiltse, *Calhoun, Nullifier*, pp. 405–7. R. M. T. Hunter to Mrs. R. M. T. Hunter, 7 Dec. 1839, Hunter Papers (U.Va.). W. B. Campbell to Gov. David Campbell, 17 Dec. 1839, Campbell Papers (D.U.L.).

18. J.H.H. to F.W.P., 27 Dec. 1839, F.W.P. (D.U.L.). F.H.E. to F.W.P., 3 Jan. 1840, Elmore Papers (L.C.). F.W.P. to F.H.E., 18 Jan. 1840, F.W.P. (W.& L.).

19. J.C.C. to Orestes A. Brownson, 30 Dec. 1839, in Calhoun, *Papers*, XV, 24–25. Hammond Diary, 6 Mar. 1840, J.H.H. (S.C.L.). Wiltse, *Calhoun, Nullifier*, pp. 51–52. F.W.P. to J.H.H., 18 June 1839, J.H.H. (L.C.).

20. F.H.E. to F.W.P., 3 Jan. 1840, Elmore Papers (L.C.). F.W.P. to F.H.E., 18 Jan. 1840, F.W.P. (W. & L.). Hammond Diary, 24 Dec. 1839, 6 Mar. 1840, J.H.H. (S.C.L.). F.W.P. to J.H.H., 18 June 1839, ibid. Wiltse, *Calhoun, Nullifier*, pp. 51–55. Merritt, *Hammond*, pp. 46–47. White, *Rhett*, pp. 41–42, 52.

21. F.W.P. to J.H.H., 15 Dec. 1839, J.H.H. (L.C.). J. P. Carroll to F.W.P., 8 Mar. 1840, F.W.P. (D.U.L.). Louis Wigfall to John L. Manning, 29 Jan. 1840, W.M.C. (S.C.L.).

22. F.W.P. to F.H.E., 3, 18 Jan., 6 Mar., 24 May 1840, Elmore Papers (L.C.).

23. James P. Carroll to F.W.P., 8 Mar. 1840, F.W.P. (D.U.L.). Louis Wigfall to John L. Manning, 29 Jan., 10 Mar. 1840, W.M.C. (S.C.L.). King, *Wigfall*, pp. 30–37.

24. Hammond Diary, 1839, J.H.H. (L.C.).

25. John P. Richardson to James Chesnut, 11 May 1840, W.M.C. (S.C.L.).

26. Hammond Diary, 27 June, 27 Aug. 1834, J.H.H. (L.C.).

27. Ibid., 17 Aug. 1839.

28. Ibid.
29. Ibid. Louis T. Wigfall to John L. Manning, 10 March 1840, W.M.C. (S.C.L.).
30. Hammond Diary, 20 Aug. 1839, J.H.H. (L.C.).
31. Wiltse, *Calhoun, Sectionalist*, pp. 51–55.
32. Ibid.
33. T. Player to J.H.H., 1 Jan. 1840, J.H.H. (L.C.).
34. Hammond Diary, 6 Jan. 1840, 7 Feb. 1841, J.H.H. (L.C.). In the latter entry Hammond recounts the entire race.
35. J.H.H. to F.W.P., Jan. 1840, F.W.P. (D.U.L.). Hammond Diary, 6 Mar. 1840, J.H.H. (S.C.L.).
36. Charleston *Mercury*, 10 Jan. 1840. J.H.H. to F.W.P., 18 Jan. 1840, F.W.P. (D.U.L.). Hammond Diary, 18 Jan. 1840, J.H.H. (S.C.L.).
37. Louis T. Wigfall to John L. Manning, 17 Feb. 1840, W.M.C. (S.C.L.). R. D. Louree to John L. Manning, 16 Feb. 1840, ibid. Merritt, *Hammond*, p. 48. F.W.P. to J.H.H., 1 Feb. 1840, J.H.H. (L.C.). Edgefield *Advertiser*, Jan.–Mar. 1840 passim.
38. F.W.P. to J.H.H., 22 Jan. 1840, J.H.H. (L.C.). J.H.H. to F.W.P., 18 Jan. 1840, F.W.P. (D.U.L.). Hammond Diary, 18 Jan., 7 Feb. 1840, J.H.H. (S.C.L.).
39. F.W.P. to J.H.H., 4 Mar. 1840, J.H.H. (L.C.). Louis T. Wigfall to J. L. Manning, 29 Jan. 1840, W.M.C. (S.C.L.).
40. F.W.P. to J.H.H., 4, 9 Mar. 1840; J.C.C. to J.H.H., 12 Jan. 1840; J.H.H. (L.C.). Wiltse, *Calhoun, Sectionalist*, p. 54.
41. J.C.C. to J.H.H., 23 Feb. 1840, in Calhoun, *Correspondence*, pp. 448–50.
42. F.W.P. to J.H.H., 28 May 1840; Sampson H. Butler to J.H.H., 29 May 1840; J.H.H. (L.C.).
43. F.W.P. to J.H.H., 9 March 1840, ibid.
44. Hammond Diary, n.d., 1840, ibid.
45. Wallace, *South Carolina: Short History*, p.423. P. M. Butler to J.H.H., 8 July 1840, J.H.H. (L.C.).
46. Wallace, *South Carolina: Short History*, p. 423.
47. Edgefield *Advertiser*, 26 Mar. 1840. Reprint from *Mercury*.
48. Hammond Diary, 6, 18 Mar. 1840, J.H.H. (L.C.). White, *Rhett*, p. 56. Wiltse, *Calhoun, Sectionalist*, pp. 50–59.
49. F.W.P. to J.H.H., 12 Jan., 23 Feb. 1840, J.H.H. (L.C.).
50. Merritt, *Hammond*, pp. 55–58. White, *Rhett*, p. 57.
51. Wiltse, *Calhoun, Sectionalist*, p. 100. White, *Rhett*, p. 57.
52. W.C.P. to Waddy Thompson, 17 Dec. 1842, W.C.P. (S.C.L.).
53. Hammond Diary, 19 Dec. 1842, J.H.H. (L.C.). The vote was 83–76. Wiltse, *Calhoun, Sectionalist*, pp. 100–102.
54. Hammond Diary, 19 Dec. 1842, J.H.H. (L.C.). Albert Rhett to Armistead Burt, 23 Dec. 1842, Armistead Burt Papers (D.U.L.).
55. Hammond Diary, 19 Dec. 1842, J.H.H. (L.C.).
56. J.C.C. to Orestes A. Brownson, 30 Dec. 1839, in Calhoun, *Papers*, XV, 24–25.
57. J.C.C. to Duff Green, 17 Jan. 1840, in Calhoun, *Correspondence*, pp. 438–40.
58. Washington *Madisonian*, 11 Jan. 1840.

59. Duff Green to J.C.C., 17 Jan. 1840; Green to F.W.P., 14 Jan. 1840; J.C.C. to Green, 17 Jan. 1840; all in Calhoun, *Papers*, XV, 50–57. *Congressional Globe*, 26th Cong., 1st sess., 13 Jan. 1840.

60. J. P. Richardson to James Chesnut, 16 May 1842, W.M.C. (S.C.L.).

61. F.W.P. to J.H.H., 10 July 1840, J.H.H. (L.C.). Pendleton *Messenger*, 2 Oct. 1840. Edgefield *Advertiser*, 5 Nov. 1840. J.C.C. to Andrew Pickens Calhoun, 5 Aug. 1840, in Calhoun, *Papers*, XV, 322–23.

62. F.W.P. to Edgefield *Advertiser*, 24, 30 June 1840.

63. Pendleton *Messenger*, 2 Oct. 1840. Waddy Thompson to F.W.P., 3 Oct. 1840, F.W.P. (D.U.L.).

64. F.W.P. to W. Thompson, 10 Oct. 1840, F.W.P. (S.C.L.). F.W.P. to W. Thompson, 12 Oct. 1840, F.W.P. (D.U.L.).

65. W. Thompson to F.W.P., 3 Oct. 1840, F.W.P. (D.U.L.). Pendleton *Messenger*, 2 Oct. 1840.

66. W. Thompson to F.W.P., 1840. Drafts of Pickens's letters to Thompson are in the Duke and W. & L. libraries.

67. Pendleton *Messenger*, 23 Oct. 1840, and a broadside published by the *Highland Sentennial*, F.W.P. (D.U.L.).

68. Hammond Diary, 13 Mar. 1841, J.H.H. (L.C.). F.W.P. to J.H.H., 16 Jan., 3 Mar. 1841, ibid. F.W.P. to J.H.H., 28 Feb., 13, 24 Apr. 1841, F.W.P. (S.C.L.). F.W.P. to F.H.E., 6 Mar. 1840, F.H.E. (L.C.).

69. Calhoun, *Papers*, XV, 52n. *Madisonian*, 3 Jan. 1840.

70. *Globe*, 13, 24 Feb. 1840.

71. Ibid., 26, 28 Feb., 11, 13 March 1840.

72. Reeves, *American Diplomacy under Tyler and Polk*, pp. 1–27.

73. F.W.P., "Remarks on the Maine Boundary Question."

74. F.W.P. to J. K. Paulding, 20 Mar. 1840, F.W.P. (S.C.L.). Edgefield *Advertiser*, 26 Mar. 1840.

75. Reeves, *American Diplomacy under Tyler and Polk*, pp. 17–19.

76. London *Times*, 9 Mar. 1840, and Committee on Foreign Affairs Report No. 162, 26th Cong., 2nd sess., 13 Feb. 1841, on the Burning of the Steamboat *Caroline* and the Imprisonment of McLeod. James Alexander Hamilton to Daniel Webster, 22 Feb. 1841, in Webster, *Papers*, V, 92.

77. Adams, *Diary*, X, 432. Pickens's Autobiographical Sketch, MS fragment, Pickens-Dugas Papers (S.H.C., U.N.C.). Corey, *Crisis of 1830–1842*, pp. 130–45. Bonham, "Alexander McLeod: Bone of Contention."

78. Andrew Stevenson, quoted from Corey, *Crisis of 1830–1842*, p. 138. U.S. Minister to Great Britian to John Forsythe, Secretary of State, 9 Feb. 1841, in Manning, ed., *Diplomatic Correspondence of the United States*, pp. 611–12. New York *Journal of Commerce*, 7 Apr. 1841. London *Times*, 16 Feb., 5 Mar. 1841.

79. *Globe*, 20, 23, 27 Feb., 20 Mar. 1841.

80. Cory, *Crisis of 1830–1842*, pp. 131–32.

81. DeConde, *History of American Foreign Policy*, pp. 153–55.

82. Pickens's Autobiographical Sketch, MS fragment, Pickens-Dugas Papers (S.H.C., U.N.C.). F.W.P. to Martin Van Buren, 9 Feb. 1842, Van Buren Papers (L.C.).

83. "Resolutions of the South Carolina House of Representatives, 19 Dec. 1840," *Globe*, 2 Jan. 1841.

84. *Globe*, 5 Apr. 1841.

85. F.W.P. to J.H.H., 8, 9 Feb., 18 June 1839, J.H.H. (L.C.). F.W.P. to J.E.C., 2 Feb. 1840, F.W.P. (S.C.L.).

86. F.W.P. to J.H.H., 13 Apr. 1841, J.H.H. (L.C.).

87. Ibid.

88. F.W.P. to J.H.H., 13 Apr. 1841, ibid. Wiltse, *Calhoun, Sectionalist*, p. 38. J.C.C. to George F. Townes, 3 Jan. 1841, Townes Papers (S.C.L.). Van Deusen, *Jacksonian Era*, pp. 153–58.

89. Speech of F.W.P. on "Bill to Distribute the Proceeds of the Public Land amongst the States," 2 July 1842, *Congressional Globe*, 27th Cong., 1st sess., p. 171. Wiltse, *Calhoun, Sectionalist*, pp. 39–41.

90. Wiltse, *Calhoun, Sectionalist*, pp. 39–41.

91. Speeches of F.W.P. on the Loan Bill, 8 July 1841, 27th Cong., 1st sess., *Congressional Globe*, Appendix, p. 107. Bill to repeal the Independent Treasury and the Creation of a United States Bank, 9 Aug. 1842, ibid., pp. 248, 267.

92. Ibid., p. 267.

93. Ibid., p. 257.

94. Wiltse, *Calhoun, Sectionalist*, pp. 39–47.

95. F.W.P. to J.C.C., 2, 7, 12 Oct. 1841, in Calhoun, *Papers*, XV, 780–82, 784, 789–90.

96. F.W.P. to J.C.C., 12 Oct. 1841, ibid., pp. 789–90.

97. F.W.P. to Maria Colhoun, 10 Apr. 1842, F.W.P. (S.C.L.).

98. F.W.P. to J.C.C., 23 Dec. 1841, J.C.C. (C.U.). F.W.P. to J.E.C., 14 Mar. 1842, F.W.P. (S.C.L.).

99. F.W.P. to J.C.C., 7 Oct. 1842, in Calhoun, *Papers*, XV, 782.

100. F.W.P. to Van Buren, 9 Feb. 1842, Van Buren Papers (L.C.).

101. F.W.P. to Levi Woodbury, 17 Oct. 1841, portion of letter in Wiltse, *Calhoun, Nullifier*, p. 90. F.W.P. to J.C.C., 7, 18 Oct. 1841, in Calhoun, *Papers*, XV, 783–84, 795–96.

102. F.W.P. to J.E.C., 30 Jan. 1842; F.W.P. to George McDuffie, 12 Mar. 1842; both in F.W.P. (S.C.L.).

103. F.W.P. to Samuel Ingham, 18 June 1842, F.W.P. (S.C.L.).

104. F.W.P. to Maria Colhoun, 10 Apr. 1842, ibid.

105. Theodore G. Weld to Angelina G. Weld, 6 Feb. 1842, in *Letters of Theodore G. Weld, Angelina Grimké Weld, and Sara Grimké*, II, 910–11. F.W.P. to J.E.C., 20 Jan., 14 Mar. 1842, F.W.P. (S.C.L.). F.W.P. to George McDuffie, 12 Mar. 1842, ibid.

106. Reeves, *American Diplomacy under Tyler and Polk*, pp. 91–113. F.W.P. to J.E.C., 30 Jan., 14 Mar. 1842, F.W.P. (S.C.L.).

107. F.W.P. to J.E.C., 30 Jan. 1842, F.W.P. (S.C.L.).

108. Ibid. F.W.P. to McDuffie, 12 Mar. 1842, ibid. Joseph A. Scoville to R. M. T. Hunter, 11 Sept. 1842, in Hunter, *Correspondence*, pp. 41–48. Dixon H. Lewis to Richard K. Crallé, 10 June 1842, in "Calhoun as Seen by His Political Friends," ed. Moore, F. W., pp. 358–60. F.W.P. to J.C.C., 19 June, 19 July 1843, J.C.C. (S.C.L.). F.W.P. to J.C.C., 4 Sept. 1843, J.C.C. (C.U.).

109. F.W.P. to McDuffie, 12 Mar. 1842, F.W.P. (S.C.L.). Wiltse, *Calhoun, Sectionalist*, pp. 80–88.
110. F.W.P. to J.E.C., 30 Jan., 14 Mar. 1842; F.W.P. to Maria Colhoun, 10 Apr. 1842; F.W.P. to McDuffie, 12 Mar. 1842; all in F.W.P. (S.C.L.). Wiltse, *Calhoun, Sectionalist*, pp. 80–88.
111. F.W.P. to J.C.C., 8 Nov. 1842; F.H.E. to J.C.C., 30 May 1842; in Calhoun, *Papers*, XVI, 534–36, 263–65. F.W.P. to McDuffie, 12 Mar. 1842, F.W.P. (S.C.L.). F.W.P. to J.H.H., 1 Dec. 1842, J.H.H. (L.C.). William Gillmore Simms to J.H.H., 30 Dec. 1842, ibid.
112. Edgefield *Advertiser*, 6, 20 July 1842.
113. J.C.C. to J.E.C., 18 Aug. 1842, in Calhoun, *Papers*, XVI, 392–93. F.W.P. to Maria Colhoun, 25 Sept. 1842, F.W.P. (S.C.L.). Anna Calhoun Clemson to Patrick Calhoun, 29 Sept. 1842, J.C.C. (S.C.L.). W. C. Preston to Waddy Thompson, 29 Aug. 1842, W.C.P. (S.C.L.). Lander, *Calhoun Family and Clemson*, p. 53.
114. F.W.P. to J.E.C., 12 Jan. 1843, F.W.P. (S.C.L.).
115. Anna C. Clemson to Patrick Calhoun, 3 Dec. 1842, J.C.C. (C.U.).
116. F.W.P. to J.C.C., 22 Apr. 1844, ibid.
117. F.W.P. to J.E.C., 18 Oct. 1843, F.W.P. (S.C.L.).
118. Pickens's Autobiographical Sketch, MS fragment, Pickens-Dugas Papers (S.H.C., U.N.C.).
119. F.W.P. to J.E.C., 6 May 1842, F.W.P. (S.C.L.). Lander, *Calhoun Family and Clemson*, pp. 36–37. J.C.C. to J.H.H., 23 Jan. 1843, in Calhoun, *Correspondence*, pp. 522–23.
120. F.W.P. to J.C.C., 15 Nov. 1842, in Calhoun, *Papers*, XVI, 548–49. F.W.P. to H. W. Conner, 26 Apr., 29 May 1843, Conner Papers (Charleston Library Society).

Chapter 4. Harbinger of Doom

1. F.W.P. to J.C.C., 8 Nov. 1842, in Calhoun, *Papers*, XVI, 534–35, 862–64.
2. Ibid. F.W.P. to J.C.C., 24 June 1843; F.W.P. to Samuel Ingham, 18 June 1842; F.H.E. to J.C.C., 30 May 1842; F.H.E. to J.C.C., 4 Sept. 1843; F.W.P. to J.C.C., 29 June 1843; F.W.P. to J.C.C., 24 June, 19 July 1843; all in J.C.C. (C.U.).
3. F.W.P. to J.C.C., 19 July 1843, ibid.
4. F.W.P. to J.C.C., 8 Nov. 1842, in Calhoun, *Papers*, XVI, pp. 862–64. F.W.P. to J.C.C., 19 July 1843, J.C.C. (C.U.).
5. F.W.P. to J.C.C., 8 Nov. 1842, in Calhoun, *Papers*, XVI, pp. 862–64.
6. Ibid.
7. F.W.P. to J.C.C., 15 Nov. 1842, J.C.C. (C.U.).
8. F.W.P. to J.C.C., 19 July, 1843, ibid.
9. F.W.P. to J.C.C., 19 July, 22 Oct. 1843, ibid. Wiltse, *Calhoun, Sectionalist*, pp. 138–49.
10. F.W.P. to R. M. T. Hunter, 27 Dec. 1843, Hunter Papers (U.Va.). F.W.P. to J.C.C., 24 Nov., 20, 27 Dec. 1843, J.C.C. (C.U.). F.H.E. to J.C.C., 4 Sept. 1843, in Calhoun, *Correspondence*, pp. 872–74. Boucher, "Annexation of Texas and the Bluffton Movement."

11. F.W.P. to J.C.C., 27 Nov. 1843, J.C.C. (C.U.). F.W.P. to R. M. T. Hunter, 27 Dec. 1843, Hunter Papers (U.Va.). Boucher, "Annexation of Texas and the Bluffton Movement."
12. F.W.P. to R.M.T. Hunter, 27 Dec. 1843, Hunter Papers (U.Va.). Boucher, "Annexation of Texas and the Bluffton Movement."
13. F.W.P. to J.C.C., 27 Dec. 1843, J.C.C. (C.U.). *Mercury*, 29 Jan., 15 Feb. 1844.
14. J. R. Poinsett to Gov. Kimble, 8 Mar. 1844, in Poinsett, "Calendar of Papers," p. 181. *Mercury*, 27 Jan. 1844.
15. F.W.P. to J.C.C., 27 Dec. 1843, J.C.C. (C.U.).
16. F.W.P. to R. M. T. Hunter, 27 Dec. 1843, Hunter Papers (U.Va.).
17. F.W.P. to J.E.C., 7 Feb. 1844, F.W.P. (S.C.L.).
18. Ibid.
19. *Congressional Globe*, Appendix, 24th Cong., 1st sess., 25 May 1836, p. 698. Adams, *British Interest and Activities in Texas*, pp. 97–233. *Congressional Globe*, 25th Cong., 1st sess., V, part 1, pp. 24–25. Reeves, *American Diplomacy under Tyler and Polk*, pp. 114–88.
20. Smith, *Annexation of Texas*, pp. 142–79.
21. Edgefield *Advertiser*, 27 Apr. 1842.
22. F.W.P. to J.C.C., 27 Nov. 1843, J.C.C. (C.U.).
23. W. G. Simms to J.H.H., 30 Dec. 1843, J.H.H. (L.C.).
24. F.W.P. to J.C.C., 27 Nov., 20 Dec. 1843, J.C.C. (C.U.).
25. *Proceedings of the South Carolina State Convention*, 1843.
26. Ibid. F.W.P. to J.C.C., 7 Feb. 1844, J.C.C. (C.U.).
27. F.W.P. to J.C.C., 3 Mar. 1844, ibid.
28. F.W.P. to J.E.C., 17 May 1844, F.W.P. (S.C.L.).
29. *Mercury*, 19 Mar. 1844. F.W.P. to J.C.C., 3, 7 Mar. 1844, J.C.C. (C.U.).
30. Lander, *Calhoun Family and Clemson*, p. 72. F.W.P. to J.E.C., 7 Feb. 1844, F.W.P. (S.C.L.), for a commentary on Pickens's view on his situation.
31. F.W.P. to J.C.C., 7 Feb. 1844, J.C.C. (C.U.). F.W.P. to J.E.C., 7 Feb. 1844, F.W.P. (S.C.L.).
32. Wiltse, *Calhoun, Sectionalist*, p. 160.
33. J.C.C. to J.E.C., 19 Mar. 1844; F.W.P. to J.C.C., 3 Mar. 1844; both in J.C.C. (C.U.). George McDuffie to J.C.C., 5 Mar. 1844; Dixon H. Lewis to J.C.C., 6 Mar. 1844; both in Calhoun, *Correspondence*, pp. 934–38. Lander, *Calhoun Family and Clemson*, p. 77–79.
34. Lander, *Calhoun Family and Clemson*, pp. 73–74.
35. J.C.C. to Anna Maria Clemson, 15 Mar. 1844; J.C.C. to J.E.C., 19 Mar. 1844; both in J.C.C. (C.U.).
36. Lander, *Calhoun Family and Clemson*, pp. 72–74. F.W.P. to J.C.C., 22 Apr. 1844, J.C.C. (C.U.).
37. F.W.P. to J.C.C., 22 Apr. 1844, J.C.C. (C.U.).
38. Ibid.
39. J.C.C. to Anna Maria Clemson, 10 May 1844, in Calhoun, *Correspondence*, pp. 585–86.
40. F.W.P. to J.C.C., 16 May 1844, J.C.C. (C.U.). Boucher, "Annexation of Texas

and the Bluffton Movement." White, *Rhett*, p. 71. Wiltse, *Calhoun, Sectionalist*, pp. 178–81. *Mercury*, May–June 1844.

41. *Mercury*, May–June 1844. Boucher, "Annexation of Texas and the Bluffton Movement."

42. F.W.P. to J.C.C., 16 May 1844, J.C.C. (C.U.).

43. Ibid. F.W.P. to J.E.C., 17 May 1844, F.W.P. (S.C.L.).

44. F.W.P. to J.C.C., 16 May 1844, J.C.C. (C.U.). F.W.P. to J.E.C., 17 May 1844, F.W.P. (S.C.L.).

45. F.W.P. to J.C.C., 28 May 1844, in Calhoun, *Correspondence*, pp. 954–60.

46. Ibid. For an excellent account of the happenings at Baltimore, see Sellers, *Polk*, pp. 85–107. Washington *Spectator*, 3, 4 June 1844. *Madisonian*, 28, 29, 30 May 1844. Pickens referred to himself as a delegate; actually he and Elmore were observers. South Carolina was not represented officially at a Democratic National Convention until 1856.

47. Baltimore *Sun*, 30 May 1844. *Madisonian*, 28, 29, 30 May 1844. *Spectator*, 28, 30 May 1844.

48. Baltimore *Sun*, 20 May 1844. *Mercury*, 4 June 1844. Washington *Spectator*, 30 May 1844.

49. F.W.P. to J.E.C., 5 June 1844, F.W.P. (S.C.L.).

50. F.W.P. to H. W. Conner, 29 May 1844, Conner Papers (Charleston Library Society).

51. James Hamilton to J.C.C., 14 June 1844, in Calhoun, *Correspondence*, pp. 962–63. Wiltse, *Calhoun, Sectionalist*, pp. 182–83.

52. J.H.H. to J.C.C., 7 July 1844, J.H.H. (L.C.).

53. F.W.P. to J.C.C., 22 Apr. 1844, J.C.C. (C.U.). See also *Correspondence Addressed to John C. Calhoun*, ed. Brooks and Boucher, pp. 222–23.

54. Pickens's Autobiographical Sketch, MS fragment, Pickens-Dugas Papers (S.H.C., U.N.C.).

55. F.W.P. to J.E.C., 16 June 1844, F.W.P. (S.C.L.).

56. F.W.P. to J.E.C., 5 June 1844, ibid.

57. Ibid. Edgefield *Advertiser*, 9 Oct. 1844. *Mercury*, 17 June 1844. F.W.P. to J.C.C., 28 July 1844; F.W.P. to J.C.C., 18 Oct. 1844; both in J.C.C. (C.U.).

58. Wiltse, *Calhoun, Sectionalist*, pp. 231–32. Hammond Diary, 2 July 1844, J.H.H. (L.C.).

59. F.W.P. to J.C.C., 28 July 1844, J.C.C. (C.U.).

60. F.W.P. to *South Carolinian*, 12 Apr. 1859, reprinted in Edgefield *Advertiser*, 17 Aug. 1859. F.H.E. to J.C.C., 30 July 1844, J.C.C. (C.U.).

61. *Mercury*, 14 June 1844.

62. F.H.E. to J.C.C., 26 Aug. 1844, in Calhoun, *Correspondence*, pp. 967–68.

63. F.W.P. to J.C.C., 28 July 1844, J.C.C. (C.U.). F.W.P. to H. M. Conner, June 1844, Conner Papers (Charleston Library Society). *Mercury*, 14, 15 June, 4, 31 July, 3, 8, 10 Aug., 3 Sept. 1844.

64. *Mercury*, 3 Sept. 1844, in Stuart's long pro-Bluffton editorial.

65. Ibid., 8 Aug. 1844.

66. F.W.P. to J.C.C., 10 Aug. 1844; F.H.E. to J.C.C., 30 July 1844; J.C.C. (C.U.). King, *Wigfall*, pp. 40–41.

67. F.W.P. to J.C.C., 28 July 1844; F.H.E. to J.C.C., 30 July 1844, J.C.C. (C.U.).
68. I. E. Holmes to J.H.H., 23 July 1844, J.H.H. (L.C.).
69. F.W.P. to J.C.C., 28 July 1844, J.C.C. (C.U.). Boucher, "Secession and Cooperation Movements."
70. I.E. Holmes to J.H.H., 23 July 1844, J.H.H. (L.C.).
71. F.W.P. to J.C.C., 28 July 1844, J.C.C. (C.U.).
72. F.H.E. to J.C.C., 26 Aug. 1844, ibid.
73. J.H.H. to Col. R. J. Colcock, 12 Sept. 1844, J.H.H. (L.C.).
74. F.W.P. to J.C.C., 10 Aug. 1844, J.C.C. (C.U.); see also *Correspondence Addressed to John C. Calhoun*, ed. Brooks and Boucher, pp. 243–44. F.H.E. to J.C.C., 26 Aug. 1844, in Calhoun, *Correspondence*, pp. 967–68. Sellers, *Polk*, pp. 123–32.
75. F.W.P. to J.C.C., 10 Aug. 1844, J.C.C. (C.U.).
76. F.H.E. to J.C.C., 30 July 1844, ibid.
77. Ibid. *Mercury*, 12 Aug., 3 Sept. 1844.
78. Sellers, *Polk*, pp. 126–28.
79. F.W.P. to J.C.C., 10 Aug. 1844, in *Correspondence Addressed to John C. Calhoun*, ed. Brooks and Boucher, pp. 243–44. F.H.E. to J.C.C., 26 Aug. 1844, in Calhoun, *Correspondence*, pp. 917–18. F.W.P. to J.E.C., 14 Sept. 1844, F.W.P. (C.U.).
80. Sellers, *Polk*, p. 123.
81. F.W.P. to J.C.C., 10 Aug. 1844, in *Correspondence Addressed to John C. Calhoun*, ed. Brooks and Boucher, pp. 243–44.
82. *Mercury*, 20, 21 Aug. 1844. F.H.E. to J.C.C., 21 Aug. 1844, in Calhoun, *Correspondence*, pp. 967–68. Wiltse, *Calhoun, Sectionalist*, p. 190. White, *Rhett*, p. 79.
83. F.W.P. to *South Carolinian*, 12 Apr. 1859, reprinted in Edgefield *Advertiser*, 17 Aug. 1859. F.W.P. to B. F. Perry, 27 June 1857, Perry Papers (Alabama Archives); see also Perry, *Reminiscences*, I, 167–68. Sellers, *Polk*, pp. 127–28.
84. F.W.P. to J.C.C., 9 Sept. 1844, in Calhoun, *Correspondence*, pp. 968–71.
85. Ibid.
86. Ibid.
87. *Mercury*, 1 Oct. 1844. McDuffie to Hammond, 22 Sept. 1844, J.H.H. (L.C.). Edgefield *Advertiser*, 25 Sept., 2 Oct. 1844.
88. Edgefield *Advertiser*, 25 Sept., 2 Oct. 1844. *Mercury*, 27 Sept. 1844. Sellers, *Polk*, p. 126.
89. F.W.P. to J.C.C., 9 Sept. 1844, in Calhoun, *Correspondence*, pp. 968–71.
90. Hammond Diary, 25 Oct., 29 Nov. 1844, J.H.H. (L.C.). Faust, *Hammond and the Old South*, pp. 247–49. F.W.P. to J.C.C., 9 Sept. 1844, J.C.C. (C.U.). F.W.P. to J.K.P., 11 Oct., 5 Nov. 1844, Polk Papers (L.C.). White, *Rhett*, p. 81.
91. Hammond Diary, 31 Jan. 1844, J.H.H. (L.C.). Hammond Diary, Dec. 1846, J.H.H. (S.C.L.). Faust, *Hammond and the Old South*, pp. 241–45.
92. Hammond Diary, 2 July 1844, J.H.H. (L.C.).
93. Ibid., 17 Nov. 1844.
94. Ibid., 24 Nov. 1844.
95. F.W.P. to J.C.C., 18 Oct. 1844, J.C.C. (C.U.).

96. Message No. 1 of His Excellency James Henry Hammond, 26 Nov. 1844, in *Niles National Register*, 4 Jan. 1845. Faust, *Hammond and The Old South*, pp. 250–51. White, *Rhett*, pp. 82–83.

97. Hammond Diary, 28 Nov. 1844, J.H.H. (L.C.). Hammond Diary, 17 July 1847, J.H.H. (S.C.L.). F.W.P. to J.C.C., 27 Nov. 1847, J.C.C. (C.U.).

98. Hammond Diary, 24, 26, 28 Nov. 1844, J.H.H. (L.C.). F.W.P. to J.C.C., 27 Nov. 1844, J.C.C. (C.U.). *Niles National Register*, 5 Jan. 1845. *S.C. Senate Journal*, Nov. and Dec. 1844, MS (S.C. Archives). F.W.P. to B. F. Perry, 24 Apr. 1844, Perry Papers (Alabama Archives). F.W.P. to J.E.C., 7 Dec. 1844, F.W.P. (S.C.L.). For a commentary on the whole affair, see Faust, *Hammond and The Old South*, pp. 250–54.

99. F.W.P. to J.C.C., 27 Nov. 1844, J.C.C. (C.U.).

100. F.W.P. to J.E.C., 7 Dec. 1844, F.W.P. (S.C.L.).

101. Hammond Diary, 27 Nov. 1844, J.H.H. (L.C.).

102. F.W.P. to J.C.C., 27 Nov. 1844, J.C.C. (L.C.).

103. Charleston *Courier*, quoted in Edgefield *Advertiser*, 4 Dec. 1844.

104. Hammond Diary, 29 Nov. 1844, J.H.H. (L.C.).

105. Ibid.

106. F.W.P. to J.C.C., 6, 18, 28 Dec. 1844, J.C.C. (C.U.).

107. W. B. Seabrook to J.C.C., 16 Dec. 1844, in *Correspondence Addressed to John C. Calhoun*, ed. Brooks and Boucher, p. 270. In a letter to Pickens which has been lost, Calhoun, acting on Seabrook's information, asked his cousin if there had been a rift between Pickens and Elmore. In his reply, Pickens was very complimentary to Elmore: "[Elmore] acted *most cordially* in everything at Columbia and did what he could to check and control others" (F.W.P. to J.C.C., 28 Dec. 1844, J.C.C. [C.U.]).

108. Hammond Diary, 29 Nov. 1844, J.H.H. (L.C.).

109. F.W.P. to J.C.C., 18 Dec. 1844, J.C.C. (C.U.).

110. F.W.P. to J.C.C., 28 Dec. 1844, in Calhoun, *Correspondence*, p. 1015.

111. Wiltse, *Calhoun, Sectionalist*, p. 195. Hammond Diary, 8 Dec. 1844, J.H.H. (L.C.). F.W.P. to J.C.C., 18, 28 Dec. 1844, J.C.C. (C.U.). J.C.C. to J.H.H., 21 Sept. 1844, J.H.H. (L.C.). F.W.P. to R. M. T. Hunter, 27 Dec. 1844, Hunter Papers (U.Va.).

112. J.H.H. to Henry Barley (Attorney General of S.C.), 5 Dec. 1844, J.H.H. (L.C.). Hammond Diary, 7 Dec. 1844, ibid. Wiltse, *Calhoun, Sectionalist*, p. 195.

113. *Niles National Register*, 4 Jan. 1845. *Mercury*, 17 Dec. 1844. *Courier*, 19 Dec. 1844. F.W.P. to J.E.C., 22, 24 June 1845, F.W.P. (S.C.L.).

114. Hammond Diary, 22 Dec. 1844, J.H.H. (L.C.).

115. F.W.P. to J.C.C., 28 Dec. 1844, J.C.C. (C.U.). Armistead Burt to J.H.H., 29 Dec. 1844, J.H.H. (L.C.). *Niles National Register*, 4 Jan. 1844. Edgefield *Advertiser*, 23 Dec. 1844. W. G. Simms to Armistead Burt, 1 Jan. 1845, in Simms, *Letters*, pp. 5–7.

116. F.W.P. to J.C.C., 28 Dec. 1844, J.C.C. (C.U.).

117. W. G. Simms to Armistead Burt, 1 Jan. 1845, in Simms, *Letters*, pp. 5–7.

118. F.W.P. to Armistead Burt, 11 Dec. 1844, Burt Papers (D.U.L.). Edgefield *Advertiser*, 11 Dec. 1844. Kibler, *Perry*, pp. 170–84. South Carolina was the only state whose presidential electors were elected by the legislature.

119. Sellers, *Polk*, pp. 165, 184–86.

120. Ibid.

121. F.W.P. to J.E.C., 7 Dec. 1844, F.W.P. (S.C.L.).

122. Ibid.

123. F.W.P. to J.C.C., 28 Dec. 1844, J.C.C. (C.U.). W. G. Simms to A. Burt, 1 Jan. 1845, in Simms, *Letters*, pp. 5–7.

124. F.W.P. to A. Burt, 26 Dec. 1844, Burt Papers (D.U.L.).

125. J.C.C. to F.W.P., 1 Mar. 1845, F.W.P. (S.C.L.). White, *Rhett*, p. 81. Wiltse, *Calhoun, Sectionalist*, p. 218.

126. J.C.C. to F.W.P., 1 Apr. 1845, F.W.P. (S.C.L.).

127. J.C.C. to F.W.P., 1 Mar. 1845, J.C.C. (C.U.).

128. Lander, *Calhoun Family and Clemson*, pp. 84–86. J.C.C. to F.W.P., 1 Apr. 1845, F.W.P. (S.C.L.). F.W.P. to J.C.C., 30 Mar. 1845; F.W.P. to J.C.C., 4 May 1845; F.W.P. to J.C.C., 20 July 1845; all in J.C.C. (C.U.).

129. Lander, *Calhoun Family and Clemson*, pp. 84–86.

130. J.C.C. to F.W.P., 1 Mar., 1 Apr. 1845, F.W.P. (S.C.L.).

131. Wiltse, *Calhoun, Sectionalist*, p. 218. White, *Rhett*, p. 81.

132. F.W.P. to J.C.C., 30 Mar. 1845, J.C.C. (C.U.). J.K.P. to F.H.E., 8 Apr. 1845, J.K.P. (L.C.). Hammond Diary, 16 Mar. 1845, J.H.H. (L.C.).

133. J.K.P. to F.W.P., 21 Apr. 1845, J.K.P. (L.C.). F.H.E. to J.K.P., 13 Apr. 1845, ibid. Hammond Diary, 11 May 1845, J.H.H. (L.C.). F.W.P. to J.C.C., 17 Apr., 4 May 1845, J.C.C. (C.U.).

134. J.C.C. to F.W.P., 6 May 1845, in Calhoun, *Correspondence*, pp. 653–54.

135. Daniel Huger to J.C.C., 24 Mar. 1845, ibid., pp. 1027–29. Duff Green to J.C.C., 21 May 1845, ibid., pp. 1035–36. Duff Green to F.W.P., 2 May 1845, J.C.C. (C.U.). D. H. Lewis to J.C.C., 9 May 1845, in *Correspondence Addressed to John C. Calhoun*, ed. Brooks and Boucher, pp. 293–94.

136. Wiltse, *Calhoun, Sectionalist*, pp. 225–27. J.C.C. to Mrs. T. G. Clemson, 22 May 1845, in Calhoun, *Correspondence*, p. 656. J. R. Poinsett to Gov. Kimble, 18 Apr., 5 July 1845, in Poinsett, "Calendar of Papers."

137. Hammond Diary, 11 May 1845, J.H.H. (L.C.).

138. James M. Walker to J.H.H., 11 June 1845, ibid.

139. F.W.P. to R. P. Treville, 27 June 1845, J.K.P. (L.C.).

140. W. A. Harris to J.C.C., 11 July 1845, in Calhoun, *Correspondence*, pp. 1038–43.

141. F.W.P. to J.K.P., 17 Apr. 1845, J.K.P. (L.C.).

142. F.W.P. to R. P. Treville, 27 June 1845, ibid.

143. J.C.C. to T. G. Clemson, 23 June 1845, in Calhoun, *Correspondence*, p. 665.

144. F.W.P. to J.E.C., 22 June 1845, F.W.P. (S.C.L.).

145. J.C.C. to J.H.H., 7 July, 2, 30 Aug., 28 Sept. 1845, in Calhoun, *Correspondence*, pp. 666–71, 672–73. J.H.H. to J.C.C., 18 Aug. 1845, ibid., pp. 1045–49.

Chapter 5. A Litany of Destruction

1. *Mercury*, July–Oct. 1845. Wiltse, *Calhoun, Sectionalist*, pp. 224–26, 247–72. Lewis S. Coryell to J.C.C., 6 Apr. 1845; Duff Green to J.C.C., 21 Mar. 1845; both in *Correspondence Addressed to John C. Calhoun*, ed. Brooks and Boucher, pp. 291–92, 287–89. Pickens and Calhoun were more fortunate than most of their fellow planters; Calhoun lost almost half of his expected crop, and Pickens had fine crops. J.C.C. to F.W.P., 21 Aug. 1845; F.W.P. to J.C.C., 18 Aug. 1845; both in J.C.C. (C.U.).

2. Dixon H. Lewis to J.C.C., 9 May 1845, in *Correspondence Addressed to John C. Calhoun*, ed. Brooks and Boucher, pp. 293–97.

3. J.C.C. to F.W.P., 6 May 1845, J.C.C. (S.C.L.), also in Calhoun, *Correspondence*, pp. 653–54. F.W.P. to J.C.C., 29 Sept. 1845, in *Correspondence Addressed to John C. Calhoun*, ed. Brooks and Boucher, p. 306. On 8 May 1845 Dixon H. Lewis, Robert Barnwell Rhett, his brother James Rhett, ex-governor James Hamilton, and Henry Gourdin, one of Calhoun's closest friends, met at Elmore's house in Charleston to plan strategy for the 1848 presidential race.

4. Dixon H. Lewis to J.C.C., 9 May 1845, in *Correspondence Addressed to John C. Calhoun*, ed. Brooks and Boucher, pp. 293–97. F.W.P. to J.C.C., 30 July 1845, J.C.C. (C.U.).

5. F.W.P. to J.C.C., 30 July 1845, J.C.C. (C.U.).

6. J.C.C. to F.W.P., 2 Aug. 1845, ibid.

7. Daniel Huger to J.C.C., 22 Feb. 1845, in *Correspondence Addressed to John C. Calhoun*, ed. Brooks and Boucher, p. 210. Daniel Huger to J.C.C., 24 Mar. 1845, in Calhoun, *Correspondence*, p. 1027–28.

8. *Mercury*, 1 July 1845.

9. *Mercury*, 1 Aug. 1845, reprinted from *South Carolinian*, n.d.

10. F.W.P. to J.E.C., 22 June 1845, F.W.P. (S.C.L.).

11. F.W.P. to J.C.C., 17 Aug. 1845, J.C.C. (S.C.L.).

12. Wiltse, *Calhoun, Sectionalist*, pp. 230–43. *Mercury*, 6 Oct. 1845.

13. *Mercury*, 7 Aug. 1845.

14. James Gadsden to J.C.C., 9 Oct. 1845; F.H.E. to J.C.C., 10 Oct. 1845; both in Calhoun, *Correspondence*, pp. 1060–63.

15. J.C.C. to F.W.P., 21 Aug., 23 Sept. 1845, J.C.C. (S.C.L.). F.W.P. to J.C.C., 18 Aug., 21, 29 Sept. 1845, J.C.C. (C.U.). Letter of 29 Sept. 1845, in *Correspondence Addressed to John C. Calhoun*, ed. Brooks and Boucher, p. 326.

16. J.C.C. to F.W.P., 23 Sept. 1845, J.C.C. (S.C.L.).

17. F.W.P. to J.C.C., 21 Sept. 1845, J.C.C. (C.U.). Jackson died on 8 June 1845.

18. J.E.C. to J.C.C., 7 Jan. 1846, J.C.C. (S.C.L.). J.C.C. to J.E.C., 16 Jan. 1846, J.C.C. (C.U.); also in Calhoun, *Correspondence*, pp. 175–77. J.C.C. to F.W.P., 23 Sept. 1845, J.C.C. (S.C.L.). F.W.P. to J.C.C., 29 Sept. 1845, J.C.C. (C.U.).

19. *Mercury*, 17, 25, 27, 28 Nov., 9 Dec. 1845.

20. F.W.P. to J.C.C., 29 Sept. 1845, J.C.C. (C.U.). White, *Rhett*, p. 91.

21. *Mercury*, 28 Nov. 1845.

22. Ibid., 29 Nov. 1845.

23. F.W.P. to J.E.C., 13 Dec. 1845, F.W.P. (S.C.L.). Wiltse, *Calhoun, Sectionalist*, pp. 240–42.

24. J.E.C. to J.C.C., 7 Jan. 1846, J.C.C. (S.C.L.). *Mercury*, 1 Dec. 1845. F.W.P. to J.E.C., 13 Dec. 1845, F.W.P. (S.C.L.).

25. F.W.P. to J.C.C., 20 Dec. 1845, J.C.C. (C.U.). J. R. Poinsett to Gov. Kimble, 18 Apr., 5 July 1845, in Poinsett, "Calendar of Papers." Duff Green, writing to Calhoun on 17 Mar. 1847, expressed the view that he (Green) had done much to promote Calhoun, "with sacrifices personal and Pecuniary," but that Calhoun had never reciprocated. See *Correspondence Addressed to John C. Calhoun*, ed. Brooks and Boucher, pp. 370–72.

26. F.W.P. to J.E.C., 23 Dec. 1845, F.W.P. (S.C.L.). *Southern Quarterly Review*, IX (Jan. 1846): 243–72. *Mercury*, 7 Feb. 1846. F.W.P. to J.C.C., 14, 17 Apr. 1846, J.C.C. (C.U.). J.C.C. to J.E.C., 2 July 1846, in Calhoun, *Correspondence*, pp. 698–702. J.C.C. to Mrs. T. G. Clemson, 11 June 1846, J.C.C. (C.U.). H. W. Conner to F.W.P., 30 Apr. 1846, F.W.P. (D.U.). Wiltse, *Calhoun, Sectionalist*, p. 242.

27. Wiltse, *Calhoun, Sectionalist*, pp. 218–20. Lander, *Calhoun Family and Clemson*, pp. 77–92.

28. Note on a letter from J.C.C. to F.W.P., 16 Mar. 1848, F.W.P. (W. & L.): "This written after Mr. Calhoun deliberately wounded my feelings . . . because his sons requested it of him." Lander, *Calhoun Family and Clemson*, pp. 79, 84, 85, 90, 98–99, 100, 103–5, 121–22.

29. F.W.P. to J.K.P., 8 Dec. 1846, J.K.P. (L.C.); see also Calhoun, *Correspondence*, pp. 698–702. F.W.P. to J.C.C., 20 Dec. 1845, J.C.C. (C.U.). J.C.C. to Mrs. T. G. Clemson, 11 June 1846, in Calhoun, *Correspondence*, pp. 694–96.

30. F.W.P. to J.C.C., 29 Sept. 1845, J.C.C. (C.U.). Reeves, *American Diplomacy under Tyler and Polk*, pp. 249–50.

31. F.W.P. to J.C.C., 20 Dec. 1845, 6 Feb. 1846, J.C.C. (C.U.). F.W.P. to James Buchanan, 15 Jan. 1856, Buchanan Papers (Historical Society of Pa.). Sellers, *Polk*, II, 364.

32. Reeves, *American Diplomacy under Tyler and Polk*, p. 253.

33. F.W.P. to J.C.C., 20 Dec. 1845, J.C.C. (C.U.).

34. Ibid. F.W.P. to J.C.C., 6 Feb. 1846, ibid.

35. Wiltse, *Calhoun, Sectionalist*, pp. 264–65.

36. F.W.P. to J.C.C., 9 Feb. 1846, J.C.C. (C.U.).

37. Ibid. Louis T. Wigfall to Armistead Burt, 17 Apr. 1846, Burt Papers (D.U.L.).

38. Wiltse, *Calhoun, Sectionalist*, pp. 270–72. F.W.P. to J.K.P., 8 Dec. 1845, Polk Papers (L.C.).

39. *Mercury*, 8, 9 July 1845.

40. Hammond Diary, 9 Mar. 1845, J.H.H. (L.C.).

41. For good accounts of South Carolina's role in the Mexican War and its effect on the state, see Lander, *Reluctant Imperialist*, pp. 1–24, and Gettys, "To Conquer a Peace."

42. Wiltse, *Calhoun, Sectionalist*, pp. 282–84. Lander, *Reluctant Imperialist*, pp. 6–12.

43. F.W.P. to J.C.C., 17 Aug. 1845, J.C.C. (S.C.L.). Gettys, "To Conquer a Peace," p. 113.
44. Edgefield *Advertiser*, 3 June 1846. Gettys, "To Conquer a Peace," p. 115.
45. King, *Wigfall*, pp. 25-35.
46. F.W.P. to J.C.C., 13 Dec. 1845, in Calhoun, *Correspondence*, pp. 1099-1102.
47. J.C.C. to Mrs. T. G. Clemson, 11 June 1846, in Calhoun, *Correspondence*, pp. 698-99.
48. Edgefield *Advertiser*, 3, 10 June 1846. Deposition of W. P. Brett of conversation between Louis T. Wigfall and F.W.P., 9 Oct. 1847, F.W.P. (D.U.L.).
49. Joseph Abney to Armistead Burt, 5 June 1846; Thomas C. Key to Armistead Burt, 15 June 1846; both in Burt Papers (D.U.L.). Edgefield *Advertiser*, 3, 10 June 1846. *Mercury*, 9, 17 June 1846. J.C.C. to J.E.C., 2 July 1846, in Calhoun, *Correspondence*, pp. 698-99. Gettys, "To Conquer a Peace," pp. 113-17. Lander, *Reluctant Imperialist*, pp. 5-24.
50. Thomas C. Key to Armistead Burt, 15 June 1846, Burt Papers (D.U.L.).
51. Joseph Abney to Burt, 23 July 1846, ibid.
52. Thomas C. Key to Burt, 16 July 1846, ibid.
53. J.C.C. to Mrs. T. C. Calhoun, 11 June 1846, in Calhoun, *Correspondence*, pp. 694-96. J.C.C. to J.E.C., 2 July 1846, ibid., pp. 698-99.
54. Perry, *Reminiscences of Public Men*, p. 49. Capers, *Calhoun—Opportunist*, p. 215.
55. F.W.P. to J.C.C., 13 Dec. 1846, in Calhoun, *Correspondence*, pp. 1099-1102.
56. J.C.C. to J.E.C., 29 Oct. 1846, J.C.C. (C.U.). Meigs, *Life of Calhoun*, pp. 116-17. Lander, *Calhoun Family and Clemson*, pp. 103-4.
57. F.W.P. to J.C.C., 13 Dec. 1846, in Calhoun, *Correspondence*, pp. 1099-1102. *Mountaineer* quote from Gettys, "To Conquer a Peace," pp. 116-17.
58. F.W.P. to J.C.C., 13 Dec. 1846, in Calhoun, *Correspondence*, pp. 1099-1102.
59. Note written in Pickens's hand on the back of a letter from J.C.C. to F.W.P., 16 Mar. 1848, F.W.P. (W. & L.). F.W.P. to J.C.C., 14 Apr. 1846, J.C.C. (C.U.).
60. R. B. Rhett to A. Burt, 3 Sept. 1846, Burt Papers (D.U.L.).
61. F.W.P. to J.E.C., 7 Oct. 1846, F.W.P. (S.C.L.). Lander, *Calhoun Family and Clemson*, pp. 104-10.
62. Hammond Diary, 25 Nov. 1846, J.H.H. (S.C.L.). Faust, *Hammond and the Old South*, pp. 284-90. Wiltse, *Calhoun, Sectionalist*, p. 291.
63. Joseph Abney to A. Burt, 23 July 1846, Burt Papers (D.U.L.).
64. J. L. Clarke to J.H.H., 15 Jan. 1845, J.H.H. (L.C.).
65. White, *Rhett*, pp. 89-93. F.W.P. to J.E.C., 7 May 1846, F.W.P. (S.C.L.).
66. J.H.H. to Nathaniel Beverley Tucker, 24 Jan. 1847, quoted in Faust, *Hammond and the Old South*, p. 286.
67. Faust, *Hammond and the Old South*, pp. 284-61.
68. F.W.P. to J.C.C., 4 Apr. 1848, F.W.P. (S.C.L.).
69. Mrs. T. G. Clemson to J.C.C., Christmas Day, 1848, J.C.C. (C.U.).
70. J.C.C. to Mrs. T. G. Clemson, 24 Jan. 1849, ibid.
71. Copy of Document "Sale of L. T. Wigfall's property to pay debts, 3, 4, 5, 6 June 1846" (Eugene C. Barker History Center, Univ. of Texas–Austin).

72. Louis T. Wigfall to A. Burt, 7 July 1846, Burt Papers (D.U.L.).
73. King, *Wigfall*, pp. 46–51. L. T. Wigfall to A. Burt, 7 July 1846, Burt Papers (D.U.L.).
74. Sellars, *Polk*, II, 476–87. Wiltse, *Calhoun, Sectionalist*, pp. 287–88.
75. Hammond Diary, 19 July 1845, J.H.H. (L.C.).
76. Ibid. A. Burt to H. W. Conner, 1 Feb. 1847, Conner Papers (Charleston Library Society).
77. Wiltse, *Calhoun, Sectionalist*, p. 303.
78. Cooper, *The South and the Politics of Slavery*, p. 239.
79. F.H.E. to J.C.C., 29 June, 25 Aug. 1847, J.C.C. (C.U.). A. P. Butler's wife was Susan Ann Simkins, who died on 22 May 1830, after a little over six months of marriage.
80. F.W.P. to J.K.P., 31 Oct. 1847, F.W.P. (D.U.L.).
81. Ibid.
82. F.W.P. to Gen. B. C. Howard, 26 Apr. 1848, ibid. Wiltse, *Calhoun, Sectionalist*, pp. 297–98.
83. Hamer, *Secession Movement in South Carolina*, pp. 7–8. Merritt, *Hammond*, pp. 90–92. *Mercury*, 10, 23 Mar. 1847.
84. J.H.H. to W. G. Simms, 27 Mar., 1 Apr. 1847, J.H.H. (L.C.). Hammond also expressed the same view to his brother, Marcellus; 16 Nov. 1849, ibid. Faust, *Hammond and the Old South*, pp. 291–97.
85. Hamer, *Secession Movement in South Carolina*, pp. 11–17.
86. F.W.P. to Gen. B. C. Howard, 26 Apr. 1848, F.W.P. (D.U.L.). A. Burt to H. W. Conner, 4 July 1848, Conner Papers (Charleston Library Society).
87. A. Burt to H.W. Conner, 1 Feb. 1847, Conner Papers (Charleston Library Society). A. Burt to B. F. Perry, 22 July 1848, Perry Papers (Alabama Archives). Hamer, *Secession Movement in South Carolina*, p. 18.
88. Edgefield *Advertiser*, 21 July 1848.
89. Ibid., 5, 19 July, 9 Aug., 20 Sept. 1848.
90. Charleston *Mercury*, 22 July 1848. Wiltse, *Calhoun, Sectionalist*, pp. 263–68.
91. Hamer, *Secession Movement in South Carolina*, p. 19. Wiltse, *Calhoun, Sectionalist*, pp. 362–68. Edgefield *Advertiser*, 9 Aug. 1848.
92. Edgefield *Advertiser*, 27 Sept. 1848.
93. *Mercury*, 26 Sept. 1848.
94. Edgefield *Advertiser*, 27 Sept. 1848.
95. F.W.P. to B. F. Perry, 24 Apr. 1859, Perry Papers (Alabama Archives). Simms to Hammond, 24 Nov. 1848, in Simms, *Letters*, p. 457.
96. Edgefield *Advertiser*, 15 Nov. 1848. Wiltse, *Calhoun, Sectionalist*, p. 372.
97. Reprinted from Columbia *South Carolinian* in Edgefield *Advertiser*, 8 Nov. 1848. McDuffie to J.H.H., 22 Aug. 1848, J.H.H. (L.C.). Letters of support from Charleston *Mercury* and Hamburg *Journal*, reprinted in *Advertiser*, 26 Oct. 1848.
98. Simms to J.H.H., 24 Nov. 1848, in Simms, *Letters*, p. 457. Wiltse, *Calhoun, Sectionalist*, p. 372. *South Carolina House Journal, 1848*, pp. 126–28. The contest was held on 12 Dec. 1848. Seabrook defeated John L. Manning on the second ballot.
99. Simms to J.H.H., 24 Nov. 1848, in Simms, *Letters*, p. 457.

Chapter 6. An Insolvable Dilemma

1. A. Burt to H. W. Conner, 1 Feb. 1847, Conner Papers (Charleston Library Society).
2. "Gathering Song of the South," Edgefield *Advertiser*, 18 Apr. 1849.
3. Ibid., 15 Nov. 1848. Wallace, *South Carolina: Short History*, pp. 505–6.
4. Schultz, *Nationalism and Sectionalism*, p. 19.
5. Wallace, *South Carolina: Short History*, p. 505.
6. Ibid. White, *Rhett*, p. 103.
7. Wallace, *South Carolina: Short History*, p. 505.
8. Edgefield *Advertiser*, 23 Apr., 23 May 1849. Open letter of the Committee of Safety, 11 Aug. 1849. Resolutions of Hon. F. W. Pickens to Committee on Public Safety, Columbia *Telegraph*, 21 June 1849, F.W.P. (S.C.L.).
9. Columbia *Telegraph*, 21 June 1849.
10. Ibid.
11. Boucher, "Secession and Cooperation Movement," p. 81. Open letter of Committee on Safety, 11 Aug. 1849, F.W.P. (S.C.L.).
12. Wiltse, *Calhoun, Sectionalist*, pp. 4–7. Schultz, *Nationalism and Sectionalism*, p. 19. *Journal of South Carolina House of Representatives*, 1848, p. 66.
13. J.C.C. to B. F. Simpson, 11 Jan. 1850, in Edgefield *Advertiser*, 29 May 1850.
14. Charleston *Mercury*, 13 Dec. 1849. Charleston *Courier*, 21 Dec. 1949. Hammond Diary, 17 Dec. 1849, J.H.H. (S.C.L.).
15. *Mercury*, 29 Nov., 1, 10, 13 Dec. 1849. Hammond Diary, 17 Dec. 1849, J.H.H. (S.C.L.).
16. J.C.C. to B. F. Simpson, 11 Jan. 1850; J.C.C.'s letter on Nashville Convention, 16 Nov. 1849; both in Edgefield *Advertiser*, 29 May 1850.
17. *Mercury*, 12 Jan. 1850.
18. Boucher, "Secession and Cooperation Movement," pp. 86–87. Kibler, *Perry*, p. 242. Wiltse, *Calhoun, Sectionalist*, pp. 448–72. *Mercury*, 19 Feb. 1850, and numerous other issues of the period.
19. Wiltse, *Calhoun, Sectionalist*, p. 464.
20. Langdon Cheves to Gov. Whitemarsh Seabrook, *Mercury*, 9, 11 Apr. 1850.
21. *Mercury*, 12 Apr. 1850.
22. Elmore died on 29 May 1850 in Washington. *Advertiser*, 5, 26 June 1850. Columbia *South Carolinian*, 5, 10 June 1850.
23. *Mercury*, 8, 11, 12, 13 Apr. 1850. Hammond delivered his eulogy of Calhoun on 21 Nov. 1850. By this time Elmore was dead.
24. Hiram Powers to H. Gourdin, 7 Apr. 1850, in *Mercury*, 13 May 1850.
25. Faust, *Hammond and the Old South*, pp. 300–303.
26. Armistead Burt to Martha Burt, 14 Mar. 1850; Ed Noble to A. Burt, 28 Feb. 1850; both in Burt Papers (D.U.L.). F.W.P. to Gen. Gilliam, 12 Apr. 1850, Edgefield *Advertiser*, 15 May 1850.
27. Edgefield *Advertiser*, 6 May 1850.
28. Boucher, "Secession and Cooperation Movement," pp. 96–104.
29. Kibler, *Perry*, p. 244. Wallace, *South Carolina: Short History*, pp. 511–13.

30. Jennings, *Nashville Convention*, pp. 152-57. Columbia *South Carolinian*, 8 June 1850.

31. Hammond Diary, 10 Aug. 1850, J.H.H. (S.C.L.). Edgefield *Advertiser*, 3 July 1850. Despite a vow of silence, Hammond did make one very mild speech advocating southern unity, but he did not advocate secession. Jennings, *Nashville Convention*, pp. 151-52. Columbia *South Carolinian*, 8, 13, 15, 18 June 1850. Kate Conyham, an observer at the proceedings, claimed Pickens's speech "surpassed anything she had seen 'in the way of fluorensic [sic] eloquence,' [Pickens's] speech fairly riddled his opponents."

32. "Resolutions prepared for the Nashville Convention in June 1850 by F.W.P.," F.W.P. (D.U.L.).

33. Hammond Diary, 10 Aug. 1850, J.H.H. (S.C.L.). F.W.P. to B. F. Perry, 30 Oct. 1850, Perry Papers (Alabama Archives). Hayne, "Politics in South Carolina," p. 23. Barnwell, *Love of Order*, pp. 104-5. White, *Rhett*, pp. 93-111.

34. Hayne, "Politics in South Carolina," p. 23. *D.A.B.*, s.v. "Pickens, Francis."

35. *Mercury*, 12, 13, 15, 20 June 1850.

36. Pickens's Nashville Resolutions, F.W.P. (D.U.L.).

37. *Mercury*, 12, 13, 15, 20 June 1850. Hammond to Simms, 16 June 1850, J.H.H. (L.C.).

38. Cooper, *The South and the Politics of Slavery*, pp. 291-321, gives an excellent picture of how the South reacted to the Compromise of 1850. See also Boucher, "Secession and Cooperation Movement," p. 105. Speech of F.W.P. in Edgefield *Advertiser*, 19 June 1850. White, *Rhett*, pp. 111-13.

39. Columbia *South Carolinian*, 10 Oct. 1850. Pickens's Nashville Resolutions, F.W.P. (D.U.L.). Barnwell, *Love of Order*, p. 135.

40. Edgefield *Advertiser*, 19 Dec. 1850.

41. W. G. Simms to J.H.H., 17 Dec. 1849, J.H.H. (L.C.). *Mercury*, 14 Dec. 1850. *South Carolina House Journal, 1850*. Barnwell, *Love of Order*, p. 137.

42. White, *Rhett*, p. 113.

43. Ibid.

44. Hammond Diary, 27 Dec. 1850, J.H.H. (L.C.).

Chapter 7. A Mere Office-Seeker

1. Boucher, "Secession and Cooperation Movement," pp. 115-29. Barnwell, *Love of Order*, pp. 106-20. On 9 July 1850 Zachary Taylor died. He had been opposed to any compromise, but Fillmore helped push the measure through Congress.

2. Ibid. *S.C. House Journal for 1850*, pp. 168, 174-75.

3. Boucher, "Secession and Cooperation Movement," pp. 114-17. Barnwell, *Love of Order*, p. 177. *S.C. House Journal for 1850*, p. 48. Hammond Diary, 29 Nov. 1850, J.H.H. (L.C.).

4. Greenville *Southern Patriot*, 28 Mar. 1851. Edgefield *Advertiser*, 20 Feb. 1851. Boucher, "Secession and Cooperation Movement," p. 117.

5. W. G. Simms to Beverley Tucker, 7 Apr. 1851, in Simms, *Letters*, p. 108.

6. Reprint from *Southern Patriot* in Yorkville *Miscellany*, 17 July 1851.

7. Yorkville *Miscellany*, 21 July 1851.
8. Edgefield *Advertiser*, 7 July 1851, a speech delivered at Edgefield. F.W.P. to B. F. Perry, 30 Oct. 1850, Perry Papers (Alabama Archives). Kibler, *Perry*, p. 247.
9. Edgefield *Advertiser*, 10, 17, 24 July 1851.
10. Ibid., 24 July 1851.
11. Yorkville *Miscellany*, 20 Sept. 1851.
12. Edgefield *Advertiser*, 23 Sept., 2, 9 Oct. 1851.
13. Barnwell, *Love of Order*, pp. 177–81.
14. Unionville *Journal*, editorial republished in Edgefield *Advertiser*, 18 Sept. 1851.
15. Edgefield *Advertiser*, 2, 9 Oct. 1851.
16. Ibid., 28 Oct. 1851. The vote was Cooperationist, 24,036; Secessionist, 16,244.
17. Ibid., 16 Oct. 1851.
18. Ibid., 9 Oct. 1851.
19. F.W.P. to J.E.C., 26 Oct. 1851, F.W.P. (S.C.L.).
20. F.W.P. to Judge Hugh Miller, 13 Nov. 1851, letter in the possession of Eulalie Salley, Aiken, S.C.
21. Pickens's Plantation Journal, 1851, F.W.P. (D.U.L.).
22. Thomas G. Clemson to F.W.P., 7 Oct. 1850, ibid.
23. White, "National Democracts in South Carolina," pp. 370–89.
24. B. F. Perry, *Reminiscences of Public Men*, pp. 389–97.
25. R. B. Rhett to Gov. J. H. Means, 30 Apr. 1852; J. H. Means to R. B. Rhett, 2, 7 May 1852; in Edgefield *Advertiser*, 20 May 1852.
26. B. F. Perry, *Reminiscences of Public Men*, p. 397. Ware, "S.C. Executive Councils," p. 10. Boucher, "Secession and Cooperation Movement," p. 135. Columbia *South Carolinian*, 30 Apr. 1852. Yorkville *Miscellany*, 8 May 1852. Barnwell, *Love of Order*, pp. 183–87.
27. Edgefield *Advertiser*, 10, 30 June, 14, 28 July, 13 Oct. 1852.
28. Ibid., 28 July 1852.
29. M. L. Bonham to Franklin Pierce, 7 June 1852, Bonham Papers (S.C.L.). F.W.P. to Abbeville *Banner*, 15 Feb. 1853. F.W.P. to Beaufort Tyler Watts, 19 June 1852, Watts Papers (S.C.L.).
30. Hammond Diary, 11 Dec. 1852, J.H.H. (S.C.L.). Edgefield *Advertiser*, 8 Dec. 1852. The votes were:

	1	2	3
J. J. Evans	41	42	50
F. W. Pickens	31	36	27
James Chesnut	24	33	41
A. G. Magrath	18	14	—
John S. Preston	15	15	18
W. F. Colcock	12	13	—

Pickens withdrew on the fourth ballot, and Evans was elected.

31. White, *Rhett*, pp. 135–37.
32. Edgefield *Advertiser*, 29 Dec. 1852. "Circular" by Preston Brooks, 6 Feb. 1853, Brooks Papers (S.C.L). "Notice" of F.W.P., 30 Jan. 1853, F.W.P. (D.U.L.). *Advertiser*, 29 Dec. 1852, 12, 19, 26 Jan., 2, 9 Feb. 1853. These issues are full of the Brooks-Pickens affair. Election results: 9 Mar. 1853.
33. Edgefield *Advertiser*, 29 Dec. 1852.
34. F.W.P. to B. T. Watts, 1 Jan. 1853, Watts Papers (S.C.L.).
35. Samuel McGowan to F.W.P., 11 Jan. 1853, F.W.P. (S.C.L.).
36. Edgefield *Advertiser*, 5, 12, 26 Jan. 1853.
37. Circular by Preston Brooks, 6 Feb. 1853, Brooks Papers (S.C.L.).
38. Ibid.
39. F.W.P. to Abbeville *Banner*, 10 Feb. 1853. Notice of F.W.P., 30 Jan. 1853, F.W.P. (D.U.L.).
40. Edgefield *Advertiser*, 9 Mar. 1853. The district was composed of Edgefield, Abbeville, Newberry, Lexington, and Laurens counties. Pickens outpolled Brooks in Edgefield and Abbeville but lost heavily to him in Lexington and Newberry. C. P. Sullivan of Laurens received the bulk of the votes in that county, and J. F. Marshall garnered the heaviest vote in Abbeville County.
41. Cauthen, *South Carolina Goes to War*, pp. 9–10.
42. Kibler, *Perry*, pp. 170–84.
43. *United States Manufacturing Census for 1850 and 1860*, Edgefield County (S.C. Archives). Edgefield County Records of the Clerk of Court. Deed transfers in Books HHH, III, JJJ, OOO, and interview with Ralph T. McClendon, who owns a pottery museum that stands on the land where Potterville was located.
44. F.W.P. to Greenville *Southern Patriot*, 13 Jan. 1854, Perry Papers (Alabama Archives).
45. Ibid.
46. F.W.P to B. F. Perry, 13 Jan. 1845, ibid.
47. Cauthen, *South Carolina Goes to War*, p. 10.
48. Schultz, *Nationalism and Sectionalism*, pp. 84–85.
49. Ibid, p. 94.
50. Ibid, pp. 94–96.
51. McClendon, *Edgefield Death Notices and Cemetery Records*.
52. F.W.P. to Thomas G. Clemson, 21 Apr. 1856, Clemson Papers (C.U.).
53. T. G. Clemson to J.C.C., 15 July 1846, J.C.C. (C.U.).
54. James Buchanan to F.W.P., 17 July 1853, in possession of A. T. Graydon, Columbia, S.C.
55. Schultz, *Nationalism and Sectionalism*, pp. 94–96.
56. *Mercury*, 5 May 1856.
57. Yorkville *Enquirer*, 17, 24, 31 Jan. 1856.
58. James L. Orr to C. W. Dudley, 23 Nov. 1855, in Yorkville *Enquirer*, 24 Jan. 1856.
59. *Mercury*, 9 May 1856.
60. Ibid. For a full text of Pickens's speech, see Edgefield *Advertiser*, 11 June 1856.
61. Cauthen, *South Carolina Goes to War*, p. 8.

62. *Proceedings of the Democratic State Convention of South Carolina*, held at Columbia on 5, 6 May 1856, for the purpose of electing delegates to the Democratic National Convention to meet in June (S.C.L.).

63. F.W.P. to J. L. Manning, 16 May 1856, W.M.C. (S.C.L.). Edgefield *Advertiser*, 14 May 1856, announced that Magrath had been appointed federal district judge for South Carolina.

64. Smith, *The Nation Comes of Age*, IV, 1090–1105.

65. Edgefield *Advertiser*, 4 July 1856.

66. Ibid., 11, 18 June, 4 July 1856.

67. P. S. Brooks to Thomas P. Slider, 19 Feb. 1856, in Yorkville *Enquirer*, 13 Mar. 1856.

68. Schultz, *Nationalism and Sectionalism*, pp. 121–24.

69. F.W.P. to J. L. Manning, 4 Aug. 1856, W.M.C. (S.C.L.). F.W.P. to A. Burt, 8 Aug. 1856, Burt Papers (D.U.L.). F.W.P. to B. T. Watts, 16 Mar. 1857, Watts Papers (S.C.L.).

70. F.W.P. to A. Burt, 8 Aug. 1856, Burt Papers (D.U.L.). F.W.P. to J. L. Manning, 4 Aug. 1856, W.M.C. (S.C.L.).

71. Election Certificate, 4 Nov. 1856, W.M.C. (S.C.L.).

72. F.W.P. to J. L. Manning, 16 Dec. 1856, ibid.

73. James Buchanan to James L. Orr, 1 Jan. 1857, Orr-Patterson Papers (U.N.C.). F.W.P. to B. T. Watts, 16 Mar. 1857, Watts Papers (S.C.L.). Nichols, *The Disruption of American Democracy*, p. 67.

74. F.W.P. to J. L. Manning, 12 Dec. 1856, W.M.C. (S.C.L.).

75. J. L. Orr to F.W.P., 6 June 1856, F.W.P. (S.C.L.). Ruffin, *Diary*, I, 38.

76. F.W.P. to J. L. Manning, 28 Jan. 1857, W.M.C. (S.C.L.). F.W.P. to B. F. Perry, 24 Apr. 1859, Perry Papers (Alabama Archives).

77. *Mercury*, 16, 27 May 1857. "Since the death of the gallant Brooks, our friend the Judge had never rallied, and the shaft which laid low the noble spirit has no doubt wounded—we fear fatally—our valued Senator" (*Mercury*, 16 May 1857).

78. Pickens's Notebook, 1835–69; 15 Apr. 1857 newspaper clipping, F.W.P. (S.C.L.).

79. F.W.P. to B. T. Watts, 16 Mar. 1857, Watts Papers (S.C.L.).

80. F.W.P. to J. L. Manning, 12 May 1857, W.M.C. (S.C.L.).

81. F.W.P. to G. N. Sanders, 14 May 1857, F.W.P. (D.U.L.). F.W.P. to J. L. Manning, 12 May 1857, W.M.C. (S.C.L.). F.W.P. to Buchanan, 4 June 1857, F.W.P. (S.C.L.).

82. Ibid. John Cunningham to J.H.H., 10 June 1857, J.H.H. (L.C.).

83. John Cunningham to J.H.H., 10 June 1857, J.H.H. (L.C.).

84. F.W.P. to James Buchanan, 4 June 1857, F.W.P. (D.U.L.).

85. F.W.P. to J. L. Manning, 12 May 1857, W.M.C. (S.C.L.). F.W.P. to G. N. Sanders, 14 May 1857, F.W.P. (D.U.L.).

86. F.W.P. to B. F. Perry, 27 June 1857, Perry Papers (Alabama Archives).

87. Ibid.

88. Lancaster *Ledger*, 8 July 1857.

Chapter 8. The Rose of Texas

1. Perry, *Reminiscences*, p. 167.
2. Pickens's Notebook, F.W.P. (S.C.L.).
3. F.W.P. to L.P.H., 10 Sept. 1857, ibid.
4. John J. Crittenden, attorney general of the United States at the time of the Lopez expedition, lost a son in Cuba. Perhaps this Lieutenant Crittenden was his son. DeConde, *A History of American Foreign Policy*, pp. 220–21.
5. Copy of work in F.W.P. (S.C.L.). Bull, "Lucy Pickens," pp. 3–4.
6. George Lee to B. L. Holcombe, 31 July 1858; Lucy Pickens to Anna Holcombe, 1858; both in Greer-Holcombe Papers, in possession of Jane Greer, Tyler, Tex.
7. F.W.P. to L.P.H., 8 Oct. 1857, F.W.P. (D.U.L.).
8. F.W.P. to B. T. Watts, 24 Oct. 1857, Watts Papers (S.C.L.). John Cunningham to J.H.H., quoted in Cauthen, *South Carolina Goes to War*, p. 10. Merritt, *Hammond*, pp. 113–15. White, *Rhett*, pp. 141–43.
9. F.W.P. to M. L. Bonham, 11 Dec. 1857, Bonham Papers (S.C.L.).
10. Ibid.
11. James Gadsden to J.H.H., 31 Jan. 1859, J.H.H. (L.C.).
12. White, *Rhett*, p. 142.
13. F.W.P. to M.L. Bonham, 2 Apr. 1859, Bonham Papers (S.C.L.). F.W.P. to B. L. Perry, 24 Apr. 1859, Perry Papers (Alabama Archives). J.H.H. to W. G. Simms, 19 Dec. 1857, J.H.H. (L.C.).
14. F.W.P. to L.P.H., 23 Sept., 5 Oct., 2, 6 Nov. 1857, 27 Jan., 13 Mar. 1858, F.W.P. (D.U.L.).
15. Pickens's Notebook, newspaper clippings, n.d., n.p., F.W.P. (S.C.L.).
16. F.W.P. to L.P.H., 27 Jan. 1858, F.W.P. (D.U.L.).
17. F.W.P. to L.P.H., 13 Mar. 1858, ibid.
18. Ibid. F.W.P. to L.P.H., 27 Jan. 1858, ibid.
19. F.W.P. to L.P.H., 9 Mar. 1858, ibid.
20. Pickens's Notebook, newspaper clippings, n.d., n.p., F.W.P. (S.C.L.). Greer, *Leaves from a Family Album*, p. 52.
21. F.W.P. to Lewis Cass (Secretary of State), 28 Feb. 1858, Secretary of State Papers (National Archives). F.W.P. to M. L. Bonham, 1 Mar. 1858, Bonham Papers (S.C.L.). Memphis *Eagle* and *Enquirer*, n.d., itinerary from clippings, F.W.P. (S.C.L.).
22. Marcellus Hammond to J.H.H., 31 Jan. 1858, J.H.H. (L.C.).
23. James Gadsden to J.H.H., 31 Jan. 1858, ibid.
24. F.W.P. to M. L. Bonham, 1 Mar. 1858, Bonham Papers (S.C.L.).
25. Ibid. Greer, *Leaves from a Family Album*, pp. 52–98.
26. Crankshaw, *The Shadow of the Winter Palace*, p. 89. Memphis *Eagle* and *Enquirer*, n.d., F.W.P. (S.C.L.). F.W.P. to Lewis Cass, 9, 31 July, 30 Aug. 1858, Secretary of State Papers (National Archives).
27. Bull, "Lucy Pickens," pp. 3–11. Graham, *Tsar of Freedom*.
28. F.W.P. to Lewis Cass, 7 Oct. 1858, Secretary of State Papers (National Ar-

chives). F.W.P. to M. L. Bonham, 24 Feb. 1859, Bonham Papers (S.C.L.). Document in Pickens's hand entitled "Resources for 1860," F.W.P. (D.U.L.).

29. F.W.P. to the editor of the *South Carolinian*, 12 Apr. 1859, reprinted in Edgefield *Advertiser*, 17 Aug. 1859. Ed Noble to F.W.P., 10 Aug. 1859, F.W.P. (D.U.L.).

30. Ed Noble to F.W.P., 10 Aug. 1859, F.W.P. (D.U.L.).

31. F.W.P. to B. F. Perry, 24 Apr. 1859, Perry Papers (Alabama Archives).

32. F.W.P. to Lewis Cass, 31 July, 16, 30 Aug., 10, 11 Sept. 1858, 26 May, 20 July, 31 Aug. 1859, Secretary of State Papers (National Archives). Notes by F.W.P. on his observations of Russian politics, history, religion, society, etc.; F.W.P. (W. & L.).

33. F.W.P. to Lewis Cass, 26 May, 20 July 1859, Secretary of State Papers (National Archives).

34. F.W.P. to Lewis Cass, 31 Aug., 14 Oct. 1859, ibid.

35. Lucy Pickens to Rev. Mr. Dunlap, 26 Nov. 1859, Pickens-Dugas Papers (S.H.C., U.N.C.). New York *Herald*, 27 Oct. 1859. F.W.P. to Lewis Cass, 23 Nov. 1859, Secretary of State Papers (National Archives). Cass to F.W.P., 14 Oct., 12 Dec. 1859, F.W.P. (D.U.L.).

36. Lucy Pickens to Mrs. Beverley Holcombe, 2 Dec. 1859, Pickens-Dugas Papers (S.H.C., U.N.C.). Lucy Pickens to Anna Holcombe, Jan. 1859; other undated letters to her sister tell of her misery and her disappointment in not giving birth to a son, Greer-Holcombe Papers (Jane Greer).

37. Lucy Pickens to Mrs. Beverley Holcombe, 2 Dec. 1859, Pickens-Dugas Papers (S.H.C., U.N.C.). John E. Bacon to Lewis Cass, 26 Sept. 1859, Secretary of State Papers (National Archives).

38. Lucy Pickens to Mrs. E. Greer, 1859, Pickens-Dugas Papers (S.H.C., U.N.C.). F.W.P. to Lucy Pickens, 21 Feb. 1861, (A. T. Graydon).

39. Lucy Pickens to Mrs. Beverley Holcombe, 2 Dec. 1859, Pickens-Dugas Papers (S.H.C., U.N.C.).

40. Ibid.

41. F.W.P. to M. L. Bonham, 11 Dec. 1857, Bonham Papers (S.C.L.)

42. F.W.P. to Bonham, 31 Dec. 1859, ibid. Several writers, citing oral tradition, have stated that Pickens fathered black illegitimate children. However, in my research I have found no evidence to corroborate these assertions.

43. F.W.P. to Bonham, 19 Oct. 1859, ibid. F.W.P. to B. F. Perry, 24 Apr. 1859, Perry Papers (Alabama Archives).

44. F.W.P. to B. F. Perry, 24 Apr. 1859, Perry Papers (Alabama Archives).

45. Ibid.

46. F.W.P. to George N. Sanders, 24 Oct. 1859, F.W.P. (D.U.L.).

47. W. M. Churchwell to F.W.P., 8 Oct. 1859, ibid.

48. W. M. Churchwell to F.W.P., 30 Dec. 1859, 12 Feb. 1860; Silas Burrows to F.W.P., 5, 12 Nov. 1859; George N. Sanders to F.W.P., 6 Mar. 1860; all ibid.

49. F.W.P. to James Buchanan, 5, 18 Feb. 1860, Buchanan Papers (Pennsylvania Historical Society). Channing, *Crisis of Fear*, pp. 269-71.

50. W. M. Churchwell (on behalf of James Buchanan) to F.W.P., 12 Feb. 1860, F.W.P. (D.U.L.).

51. F.W.P. to ?, 6 May 1860, portion of letter, F.W.P. (W. & L.).
52. George N. Sanders to F.W.P., 6 Mar. 1860; Isaac R. Diller to F.W.P., 14 May 1860; Judge John T. Mason to F.W.P., 9 Mar. 1860; Thomas Hart Seymour to F.W.P., 28 Apr. 1860; J. Durrell Green to F.W.P., 21 May 1860; all in F.W.P. (D.U.L.). New York *Journal of Commerce*, 28 Apr. 1860.
53. New York *Journal of Commerce*, 28 Apr. 1860.
54. Nichols, *The Disruption of American Democracy*, pp. 288–304. Wallace, *The History of South Carolina*, III, 149–50.
55. J. Durrell Green to F.W.P., 21 May 1860; W. M. Churchwell to F.W.P., 10 May 1860; both in F.W.P. (D.U.L.).
56. F.W.P. to Lewis Cass, 17 Apr. 1860, Secretary of State Papers (National Archives). F.W.P. to M. L. Bonham, 15 June 1860, Bonham Papers (S.C.L.). F.W.P. to ?, 6 May 1860, F.W.P. (W. & L.).
57. F.W.P. to Lucy Pickens, 18 Aug. 1860, F.W.P. (D.U.L.). Lucy Pickens to Mrs. Beverley Holcombe, 31 Aug. 1860, (A. T. Graydon). F.W.P. to M. L. Bonham, 14 Oct. 1859, Bonham Papers (S.C.L.).
58. F.W.P. to F. S. Claxton, 22 June 1860; C. Mortimer to F.W.P., 27 June 1860; both in F.W.P. (D.U.L.). F.W.P. to Lewis Cass, 17 July 1860, Secretary of State Papers (National Archives).
59. F.W.P. to M. L. Bonham, 14 Apr. 1860, Bonham Papers (S.C.L.).
60. F.W.P. to M. L. Bonham, 15 June 1860, Bonham Papers (S.C.L.). In Pickens's entourage was his manservant Lorn. Pickens told Bonham that "Lorn goes in full livery and is very much courted. He has been to parties full of white people and danced with white ladies."
61. J. Durrell Green to F.W.P., 21 May 1860, F.W.P. (D.U.L.).
62. Charleston *Mercury*, 2 Aug. 1860.
63. Ibid., 7 July 1860.
64. *Mary Chesnut's Civil War*, p. 4.
65. F.W.P. to Arthur Simkins, 19 Sept. 1860, Edgefield *Advertiser*, 31 Oct. 1860.
66. George D. Tillman to J.H.H., 9 Oct. 1860, J.H.H. (L.C.). Channing, *Crisis of Fear*, pp. 269–71.
67. *Mercury*, 3 Nov. 1860.
68. Ibid., 3, 5 Nov. 1860.
69. Ibid., 8 Nov. 1860.
70. F.W.P. to Arthur Simkins, 19 Sept. 1860, Edgefield *Advertiser*, 31 Oct. 1860.
71. Strong, *Diary of the Civil War*, p. 76.
72. Edgefield *Advertiser*, 17 Dec. 1860.

Chapter 9. A Fire-Eater Down to the Ground

1. Craven, *The Growth of Southern Nationalism*, p. 349.
2. W. P. Miles to J.H.H., 5 Aug. 1860, J.H.H. (L.C.).
3. R. S. Holt to Joseph Holt, 20 Nov. 1860, Joseph Holt Papers (L.C.).
4. *Mercury*, 8, 9 Nov. 1860.

5. Craven, *The Growth of Southern Nationalism*, pp. 349-60.
6. F.W.P. to James Buchanan, 4 Sept. 1860, Buchanan Papers (Historical Society of Pa.).
7. White, *Rhett*, p. 185. Crawford, *History of the Fall of Fort Sumter*, p. 80. For an excellent study of Pickens's role as governor, see Cauthen, *South Carolina Goes to War*. Swanburg's *First Blood* is an entertaining work mainly researched from published sources.
8. Edgefield *Advertiser*, 28 Nov. 1860.
9. Keel, "Pickens, Governor," p. 17.
10. Edgefield *Advertiser*, 28 Nov. 1860.
11. Charleston *Courier*, 24 Nov. 1860. *Mercury*, 26 Nov. 1860. Edgefield *Advertiser*, 21, 28 Nov., 5 Dec. 1860.
12. Edgefield *Advertiser*, 21, 28 Nov. 1860. M. L. Bonham to F.W.P., 17 Jan. 1861, F.W.P. (S.C.L.).
13. *Mercury*, 4 Dec. 1860. Charleston *Courier*, 3 Dec. 1860. White, *Rhett*, p. 185. Ironically, in the column next to Pickens's Edgefield speech (which was published in Edgefield *Advertiser*, 28 Nov. 1860) is an announcement that the local general store has a large supply of burial cases.
14. Strong, *Diary of the Civil War*, p. 76.
15. *Mary Chesnut's Civil War*, p. 40. L. T. Wigfall was at this time a U.S. senator from Texas. Mrs. Chesnut wrote her husband: "What a fulminating message the fair Lucy and himself [Pickens] will concoct—Mrs. Wigfall writes me a very affectionate letter—says Pickens was utterly opposed to secession until he got to Columbia. . . . She says the fair Lucy is utterly intrigante [sic] and ambitious and was always in *these* rows in Texas" (Mary Chesnut to James Chesnut, n.d. [1862], W.M.C. [S.C.L.]).
16. *Mercury*, 13, 14, 15, 17, 19, 20, 21 Dec. 1860.
17. D. L. Wardlaw to Samuel McGowan, 3 Dec. 1860, McGowan Papers (S.C.L.).
18. Edgefield *Advertiser*, 19 Dec. 1860. Charleston *Mercury*, 12, 13, 14, 15 Dec. 1860. *South Carolina House Journal*, 1861, pp. 164, 167, 176, 180, 198. White, *Rhett*, p. 185. The vote was 83-67.
19. Charleston *Courier*, 17 Dec. 1860.
20. Ibid., 18 Dec. 1860.
21. Ibid., 21 Dec. 1860, and Charleston *Mercury*, 21 Dec. 1860.
22. Hooker, "Excerpts from the Diary."
23. F.W.P. to Lucy Pickens, 23 Feb. 1861, (A. T. Graydon).
24. M. L. Bonham to W. H. Gist, 16 Dec. 1860, Bonham Papers (S.C.L.).
25. B. T. Watts to J.H.H., 1 Dec. 1860, Watts Papers (S.C.L.). *Mary Chesnut's Civil War*, p. 4.
26. Ware, "South Carolina Executive Councils," p. 27.
27. *Mercury*, 13, 18 Dec. 1860. R. B. Rhett to James Buchanan, 27 Nov. 1860, Buchanan Papers (Historical Society of Pa.).
28. F.W.P. to Buchanan, 17 Dec. 1860, Harris, *Record of Fort Sumter*, pp. 7-8. Crawford, *Genesis of the Civil War*, pp. 39-40.
29. W. H. Trescot to F.W.P., 21 Dec. 1860. Harris, *Record of Fort Sumter*, pp. 9-

11. Crawford, *Genesis of the Civil War*, pp. 39–40. *The War of the Rebellion: A Compilation of the Official Records of the Union and Confederate Armies*, 1st ser., I, 94–103 (hereafter cited as *O.R.*).

30. Message Number 1 of His Excellency Governor Pickens to the Legislature, 5 Nov. 1861.

31. Fuess, *Life of Caleb Cushing*, II, 272–74. Keel, "Pickens, Governor," pp. 25–26. Olsberg, "William Henry Trescot," p. 79.

32. A. P. Hayne to Buchanan, 22 Dec. 1861, Buchanan Papers (Historical Society of Pa.).

33. W. H. Trescot to F.W.P., 21 Dec. 1860. Harris, *Record of Fort Sumter*, pp. 9–11.

34. Feuss, *Life of Caleb Cushing*, II, 273.

35. Charleston *Daily Courier*, 25 Dec. 1860.

36. Ibid., 22 Dec. 1860. Keel, "Pickens, Governor," p. 23.

37. *Journal of the Secession Convention*, 27 Dec. 1860, MS (S.C. Archives). For an excellent short study of the role of the convention, see White, "The Fate of Calhoun's Sovereign Convention." See also Ware, "South Carolina Executive Councils."

38. Keel, "Pickens, Governor," pp. 26–29.

39. W. H. Trescot to F.W.P., 21 Dec. 1860. Harris, *Record of Fort Sumter*, p. 9. Swanburg, *First Blood*, pp. 84–85.

40. Swanburg, *First Blood*, pp. 83–101.

41. *Mary Chesnut's Civil War*, p. 5.

42. Ibid. Charleston *Courier*, 28 Dec. 1860.

43. Charles Macbeth to F.W.P., 30 Dec. 1860, F.W.P. (D.U.L.).

44. Swanburg, *First Blood*, pp. 103–6. Keel, "Pickens, Governor," pp. 38–40.

45. Col. Walter Gwynn to F.W.P., 31 Dec. 1860, F.W.P. (D.U.L.).

46. Note on bottom of Gwynn's letter to F.W.P., 31 Dec. 1860, dated 8 Jan. 1861, ibid.

47. F.W.P. to J. Johnston Pettigrew, 27 Dec. 1860. Harris, *Record of Fort Sumter*, p. 12.

48. Swanburg, *First Blood*, p. 123. Crawford, *Genesis of the Civil War*, p. 116. F.W.P. to Gen. Schnierle, 30 Dec. 1860, F.W.P. (D.U.L.).

49. Olsberg, "William Henry Trescot," pp. 80–84.

50. *Journal of the South Carolina Executives Councils of 1861 and 1862*, p. 3 (S.C. Archives). Ware, "South Carolina Executive Councils," pp. 8–19.

51. F.W.P. to Baron Edward de Stoekle (Russian Minister to the United States), 12 Jan. 1861, F.W.P. (D.U.L.). Jokingly the Baron called the Carolinians the subjects of Pickens I.

52. Captain Abner Doubleday to General Legoine, 6 Jan. 1861. *Mercury*, 19 Jan. 1861, reprinted from Auburn (N.Y.) *Union*.

53. F.W.P. to Baron Edward de Stoekle, 12 Jan. 1861, F.W.P. (D.U.L.).

54. Crawford, *Genesis of the Civil War*, pp. 174–75.

55. Louis Wigfall to F.W.P. (telegram), 8 Jan. 1861, F.W.P. (S.C. Archives). *O.R.*, 1st ser., I, 120–25. J. L. Orr to W. S. Ashe (telegram), 8 Jan. 1861, *Journal of the Executive Council*, p. 10.

56. Major Robert Anderson to F.W.P., 9 Jan. 1861. F.W.P. to Anderson in Edge-

field *Advertiser*, 16 Jan. 1861; in Charleston *Courier*, 10 Jan.; in *Mercury*, 10–16 Jan. 1861. *O.R.*, 1st ser., I, 135–36. Crawford, *Genesis of the Civil War*, pp. 178–86.

57. Robert Toombs to F.W.P., 11 Jan. 1861, F.W.P. (D.U.L.).
58. *South Carolina Journal of the House of Representatives, 1861*, pp. 310–12. Keel, "Pickens, Governor," pp. 39–40.
59. Keel, "Pickens, Governor," p. 40.
60. Harris, *Record of Fort Sumter*, pp. 28–29.
61. Ibid.
62. Executive Documents No. 2, *Correspondence and Other Papers Relating to Fort Sumter*, including correspondence of the Honorable Isaac W. Hayne with the President, pp. 3–8. Crawford, *Genesis of the Civil War*, pp. 191–94. Edgefield *Advertiser*, 13 Feb. 1861. *Journal of the Executive Council*, pp. 27–31.
63. F.W.P. to Cols. Gwynn, White, and Tropier, 9 Jan. 1861. Harris, *Record of Fort Sumter*, p. 21.
64. Keel, "Pickens, Governor," p. 71.
65. *Mercury*, 16–21 Jun. 1861. Crawford, *Genesis of Civil War*, pp. 219–20. I. W. Hayne to A. G. Magrath, 16 Jan. 1861, Pickens-Bonham Papers (L.C.).
66. Crawford, *Genesis of Civil War*, pp. 226–34.
67. Swanburg, *First Blood*, p. 193.
68. *Mercury*, 21 Jan. 1861.
69. Ibid., 19 Jan. 1861.
70. William L. Yancey to F.W.P., 27 Feb. 1861, Yancey Papers (Alabama Archives). Jefferson Davis to F.W.P., 20 Jan. 1861. McElroy, *Jefferson Davis*, I, 255.
71. Crawford, *Genesis of the Civil War*, p. 266.
72. F.W.P. to Jefferson Davis, 23 Jan. 1861, in Davis, *Jefferson Davis, Constitutionalist*, V, 95–96.
73. Columbia *Southern Guardian*, n.d., quoted in Edgefield *Advertiser*, 30 Jan. 1861.
74. S.W.B. [not identifiable] to Mrs. Coleman, 27 Jan. 1861, William Dunlap Simpson Papers (D.U.L.).
75. Ravenel, *Journal*, p. 51.
76. I. W. Hayne to A. G. Magrath, 16 Jan. 1861, Pickens-Bonham Papers (L.C.).
77. Ware, "South Carolina Executive Council," p. 20.
78. *Journal of the Executive Council*, p. 23. Keel, "Pickens, Governor," pp. 46–47.
79. *Journal of the Executive Council*, pp. 38–41. Keel, "Pickens, Governor," pp. 47–48.
80. F.W.P. to John Tyler, 7 Feb. 1861, F.W.P. (D.U.L.). *Journal of the Executive Council*, pp. 38–41. Crawford, *Genesis of the Civil War*, pp. 267–68. Keel, "Pickens, Governor," p. 48. *Mercury*, Jan., Feb. 1861 passim.
81. Edgefield *Advertiser*, 13 Feb. 1861.
82. F.W.P. to J. Thompson Mason, 7 Feb. 1861, in Swanburg, *First Blood*, pp. 192–93.
83. Cauthen, *South Carolina Goes to War*, pp. 103–6.
84. Crawford, *Genesis of the Civil War*, p. 266.

85. F.W.P. to Robert Toombs, 9 Feb. 1861, in Crawford, *Genesis of the Civil War*, p. 267.
86. *Journal of the Congress of the Confederate States of America, 1861–1865*, I, 48–49, 56–59.
87. *O.R.*, 1st ser., I, 258–59. Keel, "Pickens, Governor," p. 50.
88. F.W.P. to General Evans, 2 Mar. 1861, F.W.P. (S.C.L.). Keel, "Pickens, Governor," p. 50. Cauthen, *South Carolina Goes to War*, p. 126.
89. F.W.P. to Lucy Pickens, 23 Feb. 1861 (A. T. Graydon).
90. Robert L. Cooper to Thomas B. Fraser, 23 Feb. 1861, T. B. Fraser Papers (S.C.L.).
91. Charleston *Daily Courier*, 12 Mar. 1861.
92. Cauthen, *South Carolina Goes to War*, pp. 127–31. Keel, "Pickens, Governor," pp. 50–51.
93. Cauthen, *South Carolina Goes to War*, p. 131. Harris, *Record of Fort Sumter*, p. 35. Robert Toombs to F.W.P., 18 Apr. 1861, Toombs Letter Book, Toombs Papers (S.C.L.).
94. Charleston *Daily Courier*, 14 Apr. 1861.
95. *Mercury*, 16 Apr. 1861. Harris, *Record of Fort Sumter*, pp. 44–50. Although Pickens talked of "Twenty Millions," the garrison of Fort Sumter consisted of 9 officers, 74 noncommissioned officers and soldiers, and 43 laborers; *Mercury*, 27 Apr. 1861.
96. *Mercury*, 16 Apr. 1861.
97. New York *Times*, 16 Apr. 1861, in *Mercury*, 18 Apr. 1861.
98. Charleston *Mercury*, 26 Apr. 1861. F.W.P. to M. L. Bonham, 21 Apr. 1861, Pickens-Bonham Papers (L.C.).
99. Cauthen, *South Carolina Goes to War*, p. 139.
100. Ibid., pp. 135–36. Charleston *Daily Courier*, 25 Apr. 1861. Keel, "Pickens, Governor," pp. 60–61. *O.R.* Serial No. 127, pp. 413–15. *Journal of the Executive Council*, pp. 76–77.
101. Cauthen, *South Carolina Goes to War*, pp. 135–36.
102. W. G. Simms to William Porcher Miles, 11 May 1861, Miles Papers (U.N.C.). and in Simms, *Letters*, IV, 362–63. *Journal of Executive Council*, pp. 76–80.
103. For a full account of Pickens's role in coastal defense, see Gwinn, "Coastal Defense," pp. 64–106, 199–329.
104. W. G. Simms to W. P. Miles, 11 May 1861, Miles Papers (S.H.C., U.N.C.) and in Simms, *Letters*, IV, 363–66. Simms to J.H.H., 14 June 1861, J.H.H. (L.C.). Cauthen, *South Carolina Goes to War*, pp. 140–41.
105. W. G. Simms to J.H.H., 14 June 1861, J.H.H. (L.C.) and in Simms, *Letters*, IV, 366–67.
106. *Mary Chesnut's Civil War*, 3 Apr. 1861, pp. 40–41.
107. *Mercury*, 28 May 1861.
108. Keel, "Pickens, Governor," p. 44.
109. F.W.P. to James Chesnut, 10 Nov. 1861, W.M.C. (S.C.L.).
110. Ravenel, *Journal*, p. 47. Ware, "S.C. Executive Councils," pp. 28–29.

111. "Message No. 1 of Governor Pickens," 5 Nov. 1861. Ware, "S.C. Executive Councils," pp. 28–29.
112. Wallace, *History of South Carolina*, III, 171.
113. Charleston *Courier*, 25 July 1862.
114. *Mary Chesnut's Civil War*, 8 Nov. 1861, p. 228.
115. Ravenel, *Journal*, 21 Nov. 1861, p. 103.
116. Langdon Cheves, Jr., to Mrs. Langdon Cheves, Sr., 16 Nov. 1861, Cheves Papers (S.C.L.). Charleston *Courier*, 25 July 1862.
117. Keel, "Pickens, Governor," p. 67.
118. Cauthen, *South Carolina Goes to War*, pp. 137–38. Speech of His Excellency the Governor to a Joint Session of the House and Senate, 4 Dec. 1861.
119. Cauthen, *South Carolina Goes to War*, p. 138.

Chapter 10. Governor and Council

1. Ware, "S.C. Executive Councils," pp. 30–32.
2. Ibid., p. 32.
3. Ibid. Keel, "Pickens, Governor," pp. 68–69. *Journal of the Convention*, pp. 793–95.
4. Ware, "S.C. Executive Councils," pp. 32–36.
5. F.W.P. to A. G. Magrath, Dec. 1861, F.W.P. (S.C.L.).
6. F.W.P. to the president and members of the convention, 8 Jan. 1862, Pickens-Dugas Papers (S.H.C., U.N.C.).
7. D. F. Jamison to F.W.P., 5 March 1862, F.W.P. (D.U.L.).
8. Ibid. Keel, "Pickens, Governor," p. 37. *Journal of the Executive Council*, Appendix, p. 299.
9. Ware, "S.C. Executive Councils," pp. 38–40. Charleston *Daily Courier*, 23 Jan. 1862.
10. *Mary Chesnut's Civil War*, 9 Jan. 1862, p. 275.
11. Ibid., 29 Jan. 1862, p. 285. The passage alludes to Milton's *Paradise Lost*. Chesnut's aversion to Moses proved not to be groundless. In South Carolina history, Moses emerges as a Judas figure, for he was the nefarious scalawag governor of South Carolina during Reconstruction.
12. J. Foster Marshall to F.W.P., 17 Jan. 1862, F.W.P. (D.U.L.).
13. Ware, "S.C. Executive Councils," pp. 38–42.
14. Keel, "Pickens, Governor," p. 76. *Mary Chesnut's Civil War*, pp. 399, 454.
15. Keel, "Pickens, Governor," p. 72. F.W.P. to General W. C. DeSaussure, 29 Feb. 1862, F.W.P. (S.C.L.).
16. F.W.P. to Lucy Pickens, 24 Jan. 1862, F.W.P. (S.C.L.).
17. Bull, "Lucy Pickens." Mrs. Chesnut, in her diary, gives numerous instances of the power of Lucy's charm. Lucy's picture was on the Confederate $100 bill issued 2 Dec. 1862, 16 Apr. 1863, 17 Feb. 1864; see Allen, "The Paper Money of the Confederate States," pp. 286, 295.
18. *Journal of the Executive Council* passim.

19. Keel, "Pickens, Governor," p. 74.
20. Ibid. p. 75. Charleston *Daily Courier*, 1 May 1862; See also 15, 16, 22, 23, 24, 27, 28 May 1862. *Mary Chesnut's Civil War*, p. 426.
21. Charleston *Daily Courier*, 15, 23 May 1862. There is evidence to suggest that some of the letters were written by Lucy and Paul H. Hayne.
22. Charleston *Daily Courier*, 19 June 1862. Keel, "Pickens, Governor," p. 76.
23. *Mary Chesnut's Civil War*, p. 426. M. B. Chesnut to James Chesnut, 1862, W.M.C. (S.C.L.).
24. Cauthen, *South Carolina Goes to War*, pp. 152-61.
25. White, "The Fate of Calhoun's Sovereign Convention,"p. 760.
26. Keel, "Pickens, Governor," p. 77. Columbia *Southern Guardian*, 8 Aug. 1862, I. W. Hayne to the editor. Mrs. Chesnut believed that Lucy and her "pet," Franklin Moses, were behind the newspaper war between Pickens and Hayne. M.B.C. to Mrs. Louis T. Wigfall, Aug. 1862; M.B.C. to James Chesnut, Aug. or Sept. 1862, W.M.C. (S.C.L.).
27. White, "The Fate of Calhoun's Sovereign Convention," p. 760.
28. Ibid.
29. *Message No. 1 of His Excellency the Governor of South Carolina*, 2 Nov. 1862. *Mercury*, 1 Dec. 1862. Edgefield *Advertiser*, 3 Dec. 1862.
30. *Mercury*, 1 Dec. 1862. F.W.P. to M. L. Bonham, 1862, Bonham Papers (S.C.L.). Cauthen, *South Carolina Goes to War*, pp. 156-63.
31. Cauthen, *South Carolina Goes to War*, p. 157.
32. F.W.P. to M. L. Bonham, 15 Sept. 1862, Bonham Papers (S.C.L.). Charleston *Courier*, 8 Dec. 1862. *Mercury*, 1 Dec. 1862. F.W.P. to B. F. Perry, 8 July 1863, Perry Papers (Alabama Archives).
33. *Mercury*, 1 Dec. 1862.
34. Charleston *Courier*, 4, 8 Dec. 1862. Cauthen, *South Carolina Goes to War*, p. 162.

Chapter 11. "There Can Lay No Peace for Me"

1. F.W.P. to M. L. Bonham, 15 Sept. 1862, Bonham Papers (S.C.L.). F.W.P. to Miss Gregg [sister of Maxcy Gregg], 29 Dec. 1862, Edgefield *Advertiser*, 15 Jan. 1863.
2. Reid, *After the War*, pp. 66-67. Simkins and Woody, *South Carolina during Reconstruction*, p. 20.
3. F.W.P. to James Pringle, 27 Apr., 29 May, 21 June, 1 Aug. 1864, Pringle Papers (D.U.L.). Rawick, ed. *American Slave*, XVII, 47-50.
4. Edgefield *Advertiser*, 6 May 1863.
5. Ibid., 10 Sept. 1863.
6. Cauthen, *South Carolina Goes to War*, p. 162. Charleston *Courier*, 5, 6 October 1864.
7. F.W.P. to Lucy Pickens, 5 June 1864 (A. T. Graydon).
8. F.W.P. to Louis Wigfall, 28 July 1863, copy in Wigfall Papers (Eugene C. Barker History Center, University of Texas).

9. Cauthen, *South Carolina Goes to War*, pp. 228-30.
10. F.W.P. to A. G. Magrath, 2 Feb. 1865, Magrath Papers (U.N.C., S.H.C.). F.W.P. to B. F. Perry, 8 July 1865, Perry Papers (Alabama Archives). F.W.P. to Lucy Pickens, 15 June 1864, (A. T. Graydon).
11. Edgefield *Advertiser*, 1 Mar. 1865.
12. J. L. Orr to F.W.P., 29 Apr. 1865 (A. T. Graydon).
13. Mary B. Chesnut Diary, 27 Feb. 1865, MS, W.M.C. (S.C.L.). *Mary Chesnut's Civil War*, p. 239.
14. Burton, "The Civil War in the Confederate Interior."
15. Simkins and Woody, *South Carolina during Reconstruction*, p. 18.
16. F.W.P. to B. F. Perry, 8 July 1865, Perry Papers (Alabama Archives).
17. F.W.P. to Lucy Pickens, 1 Sept. 1863, F.W.P. (W. & L.).
18. Edgefield *Advertiser*, 24 May 1865.
19. Ibid., 28 June 1865.
20. W. H. Yeldell to F.W.P., 13 June 1865, F.W.P. (D.U.L.).
21. F.W.P. to President Andrew Johnson, 8 July 1865, Andrew Johnson Papers (L.C.). F.W.P. to B. F. Perry, 8 July 1865, Perry Papers (Alabama Archives).
22. Perry, *Reminiscences*, p. 166.
23. F.W.P. to B. F. Perry, 8 July 1865, 9 Jan. 1866, Perry Papers (Alabama Archives).
24. Agreements between F.W.P. and his former slaves, F.W.P. (D.U.L.), and numerous contracts (A. T. Graydon).
25. F.W.P. to Lucy Pickens, 4 Sept. 1865, F.W.P. (D.U.L.).
26. Ibid.
27. F.W.P. to B. F. Perry, 7 Sept. 1865, Perry Papers (Alabama Archives). Certificate that Ex-Governor Francis W. Pickens has taken the oath prescribed by President Johnson, 18 Aug. 1865, F.W.P. (W. & L.).
28. Andrews, *The South since the War*, pp. 39-41.
29. *Journal of the Convention of the People of South Carolina*, Sept. 1865, p. 7.
30. Andrews, *The South since the War*, p. 43.
31. Ibid., p. 50.
32. Columbia *Daily Phoenix*, 13, 15, 16, 21, 28 Sept. 1865.
33. *Journal of the Convention*, Sept. 1865, pp. 134-35.
34. "Proceedings of the Board of Trustees," University of South Carolina, Minutes for 20 Sept. 1865, *Proceedings of the Board of Trustees 29 Nov. 1865-8 July 1873* (University of South Carolina Archives).
35. *Journal of the General Assembly for 1865*, p. 44. Perry received 104 votes; J. L. Manning, 24; William Trescot, 4; Pickens, 4; W. W. Boyce, 2; R. W. Barnwell, 1. Perry was elected for the long term and Manning for the short term. Edgefield *Advertiser*, 15 Nov. 1865.
36. B. F. Perry to President Andrew Johnson, 7 Nov. 1865. Edgefield *Advertiser*, 15 Nov. 1865. F.W.P. to James L. Orr, 25 Nov. 1865, Orr Papers (S.C. Archives). F.W.P. to B. F. Perry, 25 Nov. 1865, Perry Papers (Alabama Archives).
37. Stampp, *The Era of Reconstruction*, p. 51.
38. F.W.P. to B. F. Perry, 25 Nov. 1865, Perry Papers (Alabama Archives).
39. F.W.P. to J. L. Orr, 4 Feb., 2 Mar. 1866, Orr Papers (S.C. Archives).

40. F.W.P. to a gentleman in New Orleans, 12 June 1866, F.W.P. (S.C.L.). Edgefield *Advertiser*, 27 June 1866, confirmed that Pickens had been ill but reported he was improving.

41. Edgefield *Advertiser*, 19 Sept. 1866.

42. P. H. Hayne to Mrs. P. H. Hayne, 27 July, 6 Aug., 9 Sept., 23 Dec. 1865, P. H. Hayne Papers (D.U.L.).

43. Notes on "Hope Not Without Cause," 1867, F.W.P. (D.U.L.).

44. Edgefield *Advertiser*, 11 Sept. 1867, and in numerous other issues, 1867–68.

45. F.W.P. to Maj. Stone, President of Provost U.S. Court [sic], 8 Nov. 1867, F.W.P. (D.U.L.).

46. F.W.P. to B. F. Perry, 9 Jan. 1868, Perry Papers (Alabama Archives).

47. Ibid.

48. F.W.P. to J. L. Orr, 25 Nov. 1865, Orr Papers (S.C. Archives). F.W.P. to a gentleman in New Orleans, n.d. Columbia *Daily Phoenix*, 3 Apr. 1867.

49. F.W.P. to Lucy Pickens, 2 Apr. 1867 (A. T. Graydon).

50. F.W.P., "Oration on the Influence of Government upon the Nature and Destiny of Man."

Bibliography

Newspapers

The Abbeville *Banner*
The *Union* (Auburn, N.Y.)
The *Merchant* (Baltimore, Md.)
The Charleston *Courier*
The *Mercury* (Charleston, S.C.)
The *Phoenix* (Columbia, S.C.)
The *Southern Times* (Columbia, S.C.)
The *Telegraph* (Columbia, S.C.)
The *Daily South Carolinian* (Columbia, S.C.)
The Edgefield *Advertiser*
The Edgefield *Carolinian*
The Edgefield *Hive*
The *Mountaineer* (Greenville, S.C.)
The *Southern Patriot* (Greenville, S.C.)
The Hamburg *Journal*
The Lancaster *Ledger*
The *Times* (London)
The Memphis *Eagle*
The New York *Herald*
The *Journal of Commerce* (New York, N.Y.)
The Pendleton *Messenger*
The *Sumter News*
The *Globe* (Washington, D.C.)
The *Madisonian* (Washington, D.C.)
Niles National Register (Washington, D.C.)
The *Reformer* (Washington, D.C.)
The *Spectator* (Washington, D.C.)
The *United States Telegraph* (Washington, D.C.)
The Yorkville *Enquirer*
The Yorkville *Miscellany*

Manuscripts

Alabama Department of Archives and History, Montgomery, Ala.
    Dixon H. Lewis Papers
    Benjamin F. Perry Papers
    William L. Yancey Papers

Bibliography

Special Collections, Clemson University Library, Clemson University
    John C. Calhoun Papers
    Thomas Green Clemson Papers
Manuscript Division, Duke University Library, Duke University
    Armistead Burt Papers
    John C. Calhoun Papers
    Campbell Family Papers
    Paul Hamilton Hayne Papers
    George McDuffie Papers
    Francis W. Pickens Papers
    James R. Pringle Papers
    William Dunlap Simpson Papers
    Richard Singleton Papers
    Waddy Thompson Papers
    William Henry Trescot Papers
Charleston Library Society, Charleston, S.C.
    Henry Conner Papers
Manuscripts Division, Library of Congress
    Richard K. Crallé Papers
    James H. Hammond Papers
    Franklin Harper Elmore Papers
    Joseph Holt Papers
    Andrew Johnson Papers
    Pickens-Bonham Papers
    James K. Polk Papers
    Waddy Thompson Papers
    Martin Van Buren Papers
New York Public Library, New York, N.Y.
    Kohn Papers
    Francis W. Pickens Papers
Pennsylvania Historical Society, Philadelphia, Pa.
    James Buchanan Papers
National Archives, Washington, D.C.
    Francis W. Pickens Papers—General Records of the Dept. of State
South Carolina Department of Archives and History, Columbia, S.C.
    Milledge Luke Bonham Papers
    James L. Orr Papers
    J. L. Petigru Papers
    Francis W. Pickens Papers
    Francis W. Pickens Governorship Papers
South Carolina Historical Society, Charleston, S.C.
    A. G. Magrath Papers
    Robert Barnwell Rhett Papers
South Caroliniana Library, University of South Carolina
    M. L. Bonham Papers
    Preston Brooks Papers

Matthew C. Butler Papers
John C. Calhoun Papers
Langdon Cheves Papers
James Edward Colhoun Papers
Thomas B. Fraser Papers
James H. Hammond Papers
Hugh Swinton Legaré Papers
McGowan Papers
Noble Family Papers
James L. Orr Papers
J. L. Petigrú Papers
Francis W. Pickens Papers
William Preston Papers
Eldred Simkins Papers
William G. Simms Papers
Waddy Thompson Papers
Robert Toombs Papers
Townes Family Papers
William Henry Trescot Papers
Beaufort Tyler Watts Papers
Williams-Manning-Chesnut Papers
Southern Historical Collection, University of North Carolina, Chapel Hill
James H. Hammond Papers
E. M. Law Papers
A. G. Magrath Papers
Christopher G. Memminger Papers
William Porcher Miles Papers
Orr-Patterson Papers
B. F. Perry Papers
Pickens-Dugas Papers
Robert Barnwell Rhett Papers
William H. Trescot Papers
William Lowndes Yancey Papers
Special Collections, University of Texas, Austin
Louis Wigfall Papers
Manuscript Division, University of Virginia, Charlottesville
R. M. T. Hunter Papers
Manuscript Division, Washington and Lee University
Francis W. Pickens Papers
Miscellaneous South Carolina Papers which contain a large number of D. F. Jamison Papers
Letters in private hands
Whitfield Brooks Diaries, Myrtle Fisher, Banner Elk, N.C.
Greer-Holcombe Papers, Jane Greer, Tyler, Tex.
Francis W. Pickens Papers, A. T. Graydon, Columbia, S.C.
Francis W. Pickens Papers, Eulalie Salley, Aiken, S.C.

Published Papers, Journals, and Diaries

Adams, John Q. *Memoirs of John Quincy Adams, Comprising Portions of His Diary from 1795–1848, IX–XII*. Edited by Charles Francis Adams. New York: AMS Press, 1970.

Bates, Edward. *The Diary of Edward Bates, 1859–1866*. Edited by Howard K. Beale. Washington: U.S. Government Printing Office, 1933.

Buchanan, James. *Works of James Buchanan*. 12 vols. Edited by G. B. Moore. Philadelphia: J. B. Lippincott, 1908–11.

Calhoun, John C. "Correspondence of John C. Calhoun." *Fourth Annual Report of the Historical Manuscripts Commission of the American Historical Association*. Edited by J. Franklin Jameson in *Annual Report of the American Historical Association for 1899*. Washington: U.S. Government Printing Office, 1900.

──────. *Correspondence Addressed to John C. Calhoun, 1837–1849*. Edited by Chauncey S. Boucher and Robert P. Brooks. *Annual Report of the American Historical Association, 1929*. Washington: U.S. Government Printing Office, 1931.

──────. *The Papers of John C. Calhoun, 1801–1843*. 16 vols. Edited by R. L. Meriwether, Edward Hemphill, and Clyde N. Wilson. Columbia: University of South Carolina Press, 1959–84.

Chesnut, Mary B. *Diary from Dixie*. Edited by Ben Ames Williams. Boston: Houghton Mifflin, 1961.

──────. *Mary Chesnut's Civil War*. Edited by C. Vann Woodward. New Haven: Yale University Press, 1981.

Davis, Jefferson. *Jefferson Davis, Constitutionalist: His Letters, Papers, and Speeches*. 10 vols. Edited by Dunbar Rowland. Jackson: Mississippi State Department of Archives and History, 1923.

Grayson, William J. "The Autobiography of William J. Grayson." Edited by Robert D. Bass. Ph.D. dissertation, University of South Carolina.

Hooker, Edward. "Excerpts from the Diary of Edward Hooker." Edited by J. Franklin Jameson. *Annual Report of the American History Association, 1896*, I. Washington: U.S. Government Printing Office, 1897.

Hunter, Robert Mercer Taliaferro. "Robert Mercer Taliaferro Hunter Papers." *American Historical Review*, II. Washington: U.S. Government Printing Office, 1916.

Mangum, Willie Person. *The Papers of Willie Person Mangum, III, 1839–43*. Edited by Henry T. Shanks. Raleigh: State Department of Archives and History, 1953.

Petigru, James Louis. *Life, Letters and Speeches of James Louis Petigru, the Union Man of South Carolina*. Edited by James P. Carson. Washington: W. H. Loudermilk, 1920.

Poinsett, Joel Robert. "Calendar of Joel R. Poinsett Papers." Edited by Grace E. Heilman and Bernard S. Levin. *Henry P. Gilpin Collection, Pennsylvania Historical Survey*. Philadelphia: Gilpin Library of the Historical Society of Pennsylvania, 1941.

Polk, James K. *Correspondence of James K. Polk. IV and V, 1837–38*. Edited by Herbert Weaver. Nashville: Vanderbilt University Press, 1977.

Ravenel, H. W. *Journal of H. W. Ravenel.* Edited by A. R. Childs. Columbia: University of South Carolina Press, 1947.
Ruffin, Edmund. *The Diary of Edmund Ruffin.* Edited by William K. Scarborough. Baton Rouge: Louisiana State University Press, 1972.
Simms, William Gilmore. *The Letters of William Gilmore Simms.* 5 vols. Edited by Mary C. Oliphant et al. Columbia: University of South Carolina Press, 1955.
Toombs, Robert; Stephens, Alexander H.; and Cobb, Howell. "The Correspondence of Robert Toombs, Alexander H. Stephens and Howell Cobb." Edited by Ulrich B. Phillips. *Annual Report of the American Historical Association.* Washington: U.S. Government Printing Office, 1911.
Trescot, William Henry. "Narrative and Letter of William Henry Trescot Concerning the Negotiations between South Carolina and President Buchanan in December, 1860." *American Historical Review*, XIII. Washington: U.S. Government Printing Office, 1908.
Van Buren, Martin. "The Autobiography of Martin Van Buren." Edited by John C. Fitzpatrick. *Annual Report of the American Historical Association for the Year 1918*, II. Washington: U.S. Government Printing Office, 1920.
Webster, Daniel. *The Papers of Daniel Webster*, V. Edited by Harold D. Moser. Hanover: University Press of New England for Dartmouth College, 1982.
Weld, Theodore G.; Weld, Angelina Grimké; and Grimké, Sara. *Letters of Theodore G. Weld, Angelina Grimké, and Sara Grimké.* Edited by Gilbert Barnes and Dwight Dumond. New York: DaCapo Press, 1970.

Published Speeches

Pickens, Francis W. "Anniversary Oration of the Clariosophic Society," 2 Feb. 1827. Columbia: Sweeny and Sims, 1827.
──────. "Speech on the Abolition Question" delivered before the House of Representatives, 21 Jan. 1836. (From notes of Henry Godfrey Wheeler.) Washington: Gales and Seaton, 1836.
──────. "Speech on the Fortification Bill" delivered before the House of Representatives, 23 May 1836. Washington: Gales and Seaton, 1836.
──────. "Remarks on the Separation of the Government from All Banks" delivered before the House of Representatives, 10 Oct. 1837. Washington: *Globe*, 1837.
──────. "Remarks on the Maine Boundary Question" delivered before the House of Representatives, 20 Feb. and 1 Mar. 1839. Washington: Gales and Seaton, 1839.
──────. "Remarks on the Bill to Repeal the Independent Treasury and on the Creation of a United States Bank," delivered before the House of Representatives, 9 Aug. 1841. n.p., n.d.
──────. "Speech on the Bill to Distribute the Proceeds of the Public Lands among the States," delivered before the House of Representatives, 2 July 1841. n.p., n.d.
──────. "Speech on the Tariff and Restrictive Policy" delivered before the House of Representatives, 22 June 1842. Washington: Blair and Rives, 1842.

———. "Address before the South Carolina Agricultural Society," 29 Nov. 1849. Columbia: A. S. Johnson, 1849.
———. "Speech delivered before a Public Meeting of the People of the District of Edgefield," 7 July 1851. Edgefield *Advertiser*, 1851.
———. "Oration on the Influence of Government upon the Nature and Destiny of Man" delivered before the Euphradian and Clariosophic Societies. Columbia: Steam Power Press of Gibbs and Johnson, 1855.
———. "Message Number 1 of His Excellency to the Legislature Meeting in Extra Session," 5 Nov. 1861. Columbia: Charles P. Pelham, 1861.
———. "Message Number 1 of His Excellency the Governor of South Carolina," 2 Nov. 1862. Columbia: Charles P. Pelham, 1862.

Official Documents

Catalogues of South Carolina College. 1806–35. University of South Carolina Archives.
Clariosophic Society Record of Debates for 1827. University of South Carolina Archives.
Clariosophic Society Record of Members for 1827. University of South Carolina Archives.
Congressional Globe, 1834–44. Washington: U.S. Government Printing Office.
Edgefield County, Records of the Clerk of Court.
Edgefield County, Probate Records.
Executive Documents No. 2, Correspondence and Other Papers Relating to Fort Sumter, including Correspondence of Hon. Isaac W. Hayne with the President. Charleston: Evans and Cogwell, 1861.
General Assembly. *Reports and Joint Resolutions of the General Assembly of the State of South Carolina. Journals of the House* and *Journals of the Senate.* 1832–63.
Journal of the Congress of the Confederate States of America, 1861–1865. I. Washington: U.S. Government Printing Office, 1904.
Journal of the Convention of the People of South Carolina, Sept. 1865. Columbia: J. A. Shelby, 1865.
Journal of the Conventions of the People of South Carolina Held in 1832, 1833, and 1852. Columbia: R. W. Gibbes, 1860.
Journal of the Convention of the People of South Carolina Held in 1860, 1861, and 1862, together with Reports and Resolutions, etc. Charleston: Evans and Cogswell, 1862.
Journal of the Secession Convention. Charleston: Evans and Cogswell, 1860.
Journals of the South Carolina Executive Councils of 1861 and 1862. Edited by Charles E. Cauthen. Columbia: South Carolina Archives Department, 1956.
Proceedings of the Democratic State Convention. Columbia: South Carolinian Office, 1843.
Proceedings of the Board of Trustees of South Carolina College. 29 Nov. 1865–8 July 1873. University of South Carolina Archives.

Proceedings of the Democratic State Convention of South Carolina, Held at Columbia, 5th and 6th of May, 1856, for the Purpose of Electing Delegates to the Democratic National Convention, to Meet in Cincinnati in June. Columbia, 1875.
Register of Debates of Congress. 24th Cong., 1st sess., 1836.
Report of the Committee on Foreign Affairs, No. 162. 26th Cong., 2nd sess., 13 Feb. 1841.
South Carolina Convention Documents, 1860–1862: Report of the Special Committee of Twenty-one on the Communication of His Excellency Governor Pickens. Columbia: R. W. Gibbes, 1862.
U.S. Bureau of the Census. 1830 (5th), 1840 (6th), 1850 (7th), 1860 (8th). Washington: U.S. Government Printing Office.
U.S. Manufacturing Census for 1850 and 1860. Edgefield District. Microfilm in South Carolina Archives.
Vestry Register of Trinity Church, Edgefield, 1834–1905.
War of the Rebellion: A Compilation of the Official Records of the Union and Confederate Armies. 70 vols. in 130 pts. Washington: U.S. Government Printing Office, 1880–1901.

Books

Abbot, Martin. *The Freedmen's Bureau in South Carolina, 1865–1872.* Chapel Hill: University of North Carolina Press, 1967.
Adams, E. P. *British Interest and Activities in Texas.* Baltimore: Johns Hopkins University Press, 1910.
Andrews, Sidney. *The South since the War as Shown by Fourteen Weeks of Travel and Observation in Georgia and the Carolinas.* Edited by David Donald. Boston: Houghton Mifflin Company, 1971.
Auchampaugh, Philip Gerald. *James Buchanan and His Cabinet on the Eve of Secession.* Lancaster: Lancaster Press, 1926.
Avary, Myrta Lockett. *Dixie after the War: An Exposition of Social Conditions Existing in the South during the Twelve Years Succeeding the Fall of Richmond.* Freeport: Books for Libraries Press, 1906.
Bailey, Thomas. *A Diplomatic History of the American People.* Englewood Cliffs: Prentice-Hall, 1980.
Ball, William Watts. *The State That Forgot: South Carolina Surrenders to Democracy.* Indianapolis: Bobbs-Merrill, 1932.
Bancroft, Frederic. *Calhoun and the South Carolina Nullification Movement.* Gloucester: Peter Smith, 1966.
Banner, James M., Jr. "The Problem of South Carolina." In *The Hofstadter Aegis: A Memorial.* Edited by Stanley Elkins and Eric McKitrick. New York: Alfred A. Knopf, 1974.
Barney, William L. *The Road to Secession.* New York: Praeger, 1972.
Barnwell, John. *Love of Order: South Carolina's First Secession Crisis.* Chapel Hill:

University of North Carolina Press, 1982.
Bemis, Samuel F., ed. *American Secretaries of State and Their Diplomacy.* Reprint. New York: Cooper Square Publishers, 1963.
Benton, Thomas Hart. *Thirty Years' View; or, A History of the Working of the American Government for Thirty Years from 1820 to 1850.* New York: Appleton, 1858.
Bleser, Carol K. Rothrock, ed. *The Hammonds of Redcliffe.* New York: Oxford University Press, 1981.
Boucher, Chauncey Samuel. *South Carolina and the South on the Eve of Secession, 1852 to 1860, VI.* St. Louis: Washington University Studies, 1919.
――――. *The Nullification Controversy in South Carolina.* New York: Russell and Russell, 1968.
Bowers, Claude G. *The Party Battles of the Jackson Period.* New York: Octagon Books, 1965.
Brantley, William H. *Banking in Alabama, 1816–1860, I.* Privately Printed, 1961.
Brodie, Fawn. *Thomas Jefferson: An Intimate History.* New York: W. W. Norton, 1974.
Brown, Norman D. *Edward Stanley: Whiggery's Tarheel Conqueror.* Tuscaloosa: University of Alabama Press, 1974.
Burton, Milby E. *The Siege of Charleston, 1861–1865.* Columbia: University of South Carolina Press, 1970.
Burton, Orville Vernon. *In My Father's House are Many Mansions: Family and Community in Edgefield, South Carolina.* Chapel Hill: University of North Carolina Press, 1985.
Capers, Gerald M. *John C. Calhoun—Opportunist: a Reappraisal.* Gainesville: University of Florida Press, 1960.
Capers, Henry D. *The Life and Times of C. G. Memminger.* Richmond: Everett Waddy, 1893.
Carpenter, Jesse T. *The South as a Conscious Minority, 1798–1861: A Study in Political Thought.* Gloucester: Peter Smith, 1963.
Cash, Wilbur J. *The Mind of the South.* New York: Alfred A. Knopf, 1941.
Catton, William, and Catton, Bruce. *Two Roads to Sumter.* New York: McGraw-Hill, 1963.
Cauthen, Charles Edward. *South Carolina Goes to War, 1860–1865.* Chapel Hill: University of North Carolina Press, 1950.
Chalmers, William Nisbet. *Old Bullion Benton: Senator from the New West, Thomas Hart Benton, 1782–1858.* New York: Russell and Russell, 1956.
Channing, Steven A. *Crisis of Fear: Secession in South Carolina.* New York: W. W. Norton, 1970.
Chapman, John A. *History of Edgefield County from the Earliest Settlements to 1897.* Newberry: Elbert H. Aull, 1897.
Coit, Margaret L. *John C. Calhoun: American Portrait.* Boston: Houghton Mifflin, 1950.
Cole, A. C. *The Irrepressible Conflict, 1850–1863.* New York: Macmillan, 1934.
Cooper, William J., Jr. *The Conservative Regime: South Carolina, 1877–1890.* Baltimore: Johns Hopkins University Press, 1968.

_____. *The South and the Politics of Slavery, 1828–1856*. Baton Rouge: Louisiana State University Press, 1978.
Corey, Albert B. *The Crisis of 1830–1842 in Canadian-American Relations*. New York: Russell and Russell, 1941.
Coulter, E. Merton. *The Confederate States of America. 1861–1865*. Vol. VII of *A History of the South*. Edited by Wendell Holmes Stephenson and E. Merton Coulter. Baton Rouge: Louisiana State University Press, 1950.
_____. *Negro Legislators in Georgia during the Reconstruction Period*. Athens: University of Georgia Press, 1968.
_____. *The South During Reconstruction, 1865–1877*, Vol. VIII of *A History of the South*. Edited by Wendell Holmes Stephenson and E. Merton Coulter. Baton Rouge: Louisiana State University Press, 1947.
Crankshaw, Edward. *The Shadow of the Winter Palace*. New York: Viking, 1976.
Craven, Avery O. *The Coming of the Civil War*. New York: Charles Scribner's Sons, 1942.
_____. *Edmund Ruffin, Southerner: A Study in Secession*. Baton Rouge: Louisiana State University Press, 1966.
_____. *The Growth of Southern Nationalism, 1848–1861*. Vol. VI of *A History of the South*. Edited by Wendell Holmes Stephenson and E. Merton Coulter. Baton Rouge: Louisiana State University Press, 1953.
Crawford, Samuel Wylie. *Genesis of the Civil War: The Story of Sumter, 1860–1861*. New York: C. L. Webster, 1887.
_____. *The History of the Fall of Fort Sumter*. New York: S. L. McLean, 1889.
Curtis, George T. *Life of James Buchanan, Fifteenth President of the United States, VII*. New York: Harper and Brothers, 1883.
Davidson, Chalmers Caston. *The Last Foray: The South Carolina Planters of 1860: A Sociological Study*. Columbia: University of South Carolina Press, 1970.
Davis, Jefferson. *The Rise and Fall of the Confederate Government, I and II*. New York: D. Appleton, 1881.
DeConde, Alexander. *A History of American Foreign Policy*. New York: Charles Scribner's Sons, 1963.
Derrick, Samuel. *Centennial History of the South Carolina Railroad*. Columbia: University of South Carolina Press, 1930.
Donald, David. *Charles Sumner and the Coming of the Civil War*. New York: Alfred A. Knopf, 1960.
Doubleday, Abner. *Reminiscences of Fort Sumter and Moultrie in 1860–1861*. New York: Harper and Brothers, 1876.
Dumond, Dwight Lowell. *The Secession Movement, 1860–1861*. New York: Octagon Books, 1973.
Eaton, Clement. *A History of the Southern Confederacy*. New York: Macmillan, 1954.
_____. *The Mind of the Old South*. Baton Rouge: Louisiana State University Press, 1967.
Edgar, Walter B., ed. *Biographical Dictionary of the South Carolina House of Representatives. I: Sessions List, 1692–1973*. Columbia: University of South Carolina Press, 1974.

Escott, Paul D. *After Secession: Jefferson Davis and the Failure of Confederate Nationalism*. Baton Rouge: Louisiana State University Press, 1979.
Faulkner, Harold Underwood. *American Economic History*. New York: Harper and Row, 1960.
Faust, Drew Gilpin. *James Henry Hammond and the Old South: A Design for Mastery*. Baton Rouge: Louisiana State University Press, 1982.
———. *A Sacred Circle: The Dilemma of the Intellectual in the Old South, 1840–1860*. Baltimore: Johns Hopkins University Press, 1977.
Fehrenbacher, Don E. *Manifest Destiny and the Coming of the Civil War, 1840–1861*. New York: Appleton-Century-Crofts, 1970.
Fogel, Robert, and Engerman, Stanley L. *Time on the Cross: The Economics of American Negro Slavery*. Boston: Little, Brown, 1974.
Foote, Shelby. *The Civil War, a Narrative, I and II*. New York: Random House, 1958.
Franklin, John Hope. *The Militant South, 1800–1861*. Cambridge: Belknap Press of Harvard University Press, 1956.
Freehling, William W. *Prelude to Civil War, 1816–1836*. New York: Harper and Row, 1966.
Freidel, Frank. *Francis Lieber: Nineteenth-Century Liberal*. Baton Rouge: Louisiana State University Press, 1947.
Fuess, Claude M. *The Life of Caleb Cushing, I and II*. New York: Harcourt, Brace, 1923.
Genovese, Eugene D. *Roll, Jordan, Roll: The World the Slaves Made*. New York: Pantheon, 1974.
Graham, Stephen. *Tsar of Freedom: the Life and Reign of Alexander II*. New Haven: Yale University Press, 1963.
Grayson, William J. *James Louis Petigru*. New York: Harper, 1866.
Green, Edwin. *George McDuffie*. Columbia: State Company, 1936.
Green, Fletcher M. *Constitutional Development in the South Atlantic States, 1776–1860*. Chapel Hill: University of North Carolina Press, 1930.
Greer, Jack. *Leaves from a Family Album*. Waco, Tex.: Texian Press, 1975.
Guess, William Francis. *South Carolina: Annals of Pride and Protest*. New York: Harper and Row, 1957.
Hamer, Philip M. *The Secession Movement in South Carolina, 1847–1852*. Allentown: H. R. Haas, 1918.
Hammond, Bray. *Banks and Politics in America from the Revolution to the Civil War*. Princeton: Princeton University Press, 1957.
Hampden. [Francis W. Pickens.] *The Genuine Book of Nullification*. Charleston: R. J. Von Brunt, 1831.
Harris, W. A. *The Record of Fort Sumter from Its Occupation by Major Anderson to Its Reduction by South Carolina Troops during the Administration of Governor Pickens*. Columbia: South Carolina Steam Job Printing Office, 1862.
Hofstadter, Richard. *The Idea of a Party System: The Rise of Legitimate Opposition in the United States, 1780–1840*. Berkeley: University of California Press, 1969.
Hollis, Daniel Walker. *South Carolina College. I, University of South Carolina*. Columbia: University of South Carolina Press, 1951.

Holt, Thomas. *Black over White.* Urbana: University of Illinois Press, 1977.
Houston, David F. *A Critical Study of Nullification in South Carolina.* Cambridge: Harvard University Press, 1896.
Huff, Archie V., Jr. *Langdon Cheves of South Carolina.* Columbia: University of South Carolina Press, 1977.
Jenkins, W. S. *Pro-Slavery Thought in the Old South.* Chapel Hill: University of North Carolina Press, 1935.
Jennings, Thelma. *The Nashville Convention: Southern Movement for Unity, 1848–1851.* Memphis: Memphis State University Press, 1980.
Jervey, Theodore. *Robert Y. Hayne and His Times.* New York: Macmillan, 1909.
Jones, Samuel. *The Siege of Charleston and the Operations of the South Atlantic Coast in the War among the States.* New York: Neal Publishing, 1911.
Julien, Carl. *Beneath So Kind a Sky: The Scenic and Architectural Beauty of South Carolina.* Columbia: University of South Carolina Press, 1948.
Keller, Norton. *Affairs of State: Public Life in Late Nineteenth Century America.* Cambridge: Belknap Press of Harvard University Press, 1977.
Kibler, Lillian. *Benjamin F. Perry: South Carolina Unionist.* Durham: Duke University Press, 1946.
King, Alvy L. *Louis T. Wigfall: Southern Fire-Eater.* Baton Rouge: Louisiana State University Press, 1970.
Klein, Philip Shriver. *President James Buchanan: A Biography.* University Park: Pennsylvania State University Press, 1962.
LaBorde, M. *History of the South Carolina College.* Columbia: Peter B. Glass, 1859.
Lamson, Peggy. *The Glorious Failure: Black Congressman, Robert Brown Elliott and Reconstruction in South Carolina.* New York: W. W. Norton, 1973.
Lander, Ernest McPherson, Jr. *The Calhoun Family and Thomas Green Clemson: The Decline of a Southern Patriarchy.* Columbia: University of South Carolina Press, 1983.
_____. *Reluctant Imperialist: Calhoun, the South Carolinian, and the Mexican War.* Baton Rouge: Louisiana State University Press, 1979.
Leemhuis, Roger P. *James L. Orr and the Sectional Conflict.* Washington: University Press of America, 1979.
Lesesne, Joab M. *Bank of South Carolina.* Columbia: University of South Carolina Press, 1976.
Lynch, Denis Tilden. *An Epoch and a Man: Martin Van Buren and His Times.* New York: Liveright, 1929.
McClendon, Carlee T. *Edgefield Death Notices and Cemetery Records.* Columbia: Hive Press, 1977.
_____. *Edgefield Marriage Records, Edgefield, South Carolina: From the Late Eighteenth Century up through 1870.* Columbia: R. L. Bryan, 1970.
McCormac, Eugene Irving. *James K. Polk.* Berkeley: University of California Press, 1922.
McElroy, Robert. *Jefferson Davis: The Unreal and the Real.* New York: Harper and Brothers, 1937.
Malone, Dumas. *The Public Life of Thomas Cooper.* Columbia: University of South Carolina Press, 1961.

Manning, William R., ed. *Diplomatic Correspondence of the United States-Canadian Relations, 1784–1860*. Washington: Carnegie Endowment for International Peace, 1940.
Meigs, William Montgomery. *Life of John Caldwell Calhoun*. New York: Neale Publishing, 1917.
Meriwether, Robert L. *The Expansion of South Carolina, 1729–1765*. Kingsport: Southern Publishers, 1940.
Merritt, Elizabeth. *James Henry Hammond, 1807–1864*. Baltimore: Johns Hopkins University Press, 1923.
Mitchell, Broadus. *William Gregg: Factory Master of the Old South*. Chapel Hill: University of North Carolina Press, 1928.
Nichols, Roy Franklin. *The Disruption of American Democracy*. New York: Free Press, 1948.
———. *Franklin Pierce: Young Hickory of the Granite Hills*. Philadelphia: University of Pennsylvania Press, 1958.
Nicolay, John G., and Hay, John. *Abraham Lincoln: A History, II*. New York: Century, 1917.
Olmstead, Frederick Law. *The Cotton Kingdom: A Traveler's Observation on Cotton and Slavery in the American Slave States*. New York: Alfred A. Knopf, 1966.
O'Neall, John Belton, and Chapman, John A. *The Annals of Newberry in Two Parts*. Newberry: Aull and Houseal, 1892.
Osterweis, Rollin G. *Romanticism and Nationalism in the Old South*. New Haven: Yale University Press, 1949.
Owsley, Frank Lawrence. *King Cotton Diplomacy*. Chicago: University of Chicago Press, 1931.
———. *Plain Folk of the Old South*. Baton Rouge: Louisiana State University Press, 1950.
Perry, Benjamin Franklin. *Reminiscences of Public Men*. Philadelphia: John D. Avil, 1883.
———. *Reminiscences of Public Men with Speeches and Addresses*. Greenville: Shannon, 1889.
Phillips, Ulrich B. *Life and Labor in the Old South*. Boston: Little, Brown, 1963.
Pickens, Andrew. *General Andrew Pickens: An Autobiography*. Edited by Lynda Worley Skelton. Pendleton: Pendleton District Historical and Recreational Commission, 1976.
Pickens, Monroe. *The Pickens Family*. Greenville: Kate Pickens Day, 1931.
Poore, Benjamin Perley. *Perley's Reminiscences of Sixty Years in the National Metropolis*. Philadelphia: Hubbard Brothers, 1886.
Potter, David. *The Impending Crisis, 1848–1861*. Completed and edited by Don E. Fehrenbacher. New York: Harper and Row, 1976.
———. *Lincoln and His Party in the Secession Crisis*. New Haven: Yale University Press, 1942.
Price, Glenn W. *Origins of the War with Mexico: The Polk-Stockton Intrigue*. Austin: University of Texas Press, 1967.
Randall, J. G. and Donald, David. *The Civil War and Reconstruction*. Lexington: D. C. Heath, 1969.

Rawick, George P., ed. *The American Slave: A Composite Autobiography.* 19 vols. and supplements. Westport: Greenwood Press, 1972.
Reeves, Jesse S. *American Diplomacy under Tyler and Polk.* Gloucester: Peter Smith, 1967.
Reid, Whitelaw. *After the War: A Southern Tour, May 1, 1865 to May 1, 1866.* London: Sampson, Lowson, and Marson, 1866.
Remini, Robert V. *Andrew Jackson and the Course of American Freedom, 1822–1832.* New York: Harper and Row, 1981.
———. *Andrew Jackson and the Course of American Democracy, 1833–1845.* New York: Harper and Row, 1984.
———. *Martin Van Buren and the Making of the Democratic Party.* New York: Columbia University Press, 1951.
Rippy, J. Fred. *Joel R. Poinsett, Versatile American.* Durham: Duke University Press, 1946.
Rose, Willie Lee. *Rehearsal for Reconstruction: The Port Royal Experiment.* Indianapolis: Bobbs-Merrill, 1964.
Schlesinger, Arthur M., Jr. *The Age of Jackson.* Boston: Little, Brown, 1953.
Schmidt, George Paul. *The Old Time College President.* New York: Columbia University Press, 1930.
Schultz, Harold S. *Nationalism and Sectionalism in South Carolina, 1852–1860: A Study in the Movement for Southern Independence.* Durham: Duke University Press, 1950.
Schultz, William J., and Caine, M. R. *Financial Development of the United States.* New York: Prentice-Hall, 1937.
Scott, Anne Firor. *The Southern Lady: From Pedestal to Politics, 1830–1939.* Chicago: University of Chicago Press, 1970.
Sellers, Charles. *James K. Polk, Continentalist, 1843–1846.* Princeton: Princeton University Press, 1966.
Simkins, Francis Butler. *Pitchfork Ben Tillman: South Carolinian.* Baton Rouge: Louisiana State University Press, 1944.
———, and Woody, Robert Hilliard. *South Carolina during Reconstruction.* Chapel Hill: University of North Carolina Press, 1932.
Smith, Alfred Glaze, Jr. *Economic Readjustment of an Old Cotton State: South Carolina, 1820–1860.* Columbia: University of South Carolina Press, 1958.
Smith, Justin H. *The Annexation of Texas.* New York: Macmillan, 1919.
Smith, Page. *The Nation Comes of Age, IV.* New York: McGraw Hill, 1981.
Spain, August O. *The Political Theory of John C. Calhoun.* New York: Bookman Associates, 1951.
Stampp, Kenneth M. *And the War Came: The North and the Secession Crisis 1860–1861.* Baton Rouge: Louisiana State University Press, 1950.
———. *The Era of Reconstruction, 1865–1877.* New York: Alfred A. Knopf, 1966.
———. *The Peculiar Institution.* New York: Random House, 1956.
Strong, George Templeton. *Diary of the Civil War, 1860–1865.* Edited by Allan Nevins. New York: Macmillan, 1952.
Swanburg, W. A. *First Blood: The Story of Fort Sumter.* New York: Charles Scribner's Sons, 1957.

Sydnor, Charles S. *The Development of Southern Sectionalism, 1819–1848.* Vol. V of *A History of the South.* Edited by Wendell Holmes Stephenson and E. Merton Coulter. Baton Rouge: Louisiana State University Press, 1948.
Taylor, George R., ed. *Jackson versus Biddle: The Struggle over the Second Bank of the United States.* Boston: D. C. Heath, 1949.
Thomas, Albert Sidney. *A Historical Account of the Protestant Episcopal Church in South Carolina, 1820–1957, Being a Continuation of Dalcho's Account, 1670–1820.* Columbia: R. L. Bryan, 1957.
Thomas, Emory M. *The Confederacy as a Revolutionary Experience.* Englewood Cliffs: Prentice-Hall, 1971.
Turner, Frederick Jackson. *The United States, 1830–1850.* New York: Holt, 1935.
Van Deusen, Glyndon G. *The Jacksonian Era.* New York: Macmillan, 1959.
———. *The Life of Henry Clay.* Boston: Little, Brown, 1937.
Wade, John Donald. *Augustus Baldwin Longstreet: A Study of the Development of Culture in the South.* Athens: University of Georgia Press, 1967.
Wallace, David Duncan. *The History of South Carolina.* 3 vols. New York: American Historical Society, 1934.
———. *South Carolina: A Short History, 1520–1948.* Chapel Hill: University of North Carolina Press, 1951.
Waring, Alice N. *Andrew Pickens: The Fighting Elder, 1739–1817.* Columbia: University of South Carolina Press, 1962.
Weir, Robert M. *Colonial South Carolina.* Millwood: K. T. O. Press, 1983.
Wellman, Manley Wade. *Giant in Gray: A Biography of Wade Hampton of South Carolina.* New York: Charles Scribner's Sons, 1949.
White, Laura A. *Robert Barnwell Rhett, Father of Secession.* New York: Century, 1931.
Williams, Kenneth P. *Lincoln Finds a General: A Military Study of the Civil War.* New York: Macmillan, 1949.
Williams, T. Harry. *P. G. T. Beauregard, Napoleon in Gray.* Baton Rouge: Louisiana State University Press, 1955.
———. *Romance and Realism in Southern Politics.* Baton Rouge: Louisiana State University Press, 1966.
Williamson, Joel R. *After Slavery: The Negro in South Carolina during Reconstruction, 1861–1877.* Chapel Hill: University of North Carolina Press, 1965.
Wiltse, Charles Maurice. *John C. Calhoun, Nationalist, 1782–1828.* New York: Bobbs-Merrill, 1944.
———. *John C. Calhoun, Nullifier, 1829–1839.* New York: Russell and Russell, 1949.
———. *John C. Calhoun, Sectionalist, 1840–1850.* New York: Russell and Russell, 1951.
Wise, Barton H. *Life of Henry A. Wise of Virginia, 1806.* New York: Macmillan, 1899.
Woodford, Francis B. *Lewis Cass, the Last Jeffersonian.* New Brunswick: Rutgers University Press, 1950.
Woodmason, Charles. *The Carolina Backcountry on the Eve of the Revolution.* Edited by Richard J. Hooker. Chapel Hill: University of North Carolina Press, 1953.

Woodward, C. Vann. *The Burden of Southern History*. 2nd ed., rev. Baton Rouge: Louisiana State University Press, 1968.
Wyatt-Brown, Bertram. *Southern Honor: Ethics and Behavior in the Old South*. New York: Oxford University Press, 1982.
Yearns, W. Buck, ed. *The Confederate Governors*. Athens: University of Georgia Press, 1985.
Youmans, LeRoy F. *A Sketch of the Life and Services of Francis W. Pickens*. n.p., n.d.

Dissertations and Theses

Bass, Robert D., ed. "The Autobiography of William J. Grayson." Ph.D. dissertation, University of South Carolina, 1933.
Edmunds, John Boyd, Jr. "Francis W. Pickens: A Political Biography." Ph.D. dissertation, University of South Carolina, 1967.
Ellen, John Calhoun, Jr. "Political Newspapers of the Piedmont Carolinas in the 1850s." Ph.D. dissertation, University of South Carolina, 1958.
Ferguson, Clyde R. "General Andrew Pickens." Ph.D. dissertation, Duke University, 1960.
Gettys, James M. "To Conquer a Peace: South Carolina and the Mexican War." Ph.D. dissertation, University of South Carolina, 1974.
Gwinn, Gilbert S. "The Coastal Defense of the Confederate Atlantic Seaboard States, 1861–1862: A Study in Political and Military Mobilization." Ph.D. dissertation, University of South Carolina, 1973.
Hendricks, Carlanna. "John Gary Evans: A Political Biography." Ph.D. dissertation, University of South Carolina, 1966.
Keel, Edward H. "Francis Wilkinson Pickens, Governor of South Carolina, 1860–1862." M.A. thesis, University of South Carolina, 1961.
Klein, Rachel. "The Rise of the Planters in the South Carolina Backcountry, 1767–1808." Ph.D. dissertation, Yale University, 1979.
Lord, Clyde W. "Louis T. Wigfall." M.A. thesis, University of Texas, 1925.
Merchant, John Holt. "Laurence M. Keitt: South Carolina Fire-Eater." Ph.D. dissertation, University of Virginia, 1976.
Olsberg, Robert Nicholas. "A Government of Class and Race: William Henry Trescot and the South Carolina Chivalry, 1860–1865." Ph.D. dissertation, University of South Carolina, 1972.
———. "William Henry Trescot: The Crisis of 1860." M.A. thesis, University of South Carolina, 1967.
Tucker, Robert C. "James Henry Hammond: South Carolinian." Ph.D. dissertation, University of North Carolina, 1958.
Ware, Lowry Price. "The South Carolina Executive Councils of 1861 and 1862." M.A. thesis, University of South Carolina, 1952.

Articles, Periodicals, and Pamphlets

Allen, H. D. "The Paper Money of the Confederate States." *The Numismatist* 31:7 (July 1919).
Bonham, Milledge L., ed. "Ante-Bellum Southerners in Russia." *Journal of Southern History* 3 (May 1937).
_____. "Alexander McLeod: Bone of Contention," *New York History* 2 (Apr. 1937).
Boucher, Chauncey S. "The Annexation of Texas and the Bluffton Movement in South Carolina." *Mississippi Valley Historical Review* 6 (June 1919): 3–33.
_____. "The Secession and Cooperation Movement in South Carolina." *Washington University (St. Louis) Studies*, ser. V, 5:15 (Apr. 1918): 65–138.
Bull, Emily. "Lucy Pickens, Queen of the South Carolina Confederacy." *Proceedings of the South Carolina Historical Association*, 1982.
Burton, Orville Vernon. "The Civil War in the Confederate Interior: From Community to Nation—The Transformation of Local Values in Edgefield, South Carolina." Paper delivered at Southern Historical Association meeting, 1983.
Calhoun, John C. "Letters from Calhoun to Francis W. Pickens." *South Carolina Historical and Genealogical Magazine* 7 (Jan. 1906): 12–19.
Carsel, Wilfred. "Slaveholders' Indictment of Northern Wage Slavery." *Journal of Southern History* 6 (Nov. 1940): 504–20.
Greenburg, Kenneth S. "Representation and the Isolation of South Carolina, 1776–1860." *Journal of American History* 44 (Dec. 1977): 723–43.
Hayne, Paul H. "Politics in South Carolina: Francis W. Pickens." Paper in South Caroliniana Library.
Jameson, J. F., ed. "Letters on the Nullification Movement in South Carolina." *American Historical Review* 6 (July 1910).
_____. "Letters on the Nullification Movement in South Carolina." *American Historical Review* 7 (Oct. 1901).
Kohn, David. "Francis W. Pickens, Governor, Lawyer, Nullification Chief." *The State Magazine*, 26 Oct. 1952.
Lander, Ernest M., Jr. "The Calhoun-Preston Feud, 1836–1842." *South Carolina Historical Magazine* 59 (1955): 24–37.
McCormick, Eugene. "Louis McLane." In *American Secretaries of State and Their Diplomacy*. IV, 281–89. Reprint. New York: Cooper Square, 1964.
Ochenkowski, J. P. "The Origin of Nullification in South Carolina." *South Carolina Historical Magazine* 83:2 (Apr. 1982).
Pickens, Francis W. "The Evacuation of Fort Sumter—Secret History of the Matter." Reprinted from Richmond *Daily Examiner*, 8 Aug. 1861, in *William and Mary Quarterly* 24 (Oct. 1911): 78–80.
_____. "The Growth and Consumption of Cotton." *Southern Quarterly Review* 13 (Jan. 1848): 103–36.
Simkins, Francis B. "Francis W. Pickens." In *Dictionary of American Biography*, (1937), XIV, 558–60.
White, Laura A. "The Fate of Calhoun's Sovereign Convention in South Carolina." *American Historical Review* 34 (1929): 757–71.

———. "The National Democrats in South Carolina, 1852 to 1860." *South Atlantic Quarterly* 28 (1929): 370–89.

———. "The South in the 1850's as Seen by British Consuls." *Journal of Southern History* 1 (1935).

Woody, Robert H. "Franklin J. Moses, Jr., Scalawag Governor of South Carolina." *North Carolina Historical Review* 10 (Apr. 1933): 111–32.

Index

Abbeville, 75, 112
Abney, Joseph, 101, 102, 105, 106
Abolitionism: growth of movement, 8, 13, 31, 37, 39, 40, 41, 42, 43, 45, 56, 60, 67, 74, 81, 89, 95, 107; as a viable political force, 112, 131. *See also* Slavery
Adams, James H., 53, 146
Adams, John, 7
Adams, John Quincy, 8, 20, 25, 26, 27; on banking issues, 35; scorns Pickens, 35, 38; introduces anti-slavery resolutions, 41; denounces South, 44, 45, 67; presents memorials on Texas and slavery, 44–45; denounces Pickens, 62; introduces reapportionment resolutions, 68–69; condemned by Pickens, 89; fights gag rule, 89
Adriatic (ship), 148
Agriculture, 23, 72, 92, 95; cotton, 7, 8, 11, 21, 31, 32, 48, 66, 75, 92, 179; corn, 23, 75; rice, 23. *See also* Pickens, Francis Wilkinson: as agriculturist
Aiken, William, 87
Alabama, 7, 11, 21, 22, 28, 47, 72, 95, 123, 128, 139, 145, 150, 160
Alamo, The, 44, 101
Alexander II of Russia, 140, 141
Allen, Thomas, 33
Allston, Robert F. W., 57
Anderson, Alexander, 76
Anderson, Robert, 159, 160; moves Union forces to Fort Sumter, 156; warns Pickens, 158; evacuates Fort Sumter, 163
Anderson *True Carolinian*, 136
Andrews, Sidney, 176
Aristotle, 5
Aroostook War, 60
Athens *Southern Banner*, 110

Bacon, James, 178
Bacon, John E., 140, 143, 145, 175
Baltimore, 178; Democratic convention of 1844, 74, 76, 78, 79, 80, 98; Democratic convention of 1852, 124, 130; Democratic convention of 1860, 145
Baltimore *Merchant*, 32, 35
Bank of Alabama, 22, 28
Bank of the State of South Carolina, 51, 104
Bank of the United States, 7, 8, 33; Jackson vetoes recharter, 25, 28; collapses, 39. *See also* Banks and banking
Banks and banking, 7, 23, 28, 36, 62, 63, 74. *See also* Independent treasury
Barnwell, Robert W.: delegate at Nashville convention, 114; appointed United States senator, 115; aversion to public office, 119
Beaufort, 51, 80, 89; Union troops occupy, 168
Beauregard, Pierre G. T., 162, 163
Benton, Thomas Hart, 141
BeVine, Ellen, 50
Biddle, Nicholas, 28, 33
Blair, Francis P., 26, 58, 83, 95; praises Pickens, 33, 38; supports Calhoun, 35, 38; opposes Calhoun, 41
Blair and Rives (Democratic printers), 58
Bluffton movement, 81, 84, 87, 90–92, 96, 98, 99, 102, 105, 115. *See also* Rhett, Robert Barnwell
Bonham, Milledge L., 101, 126, 127, 134, 140, 143, 145; elected to South Carolina convention, 120; influence on Pickens, 125, 154; succeeds Pickens as governor, 171, 172, 174; receives amnesty, 177

Boston *Daily Advertiser*, 176
Boyce, Ker, 104
Brooks, Preston S., 23, 101, 127; in duel, 52; as cooperationist, 121, 123, 124; furious with Pickens, 125–26; defeats Pickens in congressional election, 126, 210 (n. 40); canes Sumner, 131; death, 133, 134. *See also* Brooks-Sumner affair
Brooks, Whitfield, 20, 23, 52, 101, 126
Brooks-Sumner affair, 52, 131
Brown, Aaron, 50
Brown, John, 142
Brown, Joseph E., 160
Brown University, 5
Buchanan, James, 63, 100, 146, 150; contests Democratic party nomination, 76; ambassador to Great Britain, 130; elected president, 132; offers Pickens ambassadorship to Russia, 134, 140; opinion of Pickens, 144–45; and secession crises, 154, 155, 157–60, 161, 162
Burke, Edmund, 5
Burt, Armistead, 81, 85, 99, 124, 125; succeeds Pickens in Congress, 74; relationship with Pickens, 102; urges southern unity, 108, 112
Butler, Andrew Pickens, 53, 57, 91, 107, 120, 125, 127, 139; militancy, 17–18; elected to United States Senate, 104–5; villified by Sumner, 131; death, 133, 134; final illness, 211 (n. 77). *See also* Brooks-Sumner affair
Butler, Matthew C., 139, 151, 153; promoted to general, 173; slaves set free, 174
Butler, Pierce M., 53
Butler, Sampson, H., 50
Butler, Susan, 128

Calhoun, Andrew Pickens, 20, 58, 92, 95
Calhoun, Anna. *See* Clemson, Anna Calhoun
Calhoun, Floride, 5, 69, 75, 104
Calhoun, James M., 22
Calhoun, John Caldwell, 4, 7, 12, 123, 128, 130, 133, 141, 148, 152, 204 (n. 25); stifles Pickens, 3; controls South Carolina politics, 4, 10, 53, 54, 86, 94, 105, 111, 114; on concurrent majority, 10; writes "Exposition and Protest," 11–12; on state sovereignty, 11; as vice-president, 12; abandons moderation, 13–15; Fort Hill address, 13; on tariff, 15; elected to United States Senate, 17; resigns vice-presidency, 17; urges Pickens to run for Congress, 19; relationship with Pickens, 20, 24, 58, 59, 60, 62; on discord following nullification, 21; alliance with Clay on tariff, 25; on relations with France, 26, 27; opposes Jackson's war preparations, 26, 27, 34; patriotism questioned, 27; relationship to Van Buren, 30, 31, 190 (n. 92); opposition in South Carolina, 31; relationship with William C. Preston and Waddy Thompson, 31, 33; relationship with Whigs, 31, 34, 39; supports measure for independent treasury, 32, 34–37; ambitions, 34; feud with William C. Preston, 34–36, 39; among South Carolina political leaders, 36; maintains support in South Carolina legislature, 36; seeks political harmony in South Carolina, 37, 56, 58; fear of abolitionist movement, 40; urges South Carolinians to oppose abolitionism, 40; advocates southern convention, 45, 47, 48; fails to support Pickens, 51; seeks presidency (for 1844 election), 56, 57, 66, 67, 68, 70, 71, 72; resigns seat in United States Senate, 57; as moderate, 63, 64, 82; withdraws from presidential race, 72, 73, 74, 75; becomes secretary of state, 75; on slavery, 76, 78; on Texas annexation, 76, 80, 81; criticized by *Mercury*, 81; on South Carolina radi-

calism, 85; refuses ambassadorship to Great Britain, 91; borrows money, 92; differences with Polk, 95; announces retirement, 96; deteriorating relationship with Pickens, 97–106 passim; advocates internal improvements, 98; as delegate to Memphis convention, 98; declining health, 99; leaves Washington, 100; opposes Mexican War, 101; urges formation of southern party, 108, 110, 111; on political parties, 108, 130; urges nonparticipation in 1848 election, 110; illness, 114; praises Mississippi for calling southern convention, 114; final speech in the United States Senate, 114–15; death, 115; political effects of death, 117, 119, 127, 136, 180
Calhoun, Susan, 22
California, 106, 116, 117
Cambreling, Churchill, 20, 33
Campbell, Robert, 37, 38, 39
Caroline (ship) affair, 61. See also McLeod affair
Carroll, James P., 52, 126, 151
Cass, Lewis, 76, 132, 142, 144; opposes Wilmot Proviso, 108–9; receives support from Pickens, 110; loses presidential election, 111
Castle Pickney, 82, 156, 157
Charleston, 5, 36, 74, 83, 87, 89, 91, 96, 110, 115, 153, 154, 155, 156, 166; Democratic convention of 1860, 144, 145, 146; harbor fortifications strengthened, 159, 161; fire of 1861, 167
Charleston Bank, 104
Charleston *Courier*, 82, 101, 121, 122, 151, 153, 171; praises Pickens, 86; criticizes Pickens, 166; attacks secession convention, 169–70
Charleston Harbor, 154, 155, 156, 157, 158
Charleston *Mercury*, 8, 10, 15, 35, 36, 37, 42, 43, 44, 51, 54, 57, 72, 73, 78, 85, 89, 91, 96, 98, 101, 104, 110, 122, 130, 133, 151, 154, 159, 160, 171; support of Calhoun, 68, 95; praises Pickens, 80; repudiates Calhoun, 81; influence of, 82; condemns Pickens, 84, 103; warns North, 114; advocates separate state secession, 118, 121; becomes more moderate, 138; announces election of Lincoln, 148
Chesnut, James, Jr., 151, 167; resigns as United States senator, 152; hostility to Pickens, 168
Chesnut, Mary Boykin, 146, 152, 153, 156, 165, 167, 168, 170, 174
Cheves, Langdon, 35, 115, 119; delegate to Nashville convention, 114, speech at Nashville convention, 118
Cheves, Langdon, Jr., 165
China, 61
Churchwell, W. M., 144, 145
Cicero, 5
Cincinnati, 95; Democratic convention of 1856, 130–31, 132
Citadel, The, 82, 163
Civil War, 3, 4, 173, 174, 175
Clariosophic Society, 9, 179
Clay, Henry, 20, 38, 73, 76, 79; introduces compromise tariff, 18; alliance with Calhoun, 25; on slavery, 36, 63; and Whig leadership, 62, 63; influence of, 64, 66; loses presidential race, 90; and Compromise of 1850, 114, 116, 118
Clemson, Anna Calhoun 20, 24, 69, 75, 92, 105, 106, 128
Clemson, Thomas Green, 70, 92, 128, 130
Cobb, Howell, 162
Colcock, William F., 87, 89
Colhoun, Floride. *See* Calhoun, Floride
Colhoun, James Edward, 24, 69, 70, 75, 76, 78, 86, 91, 94, 97, 98, 99, 104, 123
Colhoun, John Ewing, 69
Colhoun, Maria, 24, 67, 69, 75, 91, 128
Colhoun, Martha Maria, 69, 90

Colleton district, 80, 89
Columbia, 5, 74, 84, 91, 103, 113, 118, 130, 166, 168, 169, 173, 177; Southern Rights convention, 112; smallpox epidemic, 152; occupied by Sherman's troops, 174
Columbia *Phoenix*, 177
Columbia *South Carolinian*, 51, 96, 121, 122, 141
Columbia *Southern Guardian*, 161
Columbia *Telescope*, 35
Compromise of 1850, 114, 116, 118, 120, 123
Confederate States of America, 157, 162; government formed, 161; Confederate Constitution ratified by South Carolina, 163
Congressional district of Pickens, 210 (n. 40)
Connor, H. W., 78
Cooper, Thomas: influence on Jefferson, 7; political philosophy, 7; and states' rights, 8; views on tariff, 8; impact of political thought, 11
Corn. *See* Agriculture
Cotton. *See* Agriculture
Cowpens, battle of, 5
Cralle, Richard K., 32, 36
"Crisis Letters," 184 (n. 16)
Crittenden, John J., 212 (n. 4)
Cuba, 137, 142
Cushing, Caleb, 42, 155

Dallas, George M., 78, 81
Davie, William F., 57
Davis, Jefferson, 159, 160, 162, 169; criticized by Pickens, 174; arrested, 175
Davis, Warren R., 25, 27, 31
Dearing, Marion Antoinette. *See* Pickens, Marion Antoinette Dearing
Declaration of Independence: quoted, 16
Democratic Association, 110
Democratic conventions. *See* Baltimore; Charleston; Cincinnati
Democratic Republican party, 74

Democrats, 58, 62, 66, 67, 89, 126, 127, 130; and Pickens, 35, 47, 57, 73, 108; control of House of Representatives, 72; split by tariff controversy, 72; convention of 1844, 74, 76, 78, 79, 80, 98; meeting at Nashville, 83, 84; electoral victories in South Carolina, 84, 111; convention of 1852, 124, 130; convention of 1856, 130–31, 132; fragmentation at Charleston, 144, 145, 146
Demosthenes, 5
DeSaussure, William F., 124, 125
Doubleday, Abner, 158
Douglas, Stephen A., 131, 132, 145
Dred Scott decision, 133
Dueling. *See* Southern culture: dueling and affairs of honor
Dunovant, R. M., 161
Dupont, Samuel F., 165
Durisoe, W. F., 115

Economy. *See* Agriculture; Banks and banking; Independent treasury; Panic of 1837; South Carolina: attitude toward the tariff, economy, resources; Tariff: national policy toward
Edgefield, 4, 7, 9, 10, 16, 19, 22, 25, 50, 67, 76, 80, 81, 91, 106, 115, 116, 121, 125, 127, 133, 139, 146, 152, 154, 172, 173, 176, 178; militia company recruited, 18; and Mexican War, 101; junto, 102; post-war problems, 174; occupied by Union troops, 175
Edgefield *Advertiser*, 43, 52, 54, 59, 101, 106, 110, 124, 125, 126, 136, 146, 151, 170, 173, 178; supports Pickens, 69, 115; advocates separate state secession, 118; radicalism of, 121, 123, 148–49
Edgefield *Hive*, 10
Edgewood (plantation), 20, 21, 22, 23, 47, 63, 69, 75, 111, 139, 140, 169, 173. *See also* Pickens, Francis Wilkinson: as agriculturist
Election (presidential): of 1832, 8; of

1836, 30; of 1840, 56; of 1844, 71–84 passim; of 1848, 108–10, 203 (n. 3); of 1852, 124–25; of 1856, 131–32; of 1860, 144–45, 146, 148–49
Elmore, Benjamin, 51, 53
Elmore, Franklin Harper, 47, 48, 51, 52, 67, 71, 78, 81, 82, 83, 84, 87, 92, 93, 94, 98, 103, 107, 113, 130; as candidate for Congress, 25; political ally of Calhoun, 37–38; opposes Pickens, 50; public animosity toward, 57; delegate to Democratic convention, 74; delegate to Memphis convention, 96; withdraws from senatorial contest, 104; delegate at Nashville convention, 114; replaces Calhoun in United States Senate, 115; death, 115, 207 (n. 22); hosts meeting in Charleston, 203 (n. 3)
Euphradian Society, 179
Evans, Josiah J., 125, 126, 209 (n. 30)
Everett, Edward, 92

Fillmore, Millard, 20, 61, 68, 123; enemy of Pickens, 64; endorses Compromise of 1850, 120, 208 (n. 1)
Fire-eaters, 40, 81–82, 84, 117, 146, 151–52, 160, 161
First Baptist Church, Columbia, 176
Force Act, 17–18. *See also* Nullification
Forsyth, John, 62
Fort Hill (plantation), 57, 72, 75, 92, 104
Fort Johnson, 82, 158
Fort Moultrie, 82, 152, 155, 156, 157, 158
Fort Sumter, 154, 156, 158, 162, 165, 176; public pressure favoring seizure, 159–61; evacuated, 163; description of garrison, 218 (n. 95)
France, 26, 27, 142
Freedmen: Pickens's opinion of, 175, 179; Freedman's Bureau, 178; labor contracts, 178; relations with yeoman farmers, 178; receive attention from Republicans, 179

Free Soil party, 110
Frémont, John C., 132
Fugitive Slave Act, 127

Gadberry, J. M., 131
Gadsden, James, 96, 113, 140
Gag rule, 42, 43, 72; rescinded, 89. *See also* Abolitionism
Gales and Seaton (Whig printers), 58
Gardner, John, 155
Garibaldi, Giuseppe, 151
Garrison, William Lloyd, 13, 40
Gary, Martin W., 151
Georgia, 50, 66, 76, 82, 83, 110, 123, 158, 176
Gibbes, Robert, 168
Gilmer, Thomas W., 75
Gist, William H., 151, 154, 167, 168
Goliad, battle of, 44
Gourdin, Henry, 203 (n. 3)
Grant, Ulysses S., 179
Great Britain, 130, launches anti-slavery crusade, 39–40, 67; attacked by Pickens, 41; relations with United States, 46, 60, 61, 62, 95, 96, 100, 101; interest in Texas, 67, 73; Pickens's dislike for, 93, 100
Great Lakes, 61
Green, Duff, 60; relationship with Calhoun, 35, 36, 58, 59, 93, 204 (n. 25)
Greenville, 90, 176
Greenville *Mountaineer*, 26, 27, 103, 110
Greenville *Southern Patriot*, 121, 122, 136; promotes Pickens for governor, 127
Griffin, N. L., 126
Gulf of Finland, 140
Gwynn, Walter, 156

Halcyon Grove (plantation), 7
Hamburg, 80
Hamburg *Journal*, 102, 106
Hamilton, James, Jr., 35, 43, 79, 115; as Nullifier, 13, 15; meeting in Charleston, 203 (n. 3)

Index

Hamilton, James Alexander, 61
Hammond, James Henry, 9, 48, 59, 60, 74, 98, 99, 164; edits Columbia *Southern Times*, 10; political ambitions, 10, 52, 53, 54, 55, 84, 86, 94, 115, 134; relationship with Pickens, 11, 12, 13, 140; praises Pickens, 16; in militia, 17; runs for Congress, 25; on European tour, 31; resigns from Congress, 31; urges end to factionalism, 37; in Congress, 40, 41, 43; denounces Rhett and Elmore, 50–51, 53; annoys Calhoun, 53, 54; depressed condition, 54; deserted by Pickens, 54, 55; loses gubernatorial race, 56; elected governor in 1842, 57; arrogance, 57, 58; as governor, 71, 79; on Texas annexation, 79, 101; on secession, 81–82, 85; takes military measures, 82; morals, 84–85, 104; failure of political plans, 86, 87, 89–90; attacks Pickens, 90, 93, 191 (n. 130); loses senatorial contests, 104, 119; relationship with Calhoun, 105; delegate at Nashville convention, 114, 117; moderation, 116, 117, 208 (n. 31); election to United States Senate, 138; conservative course, 143; on political parties, 206 (n. 84); delivers eulogy on Calhoun, 207 (n. 23)
Hammond, Marcellus, 140
Hampton, Wade, II, 33, 85
Hampton, Wade, III, 53, 113, 177
Harllee, W. W., 157, 167, 168
Harpers Ferry raid, 142
Harrison, William Henry, 61–62; elected president, 56; attacked by Pickens, 59; death, 63
Hayne, Arthur P., 155
Hayne, Isaac W., 159, 160, 161, 162, 165, 167, 168, 169, 171, 220 (n. 26)
Hayne, Paul Hamilton, 164, 178
Hayne, Robert Y., 35, 82; as Nullifier, 15, 18; becomes governor, 17; death, 71
Hayne-Webster debate, 12

Herodotus, 179
Hibernian Hall, Charleston, 110
Hoar, Samuel, 89
Holcombe, Beverley, 139
Holcombe, Lucy Petaway. *See* Pickens, Lucy Petaway Holcombe
Holmes, Isaac, 81, 85, 101, 110
Holt, Joseph, 157
Holt, R. S., 150
Honor. *See* Southern culture: concept of honor, dueling and affairs of honor
Hooker, Edward, 5
Hopewell (plantation), 5
Huger, Alfred, 19
Huger, Daniel, 74, 80, 87, 94, 97; reputation, 57; elected United States senator, 58; offers resignation, 95; resigns, 98
Hunter, Robert M. T., 34, 47, 48, 71, 73, 157; elected Speaker of the House of Representatives, 50; supports Calhoun, 67, 68; arrested, 175

Independent treasury, 32, 34, 38, 39, 60, 62, 63, 64
Indians, 5, 12
Ingham, Samuel, 67
Internal improvements. *See* South Carolina: attitude toward internal improvements
Iowa, 107

Jackson, Andrew, 78, 79, 91, 97; and election of 1828, 8; on tariff, 10, 13; undermines Calhoun, 12; vetoes Maysville Road bill, 13; and nullification crisis, 15, 16, 18, 19; vetoes recharter of Bank of the United States, 25; foreign policy, 26; attempted assassination, 27; monetary policy, 28; issues specie circular, 30; advocates strengthening of coastal fortifications, 31; supports Van Buren, 72; visited by Pickens, 84
Jackson, William, 41
Jamison, David F., 157, 167; president

of secession convention, 153; criticizes Pickens, 164; reassures Pickens, 168; reconvenes secession convention, 171
Japan, 139
Jefferson, Thomas, 3, 7, 11
Jeter, John S., 80
Johnson, Andrew, 175; refuses to pardon Pickens, 177
Johnson, Benjamin J., 153
Johnson, David, 53, 56
Jones, John, 51

Kansas, 131, 133, 142
Kansas-Nebraska Act, 127, 131
Keitt, Laurence, 133, 140
Kentucky, 66
Kentucky Resolutions, 11
Key, Thomas C., 101, 102

Lancaster *Ledger*, 136
Land Distribution Act, 63, 68
Lander, Ernest M., 70
Lee, George, 138
Legaré, Hugh Swinton, 37, 38, 39, 43, 45
Lewis, Dixon H., 55, 71, 83; supports Calhoun, 38, 68; and speakership contest, 47, 48, 50, 52; meeting in Charleston, 203 (n. 3)
Liberator, The, 13, 40
Lincoln, Abraham, 146, 152, 153, 162; elected president, 148; inaugurated, 163
London, 130
London *Times*, 62
Lopez Expedition, 137, 212 (n. 4)
Lorn (manservant of Pickens), 214 (n. 60)

Macbeth, Charles, 156
McCord, David J., 113
McDuffie, George, 13, 20, 27, 53, 69, 71, 81, 85, 95, 98, 99, 102, 103, 143, 186 (n. 74); elected governor, 19; as leader of Nullifiers, 19, 25; supports Bank of the United States, 28; warns of dangers of factionalism, 36; elected United States senator, 57; ill health, 74, 80, 83, 87, 89, 97, 104; radicalism, 82, 83, 87; as orator, 84; denounces Pickens, 84; suffers stroke, 94; condition improves, 96; nominates Pickens for governor, 111; on power of nullification, 186 (n. 73)
Machiavelli, 55
McLane, Louis, 93
McLeod, Alexander, 61, 62
McLeod affair, 61, 62, 63, 79, 100
Madisonian, 33, 58
Magrath, Andrew G., 131, 157, 161, 164, 167; resigns as federal judge, 150; becomes governor, 174; flight from Union troops, 174; arrested, 175; appointed federal judge, 211 (n. 63)
Maine: boundary dispute, 61, 79, 100
Mallory, Francis, 34
Manning, John L., 52, 54, 126, 131, 132, 134, 177, 221 (n. 35)
Manning, Richard I., 12, 13, 19
Marion, Francis, 141
Marion *Star*, 124
Marshall, Foster, 168
Marshall, Texas, 106, 137
Martial spirit. *See* Southern culture: martial spirit
Massachusetts, 41, 42, 66, 89, 131
Mason, J. Thompson, 162
Mason, James, 114
Maxcy, Virgil, 75
Maysville Road bill: vetoed, 13
Means, John H., 119, 124
Memminger, Christopher G., 157, 169
Memphis convention, 96, 97, 98, 99
Methodist Episcopal Church, 81
Mexican War, 101, 107, 108, 110
Mexico, 95, 106, 107, 112, 133, 142. *See also* Mexican War
Middleton, Henry, 12
Miles, William Porcher, 150, 165
Militarism: *See* Southern culture: martial spirit

Miller, Hugh, 123
Miller, Stephen Decatur, 13
Millwood (plantation), 75
Minute men, 146, 155
Mississippi, 11, 22, 76, 123, 139, 150; calls southern convention, 114; secession of, 159
Missouri Compromise, 117, 121
Mobile, 95
Montgomery: formation of Confederate government, 160, 161, 162
Morning Chronicle, 62
Morris Island, 157, 158
Moses, Franklin J., 164, 168, 220 (n. 26)

Nance, Drayton, 123
Napoleon, 111, 140
Napoleonic Wars, 26
Nashville, 95, 98; Democratic party meeting, 83, 84; southern convention, 114, 116, 117, 118, 120; failure of southern convention, 121
Nesbitt Iron Manufacturing Company, 51
New Hampshire, 128
New Orleans, 95, 138, 143, 158, 178
Newport, 128
New York, 23, 61, 62, 90, 128, 137, 140, 145
New York *Journal of Commerce*, 145, 146
New York *Observer*, 62
New York *Sun*, 67
Niles, Ogden, 33
Niles Register, 33
Noble, Edward, 141
Noble, Patrick, 26, 38, 51, 53
North Carolina, 62, 64, 76, 121, 174
Nullification, 3; origins, 9, 10; doctrine, 10, 11, 12, 186 (n. 73); sentiment increases, 13; ordinance passed, 15, 16; convention, 15, 17, 18, 21; military preparations, 17; danger of war, 17; ordinance repealed, 18; controversy subsides, 19; legacy of discord in South Carolina, 21; repercussions, 40; remembered, 113, 148. *See also* South Carolina: attitude toward the tariff, economy, Nullifiers

Ohio, 60, 66
O'Neill, Peggy: affair, 12
Ordinance of Nullification. *See* Nullification
Ordinance of Secession. *See* Secession
Oregon, 73, 74, 76, 79, 93, 95, 96, 97, 100, 105
Orr, James L., 136, 177; rise in politics, 124, 125, 126; aligns with Democrats, 127, 128, 130, 132; mission to Kansas, 133; political aspirations, 134; presidential prospects, 144; move to radicalism, 150; Confederate senator, 171; reputation, 176; governor, 178

Palmerston, Lord, 61
Panic of 1837, 45; preliminary conditions, 28; impact in following years, 62
Paris, 140
Pendleton district, 25, 27, 84
Pendleton *Messenger* 20, 35, 59, 110
Pennsylvania, 23, 67, 78, 81, 90
Perry, Benjamin F., 134, 136, 179; disagreement with Pickens, 90; *Reminiscences*, 103; alignment with Democrats, 108, 126, 127, 128; opposition to separate state secession, 121; political rise, 124, 125; appointed provisional governor, 175; attempts to secure amnesty for Pickens, 176, 177; candidate for United States senate, 221 (n. 35)
Perry, Matthew C., 139
Petigru, James Louis, 12, 34, 35, 40, 43, 183 (n. 1)
Pettigrew, J. Johnston, 156
Pickens, Andrew (grandfather), 5
Pickens, Andrew, Jr. (father), 5; as governor, 7; personal characteristics, 153
Pickens, Andrew (son), 47, 128
Pickens, Eldred (son), 47, 69, 128

Pickens, Eliza (daughter), 47, 128
Pickens, Eugenia (daughter), 141, 145
Pickens, Ezekiel (uncle), 5
Pickens, Frances (daughter), 47, 128
Pickens, Francis Wilkinson: importance, 3; influenced by Jefferson, 3; political ambitions, 3, 9, 10, 55, 56, 57, 86, 87, 95, 96, 97, 98, 99, 104; birth, 4; early education and religious training, 5; relatives, 5, 7; oratory, 7, 41, 59, 60, 64, 78, 117, 118, 151, 152, 163, 191–92 (n. 150), 208 (n. 31); student at South Carolina College, 7–9; influenced by Thomas Cooper, 8; writes letters to Charleston *Mercury*, 8, 10; attitude toward the tariff, 8, 12, 79; embraces states' rights philosophy, 8, 17; defends planter society, 9; leaves South Carolina College, 9; marriage to Eliza Simkins, 9; on the debased nature of politics, 9, 31, 55, 60, 67, 73, 75; practices law, 9, 10; relationship with Calhoun, 9, 10, 20, 25, 31, 45, 73, 75, 92, 96, 97, 98, 99, 100, 101, 106; writes letter to Columbia *Southern Times*, 10; advocates nullification, 10, 11, 186 (n. 73); personal characteristics, 10, 50, 53, 54, 73, 103, 126, 128, 131, 153, 154, 161, 163, 164, 165–66, 172, 176–77; becomes a member of Nullifier faction, 12; relationship with Nullifiers, 15; urges calling of Convention, 15; chairman of committee on federal relations, 16; elected to the South Carolina House, 16; embraces radicalism, 16; on Declaration of Independence, 16; speaks against Jackson's proclamation, 16; chairman of judiciary committee, 17; emerges as leader of state, 17; supports Test oath, 17, 19; aide-de-camp to Governor Hayne in militia, 17, 18, 185 (n. 64); advocates rebellion, 17, 117, 152; gains national fame, 19; urged to run for United States Congress, 19; elected to United States Congress, 20; moves to Edgewood plantation, 21; ownership of property, 21, 22, 127, 187 (n. 13); inherits estate, 22; as agriculturist, 22, 23, 31, 45, 47, 66, 75, 76, 80, 92, 124, 126–27, 128, 178, 179, 203 (n. 1); treatment of slaves, 22, 31; aversion to banks, 23; religious attitudes, 23; defends slavery, 23, 44, 79, 90, 148; female correspondents, 24; arrival in Washington, 25; spokesman for Calhoun, 25; on relations with France, 26, 27; opposed to Jackson, 26, 27, 34; anti-bank sentiments, 28–38 passim; relationship with Van Buren, 30, 31, 32, 35, 45; fires overseer, 31; relationship with other South Carolina congressmen, 31; urged to become Unionist candidate for governor, 31; illnesses, 31, 44, 142, 222, (n. 40); on federal relations, 32; urges Nullifiers to change national party affiliation, 32; leads battle for House printer, 33; supported by Henry Wise, 33; on federal economic policies, 33, 34, 35; helps heal Calhoun-Van Buren feud, 34; supports independent treasury, 34, 35, 36, 37, 38, 39; debates against Whigs, 35; on economic sectionalism, 35; scorned by John Quincy Adams, 35; enmity between Pickens and Waddy Thompson, 36, 37; enmity between Pickens and William C. Preston, 36, 37, 38; advocates peaceful separation of North and South, 37; declines ambassadorship to Austria, 39; seeks Speakership of the House, 39; supports use of specie by government, 39; reelected to congress, 40, 44; speaks on Biblical support of aristocracy, 41; speaks on emancipation in the West Indies, 41; denounces abolitionists, 41–43; on northern capitalism, 42; opposes gag rule, 42–43; attacks Henry L. Pickney as a traitor, 43; political despondency, 44; urges

recognition of independence of Texas, 44; rivalry with Robert Barnwell Rhett, 45, 48–57 passim, 75; financial problems, 45, 66, 76, 126, 141, 150, 173, 175, 187 (n. 13); denounced as opportunist, 46; candidate for Speaker of the House, 47, 48, 50; feels betrayed by friends, 50, 51, 52, 144, 169; deteriorating relationship with Calhoun, 51, 54, 58, 59, 60, 62, 102, 103, 104, 105, 106; supports Hammond, 53, 54; supports Daniel Huger for United States Senate, 58; on vacation in Virginia, 59, 125, 137; against internal improvements, 60; becomes chairman of the House committee on foreign affairs, 60; makes apology to Waddy Thompson, 60; and McLeod affair, 61, 62, 63; anti-British attitude, 61, 62, 73; opposes Clay's economic measures, 63, 64; Calhoun's campaign manager, 66, 67, 68, 70, 72; courtship refused by Martha Colhoun, 69; death of first wife and son, 69; depressed state, 69, 105, 138, 169, 173, 175; declines ambassadorship to France, 70; retires from politics, 70; concern for Calhoun, 70, 71; describes Calhoun's political associates, 71; views on Texas annexation, 73, 74, 76, 79; arrogance, 73, 103; accuses Rhett of deceit, 75; opinion of Tyler, 75; supports Polk, 78, 79, 80, 83, 84, 86, 90, 92, 199 (n. 46); believes Calhoun to be obstacle to poltical advancement, 79; opinion of Democratic party, 79, 108; elected to South Carolina Senate, 80; advises Calhoun, 82; at Nashville, 83; visits Jackson, 84; condemns Rhett and Hammond, 85; foils secession message, 85; marriage to Marion Antoinette Dearing, 91; refuses ambassadorship to Great Britain, 92–93; attacked by Hammond, 93; anglophobia, 93, 100; loyalty to South Carolina, 94; aspires to become a United States senator, 94, 96; hopes for United States Senate seat demolished, 99; supports Mexican War, 101, 103; attempted reconciliation and final split with Calhoun, 106; denounces Wilmot Provso, 107; embraces Polk administration, 107–8, 110; supports Lewis Cass for president, 110, 111; nominated for governor, 111; worried by South Carolina radicalism, 112; serves on committee of safety, 113, 118; advocates cooperationism in 1850–1851, 113, 114; represents Edgefield district at Nashville convention, 116, 117; advocates rights to slave property in territories, 117, 118; defeated by John H. Means in gubernatorial contest, 119; elected to South Carolina convention of 1852, 120; opposed to Compromise of 1850, 121; attitude on separate state secession, 121–22, 123; supports Franklin Pierce for president, 124–25; defeated for seat in United States Senate by Josiah J. Evans, 125, 210 (n. 30); endorses National Democratic party, 127; establishes pottery works at Potterville, 127; deaths of Marion (second wife) and other relatives, 128; relationship with Thomas Clemson, 128, 130; invited to visit London by James Buchanan, 130; speaks before Democratic state convention, 130; supports Buchanan for president, 132; opinion of the radicals, 133; appointed ambassador to Russia, 133, 134, 140; defeated for United States Senate by Hammond, 134, 136, 138; distrusted on slavery issue, 136; courtship with Lucy Holcombe, 137, 138, 139, 140; marriage to Lucy Holcombe, 140; voyage to St. Petersburg, 140; sojourn in St. Petersburg, 140, 141, 142, 143, 145; opinions on foreign policy of the United States, 142; illegitimate son, 143; aspirations for United States presidency, 144–45; leaves St.

Petersburg, 145–46; arrives in New York, 148; meeting with Buchanan concerning secession, 150, 215 (n. 15); abandons all moderation, 151; plays role of elder statesman of "Mother Carolina," 151–52; elected governor in 1860, 153; participates in ceremonies of secession convention, 153; correspondence with Buchanan regarding Charleston harbor forts, 154–55; commands military forces of South Carolina, 155–57; orders seizure of federal property, 156–57; selects cabinet, 157; attempts to gain recognition from foreign powers, 157–58; correspondence with Robert Anderson on the firing on the *Star of the West*, 158; actions concerning Fort Sumter situation, 158–63; delays actions to allow Confederate government to take responsibility, 161–62; urges Confederate officials to take Fort Sumter, 162; speech at Charleston Hotel, 163; speech to Citadel cadets, 163; plans for coastal defense, 164; sends South Carolina troops to Virginia, 164; administration of military forces, 165, 166; receives blame for fall of Port Royal area, 165–66; executive powers usurped by the convention, 167–68, 168–71; defies the Executive Council, 171; succeeded as governor by Milledge L. Bonham, 171–72; returns to Edgewood, 173; trip to Richmond, 173–74; advises Governor Magrath not to continue war effort, 174; concern over public and personal conditions following the war, 176–77; active in public affairs despite lack of pardon, 177; attitudes on Reconstruction, 177, 178, 179; relations with freedmen, 178; on the future of the South, 178, 179–80; death, 180; legacy, 180–81; impact of death on Trinity Church, 187 (n. 18); on good literature, 187 (n. 21); rift with Franklin H. Elmore, 201 (n. 107); queston of black illegitimate children, 213 (n. 42); rift with Isaac W. Hayne, 220 (n. 26)

Pickens, Israel (cousin), 7
Pickens, Jennie (daughter), 104, 128, 145
Pickens, Lucy Petaway Holcombe (third wife), 145, 162, 165, 176; Pickens's infatuation with, 137; beauty, 139; marriage, 140; fascinates Alexander II of Russia, 140–41; homesickness, 141, 142; disappointment at not giving birth to son, 142, 213 (n. 36); personal characteristics, 142–43; reputation, 153, 168, 169; social life, 168, 169, 173; relationship with Franklin J. Moses, 168, 220 (n. 26); image on Confederate currency, 169, 219 (n. 17)
Pickens, Margaret Eliza Simkins (first wife), 24, 48, 91, 128; marriage, 9; illness, 45, 47; death, 69
Pickens, Maria (daughter), 47, 139
Pickens, Marion Antoinette Dearing (second wife): marriage, 91; gives birth, 104; ill health, 124, 128; death, 128
Pickens, Rebecca (daughter), 47, 128, 143
Pickens, Susan (daughter), 47, 128
Pickens, Susan Wilkinson (mother), 5
Pierce, Franklin, 20, 130, 131, 132; nominated for presidency, 124; supports Fugitive Slave Act, 127
Pinckney, Henry L., 8; introduces gag rule resolutions, 42, 43, 72; elected mayor of Charleston, 44
Planter society, 3, 4, 7, 9, 10, 23; relationships, 4, 7, 99; life style, 4, 9; family landholding, 7; and legal profession, 9; treatment of slaves, 22, 31; plantation management, 47. *See also* Agriculture; Slavery; Southern culture; Southern nationalism
Plato, 5

Poindexter, George, 27
Poinsett, Joel R., 12, 19, 32, 72
Politics: fundamental nature of, 9, 25, 55, 60
Polk, James K., 20, 85, 86, 89, 92, 94, 132, 141, 144; speaker of the House, 33; leaves Congress, 47; presidential nominee, 78, 79, 81, 82; supported by Pickens, 83, 84, 99, 110; elected president, 84, 90; differences with Calhoun, 87, 91, 93, 95, 102, 105; vetoes internal improvements bill, 100; advocates war with Mexico, 101; expansionist, 106, 107
Pope, Alexander, 122
Port Royal, 156; captured by Union troops, 165–66
Potterville, 127
Powers, Hiram, 70, 115
Pressly, John S., 20
Preston, John S., 33
Preston, William C., 9, 94; elected United States senator, 16; hostility to Calhoun, 26, 31, 34, 37, 38, 56, 59; attacked by Washington *Globe*, 33; opposition to independent treasury plan, 35; denounces Pickens, 36; resignation from United States Senate, 39, 57
Preston, Mrs. William C., 35, 38
Princeton University, 5

"Rape of the Lock," 122
Ravenel, William Henry, 161, 165
Reconstruction: impact on South Carolina, 178
Religion, 5, 23, 81; fundamentalism, 4; among slaves, 22; revivalism, 24
Republican party, 132; threat to slavery, 131, 148; increasing strength, 142, 145; and election of 1860, 145, 146. *See also* Abolitionism; Election (presidential): of 1856
Rhett, Albert, 37, 51, 57
Rhett, James, 51, 203 (n. 3)
Rhett, Robert Barnwell, 9, 47, 53, 67, 99, 104, 105, 111, 114; political ambition, 10, 56, 57, 86; support for Calhoun, 34, 35, 37–38; calls for southern convention, 45; rivalry with Pickens, 45, 51, 55; allies with Elmore, 48, 50, 52, 83; favored by Calhoun, 54; reconciliation with Pickens, 56; defeated in contest for United States Senate, 58; Pickens's opinion of, 71, 75, 85, 89; initiates Bluffton movement, 81; radicalism, 82, 116; reelected to Congress, 84; anti-Whig speech, 110; rivalry with Hammond, 115; elected to United States Senate, 116, 119; advocates separate state secession, 117; delegate to Nashville convention, 117; ridiculed, 122; resigns from Senate, 124; reenters politics, 134; defeated by Hammond in senatorial contest, 138; as fire-eater, 146, 152, 159; withdraws from gubernatorial contest, 153; issues warning to Buchanan, 154; changes name, 189 (n. 82); meeting in Charleston, 203 (n. 3)
Rhett, Robert Barnwell, Jr., 146
Richardson, J. R., 12
Richardson, John P., 52, 54, 57, 58, 59, 87, 124; urges Pickens to desert Calhoun, 31; Unionist sentiments, 53; elected governor, 56
Richland district, 113
Romanticism. *See* Southern culture: romanticism
Russia, 143, 144, 150; ambassadorship offered to Pickens, 133, 134; Pickens arrives as ambassador, 140; Pickens's impression of, 141, 142; Pickens resigns ambassadorship, 145; Pickens seeks foreign recognition for South Carolina, 157

St. Andrew's Hall, Charleston, 153
St. Augustine, Florida, 128
St. James, Court of, 98, 133
St. Louis, 95

St. Petersburg, Russia, 140, 145
Sanders, George N., 144
San Jacinto, battle of, 44
Schlesinger, Arthur M., Jr., 20
Scott, Winfield, 125
Seabrook, Whitemarsh, 87, 124; wins gubernatorial race, 111, 113; selects United States senator, 115; urges caution, 120
Secession, 3, 4, 118, 148–49, 153; advocated, 11, 81, 82, 84, 85, 113, 117, 118, 120, 121, 123, 146, 148, 151; cooperation with rest of South advocated, 113, 120, 121, 122, 123, 124, 148; delayed, 118; separate state action advocated, 121, 122, 123; cooperationists urge moderation, 123, 124; sentiment subsides, 124; cooperationists gain control, 127; final rhetoric, 151; Ordinance of Secession passed, 153; postsecession passion, 154, 159–61; glories recalled, 165; Ordinance of Secession repealed, 176; results of 1851 vote, 209 (n. 16). *See also* South Carolina secession convention; Southern nationalism
Sectionalism, 3, 8, 11, 13, 40, 42, 67, 72, 79, 81, 107, 108, 131. *See also* Abolitionism; Nullification; Secession; Slavery; South Carolina; Southern culture; Southern nationalism
Selma, Alabama, 7, 21
Seward, William, 145
Seymour, Robert, 86
Sherman, William T.: march through South Carolina, 174
Sickles, Daniel E., 178
Simkins, Arthur, 24, 91, 92, 121, 124, 146, 173
Simkins, Eldred, 9, 13, 21, 24
Simkins, Margaret Eliza. *See* Pickens, Margaret Eliza Simkins
Simms, William Gillmore, 74, 90, 91, 111; criticizes Pickens, 164–65
Slade, William, 45
Slavery: plantation, 4, 23, 28; abolitionist assaults on, 13, 67, 72, 95; defended by Pickens, 18, 23, 90; and banks, 28; in the District of Columbia, 30, 37, 40, 41, 42, 43, 45, 113–14; and Texas issue, 39, 44; the politics of, 40–45, 108; British attitude toward, 60–61; in the territories, 106, 107, 108, 113, 114, 117; popular sovereignty, 110; Republican threat to, 148. *See also* Abolitionism; Compromise of 1850; Kansas; Kansas-Nebraska Act; Missouri Compromise; Planter society; South Carolina; Southern culture
Slave trade (domestic), 60–61
Smith, William, 13
Southampton, England, 146
South Carolina: political culture, 3, 4, 7, 9, 10, 12, 52, 55, 56, 59, 102, 103, 104, 105, 116, 131, 202 (n. 118); radicalism, 3, 4, 7, 11, 12, 15–18, 56, 63, 71, 72, 76, 84, 85, 86–87, 91, 98, 112, 116, 118, 119, 126, 138, 146, 148, 149, 150, 184 (n. 28); provincialism, 3, 4, 79, 110, 113, 114, 122, 132, 146, 148; states' rights philosophy, 3, 7, 8, 10, 12, 15, 54, 62, 82, 86, 136; factionalism, 3, 12, 36, 37, 52, 53, 54, 55, 68, 73, 82, 83, 84, 85, 90, 91, 92, 93, 102, 105, 116, 131; relationship to national political structures, 3, 12, 89, 90, 108, 110, 124, 126, 127, 130, 131, 138; resources, 3, 18, 157; electoral processes, 4, 13, 50–59, 90, 120; suppression of dissent, 4, 112, 113, 114, 146, 148; attitude toward the tariff, 7, 8, 11, 12, 15, 56, 60, 62, 63, 64, 67, 68, 74, 76, 84, 85, 91, 93, 100, 110, 127; attitude toward internal improvements, 8, 98, 100, 110; Nullifiers, 11, 12, 13, 16, 25, 26, 32, 53, 54, 56, 58, 59, 64; Unionists, 12, 13, 17, 31, 36, 56, 59, 90, 113, 121, 123, 124, 127, 128, 130, 138; economy, 18, 67, 92, 95, 178, 179; quest for political har-

mony, 37, 40, 53, 56, 63, 68, 74, 84, 85, 94, 106, 122, 130, 143–44; occupation by Union troops, 174–75, 176; Radical Republican rule, 178–79. *See also* Agriculture; Banks and banking; Nullification; Planter society; Secession; Slavery; Southern culture
South Carolina College, 8, 9, 177, 180; influence on Pickens, 7
South Carolina convention of 1852, 112, 113, 120, 121, 122, 124
South Carolina Executive Council: conflict of authority with Pickens, 167–71; abolished, 171
South Carolina General Assembly: control of elections, 4; dominated by Nullifiers, 15; upholds test oath, 21; suggests states' rights convention, 113; opposes Wilmot Proviso, 113–14; elects delegates to Nashville convention, 114; schedules election for state convention of 1860, 150; addressed by Pickens, 151–52; change in attitude, 152; abolishes executive council, 171
South Carolina House of Representatives: supports Calhoun's leadership, 163. *See also* South Carolina General Assembly
South Carolina nullification convention, 15, 17, 18, 21. *See also* Nullification
South Carolina secession convention, 155; passes Ordinance of Secession, 153; proclaims state independence, 154; creates executive council, 157; ratifies Confederate Constitution, 163; temporarily adjourns, 164; creates second Executive Council, 167; accused of usurping power, 169–71; reconvenes and adjourns, 171. *See also* Secession
South Carolina Senate: rejects Hammond's disunionist messsage, 85; accepts Pickens's resolutions, 86. *See also* South Carolina General Assembly
Southern culture: planter psychology, 3; romanticism, 3, 4, 10, 24, 127–28, 152; education, 4; intellectual pursuits, 4; concept of honor, 4, 10, 59–60, 62, 102, 107, 122; dueling and affairs of honor, 4, 52, 62, 102; martial spirit, 17, 18, 23; masculinity, 23, 24, 25; femininity, 24; egotism, 122. *See also* Planter society; Slavery; South Carolina
Southern nationalism, 37, 98, 107, 112, 114, 117. *See also* Sectionalism
Southern Quarterly Review, 99, 102, 105
Southern Rights Associations, 112
Spain, 133
Spartanburg, 121
Stanly, Edward, 62
Star of the West (ship), 158, 159, 160
States' rights. *See* South Carolina: states' rights philosophy
States' Rights Democrats, 50
Stoekle, Baron Edward de, 158, 216 (n. 51)
Strong, George Templeton, 152
Stuart, John A., 36, 51, 81, 82, 85, 86
Sullivan, C. P., 210 (n. 40)
Sullivan's Island, 158
Summer, Henry, 123
Sumner, Charles, 52, 131
Sumter, Thomas, 141

Tariff: national policy toward, 60, 68, 71, 72, 78, 79, 83, 84, 98, 100, 110, 127
Tariff Act, 8, 68
Tariff of Abominations, 10, 11
Tariff of 1842, 71, 85, 98
Tariff of 1832, 11
Taylor, Zachary, 112; and Mexican War, 101; defeated by Cass in South Carolina; 110; on slavery issue, 110; receives presidential nomination, 110; elected president, 111; death, 208 (n.1)
Tennessee, 91
Test oath: controversy, 17; supported by Pickens, 19; declared unconstitutional, 21
Texas, 37, 137, 142, 162, 176, 178; as

annexation issue, 39, 44, 72, 74–91 passim, 93, 100; Great Britain's desire for, 67; as campaign issue in election of 1844, 73; annexed to United States, 101

Thompson, Waddy, 35, 37, 127; relationship with Pickens, 31, 36, 59–60; elected to United States House, 31, 39; attacks gag rule, 43

Thucydides, 179

Toombs, Robert, 158, 162

Trescot, William H., 164; role in secession crisis, 152, 154, 156, 157

Trinity Episcopal Church, Edgefield, 23, 102, 120

Turnbull, Robert, 8, 184 (n. 16)

Turner, Nat, 13, 40

Tyler, John, 61, 66, 70; becomes president, 63; vetoes bank bill, 64; interest in Texas, 67; vetoes tariff bill, 68; seeks presidential nomination 72, 73, 76, 79; Pickens's opinion of, 75; cautions Pickens, 161

Unionists: *See* South Carolina: Unionists

Unionville *Journal*, 123

United States: relations with France, 26, 27; relations with Great Britain, 46, 60, 61, 95, 96, 100, 101; relations with China, 61; relations with Mexico, 95, 106, 107, 112, 142; war with Mexico, 101, 107, 108, 110; relations with Latin America, 142. *See also* McLeod affair; Maine; Oregon; Texas

United States Colored Troops, 33rd Regiment: occupies Edgefield, 175

United States Congress: special session of September 1837, 31; controversy over seating of New Jersey Whigs, 48; domination by Henry Clay, 63; special session of 31 May 1841, 63; confusion in, 67

Upshur, Abel P., 70

Van Buren, Martin, 12, 54, 61, 62, 63, 68, 78, 93; elected president, 30; placates the South, 30; relationship with Calhoun, 30, 34, 38, 45, 59; efforts to bolster the economy, 30–32; supports plan for independent treasury, 32; position on slavery, 41, 43; fails in bid for reelection, 56; control of Democratic party, 66, 71; policy on tariff, 72; opposes annexation of Texas, 76; nominated for presidency by Free Soil party, 110

Victoria, Queen, 73, 140

Virginia, 66, 71, 72, 76, 82, 164; and Nat Turner insurrection, 13; pro-Calhoun sentiment, 64; opposes Wilmot Proviso, 113; becomes more moderate, 116

Walker, Leroy P., 162

Walker Tariff, 100

War of 1812, 7

Wardlaw, David L., 152, 176

Wardlaw, Frank H., 80, 101–2, 120

Wardlaw, J. J., 123

Warsaw, Poland, 146

Washington *Globe*, 26, 33, 35, 36, 38, 41, 47, 48, 68, 83, 95

Washington *Reformer*, 32

Washington *Spectator*, 68, 78

Washington *Union*, 95

Washington *United States Telegraph*, 36, 44

Watts, Beaufort T., 125, 164

Webster, Daniel, 12, 20, 61, 62, 114

West Indies, 41, 61, 76

Whigs, 33, 40, 50; Pickens's distaste for, 34; in South Carolina, 36, 39, 59, 80; and New Jersey election controversy, 48; strengthened, 62; conflict within, 63; division within, 64; advocate new tariff measure, 68; control of United States House, 110; nominate Zachary Taylor for president, 110; success in Charleston, 110

White Sulphur Springs, Virginia, 59, 125, 128, 137, 138, 178

Wigfall, Arthur, 23, 102

Wigfall, Louis T., 23, 54, 139, 152, 174;

duel, 52; advocates disunion, 81; enmity towards Pickens, 94, 101–2; migrates to Texas, 106; serves as United States senator, 158, 187 (n. 18); opinion of Pickens, 191–92 (n. 150)
Wilmot, David, 106, 107
Wilmot Proviso, 106, 107, 112; reaction in South Carolina, 108, 114; condemned by Virginia legislature, 113, 116

Wisconsin, 107
Wise, Henry A., 33, 35, 40, 41, 43
Woodbury, Levi, 67
Woolens, Bill, 8, 10
Wright, Silas, 67

Yancy, William L., 160
Yeadon, Richard, 82
Yorkville *Enquirer*, 130
Yorkville *Miscellany*, 121, 122, 136

www.ingramcontent.com/pod-product-compliance
Lightning Source LLC
Chambersburg PA
CBHW021358290426
44108CB00010B/291